Microfinance, EU Structural Funds and Capacity Building for Managing Authorities

Palgrave Studies in Impact Finance

Series Editor: **Mario La Torre**

The *Palgrave Studies in Impact Finance* series provides a valuable scientific 'hub' for researchers, professionals and policy makers involved in impact finance and related topics. It includes studies in the social, political, environmental and ethical impact of finance, exploring all aspects of impact finance and socially responsible investment, including policy issues, financial instruments, markets and clients, standards, regulations and financial management, with a particular focus on impact investments and microfinance.

Titles feature the most recent empirical analysis with a theoretical approach, including up to date and innovative studies that cover issues which impact finance and society globally.

Titles include:

Manuel Stagars
IMPACT INVESTMENT FUNDS FOR FRONTIER MARKETS IN SOUTHEAST ASIA
Creating a Platform for Institutional Capital, High-Quality Foreign Direct Investment, and Proactive Policy Making

Roy Mersland and R. Øystein Strøm (*editors*)
MICROFINANCE INSTITUTIONS
Financial and Social Performance

Paola Leone and Pasqualina Porretta
MICROCREDIT GUARANTEE FUNDS IN THE MEDITERRANEAN
A Comparative Analysis

Palgrave Studies in Impact Finance series
Series Standing Order ISBN: 978-1-137-38961-9

(*Outside North America only*)

You can receive future titles in this series as they are published by placing a standing order. Please contact your bookseller or, in case of difficulty, write to us at the address below with your name and address, the title of the series and the ISBN quoted above.

Customer Services Department, Macmillan Distribution Ltd, Houndmills, Basingstoke, Hampshire RG21 6XS, England

Microfinance, EU Structural Funds and Capacity Building for Managing Authorities

A Comparative Analysis of European Convergence Regions

Edited by

Giovanni Nicola Pes
Director of the Capacity Building Project in Microfinance Financial Instruments (The Italian National Public Agency for Microcredit) and Member of the fi-compass expert group on the advisory platform for financial instruments under the ESIF and EaSI (European Commission)

and

Pasqualina Porretta
Senior Lecturer in Banking and Finance, La Sapienza University of Rome, Italy

Introduction by

Mario Baccini

Except where otherwise noted, this work is licensed under a Creative Commons Attribution 3.0 Unported License. To view a copy of this license, visit http://creativecommons.org/licenses/by/3.0/

Editorial matter, introduction and selection © Giovanni Nicola Pes and Pasqualina Porretta 2016
Individual chapters © Contributors 2016
Introduction © Mario Baccini 2016

The authors have asserted their rights to be identified as the authors of this work in accordance with the Copyright, Designs and Patents Act 1988.

Open access:

 Except where otherwise noted, this work is licensed under a Creative Commons Attribution 3.0 Unported License. To view a copy of this license, visit http://creativecommons.org/licenses/by/3.0/

First published 2016 by
PALGRAVE MACMILLAN

Palgrave Macmillan in the UK is an imprint of Macmillan Publishers Limited, registered in England, company number 785998, of Houndmills, Basingstoke, Hampshire RG21 6XS.

Palgrave Macmillan in the US is a division of St Martin's Press LLC, 175 Fifth Avenue, New York, NY 10010.

Palgrave is the global academic imprint of the above companies and has companies and representatives throughout the world.

Palgrave® and Macmillan® are registered trademarks in the United States, the United Kingdom, Europe and other countries.

DOI: 10.1057/9781137536020
E-PDF ISBN 9781137536020
E-PUB ISBN 9781137536013

Hardback 9781137515124
Paperback 9781137557230

This book is printed on paper suitable for recycling and made from fully managed and sustained forest sources. Logging, pulping and manufacturing processes are expected to conform to the environmental regulations of the country of origin.

A catalogue record for this book is available from the British Library.

Library of Congress Cataloging-in-Publication Data

Microfinance, EU structural funds and capacity building for managing authorities : a comparative analysis of European convergence regions / [edited by] Giovanni Nicola Pes, Director of the Capacity Building Project in Microfinance Financial Instruments (The Italian National Public Agency for Microcredit) and Member of the fi-compass expert group on the advisory platform for financial instruments under the ESIF and EaSI (European Commission), Pasqualina Porretta, Senior Lecturer in Banking and Finance, La Sapienza University of Rome, Italy.
    pages cm.—(Palgrave studies in impact finance)
    Includes bibliographical references.
    ISBN 978–1–137–51512–4 (hardback)
    ISBN 978–1–137–55723–0 (paperback)
        1. European Union. 2. European Union countries – Economic policy – 21st century. 3. Regionalism – European Union countries. 4. Microfinance – European Union countries. I. Porretta, Pasqualina, 1974- editor. II. Pes, Giovanni, 1977– editor.
HC240.M625 2015
332—dc23   2015018309

Contents

List of Boxes	xi
List of Charts	xii
List of Figures	xiv
List of Tables	xv
Introduction Mario Baccini	xvii
Preface Giovanni Nicola Pes	xx
Notes on Contributors	xxiv

Part I EU Structural Funds, Microenterprise and Non-financial Services

1		**Financial Crises and EU Credit Access Policy** *Francesco Minnetti, Pasqualina Porretta and Ervin Sinani*	3
	1.1	Methodology and purposes of the research	3
	1.2	Small businesses and microenterprises in the EU economy: introduction	9
	1.3	The importance of the SMEs in the European economy	11
	1.4	Typical financial profiles, in particular with regard to microenterprises	20
	1.5	The supply of credit in the years of crisis	26
	1.6	Some summary considerations on data examined	38
	1.7	Access to credit in the European Commission's view	39
	1.8	European Investment Bank: mission and operating methods	40
	1.9	What is the EIF?	41
	1.10	The main financial instruments 2007–2013	43
	1.11	GIF	45
		1.11.1 Statistical data	47
	1.12	The SMEG	48
		1.12.1 Statistical data	48

	1.13	The CBS	49
	1.14	Financial engineering instruments	51
		1.14.1 JEREMIE	51
		1.14.2 The advantages of the JEREMIE programme	53
		1.14.3 JESSICA	53
		1.14.4 JASPERS	56
		Statistical data	58
		1.14.5 JASMINE	58
		Summary of data collected on financial engineering instruments	61
	1.15	COSME 2014–2020	62
	1.16	EFG	63
	1.17	LGF	64

2 EU Cohesion Policy and Microfinance — 74
Giorgio Centurelli, Pasqualina Porretta and Fabrizio Santoboni

    2.1 Cohesion policy, EU structural funds and financial engineering instruments: regulatory framework and operational features under the programming periods 2000–2006 and 2007–2013 — 74

        2.1.1 The regulatory framework in the programming period 2000–2006: first implementing provisions in regulation (EC) no. 448/2004 — 75

        2.1.2 The regulatory framework of the programming period 2007–2013: specific features of the financial engineering instruments — 76

        The general regulation (EC) no. 1083/2006 and implementing provisions in regulation (EC) no. 1828/2006 — 76

        The Coordination Committee of the Funds (COCOF) notes — 79

    2.2 Financial instruments in the cohesion policy 2014–2020: regulatory framework — 80

        2.2.1 The main amendments compared to previous programming periods — 82

    2.3 The control system — 84

    2.4 Structural funds and microfinance — 90

    2.5 Implementing a microfinance programme through the structural funds — 92

        2.5.1 Some examples in Europe — 95

3	EU Financial Engineering and Microfinance Non-financial Service: A Case Study		102
	Maria Claudia Costantini, Maria Doiciu, Stefanie Lämmermann, Andrea Nardone and Giovanni Nicola Pes		
	3.1	The ESF and the credit access of microenterprises	102
		3.1.1 The problem of access to credit for microenterprises	102
		3.1.2 European Social Fund and access to credit of microenterprises	105
	3.2	The ESF and access to credit for microenterprises: a case study from Germany	110
		3.2.1 History of microfinance in Germany	110
		The pilot phase (2000–2004)	110
		The consolidation phase (2005–2009)	111
		Roll-out (2010–today)	113
		Appraisal of ESF support for microcredit in Germany	113
	3.3	Microfinance and non-financial services: the European resources to sustain non-financial services	115
	3.4	The new European plans	118
	3.5	Non-financial services: advantages and operational features	126
		3.5.1 Types of non-financial services	128
		3.5.2 Who funds the non-financial services?	132
	3.6	Partnerships in delivery financial and BDSS services to the microcredit beneficiaries in Romania	132
		3.6.1 Case study 1. Partnership in the delivery of integrated financial and business development services: FAER NBFI and FAER Foundation	134
		3.6.2 Case study 2. Partnership in the delivery of integrated financial and BDS services: RoCredit-NBFI and Eurom business consulting company	135
		Brief description of the BDS services	136
		First phase	137
		Second phase	138
		Third phase (ongoing)	138
		Sustainability	140
		Sustainability of the "client first" initiative	140
		Impact	141

4 Microfinance and Capacity Building in the EU Policy — 148
Alessandro Cardente, Perrine Lantoine, Fulvio Pellegrini, Giovanni Nicola Pes, Pasqualina Porretta, Paolo Rita and Fabrizio Santoboni

- 4.1 Microcredit in the new EU programmes: the role of the Italian National Agency for Microcredit and the Capacity Building project — 148
  - 4.1.1 Microcredit in the new EU programmes — 148
  - 4.1.2 The role of the Italian National Agency for Microcredit in the Capacity Building project — 150
- 4.2 Microleasing, microinsurance, social housing: the new frontiers for European microfinance — 154
- 4.3 Microleasing: introduction and Capacity Building project issues — 161
- 4.4 Microinsurance: a solution just for the "developing countries"? — 167
  - 4.4.1 Introduction — 167
  - 4.4.2 Microinsurance: definition, literature and regulatory profiles — 169
  - 4.4.3 Microinsurance: subjects involved — 173
        Provision of microinsurance — 173
  - 4.4.4 Demand for microinsurance — 173
  - 4.4.5 Microinsurance: products and distribution channels — 176
  - 4.4.6 Microinsurance in the developed countries: strengths and weaknesses — 179
  - 4.4.7 Some conclusions on microinsurance — 182
- 4.5 Social housing: introduction and the Capacity Building project issues — 183
  - 4.5.1 New developments of housing policies in the European Union — 183
  - 4.5.2 Social housing and housing microfinance — 186
  - 4.5.3 The Capacity Building project. Social microcredit to support local housing policies: new instruments for social inclusion — 191
  - 4.5.4 Possible developments within the programming period 2014–2020: the Italian case — 194
- 4.6 Housing microcredit: the French case — 196
  - 4.6.1 Introduction — 167

		4.6.2	Context of the experimentation	196

			General overview of personal microcredit in France	196
			Energy poverty: a rising problem	197
		4.6.3	Main characteristics of housing microcredit	198
			Target group	198
			Amount, duration, cost	198
			Eligible works	199
			Credit assessment methodology: combining energy efficiency and financial expertise	199
		4.6.4	A shared-value approach	200
			Expected impacts	200
			Environmental impact	200
			Impact on the beneficiaries	200
			Financial impact	201
			Sustainability: a multistakeholder approach	201
		4.6.5	Lessons learned: first insights	201
			An important demand	201
			Clients' profile	201
			Types of projects	201
			Some obstacles	202
			New stakeholders, mainly suppliers	203

Part II The Capacity Building Surveys: Results and Reflections

5 Capacity Building Surveys   213
Riccardo Graziano, Pasqualina Porretta, Giovanni Nicola Pes, Cristiana Turchetti and Matteo Re

	5.1	Methodological framework: aims, questionnaires	213
	5.2	The managing authorities' interest and needs in capacity building activities	216
	5.3	The questionnaire: the investigation area	217
	5.4	The sample used	220
	5.5	Main results	222
		5.5.1 Thematic objectives	223
		5.5.2 Ex ante conditionalities	225
		5.5.3 Programming	228
		5.5.4 Management	239
		5.5.5 Evaluation and monitoring	231
		5.5.6 Financial management and control of the operational management	232

5.6		Conclusions on first survey	235
5.7		Second survey: aims, investigation areas and sample used	235
5.8		The main results of the survey: first considerations	237
	5.8.1	Analysis of the main results of the microcredit/microfinance programming activity	237
	5.8.2	Monitoring and reporting activities	243
	5.8.3	Regulatory framework of microcredit/microfinance sector and other	243
5.9		Reflections on the second survey	247

Final Reflections — 252
Gianfranco Verzaro

Conclusions — 255
Riccardo Graziano

Bibliography — 260

Index — 279

List of Boxes

3.1	Thematic objectives and investments priorities of the European Social Fund	106
3.2	For ESF Italy 2007–2013 providing from microcredit measures	108
4.1	Capacity Building project: initial considerations on microleasing, microinsurance, housing microfinance	156

List of Charts

1.1	Number of SMEs, employment and value added change, EU-27	18
1.2	Number of enterprises, EU-27, 2008–2012	19
1.3	Number of SMEs, year-on-year percentage change, EU-27, 2008–2012	20
1.4	Outstanding loans to non-financial corporations in the euro area	27
1.5	SME access to finance (SMAF), index and its sub-indices for the EU	28
1.6	Enterprises having used different financing sources (by enterprise size class, April to September 2013)	29
1.7	Financial health of euro area SMEs compared with large firms	30
1.8	Perceived change in the external financing gap (by firm size)	31
1.9	Evolution of monetary financial institutions interest rates on new loans to non-financial corporations	33
1.10	Pressingness of access to finance as perceived by SMEs across euro area countries	34
1.11	Applications for bank loans by SMEs across euro area countries	35
1.12	Change in terms and conditions of bank loans granted to euro area SMEs	36
1.13	Companies' use of internal and external financing in the past six months	37
1.14	Projects financed by EIB	43
1.15	Yearly signatures (€ millions)	44
1.16	JASPER budget, 2006–2013 (€ millions)	59
3.1	Main criticalities perceived by European SMEs, 2013 (percentage values)	104
3.2	European SMEs regarding access to credit as the most pressing problem, 2013 (percentage values)	104
5.1	Geographical distribution of replies	222
5.2	Thematic objectives	224
5.3	Ex ante conditionalities	226

5.4	Programming, management, implementation, evaluation and monitoring and financial management and control of the operational management	228
5.5	Management	229
5.6	Implementation	230
5.7	Evaluation and monitoring	233
5.8	Financial management and control of the operational management	234

List of Figures

2.1	Control process	87
2.2	The monitoring process: phases	90
3.1	Overview of DMI MIS Intherpro	112
4.1	Shared-value approach	200
5.1	The management of structural funds: the main action	214
5.2	First questionnaire: investigation areas	215
5.3	Second questionnaire: investigation areas	215
5.4	The sample used	221

List of Tables

1.1	Small business definition	13
1.2	Enterprises, employment and gross value added of SMEs in the EU-27, 2012	17
1.3	Projects financed by EIB	42
1.4	Yearly signatures (€ millions)	44
1.5	The main financial instruments, 2007–2013	46
1.6	Types of agreements	47
1.7	Number of final beneficiaries (SMEs) as of 31 December 2012	48
1.8	Amount of commitments/guarantees	49
1.9	Output SMEG	49
1.10	SMEG results	50
1.11	JASPERS performance	58
1.12	JASPERS budget, 2006–2013 (€ millions)	58
1.13	Number of FEIs reported at the end of 2011 and 2012	61
1.14	Summary of the instruments examined	66
2.1	Differences between 2007–2013 and 2014–2020 and between the programming periods 2007–2013 and 2014–2020	85
2.2	Use of ERDF and ESF for microfinance programmes	97
3.1	Enterprises, employees and added value, EU-27, 2012	103
3.2	Loan volumes since 2005 (preliminary numbers)	114
3.3	Main actions recommended by the European Commission to the member countries: action no. 1 – entrepreneurship education and training	120
3.4	Main actions recommended by the European Commission: action no. 2 – strengthening the entrepreneurial environment	121
3.5	Main actions recommended by the European Commission: action no. 3 – reigniting the entrepreneurial spirit in Europe through the involvement of specific groups (women)	123
3.6	Main actions recommended by the European Commission: action no. 3 – reigniting the entrepreneurial spirit in Europe through the involvement of specific groups (senior entrepreneurs)	124

3.7	Main actions recommended by the European Commission: action no. 3 – reigniting the entrepreneurial spirit in Europe through the involvement of specific groups (immigrants)	124
3.8	Main actions recommended by the European Commission: action no. 3 – reigniting the entrepreneurial spirit in Europe through the involvement of specific groups (youth)	125
3.9	Main actions recommended by the European Commission: action no. 3 – reigniting the entrepreneurial spirit in Europe through the involvement of specific groups (unemployed individuals)	126
3.10	Non-financial services in the different phases of the enterprise life cycle	131
3.11	Methods of provision of non-financial services and financial support	133
3.12	Impact indicators' outputs and results/outcomes obtained and targets for 2014	142
4.1	Microinsurance vs conventional insurance	172
4.2	Insurance providers according to their legal status	174
4.3	Capacity Building project: main characteristics for housing	192
4.4	Operational proposals of the Capacity Building project	193
4.5	Contribution for different stakeholders	202
5.1	Programmes activated	238
5.2	Total amount of programmes activated	239
5.3	Other main results	239
5.4	Target of the microcredit programmes	241
5.5	Financing methods	242
5.6	Reporting activity: details	244
5.7	Websites of the microcredit programmes activated	245

OPEN

Introduction

The strengthening of the administrative capacity, both at central and regional level, represents an essential condition to ensure the successful outcome of any programme aimed at achieving economic growth and social cohesion. Emerging also from Europe 2020, the strategy to generate growth and development elaborated by the European Union is aimed at overcoming the current economic crisis as well as substantially improving the current development model, creating thus the conditions for a smart, sustainable and inclusive economic growth.

The Capacity Building issue involves in particular the programming and management processes of the so-called financial engineering instruments, including microcredit and microfinance. It is a well-recognised fact, both at national and European level, that such instruments can play a key role in tackling the effects of the crisis by facilitating access to the labour market for a number of disadvantaged subjects and ensuring the necessary support for start-ups and self-employment initiatives. The current European scenario is characterised by credit crunch and increasing cuts to the welfare systems due to debt reduction objectives pursued by several EU countries. At the same time, microcredit has proved an effective mechanism to facilitate the financial inclusion of individuals (including their households) particularly hit by the economic downturn: young people, women, subjects over 50 years of age, those ejected from the labour market, off-workers and immigrants.

We should not forget that microcredit lies at the opposite pole to grant-based policies; it facilitates the creation of enterprises by promoting self-responsibility instead of dependence on public subsidies or aid. Moreover, the current economic and employment crisis calls for integrated action through a plurality of interventions and measures aimed at mitigating the effects of the crisis on human capital, protecting the capacity to act and the professionalism of individuals and ensuring social inclusion and employment. To this end, a joint and coordinated action by a number of public and private actors is highly recommended, including policymakers, financial intermediaries and subjects engaged in the service sector, who should be able to design and implement intervention policies and provide sources of funding as well as non-financial services to support microcredit.

In this context, the Capacity Building project on the microcredit financial instruments developed by the National Agency for Microcredit over a two-and-a-half-year period (September 2012 to March 2015) represents an absolute positive experience at European level as, for the first time, the focus was put on the need to provide a direct solution to the issues faced by the European regions involved in the former Convergence Objective, where operational programmes have been implemented in the design, initiation and implementation of financial engineering instruments related to microcredit and microfinance and co-financed by resources made available through the EU structural funds.

The project – implemented thanks to the sacrifice and expertise of the authority personnel, professionals and academics working in close synergy with the Department of Public Service – has achieved the objectives expected, including the following: implementation of activities aimed at developing the expertise of managers and officers operating in the regions involved in the former convergence programme and dedicated to the economic/financial planning and development of microcredit and microfinance financial instruments; creation of local networks in support to regional government administrations and, consequently, improvement of the public administration capacity to exchange and interact with the operators on the territory; development of new microfinance products such as microleasing, microinsurance and housing microfinance in collaboration with market operators; and e-learning courses on microcredit and microfinance topics, dedicated to the regional representatives and extended also to the network of stakeholders.

This study was initiated as a corollary to such activities and with the purpose of emphasising the European dimension and relevance of microcredit-related issues, in order to acquire expertise on the programmes co-financed by the EU structural funds and implemented by the various EU regions involved in the former convergence programme for the microcredit sector and to provide reflections and comparative analysis of possible trends on the use of the financial engineering instruments within the European operational programmes.

Without further elaborating on the outcomes of our research, I would like to stress that this study has the unequivocal merit of providing some useful indications on a more effective planning of microcredit and microfinance measures within the current programming period, 2014–2020. In Italy, the new European programming period basically kicked off in January 2015, with a delay of more than a year due to lengthy negotiation procedures between Italy and the European Commission.

Consequently, also, the future programmes of the agency that could be co-financed by the structural funds within the programming period 2014–2020 (in particular the ESF) will be postponed. However, this delay gives us the opportunity to consider new ideas and initiatives that have been developed, also thanks to the experience gained within the Capacity Building project. The activities implemented, the results achieved and the relevant number of relations and contacts built with this project should in no way go missing; quite the opposite, they should be valorised on the national territory and presented as best practices also at European level.

Mario Baccini
President of the National Italian Agency of Microcredit

Except where otherwise noted, this work is licensed under a Creative Commons Attribution 3.0 Unported License. To view a copy of this license, visit http://creativecommons.org/licenses/by/3.0/

OPEN

Preface

The action plan Europe 2020 sends a clear message with regard to economic and social growth in Europe: growth must be smart, sustainable and, most of all, inclusive. In other words, growth must be able to *promote an economy that is characterised by high employment and facilitates economic, social and territorial cohesion.*

The economic crisis that has hit the global economy so severely in recent years prompted the development of policies, especially in Europe, focusing on the fight against increasing social disintegration due to the continuing and worsening employment situation, which has driven a growing number of subjects into conditions of poverty and social exclusion. Such disintegration is leading an increasing number of segments of the population (especially young people, women, immigrants, the elderly) to a general worsening of conditions related to fundamental citizenship rights: employment, housing, a satisfactory social life, territorial mobility, new technology and others. These processes of exclusion involve new sectors of the society that, until a few years ago, enjoyed conditions far from what today are perceived as severe social risks. The need to prevent the further spread of social inequities and the risk of a two-speed Europe, between the EU member states or within them, calls for improved public policies that can identify the needs of the European population, especially those segments at risk of social exclusion, and thus implement instruments and programmes to meet such needs, starting from a solid and shared idea of European social citizenship. To support this pattern of growth, based on social equality and cohesion, national and local government authorities should be equipped with intervention instruments – more flexible, customisable, integrated, easy to access – which, on one side, can effectively reach out to the growing number of disadvantaged subjects and, on the other, may benefit from the increased expertise of the public administration to channel and govern within innovative strategies and practices. The programming period 2007–2013, just ended, suggested and partly introduced a number of innovative instruments, especially financial engineering instruments, that allowed for a more flexible, effective and efficient use of the EU structural funds through a series of measures targeting areas characterised by severe social distress and the implementation of active policies of social inclusion. In addition to the traditional measures to promote employment (i.e., training programmes), such interventions seem to rely also on the use of instruments such as self-employment and promotion of a new kind of entrepreneurship, supported by the provision of non-financial services to facilitate their long-term sustainability. These measures should be accompanied by broader programmes aiming at improving the quality of living and urban spaces (urban regeneration), which constitute the basic conditions to enhance the ordinary living conditions of European citizens. As this volume will show, the new programming period 2014–2020 calls for a more innovative, fair, forward-looking and sustainable use of the aforementioned financial engineering instruments, facilitated access to financial resources by individuals long excluded by the traditional financial circuits (non-bankable subjects) and measures to support enterprises and improve housing conditions. The instruments of microfinance, including microcredit, microleasing, microinsurance and housing microfinance, are part of a generation of financial products that have already been widely used and produced surprising results in the so-called developing countries. They are created and provided with financial resources aimed at supporting cohesion policies and designed and structured according to local social and economic contexts and requirements. These products, in light of a bold and renewed move by the European Union, can now be applied also within the EU employment and housing policies and, more generally, all EU policies for social inclusion. The Capacity Building project was developed by the Italian National Agency for Microcredit in collaboration with the regions involved in the former convergence objective with the ambitious object of providing European public policies with a number of concrete results that may show that it is possible

- to encourage the public administration to consider the use of innovative financial instruments;
- to promote convergence between different actors and stakeholders (networks for microcredit and microfinance) which can operate in synergy to build the best conditions for an adequate development of opportunities to access and use the above financial instruments;
- to lay the conditions for an improved planning and management capacity of the public administration in supporting individuals (especially subjects at risk of social exclusion) in programmes that may

enhance their creative potential, their contribution to the local economies and a perception of a future in which they may envisage more equitable and fair living conditions;
- to promote a different idea of local social development based on reciprocal cooperation and trust between different actors (public, private, non-profit organisations) able to work together to generate social innovation and inclusion.

The Capacity Building project has enabled us to acquire a considerable amount of data and information on microcredit programmes that have been and are in the process of being implemented at the national and international level and to create territorial networks of exceptional importance and competence.

Among the main merits attributable to the project, one primarily to be highlighted is that we have been able to identify new solutions to problems that Italy shares with most European countries; in the first place, the underutilisation of community funds. In this context, it was possible to model microfinance instruments for the benefit of developed countries – we think particularly of microinsurance, microleasing and housing microfinance – thus far widely used in emerging economies. But an even more important aspect, which makes capacity building unique at the European level, was to provide to the regional authorities the instruments to be able to proceed to the launch of such products on the market of microfinance through a significant intervention of the 2014–2020 structural funds.

To this end, each initiative was developed in synergy with the parties, institutional, private or not-for-profit, in various competent ways in relation to the different products/services.

Certainly, a thank you for the support provided on credit matters goes to ABI and ACRI, represented within the scientific committee of the project, as well as to ANIA and ASSILEA, for their collaboration, respectively, on microinsurance and microleasing, and to all the organisations of the housing world, Italian and foreign, that have worked with the project for the definition of housing microfinance products.

Finally, the Capacity Building project has allowed the development of the idea for this study, which is dedicated to microfinance within the context of the EU structural funds and the capacity building of the managing authorities (MAs). This book is the result of a progressive research over time; it has been designed and developed jointly by a research team composed of experts of the National Agency for

Microcredit, academics and microfinance professionals, as well as representatives of EIPA and other important European institutions. This volume is, therefore, the product of consideration and analysis developed by authors and co-authors who shared their knowledge and operational experience over time.

Giovanni Nicola Pes

Except where otherwise noted, this work is licensed under a Creative Commons Attribution 3.0 Unported License. To view a copy of this license, visit http://creativecommons.org/licenses/by/3.0/

Notes on Contributors

Mario Baccini graduated from Lumsa, Free University Maria SS dell'Assunta, of Rome in Communication Sciences with a thesis on Amintore Fanfani's eschatological vision of the social economy. He is the President of the National Italian Agency of Microcredit, a public entity and institution promoted by the UN General Secretary. He was elected as an MP in the 12th, 13th, 14th and 16th term and held several prestigious institutional posts. He participated in the parliament's sessions as a member of the Budget Committee and the Bicameral Committee for the Simplification of Legislation and as a deputy-president of the Elections Committee. He was of Deputy Minister of Foreign Affairs, entrusted with supervising the relations with the Americas, and chairman of the National Committee for the Promotion of Italian Language and Culture in the World, with representation at the United Nations. He was also minister of the Public Function from 3 December 2004 to 8 May 2006. He was elected senator in the 15th term and was vice-president of the Senate and member of the 3rd Committee (Foreign Affairs), 14th Committee (UE Policies) and Antimafia Committee. As for his social commitment, he is the Chairman of the Foedus Foundation, created to promote a synergy between culture, solidarity and business in Italy and abroad. He is also Emeritus Professor at the Catholic University of Honduras, Our Lady Queen of the Peace, and Knight of Grand Cross of the Papal Order of St Sylvester. He has written several articles and essays on ethical finance and preventive diplomacy action.

Alessandro Cardente has political experience that started within the CGIL union of creating and managing a department for the citizenship rights of workers and citizens. An expert on territorial administration, he was elected president of a municipality of the city of Rome. Following that, he was elected a councillor of the city of Rome and later, in Sicily, of the municipal council of Castelmola. He has collaborated with the National Italian Agency of Microcredit, having earlier been part of the Board of Directors, and then went to Sicily as coordinator of the project Capacity Building and Housing Microfinance, on which he worked. He is the co-author of two publications related to citizenship rights and a delegate for UNESCO (Club Taormina Valli d'Alcantara and d'Agro) for Human Rights and Citizenship.

Giorgio Centurelli is a senior expert on cohesion policies, with particular reference to programming, management and control of structural funds and financial instruments. He has completed his thesis on political development and cohesion and evaluation of public investment. He has collaborated with central and regional public authority holders of operational programmes, for which he has assumed positions of responsibility and coordination in co-financed projects. He has contributed many articles and essays and has been a teacher in the field of development policies and a member of the Commission for Consumer Credit, Microcredit and the Structural Funds of the National Association for the Study of Problems of Credit (ANSPC).

Maria Claudia Costantini has been a project designer and project manager of the Fondazione Risorsa Donna since 2004. She is engaged in promoting and developing microcredit in Italy and in promoting women's entrepreneurship and their social and economic inclusion.

Maria Doiciu has 20 years of management and consulting experience in the area of business development and microfinance. She works with organisations to implement projects aimed at creating an enabling environment for business development and access to finance in Romania, the Balkans, central and eastern Europe and the central Asian countries. For the past ten years Maria has held a management position at Eurom Consultancy and Studies Ltd, acting as key expert in research and training in business development and microfinance in projects funded by EC, EIF/EIB, UNDP and USAID. Maria's professional commitment to private sector development, microfinance and sustainable development of countries in eastern and central Europe is affirmed by her service on the board of administration of the European Microfinance Network, as vice-president in charge of the central and eastern European region (2007–2012) and as a member of the BoA of FAER NBFI (2007–2013), a medium-size MFI located in Transylvanian Romania.

Riccardo Graziano has been running two law firms, located in Milan and Rome, for ten years. He specialises in corporate law, transportation law and labour law and provides legal services to several leading Italian and international companies. His consolidated background, combined with his academic collaboration with the universities La Sapienza of Rome and Roma Tre, confer upon Attorney Graziano the ability to interpret the legal profession as a tool for researching the most effective solutions for his customers' needs. Particularly active in community life, he is a member of the Rotary Club of Rome, the Palm Beach

Club of London and the Magna Grecia Association. In addition, he is the representative of the Foedus Foundation for the North of Italy, as well as a founding and board member of the Association Ubi-Maior. Due to his deep social commitment, he was awarded the Paul Harris Fellow Recognition by the Rotary Foundation of Rotary International. He is secretary general of the National Agency for Micro-credit, the President of Assoespressi (National Association of Express Couriers), Chairman of the CIRF board (the company currently building the Rome Fiumicino airport), a member of the Council of Confetra (National Confederation of Road Transport), a corporate and transport law consultant for the Justice Committee and a member of the Bar Examining Committee at the Court of Appeal of Rome.

Stefanie Lämmermann has been working as a project manager at Deutsches Mikrofinanz Institut (DMI), the German nationwide network of microfinance organisations, since 2012. There, she is mainly in charge of managing the EU-related network activities. Earlier, she had been in charge of programme and research management at the European Microfinance Network (EMN). She holds a Master's in European Project Management from University Paris 3, France as well as in Social Anthropology, Sociology and Psychology from Albrecht-Ludwigs-University Freiburg, Germany.

Perrine Lantoine is Microfinance and CSR project manager at the Federation of French Savings Banks (FNCE). She coordinates, at a national level, the actions implemented by Caisses d'Epargne in the fields of both personal and business microfinance. Through their Parcours Confiance and Créa-Sol programmes, launched in 2005, Caisses d'Epargne are leading actors in microfinance France. In particular, they have been a forerunner in financial literacy and personal microcredit. Perrine holds a Master's in Public Affairs from Sciences Po Paris and in Social Science from the Universidad Complutense de Madrid, Spain. A member of the European Savings Banks Group's CSR committee, she has participated in the last several years at the EMN Social Performance Working Group, the pilot phase of the JASMINE – European Code of Good Conduct for Microcredit Provision and the European project on Cooperation for Affordable Inclusive Personal Credit (CAPIC).

Francesco Minnetti is Associate Professor of Banking and Finance at the University of Cassino and Southern Lazio, where he teaches the economics of financial intermediaries, economics and bank management, and corporate banking. His main research interests are the relationship between banks and corporate enterprises, investment banking, local banks, credit to small and medium-small companies and strategies and organisational models in bank. He also acts as board member, auditor and consultant for companies, banks and other financial institutions.

Andrea Nardone is a senior expert on the microfinance sector, social inclusion and women's entrepreneurship. He is Secretary General of Fondazione Risorsa Donna, a non-profit organisation, and since 2003 has been coordinator of a microcredit project managed by FRD and a technical assistance project on microcredit. A consultant and trainer for the National Italian Agency for Microcredit and various Italian universities, he is the co-author of the chapter "La realtà del microcredito in Europe", in *Donne e Microfinanza: Uno sguardo ai paesi del Mediterraneo*, edited by Marcella Corsi-Aracne.

Fulvio Pellegrini holds a PhD in Social Systems and Public Policies Analysis, a Master's in Intercultural Dialogue and teaching and a in Sociology. He has worked for more than 15 years as an expert in the fields of education and training, employment, social, human resources and labour market active policies. A Professor of Economic Sociology and a senior expert, he has been in charge of implementing and evaluating several programmes addressed towards different target groups of beneficiaries (in the earlier programming periods ESF 2000–2006 and ESF 2007–2013). Since the mid-2000s he has worked as team leader and professional evaluator with the most important Italian public state-owned agencies. He has been one of the independent evaluators in charge of the evaluation of the Italian National Agreement in the framework of the programming period 2014–2020.

Giovanni Nicola Pes is the Head of the President's Office, Ente Nazionale per il Microcredito (National Italian Agency for Microcredit), and Director of the Planning and Research Department of the Ente. He is Director of the European Capacity Building project for the public administration and is President of the Consumer Credit, Microcredit and Structural Funds Committee of the National Association for the Study of Credit Issues. He has acted in the capacity of manager and consultant with international organisations, among them the International Organization for Migration (OIM) and the International Management Group (IMG). He was also Chief Editor of the microcredit and development policies observatory of the journal *MicroFinanza* and contributes articles to various dailies, press offices and national specialised journals. He is a member of the fi-compass expert group on the advisory platform for financial instruments under the ESIF and EaSI (European Commission). He graduated with honours in Political Science from the University of Cagliari and the Sorbonne University. He holds a Master's in European Political Studies obtained jointly at the Institut d'Études Politiques in Rennes and the Centre for European Studies of Exeter University. He later obtained a postgraduate diploma in Sustainable Development at Cardiff University and then specialised in microfinance at the Boulder Institute, World Bank.

Pasqualina Porretta is Senior Lecturer in Banking and Finance at Sapienza University of Rome, where she teaches risk management in banking and insurance and derivatives. She is a member of the academic board for the PhD in management, banking and commodity science at Sapienza, and her main research interests are risk measurement and management (credit risk, market risk, liquidity risk, counterparty risk), capital regulatory framework, financial derivatives, credit guarantee institutions and microcredit. She acts as consultant and trainer for various financial intermediaries, microfinance institutions, public entities and consulting firms.

Matteo Re is employed as a project assistant at the European Institute of Public Administration. He is a graduate of the United Nations University-Maastricht Economic and Social Research Institute on Innovation and Technology (UNU-MERIT). He assists in developing research and training activities on administrative capacities building and on implementation of financial engineering and microcredit facilities relating in particular to structural funds. Clients for these seminars include EU member states and regions, as well as the European Commission's DG REGIO and DG EMPL.

Paolo Rita is a senior researcher. He has been the head of the Office of Artigiancassa SpA, a bank specialising in lending to small businesses and in management of public funds. At the bank he was in charge of carrying out studies and quantitative research on credit and finance, with particular reference to facilitation and financial services to small businesses and microenterprises. He has collaborated with the magazine *Credito Artigiano*. Starting in 2005, the International Year of Microcredit, he began collaborating with the National Italian Agency of Microcredit as a senior researcher within the project "A.MI.CI" (microcredit for immigrants) and the project "Capacity Building".

Fabrizio Santoboni is Senior Lecturer in Banking and Finance at Sapienza University of Rome, where he teaches economics and management of insurance undertakings and financial markets and intermediaries. He is a faculty board member of the PhD course "Financial System and Risk Management" at the Università degli Studi Guglielmo Marconi. His main research interests are regulation and supervision of financial institutions, insurance and reinsurance, financial conglomerates, insurance companies, solvency, pension funds, corporate insurance and debt capacity and microinsurance. He acts as consultant and trainer for various financial intermediaries, microfinance institutions, public entities and consulting firms.

Ervin Sinani is an EU funding expert with experience and management skills; his work is particularly focused on special instrument of financial engineering. After receiving a degree in Economics, his desire to enhance his knowledge and competence in issues related to European cohesion policies led him to pursue a Master's in European Funding and Grants at the University Roma Tre. The international aspects of his studies reflect his great interest in, and curiosity about, global education and foreign languages. Sinani regularly collaborates with a variety of organisations public and private. The working time he spends at IGRUE, the Ministry for the Economy and Finance, provides him with indispensable quality experience.

Cristiana Turchetti is the Head of the Public Management and Comparative Public Administration Unit at the European Institute of Public Administration. She holds a Master's in Development and International Cooperation. She has more than 17 years of professional experience related to European integration and capacity building of public administrations and has worked with EU institutions and national and regional governments and in the field of regional development and strategic use of EU funds and EU community programs for regional growth, job creation and private sector promotion. She has direct experience in design and management of EU regional cooperation projects with VET schools, private enterprises, employment offices, regional development agencies, municipalities and NGOs. She also has extensive experience in building administrative capacity and training public officials. In particular, she has focused on preparation of reform processes regarding regional development, employment, social inclusion and vocational and education training.

Gianfranco Verzaro, a lawyer, is on the Board of Directors of the Italian National Agency of Microcredit and is a member of the Board of Directors of MEFOP SpA (a company for developing the market for pension funds), a member of the steering committee of the Italian Association for Complementary Pensions – Assoprevidenza, Vice President of Previdenza Italia – Committee for the Promotion and Development of Social Security in Italy, a consultant to the bicameral Parliamentary Control Commission on Social Security and Social Assistance, a member of the Social Impact Investment task force for the G8 in 2014 and Vice President of NEMETRIA – Training Centre regarding the factors involved in retirement. He was the chairman of the staff pension fund of BNL/BNP Paribas Italy until 31 July 2014; he retired from the post after completing the maximum number of mandates.

Except where otherwise noted, this work is licensed under a Creative Commons Attribution 3.0 Unported License. To view a copy of this license, visit http://creativecommons.org/licenses/by/3.0/

Part I
EU Structural Funds, Microenterprise and Non-financial Services

OPEN

1
Financial Crises and EU Credit Access Policy

Francesco Minnetti, Pasqualina Porretta and Ervin Sinani

1.1 Methodology and purposes of the research

The European Commission's proposals for the 2014–2020 legislative framework aim to increase the flexibility of the regulation, taking into account national and sectorial peculiarities; they further seek to improve the coherence and consistency between instruments, raise visibility and transparency and reduce the number of instruments in order to ensure a sufficient critical mass in a context where the amount of funding available is scattered across a large number of regions and recipients.[1]

Moreover, the European Commission attributes increasing importance to the use of financial engineering instruments, which are considered a more efficient and viable alternative to traditional grant-based financing. In fact, one of the main targets of the European Commission is to improve the level of knowledge that European resource management authorities should possess on financial engineering instruments (European Parliament, 2013, *Financial Engineering Instruments in Cohesion Policy*). The use of financial engineering instruments is an innovative way of spending the EU budget, in addition to grants and subsidies. In fact, under the cohesion policy, structural funds (SF) have typically been allocated to beneficiaries (organisations or projects) through (non-repayable) grant funding in order to achieve the objectives and outcomes defined in the national or regional operational programmes (OPs) priorities.

The literature and field research helped identify the main advantages of using financial engineering instruments: leverage effect, sustainability, capacity building, risk coverage, speeding up programme implementation, promoting urban development.

However, in the programming period 2007–2013, the managing authorities (MAs) increased the use of the structural funds through commercial practices in the form of equity, loans or guarantees (operated on a repayable basis, unlike grants), although the diffusion of financial instruments is again limited to a specific sector. Many of these instruments are designed to improve the financial sustainability of *microfinance/microcredit* schemes that can be pursued also by way of market-oriented instruments (such as securitisation and structured finance).

Microcredit, and microfinance in general, can be seen as a political tool in some countries, where politicians often intervene in favour of individuals who struggle to repay loans during times of economic stress. Microfinance can be an appropriate solution against financial and social exclusion by ensuring the availability of suitable loans, savings and other financial products or services. The EU has set up several policies that address social inclusion and highlight the efficacy of microloans in reducing poverty, boosting economic growth and increasing job creation.

In this perspective, we should keep in mind that while "there is no internationally accepted definition of *microfinance*", the term is generally used to indicate a range of financial services/products (of small amounts) offered to low-income/non-bankable customers and microenterprises. Microfinance targets those individuals who are denied credit by formal financial and banking institutions because of financial illiteracy or lack of knowledge of the formal rules that they should follow to access credit provided by these institutions (Leone and Porretta, 2014, p. 1).

Microfinance covers a wide range of financial services; while it is often confused with microcredit, the latter is actually just one of the products in microfinance (albeit the most important), which includes also a number of other financial products/services that can be synthetically grouped in the following areas: small loans (microcredit), microinsurance products/services, microleasing instruments/products, social housing products/services, forms of deposit collection and management, payment services, remittance services.

Over the past decade, the microfinance universe has undergone several changes (Leone and Porretta, 2014, p. 4). Generally, microfinance is associated with developing countries, where large segments of population need to access these types of financial services; however, microfinance includes a number of activities that extend to developed countries too, where – especially after the international economic and financial crisis – an increasing number of people deal with poverty issues due to factors such as immigration, unemployment, inactivity and marginalisation.

By "microcredit" we refer here to "microcredit for businesses/entrepreneurs", although the term is normally used to designate two types of financial activities: the so-called *social microcredit* (mainly aimed at social inclusion of *excluded* subjects through the provision of financial support to their current expenditure as well as social services, training courses, etc.) and *microcredit for businesses* (supporting start-ups and self-employment initiatives), which obviously has different goals. The traditional microcredit target groups are highly risky and cost-intensive; as a result, commercial banks are not interested in catering to some customer segments, which thus end up being *non-bankable*. This means that the microcredit business is quite different from traditional banking. It includes innovative and customised elements such as different collateral requirements or no collaterals at all, as well as alternative methods for creditworthiness assessment. In many cases, microcredit is granted not only for economic reasons and/or to make a profit but also to serve a broader purpose of social cohesion by trying to reintegrate disadvantaged people into their communities (Leone and Porretta, 2014). In fact, different kinds of credit guarantee schemes, usually created with EU structural fund, support microcredit initiatives in several EU countries.

As is known, under the programming period 2014–2020 of the EU structural funds, the role of the European Social Fund (ESF) is further enhanced, in the attempt to promote social inclusion and prevent and fight poverty, through the mobilisation of a number of policies dedicated to economically and socially disadvantaged individuals. Among the latter, there are long-term unemployed, people affected by disabilities, migrants, ethnic minorities – as well as new sectors of the society, such as women, young couples, single-parent families – who, until a few years ago, enjoyed conditions far from what today are perceived as severe social risks. The current economic crisis has severely hit the Italian economy and prompted policymakers to implement public policies focusing on the increasing risk of social disintegration, which is leading large sectors of the population towards a deterioration of the conditions to access fundamental citizenship rights, such as employment, housing, a satisfactory social life, territorial mobility and new technology. The need to prevent further social inequalities strongly calls for improved public policies able to identify the needs of the European population, especially those segments at risk of social exclusion, and thus implement instruments and programmes to meet such needs, starting from a solid and shared idea of European social citizenship. To support this pattern of growth, national and local government authorities should be equipped with intervention instruments characterised by a greater flexibility, customisable, integrated and easy to access, which, on one side, can effectively reach out to the growing number of disadvantaged subjects and, on the other, may benefit from the increased expertise of the public administration to be channelled and governed within innovative strategies and practices. To this end, the MAs must possess an efficient capacity to plan and organise the European resources; in our opinion, such capacity should originate from a detailed knowledge of local issues and requirements as well as increased information on: EU cohesion policy, thematic objectives, types and features of EU structural funds and other instruments introduced by the European Commission, financial engineering instruments that can be activated and supported by these European financial resources, characteristics of the microfinance business.

In this perspective, this editorial project developed by the Italian National Public Agency for Microcredit[2] within the project "Capacity Building"[3] focuses on the capacity building of public managing authorities (in relation to structural funds) also with regard to the microcredit sector. The study aims to provide a clear picture of the European managing authorities' capacity building also with regard to the microcredit sector in the current scenario, as well as identify best practices and perspectives in this sector.

In our opinion, it is particularly interesting to examine the principal guidelines of the EU cohesion policy, the EU financial instruments in the new regulatory framework and how structural funds have been managed and used so far by policymakers in the European convergence regions with regard to the microcredit sector. Selected case studies on a specific topic will provide a better idea of the scope of this work.

Moreover, this study aims to highlight, through two surveys, strengths and weaknesses of the MAs' capacity building as well as formulate a number of strategic and operational recommendations on the use of the structural funds in the microfinance sector, in the context of ongoing planning processes regarding the implementation of financial instruments in the programming period 2014–2020 (cohesion policy).

In this perspective, this book aims to investigate and provide an answer to the following questions:

- What uses can be made of structural funds and what are their operational features?
- What are the financial instruments used under the EU 2007–2013 regulatory framework?

- What are the new financial instruments available under the new programming period (2014–2020)? What are the goals and differences compared to the previous regulatory framework?
- What are the capacity building requirements related to financial instruments in the new EU regulatory framework (2014–2020)?
- What are the microcredit instruments available under the new EU regulatory framework (2014–2020)?
- What are the main operational features of the microcredit programmes activated thanks to the EU structural funds?
- What are the main results achieved by the microcredit programmes activated thanks to the EU structural funds?
- What are the strengths and weaknesses of the managing authorities' capacity building in the EU convergence regions?
- What are the perspectives of the microcredit activities to be supported by the EU structural funds in the ongoing planning processes with regard to the implementation of financial instruments in the programming period 2014–2020?

The *methodological approach* of this research is based on three separate "tools":

1. A review of the EU regulatory framework on microcredit instruments in the 2014–2020 cohesion policy.
2. Selected case studies on specific topics (non-financial services, housing microcredit, etc.) related to some countries (Italy, France, Germany).
3. Two questionnaires concerning the managing authorities' capacity building in the microcredit sector and their capacity building in relation to financial instruments in the new EU regulatory framework.

This study is divided into two parts and five chapters; they are briefly described below.

In this chapter, after the introduction of the aims and the methodology of the research, we provide an introduction to trends and perspectives of credit and finance for the SMEs in Europe during the financial crisis as well as an overview on a number of EU financial instruments (EIB, EIF and other initiatives). In the context of the financial crisis, microenterprises generally play a crucial role in fostering economic dynamism in the regional and national economic systems by stimulating competitiveness and productivity. Access to finance is a well-recognised problem in the current context. Access of microenterprises to finance has become increasingly difficult, especially in times of recovery from the economic downturn. In this perspective, the chapter offers some considerations on the use of EU instruments to support microenterprises in gaining access to credit explain why those instruments may be used, in the current scenario, in the small and micro enterprises.

In Chapter 2, "EU Cohesion Policy and Microfinance", the reader is given an insight into the main features of the cohesion policy, EU structural funds and the financial engineering instruments: regulatory framework and operational features under the programming periods 2000–2006 and 2007–2013. The chapter outlines advantages and disadvantages in the use of financial instruments as well as the new EU regulatory framework (Horizon 2014–2020); it offers also a comparative analysis with the previous regulatory framework. Finally, it examines the role of the structural funds with regard to microfinance.

The third chapter, "EU Financial Engineering and Microfinance Non-financial Service: A Case Studies", focuses on non-financial services in the microcredit sector: the use of European funds to support non-financial services, advantages and operational features. The non-financial services, usually named business development services (BDS), traditionally associated with the provision of microfinance services (microcredit, microguarantee, microinsurance, etc.) are aimed to assist the microcredit borrowers, potential and existing entrepreneurs, to overcome difficulties in the appropriate use of the financial products contracted. They are also a useful tool to start and/or develop their income-generating activities and/or businesses. Operational features of a non-financial service offered in some European countries are analysed through a number of selected case studies (Romania, Italy).

In the fourth chapter, "Microfinance and Capacity Building in the EU Policy", we present the role of the National Agency for Microcredit in the EU Capacity Building project. In particular, we introduce the main issues of the Capacity Building project managed by ENM with regard to microleasing, microinsurance and microcredit for social housing. For each of these financial instruments, we try to explain their main operational features as analysed during the aforementioned project.

The second part of the book is dedicated to MAs' capacity building surveys; in the fifth chapter, "Capacity Building Surveys", we present the methodology and the questionnaires used in the survey. We provide an explanation of objectives and structure (investigation area) of the questionnaires, the main content of each investigation area and the selected survey sampling of the convergence regions involved.

The first questionnaire ("The managing authorities' interest and needs in capacity building activities") focuses on three investigation areas dedicated respectively to

- the managing authorities' interest in capacity building activities;
- capacity building area where support is needed;
- types of support activities.

The second questionnaire ("The capacity building of managing authorities in the microcredit sector") focuses on four key investigation areas dedicated respectively to

- analysis of the main results of the microcredit/microfinance programming activity;
- target groups and other operational features;
- monitoring and reporting activities;
- regulatory framework of the microcredit/microfinance sector and others.

This chapter also illustrates the survey sampling. Finally, it offers an outlook on the perspectives of the programming activities for the microcredit sector with the use of EU structural funds in the context of ongoing planning processes with regard to the implementation of financial instruments in the programming period 2014–2020 (Horizon); it also suggests actions and strategies to be followed in promoting the development of sustainable forms of microcredit by managing authorities in the convergence regions in Europe.

1.2 Small businesses and microenterprises in the EU economy: introduction

Small and medium-sized enterprises (SMEs) constitute the connective fabric of the European economy, as they represent its backbone and the true driving force in terms of turnover and employment. Their relevant, structural and strategic importance has contributed to shape a number of development policies promoted by European institutions whose efforts, in recent years in particular, are directed towards increasing their competitiveness on other international markets.

Within the SMEs' world, a considerable role is played by microenterprises; namely, small businesses employing ten people or less and characterised by a turnover below €2 million.[4] They represent by far the most widespread type within the SME macrogroup and have shown a remarkable capacity of adaptation in times of economic crises and cyclic slowdown, taking advantage of their quick decisional capacity and operational flexibility to face the new general and economic conditions as well as the changes in their reference markets. Yet as is widely known, microenterprises are also affected by some critical elements hindering their growth and development; such criticalities, if not timely addressed, might jeopardise all policies that are aimed, in various forms, at supporting them. One of the most critical aspects, as will be illustrated, concerns their financial profile, a recurring issue affecting the whole category of small and medium-sized enterprises (SMEs), which often relegates them only to forms of self-financing and at the same time is characterised by the absence or insufficient provision of external capital.

To overcome these problems, European institutions have put much effort in stimulating the adoption of a number of financial measures and, within the sector, have actively supported microfinance instruments.

We would like to stress that while there is no internationally accepted definition of microfinance, this term is generally used to indicate an array of financial services/products (of small amounts) offered to low-income/non-bankable customers and microenterprises. Microfinance thus covers a variety of financial services, including savings, credit, insurance and remittance, and targets those subjects who are usually denied credit by formal financial and banking institutions due to their lack of awareness as well as stringent formal regulations, which they necessarily must abide by in order to access credit from the traditional commercial circuit.[5] In other words, microfinance, through a number of measures generally characterised by small amounts and reasonable costs, is able to support the most needy individuals as well as entrepreneurs struggling to create or keep their businesses afloat, in particular relying on the responsibility and commitment of the lenders, thus allowing for the development of local economies where such businesses are located. Traditionally, individuals who benefit from microfinance are citizens living in developing countries who struggle to provide for themselves – those unfortunately known as "the poorest of the poor". Within this category, women are of particular significance, since they constitute the group mostly affected by financial exclusion in several developing countries. More recently, microfinance has turned its attention also to self-employed workers and individuals in charge of small and often family owned businesses, who are unable to obtain bank credit. For microentrepreneurs, microfinance represents instead an alternative to borrowing from banks and often constitutes a way out of the moneylending system (La Torre and Vento, 2006, p. 3).

Financial Crises and EU Credit Access Policy 11

This first part of the study intends to present an overview of the typical profiles of the European SMEs, in particular focusing on their finance, which is assuming an increasingly crucial role in strengthening their management balance and determining their competitiveness in the market; in addition, this research provides a number of considerations specifically dedicated to microenterprises, as they are by far the most significant component within the broader group of the small businesses. To this end, Section 1.3 herein describes the main distinctive features of small and medium-sized enterprises, offering also a brief representation of a number of aggregates of their positioning within the general economic system in Europe. Section 1.4 focuses on the financial aspects that characterise such enterprises, including their limits and constraints, with particular attention to their relationship with the banking system, which – as will be examined in Section 1.5 – has grown increasingly problematic in recent years due to the effects of the financial and economic crisis and the credit crunch, which affected all business sectors in several EU member countries. Finally, Section 1.6 presents some summary reflections on possible financial measures and interventions to support SMEs, in general, and, more specifically, microenterprises.

1.3 The importance of the SMEs in the European economy

As previously mentioned, the SMEs constitute the bulk of European enterprises and play a particularly important role in terms of turnover and employment, contributing to the global competitiveness of national economies as well as to the development of innovation processes. As this macrocategory includes a wide range of businesses, we have decided to lay out some general considerations applicable to them all and then focus specifically on the microenterprises sector, which represents the area of investigation of this work.

The scientific literature unanimously acknowledges the importance played by SMEs in the economic and social fabric of nations (Keeble and Wilkinson, 1999; O'Donnell et al., 2002; Floyd and McManus, 2005; Lukacs, 2005), pointing out that:

- Proportionally, their economic significance is greater than their size and constitutes the main drive behind the creation of jobs (Caree and Klomp, 1996; Davis et al., 1996).
- They are one of the main vehicles for the creation and dissemination of innovation, especially when entrepreneurs show a strong propensity for entrepreneurship and are able to transfer their entrepreneurial

culture into their businesses, specifically in those sectors characterised by knowledge-intensive and high-added-value productions such as computing or biotechnology[6] (Edwards et al., 2005; Massa, 2008; Vrande et al., 2008; Love and Roper, 2013).
- They have the capacity of exploiting the synergies offered by the territory, given the greater flexibility of their operational structure and the competitive advantage gained by establishing profitable relations with local universities and research centres.

Whereas the presence of a high number of SMEs is a necessary requirement to strengthen the competitiveness of national economies, it is not a sufficient condition; their potential, in fact, can only be fully exploited if adequate policies to promote their growth and development are put in place; other important factors are the characteristics of the sectors they operate in and their distribution within the broader economic system (Symeonidis, 1996; Kuman et al., 1999; Cabral and Mata, 2003; Nunes et al., 2013).

First of all, it is necessary to properly understand the concept of SME, as the category includes types of businesses with totally different features and requirements. In fact, there are both enterprises operating at a local or national level and businesses boasting a strong international vocation; enterprises that cover the whole supply chain and others specialised only in some specific products; enterprises having internationally renowned brands and enterprises that make a *private label* their main commercial channel; companies targeting end consumers and others that operate only on a B2B basis; enterprises that introduce effective management tools and methods and others that carry on their business by relying exclusively on intuition and experience. From this variety of models and businesses inevitably arise different needs and requirements in terms of know-how development, investments and priorities to be addressed in order to continue developing their capacity and exploit new business opportunities.

To this end, the aforementioned EC Recommendation no. 1442 of 6 May 2003 – while pointing out that all entities involved in an economic activity should be regarded as enterprises, regardless of their legal status – has defined the following requirements for the categories of small, medium and microenterprises (Table 1.1).

As already mentioned, microenterprises represent the most relevant group within the macrocategory of SMEs, both in terms of employment and turnover; this is also the reason why institutions, operators and academics have turned their attention to their development in recent years. For some

Table 1.1 Small business definition

Type of enterprise	Number of employees	Turnover (€ millions)	Total value of balance sheet (€ millions)
Medium	250	50	43
Small	50	10	10
Microenterprise	10	2	2

Source: Authors' elaboration of European Commission Recommendation (2003) Commission Recommendation of 6 May 2003 concerning the definition of micro, small and medium-sized enterprises (notified under document number C(2003) 1422), *Official Journal of the European Union*, http://eur-lex.europa.eu/legal-content/EN/TXT/PDF/?uri=CELEX:32003H0361&from=IT.

time now, an emerging doctrine has disputed the positions of that school of thought that saw only large companies and corporations at the core of any economic system, regarding them as the only subjects having the capacity to compete on international markets and able to achieve economies of scale and certain levels of productivity, while considering small and medium-sized enterprises as a limit to the system's economic development. According to this theory, the paradigm is especially true in those countries whose economic systems are mainly based on the SMEs. More specifically, since the 1990s, several countries started to rethink the "myth" of the large corporation (Cameron, 1994; Dowgherty and Bowman, 1995; Baily et al., 1996; Ryan and Macky, 1998; Mirabal and De Young, 2005; Gandolfi and Neck, 2007) and acknowledged instead the growing socio-economic role played by the SMEs. As a matter of fact, this trend was facilitated by the concomitant occurrence of a number of key factors:

- The *organisational crisis of large companies*, determined by their excessive bureaucratisation and resulting in a consequent and progressive loss of motivation and productivity.
- The *abandonment of the vertical integration in the productive process*, through the identification and preservation of the core business, the central activity characterised by high added value and outsourcing of all other phases of production.
- The *diversification of productive activities*, specifically the advent in the market, due to the prevalence of financial management over production, of large groups and corporations in areas of business that are totally different from their products and/or services, which has often led to a decay of their core business.

- A *reduction of scale economies* and, therefore, of the minimum production levels for the various industrial compartments.
- The *creation of new businesses* characterised by small size and high added value.

At the end of the 1990s, when in particular the importance of the role played by the small enterprises in terms of job creation was definitely acknowledged by all member countries, EU institutions started to modify their policies and legislation to support this sector.

The importance of the micro- and small-sized enterprises is sustained by many points of view. It has been argued that a dynamic and growing micro- and small-sized enterprise sector can contribute to the achievement of a wide range of development objectives, including the attainment of income distribution and poverty reduction (DFID, 2000); creation of employment (Daniels, 1999); provision of the seedbed of industrialisation (Grosh and Somolekae, 1996); savings mobilisation (Beck et al., 2005a) and production of goods and services that meet the basic needs of the poor (Cook and Nixson, 2005). In general, micro- and small-sized enterprises are seen as an integral component of the informal sector in most developing countries. In the majority of cases, these enterprises are initially informal, but some of them survive and gradually turn into formal businesses, thereby providing the foundations of modern private companies (Mkandawire, 1999). Hence, their growth is part and parcel of a dynamic process in the corporate sector, as asserted by Prasad et al. (2005).

In recent years, increased knowledge of the micro- and small-sized enterprises system has improved and a number of basic databases have been made available for empirical studies aimed at identifying the constraints hindering their growth and development (Levy, 1993). According to such researches, the main factors inhibiting their development are represented by limited access to finance, poor managerial skills, lack of training opportunities and high input costs. Significantly, further studies, especially those conduced in the late 1990s and thereafter, suggested that finance represents the main obstacle for the whole micro- and small-sized enterprise sector (Green et al., 2002).

From a theoretical perspective, we have different paradigms. The main proposition, which goes back to the seminal work by Lewis (1955), goes under the name of labour supply theory, according to which the driving force behind micro- and small-sized enterprises is an excess of labour supply that cannot be absorbed by the public sector or large private enterprises. Arguably, the micro- and small-sized enterprises sector develops as a response to the growth in unemployment, functioning as a place of last resort for those subjects who are unable to find employment in the formal sector. In this sense, micro- and small-sized enterprises are expected to grow in periods of economic crisis, whereas the formal sector contracts or grows too slowly to absorb the labour force in excess. The second scientific thesis is the so-called output-demand theory, which postulates that the existence of a market for their products and services is a prerequisite for the development of micro- and small-sized enterprises. Consequently, these companies tend to develop a cyclical relationship with the economy as a whole. The third investigation, known as firm-growth theory, asserts that as a result of industrialisation and economic growth, micro- and small-sized enterprises are likely to disappear and be replaced by modern large-scale industries. This theory, however, proved to be inaccurate, as micro and small enterprises normally do not compete directly with large companies; on the other hand, they often tend to retain their micro and small dimensions and coexist with large multinational businesses. Generally, although each of the aforementioned theories has developed into some variants, they all share the belief that the development and growth of micro- and small-sized enterprises can significantly contribute to poverty reduction.

From an operational standpoint, microenterprises give birth to their own peculiar management and behavioural model (Liedholm and Mead, 1999; Hillary, 2004; Barricelli and Russo, 2005), and only by analysing it can we fully understand and examine their specific nature and propose effective measures and solutions aimed at supporting them.

One of the most relevant aspects here, shared also by other types of SMEs, is the central role played by the entrepreneurs, who often represent the main driver and decisional force behind the business, besides the main engine of any form of strategic innovation. This model is characterised by quick-decision-making capacity and operational flexibility;[7] conversely, it can be affected by situations in which decisions must be taken on unfamiliar issues or situations, where entrepreneurs and their collaborators do not possess specific and adequate skills and know-how. The second peculiar feature of microenterprises, as a direct consequence of the first, lies in their organisational structure, which in most cases is poorly articulated and shows a preference for a centralised organisational model, reflected in both their communication and management style, where entrepreneurs are often involved in all aspects of the business, often ignoring specific management elements and the importance of developing internal skills and competences. This model is also often characterised by the overlapping, in various forms and degrees, of business and family dimension, which may translate into "confusion" in terms of assets, resources and management methods. A further characteristic of microenterprises is given by their limited range of operations, often restricted to narrow, highly competitive markets; as a result, smaller companies tend to limit their strategies with regard to their space of business, the geographical area, the range of products on offer and the degree of vertical integration, moving towards highly focused strategic choices. Finally, as several microenterprises are interconnected and part of industrial clusters or company networks (Parkhe, 2006; Cafaggi, 2011; Gronum et al., 2012), in order to define their positioning it is necessary also to examine the intrinsic elements of their reference networks, markets or supply chain.

Whereas the life cycle of microenterprises is articulated in the classic business phases (creation, development, maturity and obsolescence), within their group we can distinguish those referred to as *topo* by physician-economist David Birch of MIT (Boston); namely, small enterprises created not to develop themselves but uniquely to generate income and alternative forms of employment and, therefore, destined to retain their small dimension, from the so-called *gazelle* enterprises (Henrekson et al., 2010), which are small enterprises created with the intent to grow and develop into larger companies, leveraging on their capacity to quickly grab the business opportunities available and sail through periods of crisis and uncertainty, including their capacity to compete on international markets.[8]

According to the extensive literature on the subject (Pal and Ferrando, 2010; EU, 2010; Artola and Genre, 2011; Coluzzi et al., 2012; OECD, 2012, 2013; Hessel and Parker, 2013), besides poor managerial skills and educational background of the entrepreneurs, the growth and development of microenterprises can be hindered by three other obstacles, which represent also their main weaknesses:

- Lack of capital or financial reserves to cope with unexpected events and the difficulty to access credit or bank loans, especially for smaller enterprises unable to offer any collaterals or that have already secured pre-existing assets to obtain financing and, therefore, are already heavily exposed and/or indebted towards banks.
- Lack of a skilled workforce, including the difficulty of training and turning generic labour into specialised work and relocating the workers already employed.
- Bureaucracy, complexities and lengthy of administrative procedures.

In light of the above considerations, the European Commission has long focused on the development of policies specifically dedicated to the SMEs and microenterprises through a number of programmes and regulations, which are considerably different from the measures applicable to large businesses, as the two types clearly show different features, economic characteristics, requirements and perspectives. Following this logic – analysed in detail in Chapter 2 – several measures and programmes were recently started to enhance the competitiveness of the European SME system in different management areas, in particular with regard to the access to credit and the capacity to attract financial resources and investments as well as training programmes to build technical and managerial skills, within a framework that favours the simplification and implementation of specifically targeted solutions. The empirical feedback to the aforementioned considerations and the importance of the microenterprises on the European area is summarised in the charts and tables below.

From a quantitative point of view (Table 1.2), at 31/12/2012, over 20 million SMEs operate in the European economy. Most of them (over 18.7 million) are microenterprises, which represent 92 per cent of the total number of businesses in Europe.

The SMEs make a significant contribution in terms of employment. They employ 66.5 per cent of the total number of workers, with a relevant role played by microenterprises, which employ 28.7 per cent of workers in Europe, a little less than a third of the total.

Table 1.2 Enterprises, employment and gross value added of SMEs in the EU-27, 2012

2012	Micro	Small	Medium	SMEs	Large	Total
Number of enterprises						
Number (mln)	18.8	1.3	0.2	20.4	0.0	20.4
%	92.1%	6.6%	1.1%	99.8%	0.2%	100.0%
Employment						
Number (mln)	37.5	26.7	22.6	86.8	43.8	130.6
%	28.7%	20.4%	17.3%	66.5%	33.5%	100.0%
Value added at factor costs						
Euros (1,000 mln)	1,242.7	1,076.4	1,076.3	3,395.4	2,495.9	5,891.3
%	21.1%	18.3%	18.3%	57.6%	42.4%	100.0%

Source: Authors' elaboration on Eurostat, National Statistical Offices, 2012, DIW, London Economics.

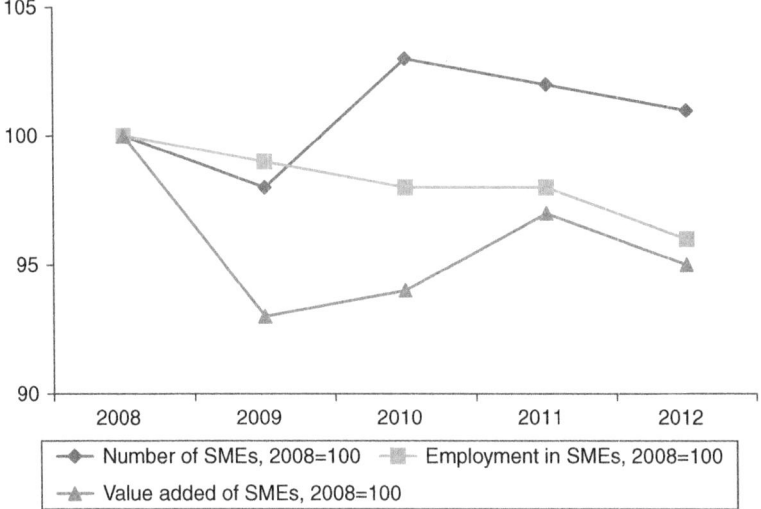

Chart 1.1 Number of SMEs, employment and value added change, EU-27
Source: Authors' elaboration on Eurostat, National Statistical Offices, 2012, DIW, London Economics.

The SMEs system is obviously fundamental also in the production of wealth. The sector generated 57.6 per cent of the gross added value produced by the non-financial private economy in Europe in 2012, for a total of over €3.4 trillion at current prices against a total added value produced by the non-financial private sector amounting to around €5.9 trillion. With this regard, microenterprises contributed to the figure by creating a value in the excess of €1.2 trillion, which translates into 21.1 per cent of the whole production in Europe.

Examining the same aggregates in the period 2008–2012 but focusing only on the SMEs (Chart 1.1), we can observe that:

- As for the number of enterprises, the trend showed a discontinuous performance in the period, reaching its lowest point in 2009, followed by a good recovery in 2010 and a further decline in 2011 and 2012, although at slightly higher levels than in 2008.
- The number of employees followed a downward trend, albeit at very low rates.
- In terms of added value, compared to the 2008 value, there was a reduction of about 10 percentage points in 2009 and a recovery in the

Financial Crises and EU Credit Access Policy 19

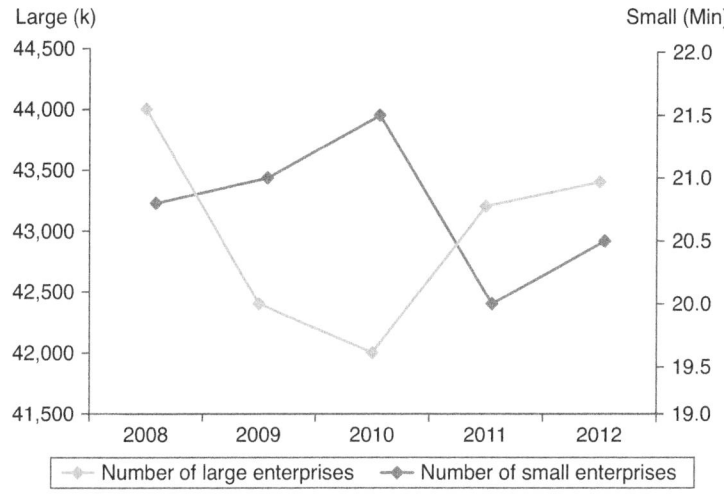

Chart 1.2 Number of enterprises, EU-27, 2008–2012
Source: Authors' elaboration on Eurostat, National Statistical Offices, 2012, DIW, London Economics.

following years, with the 2012 value standing at 95 per cent of the initial value at the beginning of the period.

In strictly demographic terms instead and making a broader comparison (Chart 1.2), the European SMEs followed a different trend than large companies. In 2009, the number of the latter dropped from almost 44,000 to approximately 42,400 and started to recover only from 2011, without reaching the pre-2009 level in 2012. On the other hand, the number of small and medium-sized enterprises grew by 1 million between 2008 and 2010, with a significant drop in 2011 and a good recovery in 2012, when it reached values very close to – albeit lower than – the 2008 figure.

Within the different segments of SMEs according to their size (see Chart 1.3), the dynamics showed considerable differences, influenced by the prevailing trend of microenterprises, which inevitably impacts the whole system.

With regard to the microenterprises, we can observe than only 2010 showed a growing trend, with a growth rate of almost 6 per cent, while the other years recorded drops of 2 per cent a year. This trend reflects the rapid market entry and exit rates typical of this particular segment, which was clearly augmented by the economic and financial crisis.

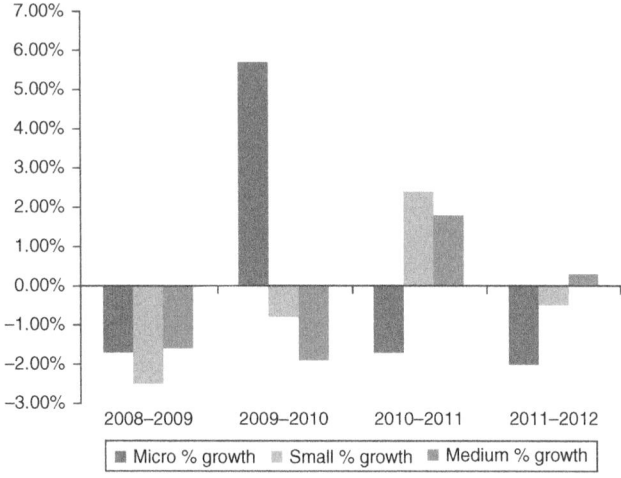

Chart 1.3 Number of SMEs, year-on-year percentage change, EU-27, 2008–2012

Source: Authors' elaboration on Eurostat, National Statistical Offices, DIW, London Economics, 2008–2012.

1.4 Typical financial profiles, in particular with regard to microenterprises

As we have just observed, it is not an easy task to determine the characteristics of the SMEs, as they do not constitute a uniform and homogeneous group, varying instead in size, business models, ownership structure, organisational complexity and propensity to growth and innovation.

The presence of multiple characteristics is reflected in the formation of different financial behaviours and approaches to finance showing different degrees of structuring (Chittenden et al., 1996; Reid, 1996; Hall et al., 2004). In other words, the higher the degree of complexity of the companies,[9] the higher their degree of financial sophistication, which in terms of relationship with the banks and the financial system, gives rise to a whole range of situations and instruments, from ordinary and standardised relationships to contexts characterised by high degrees of customisation and uniqueness (Guelpa, 2005). Hence, it is clear that SMEs cannot be regarded as a macroaggregate to be examined as a whole in an undifferentiated way. The system, in fact, is made of at least two different archetypes, simple firms and complex enterprises, which while having some points in common, show different financial needs and requirements and therefore approach the financial system with different kinds of requests for support.

Microenterprises fall in the first category and feature some peculiar operational characteristics that impact also their financial management. Besides the typical operational risk of new ventures, small businesses with growth targets are generally exposed to high financial risks due to scarce availability of own resources. The need to resort to external financing sources exposes them, in fact, to the risks of fund rationing or high and unsustainable borrowing costs. Such risks are particularly relevant when loans are granted to small or new enterprises whose products or services are highly dependent on the application of scientific or technology know-how and characterised by high expected returns matched by equally high level of risk (Storey, 1994).[10]

Financial risks borne by new and small firms originate from some imperfections in the capital markets, which the reference literature ascribes to fiscal burdens and information-related factors, banking and transaction costs and, more generally, the inadequacy of the structure of some financial systems to support the activity of the SMEs and their most innovative projects (Beck et al., 2006). In particular, situations of information asymmetries, due to imperfect knowledge of the business projects by the lenders, may result in particularly severe financial constraints.[11] This is aggravated by the poor development of the main areas of the business management inside such companies (administration, finance, marketing), resulting in an objective difficulty to provide the lenders with sufficiently clear and articulated information on the company's projects (Devereux and Schiantarelli, 1989; Beck et al., 2005b); a further critical issue is represented by the overlapping of management and ownership, often giving birth to opaque economic and financial situations of both, which prompts lenders to put a greater emphasis on the collateral requirements of entrepreneurs-owners than on the earning prospects of the businesses (Atanasova and Wilson, 2004).

A structurally weak financial profile, poorly equipped to support important development projects, inevitably affects the research of funds and forms of financing, a common issue shared also by other types of SMEs. With this regard, a number of general considerations applicable to the whole category can be outlined. Firstly, the SMEs generally show a limited capacity to fund their projects with their own capital and, conversely, manifest a preference for borrowing, with an inevitable impact on their debt ratio and the level of risk of their business investments, which clearly does not contribute to strengthen their position towards banks and lenders (Pissarides, 1999; Becchetti and Trovato, 2002). While this aspect of their financial structure is driven by correct economic motivations, as borrowing is cheaper than using their own capital, also due to the tax deductibility of financial expenses, it is also justified by an element connected with the attitude of entrepreneurs, namely their reluctance to open their capitals to third parties, which could limit their capacity to control and manage the companies. A second peculiarity is represented by the prevalence, among debts, for short-term loans. Here, given the higher costs of this kind of borrowing, this choice appears to be the result of a lack of planning and limited financial knowledge, which both constitute a relevant obstacle to the use of alternative instruments to the traditional forms of financing.

The above-described characteristics are consistent with the indications of the so-called *Pecking Order Theory*, a financial theory that defines a hierarchy of forms of financing chosen by companies (*financial hierarchy*), assuming the existence of an order of preferences (Myers, 1984; Myers and Majluf, 1984; Fazzari et al., 1988), where the first choice is represented by self-financing, regarded in its broadest definition and including also personal funds, followed by bank debt and direct issuance of shares. This traditional hierarchy of preferences, though, may be subject to changes according to a number of factors, such as the size, longevity and characteristics of businesses. This leads to the introduction of another proposition, the so-called theory of the *Financial Growth Cycle* (Berger and Udell, 1998), which relates the types of investors and methods of financing to the aforementioned elements, assuming the existence of a causal link between the use of different financial instruments and contracts and the role of the various institutional financiers/investors in the funding of companies on one side and, on the other one, the observation of their financial needs throughout the various phases of their development.

The transition from a financial structure characterised solely by self-financing to another one that includes also other forms of financing constitutes, in another respect, a relevant organisational change, which involves managing increasingly complex situations according to the kind of financing sources used. The reasons are essentially threefold: first of all, companies take on the challenge of interacting with different financial subjects whose interests and objectives are different from their own, therefore enterprises need to engage in a conduct able to match such plurality of targets as much as possible. In addition, the information flows they need to produce are larger and more detailed, resulting in increased burdens for their administration offices or "forcing" them to undesirable disclosure levels. Finally, more market-oriented forms of financing require governance forms of greater complexity and, in any case, a number of costs to improve and adjust the firms' organisational structure. In addition, a further distinctive feature shared with other SMEs, especially micro- and small-sized enterprises, is represented by the considerable difficulties in gaining access to financial markets and venture capitals; this inability may result in financial and equity imbalances, such as higher debt levels, lower capitalisation and unbalanced financial statements. Such problems are common in all EU member countries, with different degrees of intensity (Cressy and Olofsson, 1997; Carpenter et al., 2002; Wagenvoort, 2003a; Hutchinson et al., 2006; Ferrando et al., 2007).

Summarising the above considerations, we can observe that the SMEs' financial profile is strongly characterised by short-term bank borrowing, limited use of debt instruments in the market, preponderance of trade payables and limited use of own resources and capital for investments. Banks have traditionally played a fundamental role in the functioning of the SMEs' and microenterprises' financial circuits (Berger et al., 2001; Wagenvoort, 2003b; Avery and Samolyk, 2004; Landi and Rigon, 2006; de la Torre et al., 2008; Beck et al., 2008), providing short-term loans that, de facto, become a long-term form of financing following the periodic renewal of the credit lines granted. The use of bank borrowing, as already pointed out, is due to the poor transparency of information provided by the SMEs, which often prevents lenders from understanding the actual creditworthiness of enterprises applying for loans and limits the number of available funding sources, thus reducing also the options for arbitrage, unlike what happens for larger and more transparent companies, which can easily fund their projects through the issuance of *information-sensitive* securities, such as shares, or by resorting to the capital markets.

In particular, local banks have always played a prominent role in financing the SMEs, as they – thanks to their operations in geographically circumscribed areas and effective distribution networks – were able to build solid long-term relationship with local enterprises based on reciprocal trust and following a relationship banking pattern (Cole et al., 2004; Berger and Udell, 2002; Prager and Wolken, 2008). Their operating model enjoys a number of consolidated advantages; specifically, the same geographical and cultural vicinity as the enterprises; good customer relationship management; the acquisition of information on the local environment and clientele, which becomes an information edge when assessing creditworthiness and credit lines; the search and use of soft information, namely quality and reserved data, a type of non-structured information which can only originate from long-term relationships with the borrowers; a light and efficient organisational structure, which facilitates their capacity to pick up information and take decisions in a timely effective fashion. The lending activity, which represents the core business of such banks, is thus strengthened by virtue of a direct and privileged knowledge of the borrowers and the possibility of a sort of social agreement and checks that go beyond the terms of formal contracts (Petersen and Rajan, 1994; Cole and Rebel, 1998; Scott, 2004; Berger et al., 2004).

While the above-illustrated characteristics are applicable to the whole category of SMEs, when the focus is put on microenterprises instead, the following peculiarities can be observed:

- Net profit levels are quite low; this limits their capacity to fund their own investments and projects by using internal resources and capital; conversely, they are most likely to resort to bank borrowing, an option driven also by their financial structure, which is weaker than other types of companies.
- Discontinuous ability to raise capital, which shows periods of relatively high investments and others when no investments at all are made.
- Debt mainly originates from bank borrowing, although it must be stressed that several microenterprises have no relationships at all with the banking system.
- The amount of funding provided directly by their members is more significant, as they tend to offset the risks of high indebtedness levels and confer greater stability to their financial structure.
- Relationship with banks is restricted to a limited number of intermediaries.

In short, all this leads to the frequent use of self-financing methods, with all the relevant limits, and the general absence of any kind of reserves, even minimal, to cope with any situation of instability that may arise from general economic issues (economic cycles, crisis in the sector), business problems (loss or failure of some key customers), extraeconomic matters (theft and breakdown of equipment and machinery) and personal occurrences (from incidents on business trips to various unforeseen circumstances).

A recent analysis carried out by the Bank of Italy (De Mitri et al., 2013) in the country, which, among the EU members, is the nation where enterprises with ten or fewer employees have the greatest relevance in terms of turnover and employment, confirms these aspects and shows that the indebtedness levels of microenterprises, calculated through the ratio of financial debt to its sum with equity, is always higher than within other types of companies. This is due to the fact that many of them do not borrow from banks (around 40 per cent) because they are unable to obtain external credit lines due to their young or opaque structure. The study highlights also how microenterprises, unlike other types of companies, are also frequently reliant on funds provided by their own members. With regard to their relationship with the banks, which is limited to a few lenders, microenterprises are burdened by the more stringent collateral requirements and application of higher interest rates. Microenterprises generally manifest different kinds of financial needs according to the various phases of their life cycle: whereas, in fact, during the start-up phase they need to make sure to have an adequate share capital, avoiding the creation of undercapitalised enterprises, which could turn into a "chronic" issue and jeopardise the balance of future financial flows, in the survival phase instead, which is common to all microenterprises, they need to be able to cope with unexpected events that may severely impact their business due to an insufficiency of financial reserves. Moreover, if we consider the growth stage, financing is required both for investment purposes and the necessary and automatic increase of their working capital.

Generally, access to credit and finance ultimately represents a critical issue for all microenterprises about to start and develop their business. With this regard, an important set of measures adopted at European level, aimed at solving a number of issues, including the credit difficulties, characterised by the relevance of its scope and institutional participation, is contained in the *Small Business Act for Europe* (SBA), which proposes, within a global strategic agreement for all the European Union and its member countries, a series of interventions revolving around ten key principles and aimed at providing long-term support to the development of this kind of enterprises.[12]

In addition, the European Commission kicked off a series of programmes that involve the allocation of funds and the development and diffusion of instruments more suitable to meet the requirements and needs of the SMEs, such as intermediate financing, collaterals and microcredit. In particular, microfinance was introduced into the development arena slightly more than two decades ago. However, the widespread adoption of the microfinance model did not occur until the early 1990s. Since the mid-1990s, microfinance programmes and institutions have become an increasingly important component within the strategies to promote micro- and small-enterprise development and especially to reduce poverty (Mosley and Hulme, 1998; Morduch, 1999; Hartaska, 2005; Green et al., 2006; La Torre and Vento, 2006; Erikkson et al., 2011;

EIF, 2012). In this perspective, the European Commission (see §§1.7ff.) consistently increased the amount of financial resources to be allocated to microcredit programmes, both through direct contributions and funds granted to the various national funds.

The projects financed through European funds must be constantly monitored in order to observe their efficacy, though – namely, whether the proposals laid out are actually implemented through the tools provided and also what kind of critical issues can be observed during the application phase.[13]

1.5 The supply of credit in the years of crisis

One of the main characteristics of the recent crisis gripping Europe has been the decline in credit granted to businesses, with different degrees of seriousness according to the single country situations. This phenomenon, known as credit crunch, affected the SMEs' capacity to raise the financial resources needed (Canton et al., 2010; Buca and Vermeulen, 2012; Buera et al., 2012; Iyer et al., 2013; Klein, 2014). The evidence commonly found in literature, in fact, agrees in indicating that the smaller enterprises – those with a lower turnover and a relatively young credit history that are most likely to resort to internal funds and operate with lower capital – were those mostly affected by the credit crunch, as they faced increasingly stringent credit constraints during the years of the financial crisis in Europe and their financial situation inevitably deteriorated (Castelli and Modina, 2010; Ferrando and Griesshaber, 2011; Dallago and Guglielmetti, 2012; Varum and Rocha, 2013). The difficulty to access credit affects not just the ordinary operations of smaller enterprises but also their capacity to grow, turning liquidity issues into permanent and chronic weaknesses. The causes of such an occurrence are partly structural and related also to the specific characteristics of the SMEs themselves, as we have seen in the previous sections, in particular to the information asymmetries that arise when dealing with them. Banks regard these enterprises as "less transparent"; as their business capacity is not easy to be assessed, their balance sheets do not offer comprehensive information and their credit history is not as long as that of larger companies. To this must be added greater fixed costs to be borne by the lenders for external assessment and monitoring activity, both before and after the provision of credit.

For these reasons, the suspicious attitude of the banks is partly justified, as – especially in times of economic recession – they generally tend to adopt cautious behaviour in the provision of credit in order to preserve the quality of their balance sheets and assets. As a result, SMEs are more prone to be

Financial Crises and EU Credit Access Policy 27

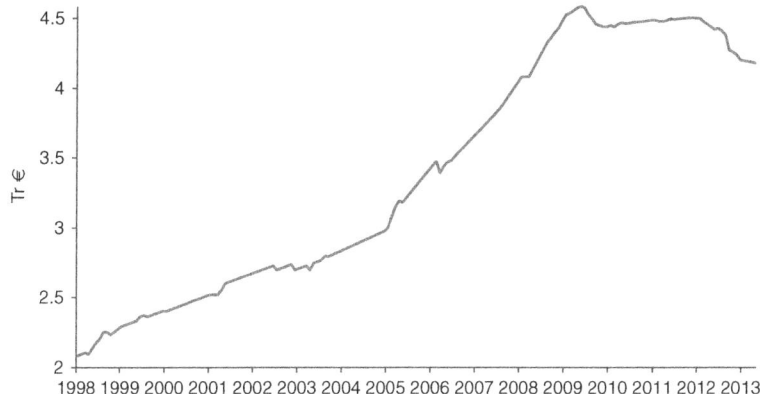

Chart 1.4 Outstanding loans to non-financial corporations in the euro area
Source: Authors' elaboration on ECB Data (2013).

affected by risk-averse banks than larger companies, since they are generally perceived as more likely to default than other companies.

Bank lending to non-financial corporations in Europe showed a constantly growing trend in Europe during the period 1998–2008 (Chart 1.4), rising progressively from €2.1 trillion at the beginning of the decade up to a peak of €4.7 trillion towards the end of 2008. The trend reversed in 2009, with a gradual decrease in the volume of loans in the following years, which – compared to the peak – fell by 9 per cent, down to €4.2 trillion, in October 2013.

In recent years the issue of access to credit has become increasingly relevant in Europe; this is confirmed also by the research and numerous studies constantly issued by interested institutions; all highlight the most significant effects of the problem, both with regard to the business point of view and its financial aspects, showing the intensity of these change over time and their effects on the different types of businesses (micro, small, medium, large enterprises) and, occasionally, also for the single countries. Our research will propose empirical evidence of some elements deemed of particularly interest in order to get an understanding of the SMEs' financial situation in the current context, drawing from contributions prepared by different European institutions and bodies and referring to them for more detailed analysis and in-depth consideration on other relevant topics.

To evaluate the access to credit for the European small and medium-sized enterprises in the same period, first of all we can take a look at the performance of the *SMAF (SMEs' Access to Finance) Index*, a parameter proposed by the European Community to monitor the developments in the sector and analyse differences in each member country. This indicator, calculated by using the EU 2007 data = 100[14] as a reference parameter so as to allow comparing both the results of different countries and the overall results over a period of time, is constructed as a weighted average of two subindices: the index of access to financial debt, which accounts for 85 per cent, and the index of access to capital funding, which accounts for 15 per cent.[15] We observe that the SMAF value significantly increased from 2008 to 2010 and then stabilised at slightly lower values in the following two years (Chart 1.5).

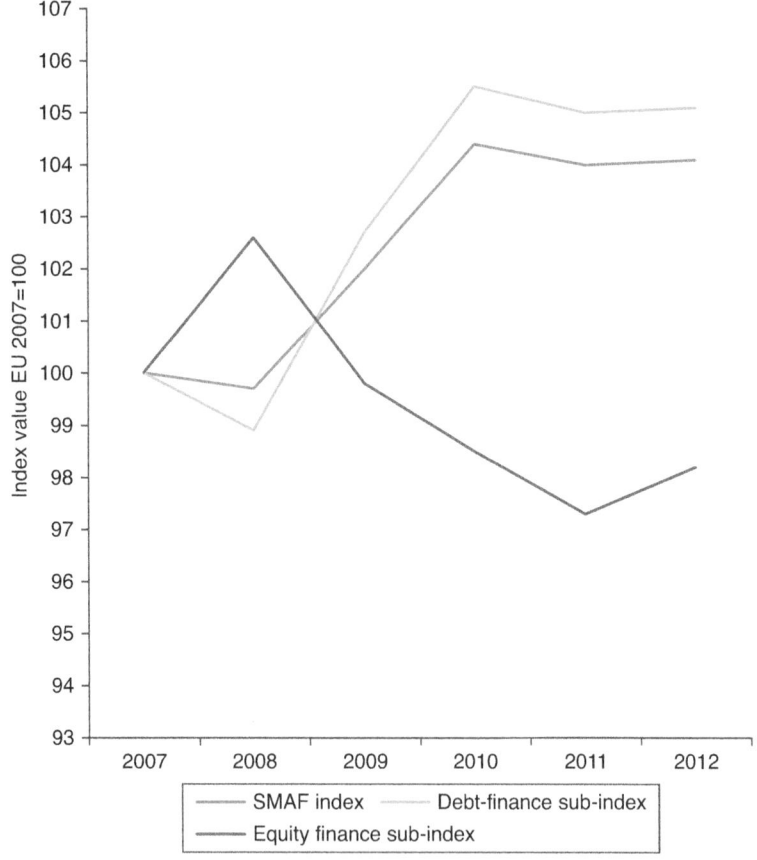

Chart 1.5 SME access to finance (SMAF), index and its sub-indices for the EU
Source: Authors' elaboration on European Commission (2013).

The trend reflects the performance of the subindex financial debt, which had a similar pattern, also due to the decrease of interest rates on loans and overdrafts recorded from 2008 onwards. Investments in venture capital by private equity operators instead significantly dropped between 2008 and 2011, then slightly picked up in 2012. In this context, it is interesting to observe through which technical forms enterprises receive financial support from the banking system. Chart 1.6 indicates how the forms of financing vary greatly according to the size of the businesses. Microenterprises show a preference for using financing sources in the likes of *bank overdrafts*, *credit line overdrafts* and *credit card overdrafts*, while forms such as *trade credits* and *bank loans* are used to a lesser extent; even lower is the use of instruments such as *leasing*, *hire purchase* and *factoring*, which are, conversely, more popular among large companies.

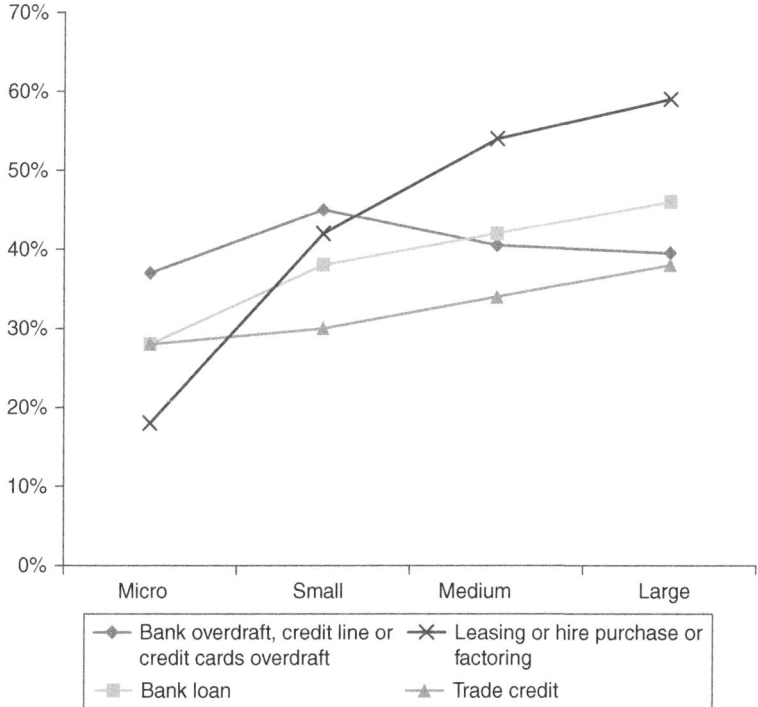

Chart 1.6 Enterprises having used different financing sources (by enterprise size class, April to September 2013)

Source: Authors' elaboration on ECB data (2013).

30 *Minnetti, Porretta and Sinani*

This highlights that with the exception of the first type of instruments, the use of other financing sources increases as the size of enterprises grows. These numbers reflect the difficulties to access credit by microenterprises, which, given their inability to enjoy more stable funding sources in a systematic way, in situations of liquidity crisis are more bound to rely on instruments that are less risky for the banks, as they involve smaller amounts, but are characterised by higher costs when the relationship is prolonged over time. Moreover, *trade credit*, leasing and factoring are strictly connected to business activities of the companies, and their function of reserve (buffer) during recessions could be limited by a reduction in the trade of goods and services.

Taking a look at the elements that determine the financial structure of enterprises, we can observe that with regard to SMEs, during the years of the crisis, profits, interventions on equity and the relationships with the banks all recorded lower values than those of large companies. As indicated by Chart 1.7, from 2008 onwards, the SMEs, although with an irregular trend, saw a drastic reduction of their profits, which fell

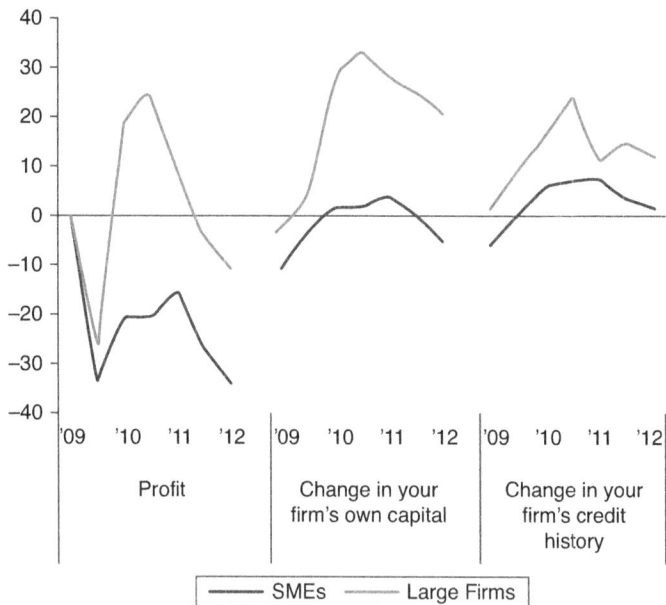

Chart 1.7 Financial health of euro area SMEs compared with large firms
Source: Authors' elaboration on ECB Statistical Data Warehouse (2013).

by approximately 35 percentage points during the period 2009–2012, a decline greater than the one of large companies, whose profits showed a fluctuating trend and were reduced by around 10 per cent if comparing the end-of-period figures and the 2009 value.

Even in terms of variations in equity, the SMEs' performance is quite different, with a gap of approximately 25 percentage points compared to large companies, which were able to improve the quality of their balance sheets. The same pattern can be observed with regard to the SMEs' credit history with the banking system.

The credit crunch of the last two years has greatly affected most SMEs, which, given their limited size in terms of turnover and geographical range of operations, are often unable to rely on funding sources other than the traditional banking system. Access to financial markets, typical of the equity and bond markets, would instead allow these enterprises to acquire the necessary capital to fund investment plans for their development and growth in an alternative way. From this point of view, it appears clear the gap in terms of perceived needs for external funding between large companies and other kinds of companies (Chart 1.8), within a general trend that saw an initial phase (until 2011) where all types of companies clearly manifested such a need and a second phase when the demand for credit decreased,

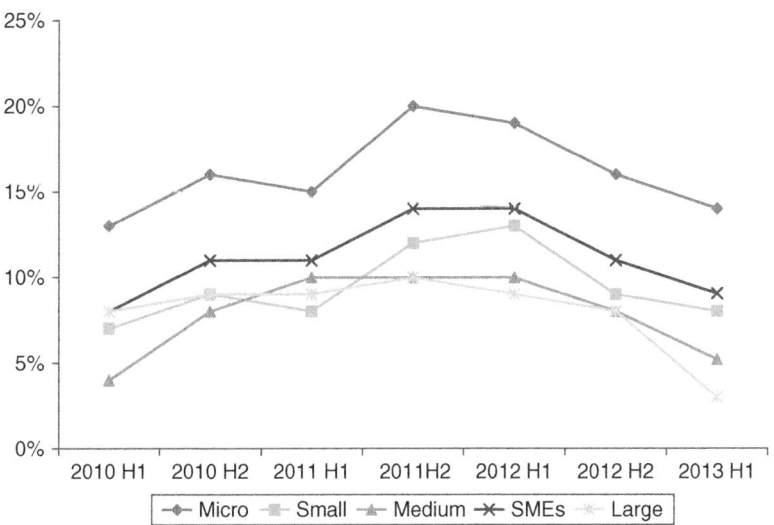

Chart 1.8 Perceived change in the external financing gap (by firm size)
Source: Authors' elaboration on ECB Statistical Data Warehouse (2013).

most likely due to a contraction in investments following the economic crisis.

Of course, it is absolutely normal that microenterprises are those businesses that, more than others, develop a perception to be in need of access to external funding; such need, after a peak reached in 2011, seems to have decreased again from the first half of 2012, with a spread of the SME average that, starting from the second half of 2011, never dropped below 5 percentage points, a further confirmation of their peculiar financial profile. The afore-examined difficulties are also related to the fact that interest rates on loans up to €0.25 million, which represent the bulk of those granted to small enterprises (so-called *small loans*), point out values generally higher than those applied to loans between €0.25 million and €1 million (so-called *medium-sized loans*) and to loans greater than €1 million (so-called *large loans*; Chart 1.9). More precisely, in the aftermath of the outbreak of the economic crisis, interest rates on loans up to €0.25 million gradually rose until they reached a 5 per cent peak in 2012.

Starting from 2012, the market has a general decrease of the interest rates: for loans greater than €0.25 million, the decrease was around 1 per cent in the period 2012–2013, while the interest rate level for loans of less than €0.25 million showed a fluctuating performance, although in a downward trend for about half a percentage point, that widened the spread in terms of borrowing costs. In particular, if we look at the difference between the interest rates applied to small loans (up to €0.25 million) and those on large loans (exceeding €1 million), we can observe that the spread progressively expanded as the crisis prolonged over time, reaching an average of around 250 bp since March 2012. This figure shows, once again, the difficulties met by SMEs in accessing credit compared to large companies. Given their incapacity to provide banks with the same level of information and the economic-financial solidity of large companies, banks see smaller enterprises as more risky and less solvent; therefore, they pay higher costs to access credit. The difference between interest rate levels is therefore the result of a difference in terms of specific business risk associated with the two types of enterprises and can also be explained by the fact that small-sized companies are greatly dependent on the national banking system, also in light of their reduced flexibility in terms of access to credit; on the other hand, large companies generally boast a more consolidated and diversified relationship with the capital market.

An effective source for examining the financial peculiarities of the SMEs are in the periodic surveys carried out at a European level by the *Survey on access to finance of small and medium enterprises in the euro area* (SAFE).

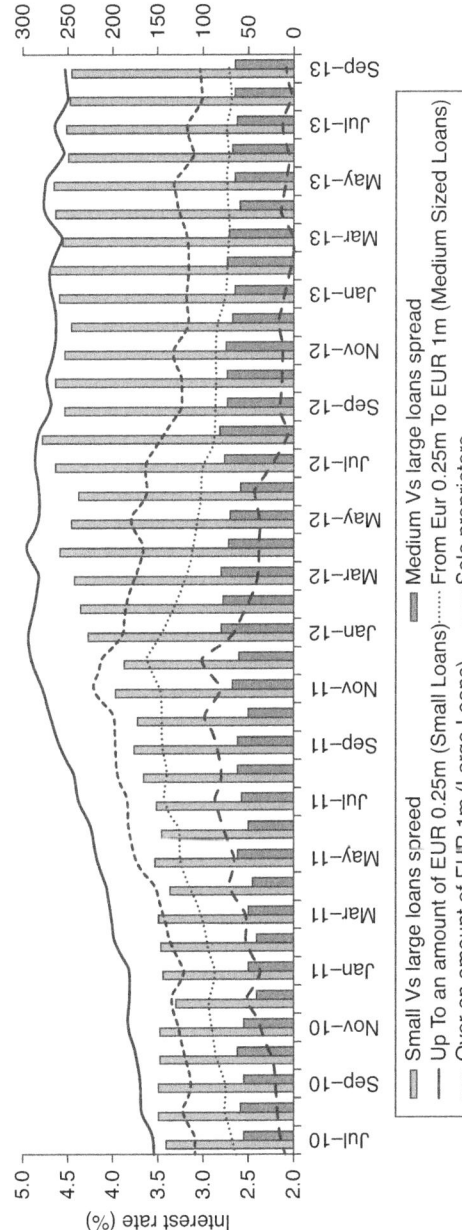

Chart 1.9 Evolution of monetary financial institutions interest rates on new loans to non-financial corporations

Source: Authors' elaboration on Huerga et al. (2012); ECB (2013a); ECB SDW.

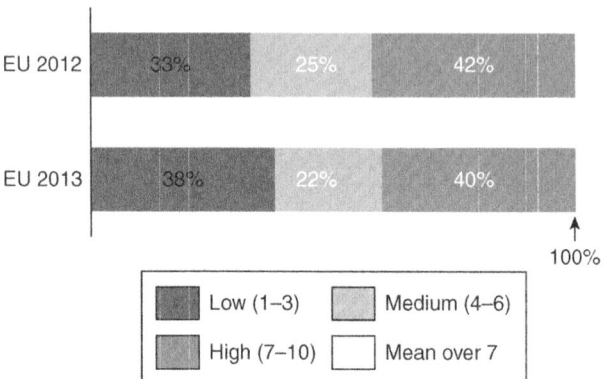

Chart 1.10 Pressingness of access to finance as perceived by SMEs across euro area countries

Source: Authors' elaboration on ECB (2014), "Survey on the access to finance of small and medium-sized enterprises in the euro area – October 2013 to March 2014".

According to the results published in the April 2014 survey,[16] it emerged that access to credit is definitely perceived by SMEs as one of the main critical aspects (14 per cent of the respondents), surpassed only by the need to win new customers (22 per cent of the sample examined).[17] This issue is even more relevant if referred solely to microenterprises, showing higher percentages of consensus than those expressed by the small and medium-sized companies with figures close to 20 per cent in the last three years, a confirmation of the credit hurdles faced by this type of business.[18]

More specifically, when companies were asked how pressing the problem of access to credit was on a scale from 1 to 10 (where 1 corresponds to "not worrying at all" and 10 to "extremely worrying"), the average value recorded was generally above 7 (Chart 1.10), further evidence that, despite some signals of economic recovery in the second half of 2013, the SMEs' perception of a reluctance by banks to fund them remains high.

The SAFE 2014 search highlights also that approximately 4 per cent of European SMEs increased their needs for a bank loan, while 7 per cent of them incremented their need for an overdraft.[19] Both these figures are slightly lower than in the period Aprilto October 2013, within a picture where, at the end of 2013, 54 per cent of European SMEs declared they resorted exclusively to external financing sources for investments. Narrowing the field to the microenterprises sector, their need for

Financial Crises and EU Credit Access Policy 35

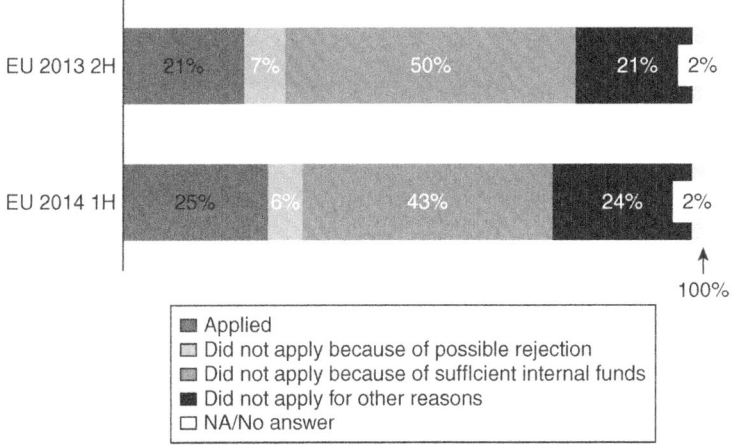

Chart 1.11 Applications for bank loans by SMEs across euro area countries
Source: Authors' elaborations based on ECB (2014) "Survey on the access to finance of small and medium-sized enterprises in the euro area – October 2013 to March 2014".

overdrafts increased in the same period by more than 10 per cent, due to a greater difficulty in raising funds through other channels.[20] The survey also indicates (Chart 1.11) that 25 per cent of the SMEs applied for a loan during the period October–March 2014 against 21 per cent of the previous report, while 43 per cent of them did not apply at all because they used their own internal funds to finance the necessary investments compared to 50 per cent of the previous group sampled, and a further 24 per cent of enterprises did not apply for other reasons. On the other hand, the percentage of companies that did not apply for loans due to fears of rejection fell from 7 to 6 per cent. Finally, as for other aspects of the SMEs-banks relationship, we can observe that:

- Around 66 per cent of enterprises were granted the loans they applied for, while 11 per cent of the applications were rejected and 10 per cent of them only partly approved.[21]
- Compared to the values of the end of 2013, the percentage of companies regarding as relevant the burden of borrowing-related costs, commissions and expenses was slightly lower (from 43 per cent to 40 per cent); likewise, the percentage of companies that pinpointed the interest rate levels as the critical element in their relationships with the banking system dropped (from 19 per cent to 9 per cent; Chart 1.12).

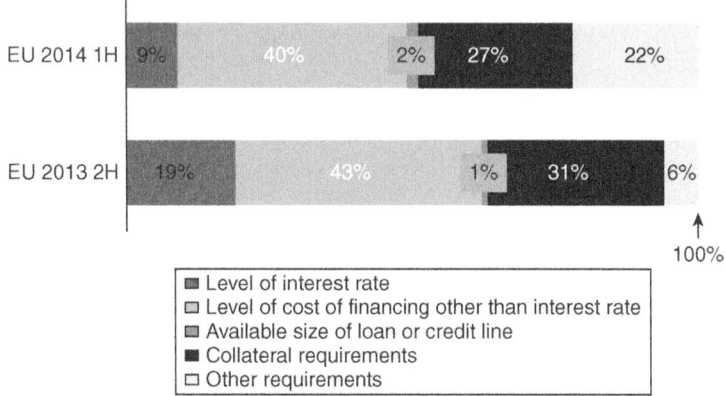

Chart 1.12 Change in terms and conditions of bank loans granted to euro area SMEs

Source: Authors' elaboration on ECB (2014) "Survey on the access to finance of small and medium-sized enterprises in the euro area – October 2013 to March 2014".

- Always comparing the percentages of the beginning of 2014 with those of the previous survey (Chart 1.12), the study recorded a reduction in the importance attributed to collateral requirements, which was indicated by 27 per cent of the interviewees at the beginning of 2014 against 31 per cent of the previous half.

Overall, qualitative analysis, too, highlights that generally all SMEs faced, and still face, problems and difficulties in accessing credit, although a number of parameters contained in the first survey carried out in 2014 have shown a slight improvement.

One more point deserves to be stressed. When the focus shifts from the use of bank loans to other financing sources, either in the form of debt or equity, the picture shows that SMEs have very limited opportunities; a few funding instruments appear basically foreclosed to them. Whereas the use of bank loans is widespread and properly known, as well as the choice for self-financing, namely the reinvestments of profits in the business or the sale of non-strategic assets or assets deemed not directly functional to the core business, alternative and more sophisticated forms of financing – such as the entry of new investors in the companies' equity, the issuance of debt securities, subordinated loans, participation loans or similar – are mostly unknown or unfeasible. Chart 1.13 clearly highlights this situation.

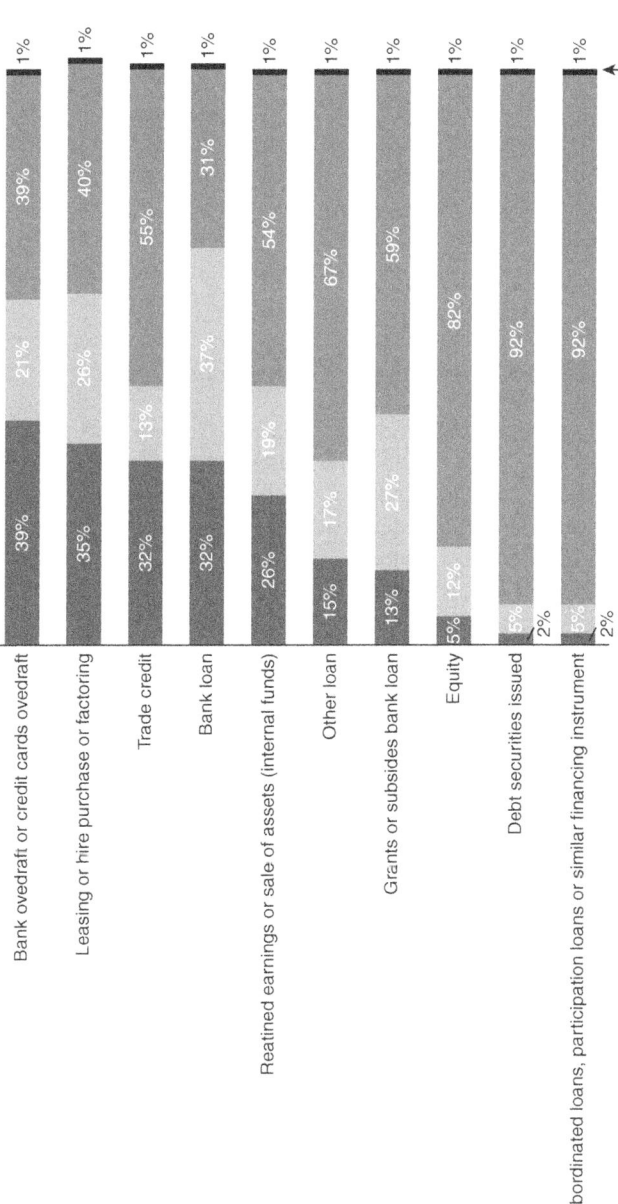

Chart 1.13 Companies' use of internal and external financing in the past six months

Source: Authors' elaboration on European Commission and Ipsos MORI (2013).

Of course, a number of financial instruments can be applied only to some types of SMEs – or rather those characterised by high performance and results, those that operate in particularly lucrative sectors or business areas showing great potential for growth, those boasting a strong propensity for development and internationalisation and those led by entrepreneurs who already improved their management quality and structure. On the other hand, we should consider that almost all companies started small before growing and reaching their definitive size, following a standardised model of development where each phase is marked, from a financial standpoint, by specific measures, needs and requirements.

1.6 Some summary considerations on data examined

The foregoing considerations and data examined show the general fragility and precariousness of the SMEs' financial profile and that of microenterprises in particular, with a strong dependence on bank borrowing on one side and a widespread difficulty accessing credit on the other. This aspect makes them particularly vulnerable or exposed to the risk of exit from their own market as it affects, in most cases, their capacity to start development and growth processes.

Consequently, in light of their specific weight within the European economy in terms of number as well as their relevant contribution to the production of wealth and employment, it is absolutely mandatory to create and strengthen the conditions to facilitate their access to credit and, generally, to additional financing sources.

The primary obvious and natural recipient of such recommendations is the banking system, which besides traditional lending activity in all its technical forms, should extend to the SMEs the provision of alternative instruments and opportunities to raise capital by promoting innovative tools and solutions, in the form of both debt and equity, including also studies on their feasibility and adapting their form to the needs and requirements of the enterprises, following an approach where the advisory part and the supply of products/services are combined in accordance with a problem-solving approach. While the SMEs could seem excluded from such instruments due to their peculiar requirements and poor transparency, their absolute relevance within the European economy is a good enough reason to prompt banks to include them in their commercial and strategic plans, starting from the smaller companies that present characteristics of excellence. SMEs led by innovative and competent entrepreneurs and with a strong propensity to grow are the ones most in need of innovative and structured financial services, as they are also the ones most likely to undergo processes of restructuring, concentration and internationalisation.

On the other hand, an additional effective support to microenterprises – which, again, represent the most widespread type of enterprises in Europe – can be provided, together with other structural measures to be implemented by banks within their ordinary lending activity as well as by other institutions involved, by microcredit and microfinance, with the obvious and adequate adjustments in terms of services, products and methods of provision. The growth of the microcredit and microfinance sectors and their systematic application among operators, both by specialised financial intermediaries and enterprises making use of them, represent a clear and explicit target of the European Commission, which has drawn an actual manifesto to shape its development policies in this direction for the years to come. The next section explains the response of the EU Commission to the different kinds of financial need of small business and microenterprises.

1.7 Access to credit in the European Commission's view

According to the report partially entitled *Access to finance* (EC, 2013),[22] published by the European Commission and the European Central Bank (ECB), access to credit (EC, 2013),[23] especially for young and small enterprises, remains one of the main concerns debated by the EC. The current economic environment has brought SME needs in particular focus, given the significantly tightened credit supply conditions arising from reduced ability and willingness of banks to provide the financing on which this sector is particularly reliant.

In 2008, the EC and the European Central Bank (ECB) joined forces to collaborate on a survey on access to finance for SMEs in the European Union and established the Survey on the Access to Finance of Small and Medium-Sized Enterprises (SAFE). The study, conducted across 37 countries, including the 28 European Union (EU) member states and 17 euro area countries, was undertaken in June–July 2009, in August–October 2011 and, most recently, in August–October 2013.

In detail, the survey[24] examines SMEs:

- financial situation, growth (past and future), innovative activities and need for external financing;
- use of internal funds and external sources of financing;
- experiences when applying for different types of external financing;

- use of loans, size and reasons behind taking out specific types of loans;
- views on the extent to which different types of financing are available to them;
- expectations regarding future loan finance with banks and other sources of funding.

The survey at issue highlighted a worsening in the terms and conditions of bank loan finance in 2013, due to an increase in interest rates and collateral requirements. Approximately one of three of the SMEs examined (EC, 2013)[25] did not get the whole bank loan finance needed for 2013; amongst the latter, small and young enterprises are more exposed to the risk of obtaining just a part of the loans they applied for or, in the worst cases, no financing at all. Scarcity of collateral and other burdensome conditions required by banks represent the most common obstacles faced by businesses seeking bank loan financing, followed by the excessive burden of interest rates. Particularly weak was also the use of venture capital financing, which involved only 5 per cent of the SMEs (EC, 2013);[26] generally, it is a scarcely used form of funding and characterised by high costs.

In order to promote access to credit under the 2007–2013 plan,[27] just ended, the EC activated several instruments: those within the Entrepreneurship and Innovation Programme, such as GIF and SMEG (EC, 2006),[28] and other innovative instruments in collaboration with the EC and the European Investment Bank and other financial institutions (JEREMIE, JASPER, JESSICA and JASMINE). In the new plan, the European Commission intends to tackle the issue of access to credit through the new programme for competitiveness (COSME,[29] *Programme for the Competitiveness of enterprises and SMEs*). Running from 2014 to 2020, this is the first EC programme exclusively dedicated to SMEs.

1.8 European Investment Bank: mission and operating methods

The European Investment Bank (EIB)[30] is the European Union bank; it contributes to the implementation of the EU objectives through investments in projects aimed at promoting integration within the EU, balanced development of countries and economic and social cohesion, as well as the development of an economy based on knowledge and innovation.

The EIB, both a bank and an independent institution within the EU, enjoys its own legal personality, financial autonomy and decision-making structure. Its task is to contribute to the balanced and steady development of the common market (EU) by financing, through the granting of loans and collaterals, the following projects on a non-profit basis in all sectors of the economy (EU, 2010):[31]

- projects for developing less-developed regions;
- projects for modernising or converting undertakings or for developing fresh activities called for by the establishment or functioning of the common market, where these projects are of such a size or nature that they cannot be entirely financed by the various means available in the individual member states;
- projects of common interest to several member states which are of such a size or nature that they cannot be entirely financed by the various means available in the individual member states.

In carrying out its activities, the bank facilitates the funding of investment programmes, in conjunction with measures provided by EU structural funds and other financial instruments, by applying interest rates (EU, 2010)[32] consistent with prevailing conditions on the capital markets and calculated so as to allow the bank to meet its obligations, cover its costs and risks and create a reserve fund (pursuant to art. 22 of the general EIB Statute; EU, 2010).[33] Table 1.3 lists amounts of EIB investments (€) made in recent years and divided by different business sectors.

1.9 What is the EIF?

The European Investment Fund (EIF)[34] was established in 1994 as the EU financial entity specialising in supporting SMEs. The EIF is the European Union body dedicated to providing risk-finance integrated development solutions for SMEs in the EU member states, countries included in the European Free Trade Association (EFTA) and EU candidate countries. It offers a variety of financial solutions to public and private intermediaries, with the aim of supporting access to credit for the SMEs as well as correcting a number of market imbalances. The EIF is committed to promoting EU objectives in terms of innovation, regional development, entrepreneurship, growth and employment. Its ownership structure was modified in June 2000; currently, the main EIF shareholder is the European Investment Bank (61.2 per cent), followed by the EC (30 per cent) and 28 public and private financial institutions from EU member countries Turkey and Croatia (EU candidate countries)

Table 1.3 Projects financed by EIB

Sectors	Years						
	2007	2008	2009	2010	2011	2012	2013
Agriculture, fisheries, forestry	–	9,100,000	373,571,217	255,000,000	1,135,341,482	350,000,000	475,562,500
Composite infrastructure	659,461,419	1,749,117,849	1,252,010,040	1,496,553,396	127,800,000	458,380,689	337,956,402
Credit lines	10,394,573,188	12,474,837,012	18,333,653,882	13,848,344,313	14,390,794,228	15,254,070,280	21,900,082,482
Education	1,877,501,459	2,419,619,408	2,458,925,821	4,015,317,965	1,453,709,020	1,462,329,000	2,811,655,679
Energy	6,556,816,214	9,204,082,582	11,110,310,727	14,591,469,851	10,622,348,889	7,250,475,352	10,615,090,817
Health	2,031,108,592	943,950,000	1,061,488,638	3,428,198,887	1,412,300,000	848,827,331	2,183,485,837
Industry	4,312,525,475	6,344,070,145	13,320,133,946	8,825,996,481	6,724,099,705	5,093,743,992	723,557,067
Services	3,067,312,849	1,730,997,399	2,854,582,422	3,990,344,202	2,144,181,024	2,358,517,218	4,126,376,062
Solid waste	89,685,475	563,275,354	626,380,023	88,500,000	419,300,000	203,800,500	195,081,692
Telecommunications	2,619,117,108	1,912,240,000	2,848,975,000	2,286,983,614	1,646,616,000	1,636,672,422	3,025,160,304
Transport	11,521,195,430	14,957,700,538	17,452,887,854	14,562,272,139	15,735,935,465	11,882,567,734	12,584,859,956
Urban development	2,083,524,058	2,567,818,098	2,902,321,368	2,104,431,867	1,226,784,556	2,179,519,946	1,573,287,372
Water, sewerage	2,285,135,367	3,036,587,765	4,250,686,658	2,352,185,166	3,876,461,759	3,411,523,503	4,671,444,281

Source: Authors' elaboration on EIB data (2013), www.eib.org/projects/loans/sectors/index.htm?start=2013&end=2013.

Financial Crises and EU Credit Access Policy 43

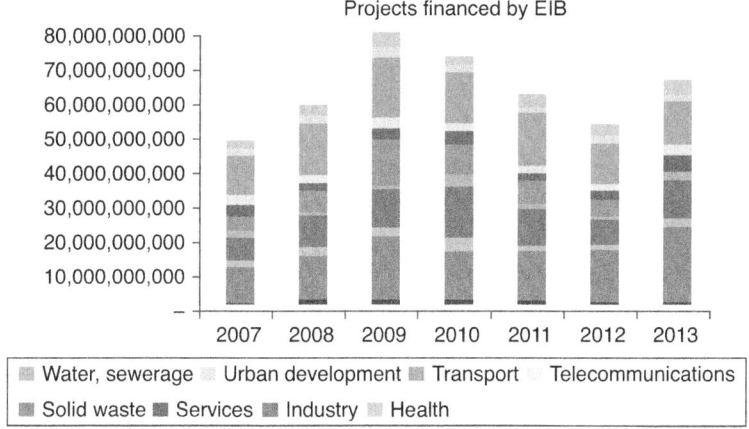

Chart 1.14 Projects financed by EIB
Source: Authors' elaboration on EIB's data (2013).

(8.8 per cent). The EIF is provided with capital of €3 billion. It uses market instruments to promote the creation and growth of European SMEs, such as venture capital, mezzanine finance and debt instruments (supported by collaterals).

With regard to debt instruments, the EIF operates through credit support activities and guarantees/counterguarantees for loan portfolios and leasing contracts entered by SMEs. The EIF helps the partner financial institutions to facilitate transfer of risk, provide part of the equity and reserve capital and diversify financing sources. EIF's guarantees contribute to strengthen the SMEs access to credit while generating further resources for their development.

The table below illustrates some statistical data related to operations and activities carried out by EIF (Table 1.4 and Chart 1.15).

1.10 The main financial instruments 2007–2013

Following decision no. 1639/2006 of the European Parliament and the European Council (24 October 2006), the EU established a Competitiveness and Innovation Framework Programme for the period January 2007 to December 2013. This programme pursues the following objectives:

- Promote the competitiveness of enterprises, in particular SMEs.
- Promote any innovation forms, including eco-innovation.

44　*Minnetti, Porretta and Sinani*

- Accelerate the development of a sustainable, innovative and inclusive information society.
- Promote energy efficiency and the use of innovative and renewable energy sources in all sectors, including transports.

The programme at issue is provided with a budget of €3,621,300,000[35] for its implementation.

Table 1.4 Yearly signatures (€ millions)

Operational highlights	Year				
	2013	2012	2011	2010	2009
Equity signatures	1,468	1,350	1,126	930	733
Equity catalysed amount	7,147	7,078	6,061	4,589	–
Guarantee signatures	1,844	1,180	1,461	611	191
Guarantee catalysed amount	8,611	5,111	7,626	3,138	–
Microfinance signatures	54	40	67	8	–
Microfinance catalysed amount	201	139	14	32	–

Source: Authors' elaboration on EIF data (2013), *Annual report 2013*, Imprimerie Centrale, Luxembourg, http://www.eif.org/news_centre/publications/eif_annual_report_2013.pdf.

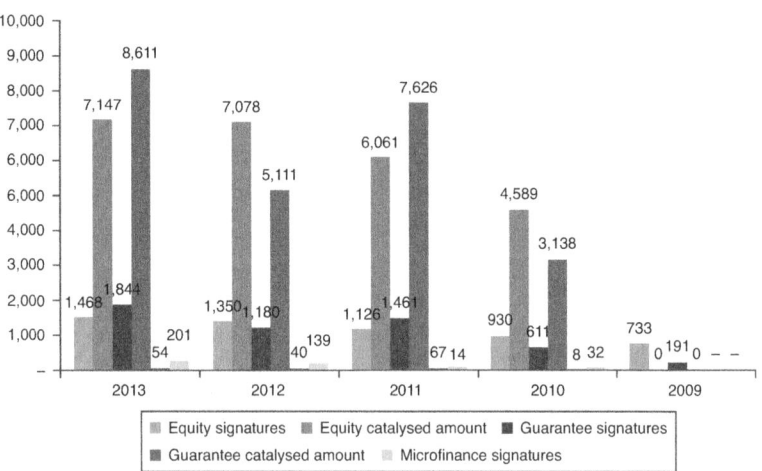

Chart 1.15 Yearly signatures (€ millions)
Source: Authors' elaboration on EIF's data (2013).

The programme's financial instruments are as follows:

- GIF (*Growth and Innovative Facility*);
- SMEG (*Small Medium Enterprise Guarantee Facility*);
- CBS (*Capacity Building Scheme*).

Table 1.5 describes in detail each of the above financial instruments, including general information on activation date, financing methods, main objectives, statistical data and primary advantages that can be obtained through their use.

1.11   GIF

The GIF (*Growth and Innovative Facility*) contributes to the establishment and financing of SMEs and reduces the lack of equity capital in the European markets. It is managed by the European Investment Fund on behalf of the European Commission and supports innovative and high-growth potential SMEs, favouring those engaged in R&D and innovation. There might also be co-investments in funds and investment vehicles promoted by intermediaries, including collaboration with national or regional programmes aimed at developing investments into small enterprises. The GIF (EP, 2006, p. 17)[36] includes two sections that support SMEs in two different stages:

- Section "GIF 1" involves the provision of risk capital for innovative SMEs in their early stages (seeding and start-up). This facility invests in the equity of intermediary capital venture funds and other investment vehicles that, in turn, invest in SMEs no older than ten years, generally during the seeding and start-up phases. EIF usually can invest (EC, 2006)[37] in 10–25 per cent of the total equity of the intermediary venture capital funds. In exceptional cases, EIF can invest up to 50 per cent of the total risk capital; this happens for new funds likely to have a particularly strong catalytic role for the development of risk capital markets for specific technologies, in a specific area or for investment instruments of formal investors. The GIF1 can co-invest using the EIF's own resources or other resources managed by the EIF. In both cases, the maximum commitment for a single fund cannot exceed €30 million (EP, 2006, p. 22).[38]
- The second section, named "GIF 2" (EP, 2006),[39] concerns the provision of risk capital for SMEs with high growth potential in their expansion phase; the EIF invests in venture capital funds that, in

Table 1.5 The main financial instruments, 2007–2013

Type of instrument	Products offered	Characteristics
GIF	GIF 1	It provides venture capital for innovative SMEs in their early stages (seeding and start-up phase). It invests in the equity of intermediary capital venture funds and other investment vehicles that, in turn, invest in SMEs no older than ten years.
	GIF 2	It provides venture capital for SMEs with high growth potential in their expansion phase, investing in the equity of intermediary venture capital funds that, in turn, provide equity or quasi-equity investments to the aforementioned innovative SMEs.
SMEG	Financing through loans or leasing	It reduces the particular difficulties met by SMEs to access finance due to the fact that investments in certain knowledge-related activities, such as technological development, innovation and technology transfer, are perceived as more risky or because they do not possess sufficient collateral.
	Microcredit	It provides loan guarantees to encourage banks to make more debt finance available to SMEs by granting small amount loans, with higher management costs for the borrowers who do not possess sufficient collateral. SMEG provides co-, counter- or direct guarantees to financial intermediaries as well as subsidies to reduce the high administrative costs related to microcredit.
	Equity or quasi-equity guarantees to support investments in SMEs	It provides equity or quasi-equity guarantees for investments to create and/or start enterprises, as well as to mezzanine finance providers, in order to reduce the particular difficulties met by the SMEs to access credit due to their weak financial structure or in the event of transfer of businesses.
	Securitisation of loan portfolios granted to SMEs	It mobilises additional debt finance resources for SMEs, within appropriate sharing agreements of eco-innovation-oriented projects.
Capacity building scheme	Seed capital	Aimed at stimulating the provision of venture capital for innovative SMEs or SMEs with high growth potential, including those involved in sectors of the traditional economy, through investments in funds that provide capital for the creation and start-up of enterprises.
	Partnership	Subsidies granted to financial intermediaries to cover technical assistance costs needed to improve procedures to assess loan applications submitted by SMEs in order to stimulate the provision of finance to SMEs in those countries where bank intermediation is weak.

turn, provide equity or quasi-equity investments in the aforementioned innovative SMEs. GIF 2 investments do not support buyout or asset-stripping operations.[40]

1.11.1 Statistical data

At the end of December 2012, 34 agreements had been signed. The net amount committed to these funds was €430.5 million.[41] A total of 289 SMEs have benefited from investments.

Overview of commitments/deals and agreements/related equity investment and final beneficiaries as of 31 December 2012:[42]

- EU GIF budgetary commitments since the beginning (2007): €499.77 million;
- EU GIF net commitments: €430.5 million;
- deals approved by EC as of 31 December 2012 (ECFIN data on deals flow): 36 deals had been approved by the EC with regard to the financial intermediaries (venture capital funds), for a total of €463.8 million in net commitments from the EU budget, corresponding to a utilisation rate of 98.5 per cent of commitments available for deals (i.e., €470.6 million over the period 2007–2012). Out of these 36 funds, 17 funds have a multicountry focus, and the remaining 19 funds target investments in specific countries. Ten venture capital funds are investing in eco-innovation projects, supported by approved EU investments for a total amount of €147.9 million (*valued at the exchange rate of the reporting date*);
- number of signed agreements (by EIF): 34 (out of the 36 funds approved), for a total amount of €430.5 million);
- including eco-innovation: 7 deals (20.5 per cent), amounting to €124.9 million (29 per cent).

The stage focus spread of the 34 agreements is indicated in Table 1.6.

Table 1.6 Types of agreements

☐ start-up/early stage	13
☐ technology transfer	5
☐ other (small caps/midmarket/balanced venture capital):	16

Source: Authors' elaboration on EC data (2013).

Table 1.7 Number of final beneficiaries (SMEs) as of 31 December 2012

Gearing effect of GIF (target intermediary size/EU GIF net commitments)	5.5[a]
Number of final beneficiaries (SMEs)	289
Contribution to long-term growth prospects of beneficiaries: nearly 95% of the final beneficiaries interviewed stated that the EIP support had a positive or fairly positive impact on their long-term growth prospects.	
Feedback from SMEs on added value, utility and relevance[b]	
– Final beneficiaries stating the EU financing scheme was the only option available	39%
– Final beneficiaries stating that they would have received only part of the funding needed without the EU financing scheme	23%
Total of beneficiaries indicating that EU support was crucial to finding the finance needed	62%
– Leverage effect assessment: final beneficiaries stating that receiving financing from EIP was easier to get additional finance	77%

[a]2,360.1/430.5; target intermediary (fund) size as of 31 December 2012: €2,360.1 million (*Source*: EIF CIP GIF Report, 31 December 2012).
[b]EIP (2011), "Final evaluation final report March 2011", questionnaire on 117 interviewees, pp. 47, 56, 57.

Source: Authors' elaboration on EIPC data (2013), http://ec.europa.eu/cip/files/docs/eip-final-evaluation-report_en.pdf.

1.12 The SMEG

The SME Guarantee Facility (SMEG) offers guarantees to encourage banks to mobilise additional resources to finance SMEs through loans by reducing their exposure to risk. The SMEG provides co-, counter- and direct guarantees to financial intermediaries providing loans, mezzanine finance and microcredit to the SMEs. The SMEG is divided into four sections (loan or leasing guarantees, microcredit, equity and quasi-equity guarantees, securitisation of loan portfolios granted to SMEs), whose operating methods have already been illustrated in Table 1.5 (EP, 2006, p. 26).[43]

1.12.1 Statistical data

At the end of 2012, 62 agreements with 45 financial intermediaries had been signed under this facility. In total, 256 341 loans were provided to 218,843 SMEs.

Table 1.8 Amount of commitments/guarantees

Commitments/guarantees	Amount
EU SMEG budgetary commitments since beginning (*Source*: ECFIN budget figures)	€510.88 million
EU SMEG total loan amount	€13,353.3 million
EU SMEG guarantee	€7,420.3 million
SMEG guarantee cap amount	€460.1 million

Source: Authors' elaboration on EIF data (2013), *Entrepreneurship and Innovation Programme Committee*, http://ec.europa.eu/cip/files/cip/eip_performance_report_2007–2013_en.pdf.

Table 1.9 Output SMEG

Number of signed agreements (by EIF)	62
Number of agreements brought about by SMEG windows	
☐ Loan window	48
☐ Microcredit window	13
☐ Equity/quasi-equity window	1
Number of SMEs benefiting as of 31 December 2012	218,483
Number of related loans as of 31 December 2012	256,341

Source: Authors' elaboration on EIF data (2013), *Entrepreneurship and Innovation Programme Committee*, http://ec.europa.eu/cip/files/cip/eip_performance_report_2007–2013_en.pdf.

Table 1.8 shows an overview of commitments/guarantees/deals and agreements/related loans and final beneficiaries financed by SMEG as of 31 December 2012.

At the end of December 2012, the EC approved deals with 46 financial intermediaries from 23 countries (including 16 from 8 new member states, one from Norway, one from Serbia and Montenegro, two from Croatia and four from Turkey), with a total of €482.9 million from the budget for guarantees or counterguarantees (Table 1.9).

Table 1.10 shows the results in terms of contributions made to long-term growth prospects of final beneficiaries/final beneficiaries' statement on the utility of the programme.

1.13 The CBS

The Capacity Building Scheme (CBS) (EP, 2006, p. 26)[44] is managed in collaboration with a number of international financial institutions, including the European Bank for Reconstruction and Development (EBRD), the EIB, the European Investment Fund and the Council of

Table 1.10 SMEG results

Gearing effect EU guarantee/guarantee cap amount[a]	16.1
Leverage (total loan amount/guarantee cap amount[b]	29
Number of final beneficiaries (SMEs)	218,843
The target of 315,750 SMEs[c] benefiting from the EIP financial instruments by the end of the programme seems therefore achievable (2013)	
– Contribution to long-term growth prospects of beneficiaries: ¾ of all interviewed final beneficiaries stated that the EIP support had a positive or fairly positive impact on their long-term growth prospects	
– Feedback from SMEs on added value, utility and relevance[d]:	
☐ Final beneficiaries stating the EU financing scheme was the only option available	46%
☐ Final beneficiaries stating that they would have received only part of the funding needed without the EU financing scheme	18%
Total of beneficiaries indicating that EU support was crucial to find the finance needed	64%
☐ Leverage effect assessment: final beneficiaries stating that receiving financing from EIP was easier than accessing additional finance	42%

[a]EU guarantee/guarantee cap amount = 7,420.3/460.1; these are the "gearing effect" figures officially released by the EIF (*Source*: EIF SMEG 2007 Report, 31 December 2012).
[b]For agreements signed by EIF under SMEG, as of 31 December 2012: Total loan amount/ guarantee cap amount = 13,353.3/460.1 (*Source*: EIF SMEG 2007 Report, 31 December 2012).
[c]EIP (2013), "Final evaluation final report", March 2011, p. 51.
[d]EIP (2013), "Final evaluation final report", March 2011, questionnaire on 117 interviewees, p. 47, 56, 57.
Source: Authors' elaboration on EIF data (2013).

Europe Development Bank (CEB). The CBS pursues the following objectives:

- Improve technical skills on investments, fund technology and those of other financial intermediaries investing in innovative or high growth potential SMEs.
- Stimulate credit supply to the SMEs by improving assessment procedures to evaluate loan applications submitted by SMEs.

The CBS comprises two parts: *seed capital* and *partnership*.

The *seed capital* action provides grants aimed at stimulating the supply of venture capital to innovative SMEs and other SMEs with high growth potential, including those operating in traditional sectors of the economy, by providing grants to venture capital funds investing in the creation or support of start-ups or similar organisations. Grants can be provided also for the long-term recruitment of staff or staff with specific investment or technology expertise.

The *partnership* action provides grants to financial intermediaries to cover the costs of the technical assistance needed to improve their assessment procedures to evaluate loan applications submitted by SMEs in order to stimulate the supply of financing to SMEs in those countries where bank intermediation is weak. For *partnership* action purposes, bank intermediation in a given country is deemed weak when the domestic credit, expressed as a percentage of gross domestic product of a country, is well below the EU average, according to data of the European Central Bank or the International Monetary Fund.

The *partnership* action supports the credit lines or risk-sharing that the international financial institutions grant to their partners (banks or financial institutions) in eligible countries. A significant portion of the action is aimed at improving the capacity of banks and other financial intermediaries to assess the loans' commercial feasibility.

1.14 Financial engineering instruments

To ensure a more efficient and sustainable use of the structural funds and cohesion funds in the period 2007–2013, the European Commission activated various programmes and numerous financial instruments. Financial engineering instruments[45] are an innovative form provided by the structural funds to achieve the cohesion policy objectives, as they are an integral part of the strategy aimed at promoting long-term sustainable growth in the European regions. For such purpose, the European Commission implemented a number of financial instruments in collaboration with EIBI, EBRD and CEB. These instruments are forms of financial support different from grants. Art. 44 (EC, 2006)[46] of General Regulation no. 1083/2006 EC is the main source regulating the various aspects of financial engineering instruments. The financial engineering instruments are the following: JEREMIE and JESSICA.

1.14.1 JEREMIE

JEREMIE (*Joint European Resources for Micro to Medium Enterprises*) is an initiative of the European Commission developed together with the European Investment Funds and the European Investment Bank. It is an opportunity offered to all EU regions to use their structural fund allocations to finance measures and programmes aimed at supporting the development of enterprises through the use of financial engineering instruments. Within the JEREMIE initiative, national and regional authorities may choose to use the financial resources allocated by the European Regional Development Fund (ERDF) in the forms of equity, loans and/or guarantees.

Unlike the assistance traditionally provided through grants, which can be spent only once, the financial instruments activated through JEREMIE have the advantage of being revolving; hence, a pool of funds can be reused several times. While global grants are reimbursements of expenditures incurred by managing authorities according with the relevant invoices, JEREMIE is instead an advance payment, according to the operations and uses planned.

JEREMIE (EIF, 2012)[47] provides for three main services:

- counselling and technical assistance;
- investments in equity and venture capital;
- loan guarantees.

The implementation of the initiative is entrusted to the individual managing authorities; they choose a fund holder, which shall subsequently select the financial intermediaries channelling the resources (revolving resources) to the enterprises. The JEREMIE programme is dedicated to the small and microenterprises controlled or owned by private subjects or enterprises in the final stage of their privatisation process. However, exclusions concern SMEs involved in the following businesses: real estate, banking, insurance, financial intermediation, gaming and all those enterprises excluded from the EIB and EIF lists. The EU member states can implement the JEREMIE initiative by creating holding funds financed by the structural funds. The management of such funds can be assigned to the EIF or other financial institutions according to the applicable EU legislation on structural funds (EC Regulation no. 1083/2006 and Executive Regulation no. 1828/2006). The managing authorities, therefore, can assign their management directly to the EIF or any national institutions or financial institutions by means of a tender. Holding funds can be set up as bank accounts managed in name and on behalf of the managing authorities or as independent legal entities (with the establishment of a specific organisation). The choice of the most suitable legal form depends on the complexity of the JEREMIE holding funds and applicable national legislation. The JEREMIE[48] initiative combines contributions from the European Regional Development Fund with loans and other forms of financing to support the creation and development of small, medium-sized and microenterprises within the regional policy of the European Union. Moreover, JEREMIE supports the transfer of technology and partnerships between enterprises, universities and R&D centres by improving access to microcredit for all those subjects excluded from the traditional lending system. Finally, the financing through instruments under the JEREMIE initiative can be combined with other instruments to support enterprises and institutions financed by the structural funds.

1.14.2 The advantages of the JEREMIE programme

Here follows a detailed description of the main advantages of using JEREMIE:

- *Flexibility*: the contributions from the operational programmes to the JEREMIE holding funds may be advanced on a provisional basis by the European Regional Development Fund (ERDF) and the European Social Fund (ESF), thus allowing the managing authorities to allocate the resources more flexibly; the contributions from the structural funds to the holding funds must be invested in the SMEs by 2015.
- *Advantages of a portfolio-approach*: the holding funds may allocate the resources in a flexible way by using several financial instruments tailored to the specific needs of particular countries or regions. The nature of holding funds with multiple compartments facilitates the diversification of risk and enhances the effectiveness of their investments in businesses.
- *Reuse of funds*: Holding funds are revolving funds, fed by the repayments made by the financial intermediaries, which are the reinvested in SMEs. Compared to the traditional assistance provided through grants, the EU structural funds thus are designed to provide a long-lasting and continuous support to the European SMEs.
- *Leverage*: one of the most relevant advantages of using JEREMIE is the capacity of boosting financial resources, with regard both to the holding funds, thanks to capital contributions from the financial institutions, and to the financial instruments through public–private co-financing, for instance in collaboration with the EIB.

1.14.3 JESSICA

JESSICA (*Joint European Support for Sustainable Investment in City Areas*) is an initiative of the EC for sustainable investments in city areas developed in cooperation with the EIB and the *Council of Europe Development*

Bank (CEB). This programme sees also the collaboration of the member states, regions, provincial and municipal authorities and other public and private investors in the implementation of the projects. Partnerships are conducted in compliance with the institutional, legal and financial responsibilities of each category of subjects. In this way, the structural fund allocations can be used in innovative ways to support urban development projects and do not represent a source of additional funding. Public–private partnerships are intended for the use and development of innovative financial engineering instruments suitable to produce repayable investments or guarantees for repayable investments or both. Thanks to this initiative, the managing authorities of the member countries, in particular regions, are authorised to use their structural fund contributions to develop urban areas, choosing to invest them in urban development funds (UDF)[49] or, alternatively, channelling them in holding funds (HF), which are set up to invest in several UDFs. These funds are financial engineering instruments that must be set up as independent legal entities or as "independent capital", accounted for separately within existing financial institutions. They can be public, private or public–private funds; they are not governed by a specific regulatory framework of their own within the European regulations for the structural funds but can invest directly in public–private partnerships and other urban projects included in an integrated plan for the sustainable urban development. JESSICA is designed for urban renewal activities, whose returns should seek to preserve the value of the investments over time and allow, through recycling of funds, reuse of the initial contributions for other similar projects. This initiative, therefore, supports the development of urban areas in their environmental, social, institutional and governance dimension through innovative methods of strategic analysis and project assessment. Physical, human and business capital is all integrated in a multidimensional and flexible dimension, with the aim of creating "sustainable communities".

The implementation of the initiative provides for the creation of an integrated plan for sustainable urban development, which is a system of interconnected interventions aimed at improving economic, physical, social and environmental conditions of city areas. As a whole, the plan should achieve better results than those that would be obtained by the single parts if independently implemented. It should not be regarded, therefore, as a closed structure but rather as a process suitable to amendments and integrations.

It is therefore essential to prepare medium to long-term plans to ensure sustainable development and the coherence of investments and their environmental quality[50] (EIB, 2008). The integrated plans must lead not just to the restoration of the territorial characteristics but to a true rebirth of the territory, with positive impact on urban and extraurban area development.

Rules on the eligibility of project expenditure, using JESSICA, are the same as those on the use of the structural funds as a whole and also need to take account of any national constraints. Apart from specific non-eligible items listed in the regulation, such as housing in some of the member states, JESSICA may allow for more flexible management of projects, respecting at the same time the eligibility rules, provided always that the projects being supported form part of Integrated Plans for Sustainable Urban Development.[51] Ineligible expenditure components might, for example, be included as a part of a larger, multisector urban development project, provided that sufficient additional funding is attracted from other public or private sources. Specifically, JESSICA promotes sustainable urban development by supporting projects in the following areas:

- urban infrastructure, including transport, water/waste water, energy;
- heritage or cultural sites for tourism purposes or other sustainable uses;
- redevelopment of brownfield sites, including site clearance and decontamination;
- creation of new commercial floor space for small and medium-sized enterprises (SMEs), IT and/or R&D sectors;
- university buildings, including medical, biotech and other specialised facilities;
- energy efficiency improvements.

Taking a look at the advantages of the JESSICA programme, we can identify a leverage effect obtained by attracting and combining structural funds with private funding sources and supporting the creation of PPP (public–private partnerships) as well as a market-oriented approach, which facilitates the effective implementation of projects. The opportunity to rely on the professional expertise of international financial institutions and specialised investment funds facilitates the development and modernisation of local financial markets, thus attracting new types of investors. With regard to the use of the European structural funds, which reduce the risks related to the complexity of the projects for sustainable urban development, JESSICA makes available a permanent financial instrument, as it allows receiving payments in advance as well as the reuse of funds. Long-term sustainability of investments is boosted by the revolving nature of the EU structural funds and the possibility of reusing the funds already obtained, thanks to the reinvestments of profits generated by the projects. Return on investments generated by the investments in projects is preferentially allocated to private investors and only at a later time to other public partners. In compliance with the national constraints, this instrument provides for the flexibility needed both for defining the general objectives and areas of interventions and for use of resources. It leads to the achievement of higher returns on investments thanks to the configuration of a global package of projects, which are coordinated with other national and regional policies. Among the other advantages in terms of resource management offered by this initiative is reduction of risk of automatic decommissioning of resources. The ERDF allocations to the Funds for Urban Development are not subject to potential limits and restrictions related to the calculation of $N + 2^{52}$ until 2013 (evidence of the actual disbursement of the funds by the UDF shall be submitted during the final certification phase by December 2015).

Resources to be allocated to interventions are made available and can be used immediately. Thanks to the support offered by the EIB, which provides specialised consulting services, JESSICA offers the opportunity to attract investments also from other international institutions, such as the Council of Europe Development Bank (CEB), which already agreed to join the programme. Last but not least, development and consolidation of a European market of qualified operators dedicated to urban renewal results in the definition of clear and standardised procedures, thus facilitating the inclusion of the JESSICA initiative in the operational programmes (on a national and regional level) and their implementation.

1.14.4 JASPERS

JASPERS[53] (*Joint Assistance to Support Projects in European Regions*) is a technical assistance facility developed in partnership between the European Commission (Directorate General for Regional Policy), the European Bank for Reconstruction and Development and the Kreditanstalt fur Wiederaufbau (KFD), dedicated to the 12 member countries which joined the EU in 2004 and 2007 (Bulgaria, Czech Republic, Cyprus, Estonia, Hungary, Latvia, Lithuania, Malta, Poland, Romania, Slovakia and Slovenia) and, from 2011, Croatia, in anticipation of its inclusion in the EU, which took place in July 2013. It provides the EU member states concerned with the technical support they need to prepare high-quality major projects, which will be co-financed by the structural funds and the cohesion fund. Specifically, this initiative

- provides technical assistance aimed at improving the preparation of investment projects eligible for funding under the EU structural funds for the period 2007–2013;
- provides technical assistance to the EU state members concerned to enable them to better prepare major infrastructure projects. In particular, JASPERS advice can cover project preparation (e.g. cost–benefit analysis, financial analysis, environmental issues, procurement planning), review of documentation (feasibility studies, grant applications, etc.) as well as advice on compliance with EU law (environmental, competition, etc.);
- coordinates, develops and re-examines the project structures, eliminating potential bottlenecks, filling gaps and identifying those issues that have not been fully resolved by the beneficiaries states, such as applications for EU grants in PPP projects, issues related to state aid and environmental impact assessment;
- operates following the country action plans prepared annually for each member in cooperation with the beneficiary state concerned and the European Commission. A managing authority acts as a central coordinator for each country, and it can request assistance from JASPERS. JASPERS professionals (EIB, 2012)[54] provide technical assistance for all the phases of the projects since their seeding stage.

During the process of preparing the annual action plans, JASPERS works in close cooperation with beneficiaries, managing authorities and relevant intermediate bodies. The member states remain the owners of the projects, and the grant application process remains always their responsibility. There is no obligation of JASPERS beneficiaries to borrow from EIB, EBRD or KFW. The JASPERS[55] structure is based on five sectors of activity: air, maritime and public transport, knowledge economy and energy, water and waste and roads. The sector-based structure meets JASPERS operational needs and ensures consistency in advice delivered across the beneficiaries' countries.

JASPERS mainly targets assistance on major infrastructure projects with total costs exceeding €25 million for environmental projects and €50 million for transport and other infrastructure projects, which can be supported also by the EU cohesion fund.

Statistical data

Table 1.11 JASPERS performance

	Total 2006 to date	2006	2007	2008	2009	2010	2011	2012	2013
Number of assignment s completed (#)	795	3	22	82	133	159	142	116	138
Number of JASPERS-supported applications submitted to the commission (#)	407	0	5	30	59	86	62	76	89
Number of JASPERS-supported applications approved by the commission (#)	310	0	0	10	35	58	68	53	86

Source: Authors' elaboration on JASPERS annual report (2013).

Table 1.12 JASPERS budget, 2006–2013 (€ millions)

Total 2006 to date	2006	2007	2008	2009	2010	2011	2012	2013
	3.6	17.8	21.2	23.5	30.2	31.9	30.4	31.6

Source: Authors' elaboration on JASPERS annual report (2013), www.jaspers-europa-info.org/attachments/article/161/JASPERS%20Annual%20Report%202013_en.pdf.

1.14.5 JASMINE

JASMINE[56] (*Joint Action to Support Microfinance Institutions*), the fourth joint initiative of the EC, the EIB and the EIF, is a pilot programme initiated in 2008 whose objective is to develop the microcredit market in the European Union by providing financial support (through loans and equity) and technical assistance, dedicated to non-bank microcredit operators. This project complements the action started by the JEREMIE programme. JASMINE can be considered the operational outcome of the EC communication of 13 November 2007, which proposed the "*European initiative for the development of*

Financial Crises and EU Credit Access Policy 59

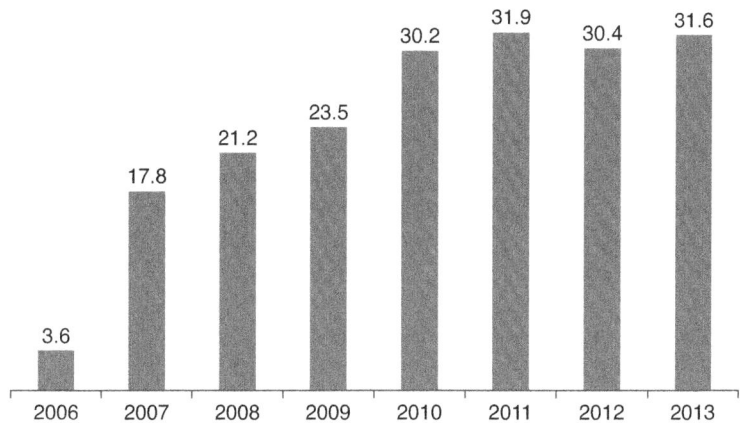

Chart 1.16 JASPER budget, 2006–2013 (€ millions)
Source: Authors' elaboration JASPERS annual report (2013).

microcredit in support of growth and employment" (EC, 2007).[57] JASMINE was created to

- support the development of microcredit providers and microfinance institutions (MFIs) in various areas, such as institutional governance, information systems, risk management and strategic planning;
- help these intermediaries become sustainable operators on commercial terms.

The project is financed by the Directorate General of EU Regional Policies in the amount of €50 million and is made available free of charge to the beneficiaries. This facility is dedicated to new and non-bank MFIs and provides

- technical assistance;
- information and publicity regarding the initiative for member states, regions, banks and MFIs in general;
- technical manuals, guides, software and organisation of seminars and conferences;
- improved access to finance.

The EIF was entrusted with the task of providing financial support and technical assistance to non-bank MFIs. Financial support (with a budget of approximately €20 million) can take the form of co-investments (in collaboration with banks, MFIs, development agencies, etc.) dedicated to microcredit operators that have almost achieved self-sustainability[58] and/or in a growth phase. Technical assistance (with a budget of €30 million) is aimed at increasing the reliability of the MFIs, facilitating access to finance and providing institutions with a free-of-charge assessment of their activity, organisation and structure.

To participate in the programme, the MFIs shall meet the following specific requirements:

- They must operate in EU member states.
- They must operate in the microcredit for at least two years.
- They must have more than 150 active customers during the last year.
- They must be engaged in social development programmes.
- They must provide evidence of their internal strategy.

Following the selection of applicants, in collaboration with the two rating agencies involved in the project, "MicroFinanza Rating"[59] and "Planet Rating",[60] assessments and estimates of the activities carried out by the MFIs are performed. Upon conclusion of such operations, the selected beneficiaries may benefit from the following services made available free of charge:

- Either an evaluation/diagnosis of their structure, organisation or operating mode or an institutional rating performed by a specialised rating agency.
- Consulting or training of a maximum duration of 12 days for the technical staff and the management provided by expert consultants of the Microfinance Centre.

From 2010 to 2013, 70 microfinance and microcredit institutions (EC, 2013)[61] were supported through this programme; as already mentioned, once selected as potential beneficiaries, the MFIs could enjoy tailored consulting, training and rating services free of charge. Implementation of these three EU initiatives proved essential for the creation and development of a healthy environment for the growth of microcredit in Europe. Moreover, these programmes prompted many institutions to improve their businesses, especially in light of the possibility of accessing the EU structural funds and thanks to greater availability of economic resources to fund valid business projects.

Summary of data collected on financial engineering instruments

At the end of 2012, a total of 870 specific loan guarantees, equity/venture capital and other funds were set up, of which 816 were for enterprises, 38 for urban development and 16 for energy efficiency/renewable energies. Compared to the data for 2011, the total number of specific funds reported for 2012 increased by 324 funds (see Table 1.12).[62]

Table 1.13 Number of FEIs reported at the end of 2011 and 2012

		Summary of data for 2012				Summary of data for 2011			
1	2	3	4	5	6	7	8	9	10
	Member No. states	No. of FEIs	of which HF	of which specific funds with a HF	of which specific funds without a HF	No. of FEIs*	of which HF	of which specific funds with a HF	of which specific funds without a HF
1	AT	2		0	2	2	0	0	2
2	BE	9	0	0	9	9	0	0	9
3	BG	9	2	6	1	5	2	3	0
4	CY	4	1	3	0	4	1	3	0
5	CZ	4	2	0	2	3	1	0	2
6	DE	41	0	0	41	42	4	4	34
7	DK	6	0	0	6	6	0	0	6
8	EE	6	0	0	6	6	0	0	6
9	EL	26	4	21	1	14	4	10	0
10	ES	15	6	7	2	9	4	4	1
11	FI	1	0	0	1	1	0	0	1
12	FR	95	2	17	76	111	3	4	104
13	HU	185	1	183	1	3	1	1	1
14	IT	95	13	15	67	80	14	14	52
15	LT	33	4	28	1	29	4	24	1
16	LV	10	1	5	4	9	1	5	3
17	MT	2	1	1	0	2	1	1	0
18	NL	8	1	2	5	5	0	0	5
19	PL	247	16	128	103	139	13	54	72
20	PT	50	3	34	13	19	3	7	9
21	RO	3	1	2	0	3	1	2	0
22	SE	11	0	0	11	11	0	0	11
23	SI	4	1	2	1	10	1	8	1
24	SK	1	1	0	0	1	1	0	0
25	UK	73	10	27	36	68	9	27	32
26	CBC	0	0	0	0	1	0	0	1
	Total	940	70	481	389	592	68	171	353

Source: Authors' elaboration on EC data (2013), "Summary of data on the progress made in financing and implementing financial engineering instruments co-financed by structural funds", http://ec.europa.eu/regional_policy/thefunds/instruments/doc/summary_data_fei_2012.pdf.

Although the total number of specific funds reported in 2012 increased by 66 per cent, the share of the three types of funds[63] remained the same – 94 per cent for funds targeting enterprises, 4 per cent for funds for urban development and 2 per cent for funds operating in the area of energy efficiency/renewable energies. Of all specific funds, 389 were implemented directly (without a holding fund), and 481 were implemented through 70 holding funds.

At the end of 2012, the total value of the 159 ERDF and 16 ESF operational programmes contributions paid by managing authorities to financial engineering instruments amounted to €12,558.23 million, of which €8,364.58 million were structural funds. The total value of contributions paid to the holding funds amounted to €5,957.16 million, including €4,314.48 million of 21 structural funds and €1,642.68 million of the national co-financing. This represents 86 per cent of the OP contributions committed in the funding agreements signed between managing authorities and holding funds. Of €5,957.15 million of OP contributions paid to the holding funds, almost a half (€2,812.20 million) was subsequently transferred to the specific funds for enterprises, meaning that €3,144.88 million of OP contributions (including €2,340.53 of structural funds and €801.30 million of national co-financing) remained at the level of holding funds at the end of 2012. In addition, €6,601.07 million of OP contributions, with €4,050.10 million of structural funds and €2,550.97 million of the national co-financing was paid directly from managing authorities to specific funds set up without a holding fund. The amounts paid to specific funds set up without a holding fund at the end of 2012 represent 62 per cent of amounts committed in legal agreements. In total, €9,413.35 million of OP contributions (including €6,024.05 million of structural funds) reached specific funds and was available to support final recipients. At the end of the reporting period (31 December 2012), 37 per cent of this amount (€4,684.33 million) was invested in final recipients. The overall absorption at the level of final recipients increased by more than 20 per cent for OP contributions and almost 30 per cent for the structural funds part in comparison to the data reported for 2011.

1.15 COSME 2014–2020

COSME[64] (*Competitiveness of Enterprises and Small and Medium-Sized Enterprises*) is the new EU programme for the competitiveness of enterprises and SMEs for the period 2014–2020. In particular, the programme is intended to facilitate SMEs' access to finance, improve their competitiveness on the European and international markets and encourage the development of an entrepreneurial culture.

In addition, COSME intends to stimulate the creation of new enterprises and targets businesses of all industrial, manufacturing and service sectors, including tourism.

The programme provides for specific and relevant financial instruments, for credit and guarantees, in the early stages of growth and development of small and medium-sized enterprises. The COSME programme is provided with a budget of €2.298.243 million (EP and EC, 2013)[65] at current prices for its implementation, of which no less than 60 per cent is dedicated to financial instruments. In fact, almost €1.4 billion of the COSME budget is dedicated to fund loans and venture capital in addition to national financial support programmes. In particular, the COSME programme will provide guarantees and counterguarantees to loans granted to SMEs and will offer an improved access to venture capital through a financial facility, with a particular focus on the SMEs' stages of growth and expansion. The financial instruments provided by the COSME programme, in accordance with Title VIII of Regulation (UE and Euratom) no. 966/2012, are used to facilitate access to credit for SMEs during the start-up, growth and transfer phases. The financial instruments under the programme may take the forms of equity and guarantees. The allocation of the funds to the various instruments takes into account the demand of the financial intermediaries. Financial instruments for the SMEs can be combined and integrated with the following:

- Other financial instruments established by the member states and the relevant managing authorities and funded with national or regional funds or included in activities financed by EU structural funds, pursuant to art. 38, paragraph 1, letter a), of EU Regulation no. 303/2013.
- Other financial instruments established by the member states and the relevant managing authorities and funded with national or regional funds not included in activities financed by EU structural funds.
- EU subsidies, including within the framework of this regulation.

1.16   EFG

The Equity Facility Growth (EFG) is a window of the Single EU Equity Financial Instrument, which supports EU enterprises' growth and research and innovation (R&I) from the early stage, including seed, up to the expansion and growth stage. The Single EU Equity Financial Instrument enjoys financial support from the programmes Horizon 2020 and COSME. EFG invests in selected funds that provide venture capital and mezzanine finance, such as subordinated and participating loans, to expansion and growth-stage SMEs, in particular those operating across borders, with the possibility of investing in early-stage funds as well as providing equity for R&I within the framework of the Horizon 2020 programme and co-investment instruments for informal investors (business angels).[66] In case of early-stage investments, the EFG investments (EP and EC, 2013, p. 43)[67] cannot exceed 20 per cent of the total EU investment. Exceptions are represented by stage funds and funds of funds, where the EFG investment and the equity facility for R&I, within the framework of the Horizon 2020 programme, are provided on a pro rata basis, according to the funds' investment policies.

The European Commission may decide to modify the 20 per cent limit depending on the evolution of market conditions. EFG support can take the form of one of the following investments:

- Directly from the European Investment Fund or other entities entrusted with the EFG implementation by the Commission.
- From funds of funds or other investment instruments that invest in cross-border projects, created by the European Investment Fund or other entities (including public and private sector managers) entrusted with the implementation of the EFG by the commission along with public and/or private financial institutions. EFG invests in intermediate venture capital funds, including funds of funds, which invest in expansion and growth SMEs. The investments under EFG are long term, namely investments in venture capital funds usually between 5 and 15 years. In any case, the duration of the investments under EFG cannot exceed 20 years from the signing of the agreement between the European Commission and the entities entrusted with their implementation.

1.17 LGF

The Loan Guarantee Facility (LGF; EP and EC, 2013, p. 43)[68] provides

- counterguarantees and other risk-sharing agreements for guarantee schemes, including co-guarantee, if applicable;
- direct guarantees and other risk-sharing agreements for other financial intermediaries that comply with eligibility criteria.

The LGF is a window of the Single EU Debt Financial Instrument, which supports European enterprises' growth and innovation by using the same implementation mechanism of the section dedicated to SMEs willing to use the debt facility for R&I within the Horizon 2020 programme (RSI II). The LGF includes the following:

- Guarantees for debt financing (including subordinated and participating loans, leasing or bank guarantees) that reduce the difficulties faced by SMEs in accessing vital credit as the investments are perceived as more risky or because enterprises do not have sufficient collateral.
- Securitisation of SME debt finance portfolios, which mobilise additional resources to finance SMEs through lending, within adequate risk-sharing agreements with the relevant institutions. The support to such securitisation operations is conditional upon a commitment by the institutions at issue to use a significant portion of the remaining liquidity or the mobilised capital to grant new loans to SMEs within a reasonable time.

The amounts of the new loans are determined according to the risk amount of the portfolios guaranteed and are negotiated on an individual basis with each institution, including the repayment terms. LGF is directly managed by the European Investment Fund or other entities entrusted with its implementation by the European Commission. The maximum duration of guarantees individually granted under LGF cannot exceed ten years. Eligibility of each intermediary for the LGF facility is assessed according to their activities and effectiveness in supporting SME access to finance for profitable projects. LGF can be used by intermediaries that support enterprises, among other things, to access debt finance to fund acquisition of tangible and intangible assets, working capital and transfer of businesses. Eligibility criteria related to the securitisation of SME debt finance portfolios include individual transactions, transactions with multiple partners and multinational transactions. Eligibility is assessed according to the best practices on the market, in particular with regard to credit quality and risk diversification of the securitised portfolios. Apart from securitised loan portfolios, the LGF covers loans up to €150,000 and with a minimum maturity of 12 months.

LGF also covers loans exceeding €150,000 when the SMEs that meet eligibility criteria according to the COSME programme, do not meet the eligibility criteria set forth by the section of the SME loan guarantee facility under the Horizon 2020 programme, with a minimum maturity of 12 months. Beyond such limits, the proof whether the SME is eligible to the SME section of the loan guarantee facility under Horizon 2020 lies in the financial intermediaries. LGF is structured so as to allow presenting an account of the beneficiary SMEs, indicating both the number and the amounts of loans.

Table 1.14 Summary of the instruments examined

Instrument	Reference website	Purposes	Beneficiaries	Products offered
GIF1	http://ec.europa.eu/enterprise/policies/finance/cip-financial-instruments/index_en.htm	Supporting innovative SMEs with high growth potential, in particular those undertaking research, development and other innovation activities Contributing to the	Innovative SMEs in their early stages	Venture capital funds such as early stage funds, funds operating regionally, funds focused on specific sectors, technology or research and technological development
GIF2	http://ec.europa.eu/enterprise/policies/finance/cip-financial-instruments/index_en.htm	establishment and financing of SMEs and reduction of the equity and risk capital market gap	SMEs with high growth potential in their expansion phase	Risk-capital funds which in turn provide quasi-equity or equity for innovative SMEs with high growth potential in their expansion phase
SMEG	http://ec.europa.eu/enterprise/policies/finance/cip-financial-instruments/index_en.htm	Providing loan guarantees to encourage banks to make more debt finance available to SMEs, by reducing the banks' exposure to risk	Financial intermediaries providing SMEs with loans, mezzanine finance and equity	Loan guarantees Microcredit Equity and quasi equity guarantees Securitisation
JEREMIE	http://www.eif.org/what_we_do/resources/jeremie/ http://ec.europa.eu/regional_policy/thefunds/instruments/jeremie_en.cfm	JEREMIE promotes the use of financial engineering instruments to improve access to finance for SMEs via structural funds interventions.	JEREMIE is an umbrella fund and, as such, targets financial intermediaries, not SMEs directly. These financial intermediaries, in turn, provide SMEs (which are the "final beneficiaries") with loans and equity instruments.	Equity, loans or guarantees

JESSICA	http://www.bei.org/products/jessica/index.htm http://ec.europa.eu/regional_policy/thefunds/instruments/jessica_en.cfm	JESSICA establishes funds for sustainable urban development and regeneration, which will finance public–private partnerships or other urban development projects	Final beneficiaries can be municipalities, local government, entrepreneurs and public–private partnerships between municipalities and private investors which invest in UDF	UDF financial products: Guarantees Investment loans Equity capital
JASMINE	http://www.eif.org/what_we_do/microfinance/JASMINE/ http://ec.europa.eu/regional_policy/thefunds/instruments/jasmine_en.cfm	JASMINE helps non-bank microfinance institutions to scale up their operations and maximise the impact of microfinance products on microenterprise development and unemployment reduction within the European Union	JASMINE technical assistance primarily targets the following type of microcredit providers: non-bank financial institution, licensed banks	Financial support in the form of funding to non-bank microfinance institutions (MFIs) and microcredit providers (EIB resources) and technical assistance (EC resources)
JASPER	http://www.jaspers-europa-info.org/ http://ec.europa.eu/regional_policy/thefunds/instruments/jaspers_en.cfm	JASPERS provides advice during project preparation to help improve the quality of the major projects to be submitted for grant financing under the structural and cohesion funds	JASPERS targets assistance on major infrastructure projects costing more than €50 million supported by the EU funds – e.g., roads, rail, water, waste, energy and urban transport projects	Project preparation (e.g., cost-benefit analysis, financial analysis, environmental issues, procurement planning) review of documentation (e.g., feasibility studies, grant applications) advice on compliance with EU law (environmental, competitiveness, etc.)
LGF	http://ec.europa.eu/enterprise/initiatives/cosme/access-to-finance-smes/index_en.htm	Providing enhanced access to finance for SMEs in their start-up, growth and transfer phases through debt instrument	SME financing up to €150,000 for any type of SME	Guarantees and securitisation on loans
EGF	http://ec.europa.eu/enterprise/initiatives/cosme/access-to-finance-smes/index_en.htm	Providing investments for SMEs typically in their expansion and growth stages	Growth-oriented SMEs	Risk-capital fund Fund of funds

Source: Authors' elaboration.

Notes

1. Although the chapter has been prepared by both authors jointly, §1.1 was written by Pasqualina Porretta, whereas §§1.2–1.6 were written by Francesco Minnetti and §§1.7–1.17 by Ervin Sinani.
2. http://www.microcreditoitalia.org/index.php?lang=it.
3. http://www.microcreditoitalia.org/capacitybuilding/.
4. This definition is contained in EC Recommendation no. 1442 issued on 6 May 2003, replacing EC Recommendation no. 280 of 1996 and entered into force on 1 January 2005.
5. According to Otero (1999, p. 8), microfinance is "the provision of financial services to low-income poor and very poor self-employed people".
6. In the most developed businesses, instead, innovative products are usually developed within large existing organisations.
7. More precisely, flexibility consists in timely adaptation of quality, quantity and characteristics of the business, such as its seasonality, the occasional need to rely on external workers, the determination of in-progress production methods, the diversification of products and services compared to market standards and other circumstances that are typical of the so-called "niche-markets", where small and microenterprises often operate.
8. The analysis of the American professor (Birch, 1993) – which moves from the fundamental premise that the American as well as the European economies are cyclically affected by a deep economic crisis every five years or so, which results in the replacement of 50 per cent of businesses and jobs – is deemed highly relevant as its observations are based on a large sample of businesses, something in the region of 22 million companies over a 22-year timeline, from the end of the 1960s to the 1980s.
9. This can be due to multiple factors, such as the high concentration of businesses in their territory, the start-up of new industrial activities, the opening of reference markets, development projects through acquisitions, delocalisation of production, the need to cope with various problems and trends that characterise their sectors.
10. Innovative projects that reach the stage of product marketing can, as a matter of fact, generate high operating profits for companies due to the competitive advantage obtained by those firms able to introduce new products in the market or manufacture existing products in an innovative way. However, the transition from the design and initial implementation phases to the subsequent development and marketing stages may result particular selective, as companies may decide to abandon their projects with the consequent loss of the capital invested.
11. A critical analysis of the main scientific contributions on this topic can be found in Bhattacharya and Thakor (1993), Dabrassi (1996) and Ongena and Smith (2000), among others.
12. The ten principles are the following: *entrepreneurship, second chance, think small first, receptive administration, public contracts and aid, access to credit, single market, innovation and skills, environment, internationalisation*. Every year, the profile of each country for each of these principles is assessed both with regard to the existing situation in the previous year and the average value recorded at EU level, in order to assess the global situation as well as identify any gap

Financial Crises and EU Credit Access Policy 69

in order to take the necessary corrective actions. See European Commission in Enterprise and Industry topics, "Small Business Act" for Europe, 2013.
13. For access to credit, among other things, the following information must be provided: rejected applications for funding and unacceptable offers for financing; access to public financial support, including public guarantees; willingness of the banks to grant loans; relative difference in the interest rate levels between loans up to €1 million and loans of more than €1 million; investments in venture capital; UIF regional funds for entrepreneurship and SMEs; UE funds for the creation and development of enterprises.
14. The reference parameter of 2007 deliberately provides a basis for assessment prior to the beginning of the financial crisis.
15. If the index shows values lower than the 2007 reference value, it means that access to credit is lower than the years before the crisis.
16. European Central Bank (2014), "Survey on the access to finance of small and medium-sized enterprises in the euro area – October 2013 to March 2014", https://www.ecb.europa.eu/pub/pdf/other/accesstofinancesmallmediumsizedenterprises201404en.pdf?da920468528300ff549d8cc95522eb81.
17. See p. 4, 5 of the Survey SAFE (2014), April http://www.ecb.europa.eu/pub/pdf/other/accesstofinancesmallmediumsizedenterprises201404en.pdf?da920468528300ff549d8cc95522eb81.
18. See p. 25 of the Survey SAFE (2014), April, http://www.ecb.europa.eu/pub/pdf/other/accesstofinancesmallmediumsizedenterprises201404en.pdf?da920468528300ff549d8cc95522eb81.
19. See p. 7 Survey SAFE (2014), April, http://www.ecb.europa.eu/pub/pdf/other/accesstofinancesmallmediumsizedenterprises201404en.pdf?da920468528300ff549d8cc95522eb81.
20. See European Commission, *2013 SMEs' access to finance survey*, p. 19, 20, http://ec.europa.eu/enterprise/policies/finance/files/2013-safe-analytical-report_en.pdf.
21. See p. 16 of the SAFE, April survey, http://www.ecb.europa.eu/pub/pdf/other/accesstofinancesmallmediumsizedenterprises201404en.pdf?da920468528300ff549d8cc95522eb81.
22. European Commission (2013), *2013 SMEs' access to finance survey – analytical report*, http://ec.europa.eu/enterprise/policies/finance/files/2013-safe-analytical-report_en.pdf.
23. European Commission (2013), *One out of three SMEs did not get the finance they needed in 2013*, Brussels, http://europa.eu/rapid/press-release_IP-13-1070_en.htm.
24. Further details of the interviewing methods, sampling and weights applied can be found in appendix 1, http://ec.europa.eu/enterprise/policies/finance/files/2013-safe-analytical-report_en.pdf.
25. The sample was selected following random criteria, albeit in a disproportionate manner and according to the following criteria:
    – Countries: 28 EU member countries and other countries participating in the Entrepreneurship and Innovation programme (EIP).
    – Enterprise size: micro (1–9 employees), small (10–49 employees), medium-sized (50–249 employees) and large (over 250 employees) enterprises.
    The enterprises surveyed operate in the following sectors: mining and quarrying; manufacturing; electricity; gas and water; construction; wholesale and

retail business; hotels and restaurants; transport, storage and communication; real estate; rental and trade; education; health-care and other social services; other public, social and personal services. *Source*: European Commission (2013), *2013 SMEs' access to finance survey – analytical report*, http://ec.europa.eu/enterprise/policies/finance/files/2013-safe-analytical-report_en.pdf.
26. The survey carried out covers multiple periods of time. In particular, June to July 2009, August to October 2011 and August to October 2013.
27. http://ec.europa.eu/cip/index_en.htm.
28. European Parliament (2006), Decision no. 1639/2006/CE of the European Parliament and of the Council of 24 October 2006 establishing a Competitiveness and Innovation Framework Programme (2007–2013), *Official Journal of the European Union*, http://eur-lex.europa.eu/LexUriServ/LexUriServ.do?uri=OJ:L:2006:310:0015:0040:en:PDF.
29. http://ec.europa.eu/enterprise/initiatives/cosme/index_en.htm.
30. http://www.eib.org/.
31. http://eur-lex.europa.eu/legal-content/EN/TXT/PDF/?uri=OJ:C:2010:083:FULL&from=IT, *Official Journal of the European Union*, C83, 30 March 2010, art. 309, TFUE, p. 182.
32. European Union (2010), "Consolidated versions of the treaty on European Union and the treaty on the functioning of the European Union, *Official Journal of the European Union*, C83, 30 March, art. 17, http://eur-lex.europa.eu/legal-content/EN/TXT/PDF/?uri=OJ:C:2010:083:FULL&from=IT; http://eur-lex.europa.eu/legal-content/IT/TXT/PDF/?uri=OJ:C:2010:083:FULL&from=IT, *Official Journal of the European Union*, C83, 30 March 2010, protocol no. 5, BEI General Statute, art. 17, p. 261.
33. Ibid., art. 22, p. 264.
34. http://www.eif.org/.
35. http://eur-lex.europa.eu/LexUriServ/LexUriServ.do?uri=OJ:L:2006:310:0015:0040:en:PDF, art. 3.
36. European Parliament (2006), Decision no. 1639/2006/CE of the European Parliament and of the Council of 24 October 2006, establishing a Competitiveness and Innovation Framework Programme (2007–2013), *Official Journal of the European Union*, art. 18, http://eurlex.europa.eu/LexUriServ/LexUriServ.do?uri=OJ:L:2006:310:0015:0040:en:PDF.
37. European Commission (2006), "CIP financial instruments, entrepreneurship and Innovation Programme", http://eur-lex.europa.eu/LexUriServ/LexUriServ.do?uri=OJ:L:2006:310:0015:0040:IT:PDF.
38. European Parliament (2006), Decision no. 1639/2006/CE of the European Parliament and of the Council of 24 October 2006 establishing a Competitiveness and Innovation Framework Programme (2007–2013), *Official Journal of the European Union*, 22, http://eur-lex.europa.eu/LexUriServ/LexUriServ.do?uri=OJ:L:2006:310:0015:0040:en:PDF.
39. Ibid., art. 18, p. 25.
40. "Asset stripping" is defined as the process of buying an undervalued company with the intent to sell off its assets for a profit.
41. European Commission (2013), *Entrepreneurship and Innovation Programme Committee*, p. 7, http://ec.europa.eu/cip/files/cip/eip_performance_report_2007-2013_en.pdf.
42. Ibid.

43. European Parliament (2006), Decision no. 1639/2006/EC of the European Parliament and of the Council of 24 October 2006 establishing a Competitiveness and Innovation Framework Programme (2007–2013), *Official Journal of the European Union*, art. 19, p. 26, http://eur-lex.europa.eu/LexUriServ/LexUriServ.do?uri=OJ:L:2006:310:0015:0040:en:PDF.
44. European Parliament (2006), Decision no. 1639/2006/EC of the European Parliament and of the Council of 24 October 2006 establishing a Competitiveness and Innovation Framework Programme (2007–2013), *Official Journal of the European Union*, art. 20, p. 26, http://eur-lex.europa.eu/LexUriServ/LexUriServ.do?uri=OJ:L:2006:310:0015:0040:en:PDF.
45. http://ec.europa.eu/regional_policy/archive/themes/financial/index_en.htm.
46. As part of an operational programme, the structural funds may finance expenditure with respect to an operation comprising contributions to support any of the following:
    a) financial engineering instruments for enterprises, esp. for small and medium-sized enterprises, such as venture capital funds, guarantee funds and loan funds;
    b) urban development funds, i.e., funds investing in public–private partnerships and other projects included in an integrated plan for sustainable urban development;
    c) funds or other incentive schemes providing loans, guarantees for repayable investments or equivalent instruments for energy efficiency and use of renewable energy sources in building, including in existing housing.

    When such operations are organised through holding funds, i.e., funds set up to invest in different venture capital funds, guarantee funds, loan funds, urban development funds, funds or other support programmes that grant loans, guarantees for repayable investments or similar instruments for energy efficiency and the use of renewable energy sources in building, including in the existing residential buildings, the member states or the managing authority shall implement them through one or more of the following forms:
    a) the award of a public contract in accordance with applicable public procurement law;
    b) in other cases, where the agreement is not a public service contract within the meaning of public procurement law, the award of a grant, defined for this purpose as a direct financial contribution by way of donation to a financial institution without a call for proposals, if this is in accordance with a national law compatible with the treaty;
    c) the award of a contract directly to the EIB or the EIF.
    European Council (2006), Council Regulation (EC) no. 1083/2006 of 11 July 2006 – laying down general provisions on the European Regional Development Fund, the European Social Fund and the Cohesion Fund and repealing regulation (EC) no. 1260/1999, *Official Journal of the European Union*, http://eur-lex.europa.eu/LexUriServ/LexUriServ.do?uri=OJ:L:2006:210:0025:0078:EN:PDF.
47. European Investment Fund (2012), "JEREMIE – a new way of using EU structural funds to promote SME access to finance via Holding Funds", Luxembourg, http://www.eif.org/news_centre/publications/Jeremie_leaflet_files/jeremie_leaflet_en.pdf.

48. Commission of the European Communities (2006), "Communication from the Commission to the Council, the European parliament, the European Economic and Social Committee and the Committee of the Regions – implementing the Community Lisbon Programme: Financing SME growth – adding European value", COM (2006) 349 final, http://eur-lex.europa.eu/legal-content/EN/TXT/PDF/?uri=CELEX:52006DC0349&qid=1403702569267&from=EN.
49. The contributions of the European Regional Development Fund (ERDF) are allocated to urban development funds (UDF), which, in turn, invest them in public–private partnerships or other projects included in an integrated plan for sustainable urban development. These investments can take the form of equity, loans and/or guarantees.
50. European Investment Bank (2008), "JESSICA – a new way of using EU funding to promote sustainable investments and growth in urban areas", Luxembourg, http://www.eib.org/attachments/thematic/jessica_2008_it.pdf.
51. An integrated plan for urban sustainable development is a system of interconnected interventions aimed at steadily improving economic, physical, social and environmental conditions of urban areas.
52. The $N + 2$ rule is referred to the automatic decommissioning of resources as governed by art. 93 of regulation no. 1083 of 2006. In particular, paragraph 1 of the regulation at issue states, "The Commission shall automatically decommission any part of a commitment included in an Operational Plan which has not been settled by the payment on account or for which it has not received an acceptable payment application pursuant art. 86, by the end of the second year following the year of commitment or, where appropriate, for the amounts concerned pursuant paragraph 2". http://eur-lex.europa.eu/LexUriServ/LexUriServ.do?uri=OJ:L:2006:210:0025:0078:EN:PDF.
53. http://www.jaspers-europa-info.org/.
54. European Investment Bank (2012), "JASPERS – European Investment Bank", Luxembourg, http://www.jaspers-europa-info.org/attachments/article/123/JASPERS%20brochure%202012.pdf.
55. http://ec.europa.eu/regional_policy/thefunds/instruments/jaspers_en.cfm.
56. http://ec.europa.eu/regional_policy/thefunds/instruments/jasmine_en.cfm.
57. Commission of the European Communities (2007), "Communication from the Commission to the Council, the European Parliament, the European Economic and Social Committee and the Committee of the Regions – a European initiative for the development of microcredit in support of growth and employment", COM (2007) 708 final, http://eur-lex.europa.eu/legal-content/EN/TXT/PDF/?uri=CELEX:52007DC0708&qid=1403707249640&from=EN.
58. The economic self-sustainability of a credit agency is its capacity to break away from the initial donations through which it starts its own business.
59. MicroFinanza Rating (MFR) is a private and independent international rating agency, specialising in microfinance, founded in 2000. Its mission is to provide the microfinance and responsible finance industry with independent, high quality ratings and information services aiming at enhancing transparency, facilitating investments and promoting best practices worldwide. http://www.microfinanzarating.com/index.php?option=com_content&view=article&id=97&Itemid=167&lang=en.

Financial Crises and EU Credit Access Policy 73

60. Planet Rating is a specialised microfinance rating agency offering evaluation and rating services to microfinance institutions (MFIs), using the Smart GIRAFE and the Social Performance methodologies. http://www.planetrating.com/EN/who-are-we-a.html.
61. http://www.eif.org/what_we_do/microfinance/JASMINE/.
62. http://ec.europa.eu/regional_policy/thefunds/instruments/doc/summary_data_fei_2012.pdf.
63. Specific funds set up according to Art. 44 §1 a), Art. 44 §1 b) and Art. 44 §1 c) of the General Regulation no. 1083/2006. http://eur-lex.europa.eu/legal-content/EN/TXT/PDF/?uri=CELEX:32006R1083&from=EN.
64. http://ec.europa.eu/enterprise/initiatives/cosme/index_en.htm.
65. European Parliament, European Council (2013), Regulation (EU) no. 1287/2013 of the European Parliament and of the Council of 11 December 2013 establishing a Programme for the Competitiveness of Enterprises and small and medium-sized enterprises (COSME) (2014–2020) and repealing Decision no. 1639/2006/EC, *Official Journal of the European Union*, art. 5, http://eur-lex.europa.eu/legal-content/EN/TXT/PDF/?uri=CELEX:32013R1287&qid=1401115426118&from=IT.
66. http://ec.europa.eu/enterprise/policies/finance/risk-capital/business-angels/index_en.htm.
67. European Parliament, European Council (2013), Regulation (EU) no 1287/2013 of the European Parliament and of the Council of 11 December 2013 establishing a Programme for the Competitiveness of Enterprises and small and medium-sized enterprises (COSME) (2014–2020) and repealing Decision no. 1639/2006/EC, *Official Journal of the European Union*, art. 18, p. 43, http://eur-lex.europa.eu/legal-content/EN/TXT/PDF/?uri=CELEX:32013R1287&qid=1401115426118&from=IT.
68. Ibid., art. 19, p. 43.

Except where otherwise noted, this work is licensed under a Creative Commons Attribution 3.0 Unported License. To view a copy of this license, visit http://creativecommons.org/licenses/by/3.0/

OPEN

2
EU Cohesion Policy and Microfinance

Giorgio Centurelli, Pasqualina Porretta and Fabrizio Santoboni

2.1 Cohesion policy, EU structural funds and financial engineering instruments: regulatory framework and operational features under the programming periods 2000–2006 and 2007–2013

The aim of ensuring a balanced development of the territory of the European Union as well as equal social and economic opportunities to all individuals in the EU member states led European Union institutions to activate a number of financial instruments that may allow reducing the current structural economic gaps between different regions in Europe and establishing a regional development policy based on the concepts of economic, social solidarity and cohesion.[1]

The regional development policy, already introduced in the early 1970s, albeit in an embryonic state, finds its milestones in the Single European Act (SEA) of 1986 and the subsequent Treaty of Maastricht on the European Union in 1992.[2]

Those were the years that gave birth to the cohesion policy and its main financial arm (ERDF, European Regional Development Fund); in addition, a careful and rational planning process started to gradually emerge. This is the origin of the EU programming cycles: multiyear plans for regional policies, initially of variable duration (1989–1993, 1994–1999), and then, from 2000 onwards, established in seven-year cycles (2000–2006, 2007–2013 and now 2014–2020).

The evolution of the EU structural funds programming has been accompanied by the introduction of increasingly detailed and stringent regulations. The regulatory framework has obviously covered also the financial engineering instruments, which while governed by a few provisions in the programming period 2000–2006,[3] are now regarded as a strategic tool within the programming period 2014–2020 and, as such, governed by specific regulations, as we will see later.

2.1.1 The regulatory framework in the programming period 2000–2006: first implementing provisions in regulation (EC) no. 448/2004

As mentioned above, the regulatory framework of the programming period 2000–2006 contained the first framework laying down detailed rules to define the financial engineering instruments.

Regulation (EC) no. 1260/1999 of the EU council of 21 June 1999[4] laying down "General provisions on the structural funds"[5] made no mention whatsoever of the financial instruments, and their regulatory framework could be only found in two rules (no. 8, Venture capital and loan funds; no. 9, Guarantee funds) of Annex no. 1, "Eligibility rules", of EC regulation no. 1685/2000 of 28 July 2000 laying down a number of implementing rules and then the following EC regulation no. 448/2004 of 10 March 2004.[6]

In particular, the regulation concerning programming period 2000–2006, defined the "venture capital funds and loan funds as investment vehicles established specifically to provide equity or other forms of risk capital (including loans) to small and medium-sized enterprises, except those enterprises in difficulty". In fact, the structural funds' participation in funds may be accompanied by co-investments or guarantees from other community financing instruments.

The legislation included some provisions that would later be reinforced in subsequent planning cycles, such as the mandatory introduction of a prudent "business plan" on which the "guarantee fund" had to be based. The business plan had to be carefully appraised and its implementation monitored by or under the responsibility of the managing authority. In addition, the text added that the fund should be set up as an independent legal entity governed by agreements between the shareholders or as a separate block of finance within an existing financial institution.[7]

The fund management costs could not exceed 2 per cent of the paid-up capital on a yearly average for the duration of the assistance programme unless, after a competitive tender, a higher percentage proves necessary. Finally, the regulation emphasised that, at the time of closure of the operation, the eligible expenditure of the fund should be the amount of paid-up capital of the fund necessary, on the basis of an independent audit, to cover the guarantees provided, including the management costs incurred. It is clear here that the legislation, albeit very basic, primarily referred to measures strictly within the scope of the ERDF and not to the European Social Fund (ESF), that is, measures related to entrepreneurial development and the competitiveness of enterprises rather than initiatives aiming at promoting social inclusion and employment (ESF area of competence), as previously explained (see Chapter 1).

2.1.2 The regulatory framework of the programming period 2007–2013: specific features of the financial engineering instruments

Within the programming period 2007–2013, the financial engineering instruments start to play a central role in the regulatory framework and implementation plans of the European Commission.

The renewed strategic importance of such instruments lays the foundations for their strong development both within the ERDF (with a primary focus on innovation and information-based economy) and the ESF through specific microcredit programmes targeting social inclusion and the creation of jobs.

The general regulation (EC) no. 1083/2006 and implementing provisions in regulation (EC) no. 1828/2006

As already highlighted, the financial engineering instruments are governed not just by EC regulation no. 1828/2006[8] setting out rules for the implementation of council regulation (EC) no. 1083/2006, but also by EC regulation no. 1083/2006[9] itself, laying down general provisions on the ERDF, as well as by the structural funds specific regulations (with regard to the ERDF, see arts 3–6 of EC regulation no. 1080/2006,[10] and for the ESF see art. 11 of EC regulation no. 1081/2006)[11] and start enjoying a systemic and satisfactory definition. In particular, EC regulation no. 1083/2006 dedicated an entire section (no. 4) to the financial engineering instruments. Art. 44 explicitly stated that, within a given operational programme, the structural funds could finance:

(a) *financial engineering instruments for enterprises*, especially small and medium-sized enterprises, such as venture capital funds, guarantee funds and loan funds;
(b) *urban development funds*, that is, funds investing in public–private partnerships and other projects included in an integrated plan for sustainable urban development;
(c) *any loans or guarantees for repayable investments from funds or other incentive schemes providing loans, guarantees for repayable investments or similar instruments* for energy efficiency and the use of renewable energy sources in housing, including existing housing.

Always with regard to the financial instruments, to the above must be added also the exception constituted by the creation of the funds dedicated to the EU reporting process. As is known, all statements of expenditure submitted to the European Commission shall include the total amount of eligible expenditure actually incurred by the beneficiaries, that is, the amounts supported by receipted invoices. The process is, therefore, dependent on the expenditure actually met, which, when duly supported by the accounting documents and complying with the regulations indicated in the documents illustrating the management and control systems adopted by each operational programme, are then certified to the European Commission in order to contribute to the achievement of the annual EU spending targets and avoid the penalty of the automatic decommissioning of resources at the end of the year. There are some exceptions to the above principle though: state aid[12] within certain limits, the simplified costs, as firstly introduced by the programming period 2007–2013 and, with regard to the financial engineering instruments, the total expenditure paid in establishing or contributing to funds under art. 44 of EC regulation no. 1083/2006 or holding funds or the expenditure paid to invest in the latter (see art. 78, paragraph 6, of EC regulation no. 1083/2006).

In other words, the amount transferred to the managing authority to create, for instance, a guarantee or revolving fund, was already regarded as certifiable expenditure, unlike the general rule imposed to wait for the transformation of the sums transferred into actual expenditure.

A broader scope combined with the relative appeal in terms of expenditure certification resulted in a relative increase in the use of such instruments already during the programming period 2007–2013, up to representing approximately 5 per cent[13] of the ERDF total resources in 2012 and reaching a considerable share also within the ESF. In particular, according to communication COM (2011) no. 662, within the programming cycle 2007–2013, nearly all member states implement a range of equity and/or debt (loan and guarantee) instruments, either directly by contributing resources from an operational programme to a venture capital fund, loan or guarantee fund or through holding funds set up to invest in several funds.[14]

In many cases, instruments are implemented through investments into holding funds. Under the JESSICA initiative (Joint European Support for Sustainable Investment in City Areas), holding funds are implemented through the EIB. Under the JEREMIE initiative (Joint European Resources for Micro to Medium-Sized Enterprises), holding funds are generally implemented through the EIF or a range of national or regional institutions. The importance of the financial instruments over time, in particular at the end of the first three years of planning, made it necessary to strengthen also their supervisory framework, and this is why in 2011, following the amendment to art. 67 of the general regulation by EU regulation no. 1310/2011 of the European Parliament and Council of 13 December 2011,[15] the latter established the obligation to give notice of the implementation of the financial instruments in the annual reports as well as in the final implementation reports. With regard to the financial engineering instruments, EC regulation no. 1828/2006, section no. 8 (arts 43–46), setting out rules for the implementation of council regulation (EC) 1083/2006, introduced also a number operational provisions, which clarified and improved the regulatory framework already existing within the programming period 2000–2006, in particular with respect to investment plan and management costs. Art. 43, in fact, established that "The terms and conditions for contributions from operational programmes to financial engineering instruments shall be set out in a funding agreement, to be concluded between the duly mandated representative of the financial engineering instrument and the Member State or the managing authority". The funding agreements were to include at least the following:

- Strategy and investment plan;
- The by-laws of the financial engineering instrument;
- The policy of the financial engineering instrument concerning exit from investments in urban projects or enterprises;
- The winding-up provisions of the financial engineering instruments, including the reutilisation of resources returned to the financial engineering instrument from investment or left over after all guarantees have been honoured, attributable to the contribution from the operational programme.

With regard to the management costs, the following limits were established:

(a) 2 per cent of the capital contributed from the operational programme to the holding funds, or the capital contributed from the operational programme or the holding fund to the guarantee funds;
(b) 3 per cent of the capital contributed from the operational programme or the holding fund to the financial engineering instrument in all other cases, with the exception of microcredit instruments directed at microenterprises;

(c) 4 per cent of the capital contributed from the operational programme or the holding fund to microcredit instruments directed at microenterprises.

The above limits could be exceeded though any time a higher percentage was proved necessary after a competitive tender.

The Coordination Committee of the Funds (COCOF) notes

In the programming period 2007–2013, in order to offer specific guidance on the issues related to the implementation of the regulations governing the structural funds and the Cohesion Fund (pursuant to art. 103 of regulation no. 1083/2006), the EU provided for the creation of a Coordination Committee of the Funds (COCOF) as a permanent committee operating within the European Commission.

This committee, which used to convene once a month, was chaired by the European Commission and would produce guidelines, called "notes", in the EU legislative jargon. As for the financial engineering instruments, the committee issued notes COCOF/07/0018/01 and COCOF/08/0002/03 and, finally, COCOF 10/0014/04 of 21 February 2011, amended by the note under the title "Guidance note on financial engineering instruments under art. 44 of Council Regulation (EC) No. 1083/2006" of 14 December 2011.[16]

Note COCOF 10/0014/04 aimed to provide some clarifications on issues related to the creation and implementation of the financial engineering instruments, in accordance with art. 44 of EC regulation no. 1083/2006, but also technical information and good practices.

The content of the aforementioned note is quite complex and addresses a number of specific issues concerning management and controls that were explicitly mentioned also by the EC decision of 20 March 2013 on the approval of guidelines on the closure of the operating programmes adopted for assistance from the European Regional Development Fund, the Social European Fund and the Cohesion Fund (2007–2013). In particular, the note anticipated the still-much-debated issue of the closure of the financial instruments. As previously mentioned, the expenditure related to this type of intervention can be immediately certified to the European Commission and contribute to achieving the annual expenditure targets, it being sufficient the establishment and transfer of the relevant amounts to the managing authority. At the partial or total closure of the programme, that is, at the end of eligible expenditure, which for the programming period 2007–2013 was established on 31 December 2015, in compliance with art. 78, paragraph 6, of the general regulation, eligible expenditure, with regard to financial engineering instruments, that can be included in the final statement of expenditure shall correspond to the sum of the following amounts:

- Any payments from urban development funds for investment in public–private partnerships or other projects included in an integrated plan for urban development.
- Any payment for investments in enterprises from financial engineering instruments directed at enterprises.
- Any guarantees provided, including amounts committed as guarantees by guarantee funds.
- Any loans or guarantees for repayable investments from funds or other incentive schemes providing loans, guarantees for repayable investments, or equivalent instruments, for energy efficiency and use of renewable energy in buildings, including in existing housing.
- Eligible management costs or fees.

For the expenditure to be considered eligible at the closure of the programme, it is not necessary that the final recipient completed the implementation of the activity supported by the financial engineering instrument, which can, therefore, continue also after 31 December 2015.

The exception to the general rule of the financial instruments under implementation is, therefore, overcome upon closure of the programme and the lack of implementation of the funds in the final statement of expenditure translates into the write-off of the expenditure not incurred.

The programming period 2007–2013, despite the relevant production of secondary regulatory legislation on eligibility issues related to financial engineering instruments, left open some interpretative doubts that resulted in several requests for opinion, which were collected by the European Commission during the meetings with the member states for the closure of the programmes in the second quarter of 2014 and are currently being assessed to provide further guidance in the last quarter of 2014.

2.2 Financial instruments in the cohesion policy 2014–2020: regulatory framework

With its communication of 3 March 2010, the European Commission launched the new ten-year political strategy Europe 2020 (see also Chapter 1) with the aim not only to overcome the economic crisis which continues to affect several EU countries but also to fill in the gaps of the

European development model and create the conditions to achieve a smart, sustainable and inclusive economic growth. The new programming period obviously includes also the financial engineering instruments, which are regarded as the main tool to deploy the resources of the cohesion policy aimed at achieving the proposed targets by 2020. The financial instruments, in fact, provide a targeted support for investments in projects that display potential economic viability and, besides the clear advantages related to the long-term reutilisation of the funds, they provide additional investments through public–private partnerships, thus correcting some imbalances of the market. Moreover, given the increasingly difficult economic crisis and scarcity of public resources, these instruments may have an even greater impact on the cohesion policy throughout the programming period 2014–2020, representing a more efficient and sustainable alternative aimed at integrating traditional grant-based forms of assistance. The previous considerations are justified in light of the relevant regulatory changes on financial engineering instruments introduced by the new EU legislation related to the programming cycle 2014–2020. Awaiting the adoption of secondary regulations, these instruments are now entirely governed by the Title IV (arts 37–46) of EU regulation no. 1303/2013 of the European Parliament and Council of 17 December 2013.

While we postpone a detailed analysis to the next paragraphs, in order to encourage and increase the use of such financial instruments in the cohesion policy, the new regulatory system

- introduces a greater flexibility;
- establishes a stable framework for their implementation based on a number of clear and detailed provisions as well as on existing guidelines and empiric experience in the business practice;
- promotes integration with other forms of assistance, such as subsidies;
- ensures compatibility with other EU financial instruments with a series of provisions on direct management.

As for the types of financial instruments to be activated with the resources from the structural funds, the European Commission lays out only some recommendations.

In particular, the aforementioned communication COM (2011) no. 662[17] provides for three options:

1. Member states continue creating tailor-made instruments under shared management principles, aligned with some common rules

inspired by the EU equity and debt platforms under development for the EU instruments.
2. Creation of "off-the-shelf instruments" under shared management principles which would facilitate the set-up of instruments for member states as well as ensure compatibility with the EU-level instruments.
3. Member states would be encouraged to invest part of their structural funds in compartments of EU level instruments "ring-fenced" for investments in regions and policy areas covered by operational programmes from which structural funds resources are contributed ("joint instruments").

2.2.1 The main amendments compared to previous programming periods

Unlike those related to the programming period 2007–2013, the regulations governing the financial instruments for the programming period 2014–2020 are not mandatory with regard to the sectors, beneficiaries, types of projects and activities to be funded. Member states and managing authorities can, therefore, use such instruments for all the 11 thematic objectives under the operational programmes and all structural funds, where appropriate, for reasons of efficiency and effectiveness. Besides the extension of the scope of the financial engineering instruments, the new regulatory framework introduces some relevant changes that could be summarily referred to the following areas: ex ante assessment; reporting; monitoring.

Firstly, art. 37 of EU general regulation no. 1303/2013[18] for the first time introduces the obligation, any time a financial instrument is activated, to prepare a specific ex ante assessment which may establish evidence of market failures and suboptimal investment situations, the estimated level and scope of public investment needs, the estimate of private resources to be potentially raised by the financial instrument and the added value of the financial instruments that are being considered for support. In addition, the ex ante assessment, which may also be reviewed and updated as required during the implementation of any financial instruments, must represent their added value as well as the consistency with other forms of public intervention addressing the same market, including lessons learnt from similar instruments and ex ante assessments carried out by member states in the past and how such lessons will be applied in the future. Moreover, the ex ante assessment may be performed in stages, but it must be, in any event, completed before the managing authorities decide to make programme contributions to a financial instrument and must also be submitted to the monitoring committee for information purposes. The summary findings and results of ex ante assessments are published within three months of their date of finalisation. With regard to reporting, the main innovation compared to the previous framework is represented by the overcoming of the equivalence between the establishment of the funds and the certification of expenditure, which, in the programming period 2007–2013, had led the financial instruments at issue to assume a leading role in the acceleration of public spending.

In this sense, art. 41 of EU general regulation no. 1303/2013 introduces phased applications for interim payments paid to the financial instrument during the eligibility period. In particular, the amount of the programme contributions paid to the financial instrument included in each application for interim payment submitted during the eligibility period (more correctly, for the revolving funds and the guarantee funds, upon the transfer of the sums to the managing authority) cannot exceed 25 per cent of the total amount of programme contributions committed to the financial instruments under the relevant funding agreements.

Subsequent payments, always within the maximum allowed limit of 25 per cent, may be included in applications for interim payment, that is, certified to the European Commission, in compliance with the following provisions:

- For the second application for interim payment, when at least 60 per cent of the amount included in the first application for interim payments has been spent as eligible expenditure within the meaning of points (a), (b) and (d) of art. 42 of EU general regulation no. 1303/2013.
- For the third and subsequent applications for interim payment, when at least 85 per cent of the amounts included in the previous applications for interim payments have been spent as eligible expenditure within the meaning of points (a), (b) and (d) of art. 42 of EU general regulation no. 1303/2013.

With regard to the financial instruments, the following are considered eligible expenditure of the financial instrument within the meaning of the above-mentioned minimum levels (see paragraph 1, points (a), (b) and (d) of art. 42 of EU general regulation no. 1303/2013):

- Payments to final recipients and, in the event of financial instruments combined with other forms of assistance under a single programme, payments to the benefit of final recipients.

- Resources committed for guarantee contracts, whether outstanding or already come to maturity.
- Reimbursement of management costs incurred or payment of management fees of the financial instrument.

Finally, as for the monitoring of the financial instruments, art. 46 of EU general regulation no. 1303/2013 provides that the new level of monitoring should not be limited to the introduction of a specific section in the annual and final implementation report (which are to replace the progress reports of the programming period 2007–2013) but imposes the obligation to send to the commission a specific report covering the operations comprising financial instruments as an annex to the annual implementation report.

Table 2.1[19] below shows a summary of the specific differences between the programming periods 2007–2013 and 2014–2020 with regard to the financial engineering instruments (figures are valid both for ERDF and ESF).

2.3 The control system

One of the key factors of the EU cohesion policy spending is represented by the decentralised management system. Programmes are managed at regional and local level, so that the projects selected are better attuned to the local specific requirements. Member states and regions take the lead role in deciding how money should be used and bearing the responsibility for managing it properly. Within the member states, hundreds of organisations are involved in managing the different parts of the operational programmes; likewise, hundreds of thousands of beneficiaries implement individual projects. Such a system of decentralised government is prone to high inherent risks, due to the great number of organisations involved in the supply chain.[20] The European Commission has supervisory role in ensuring that expenditure is in line with the agreed strategic priorities and financial rules; it is accountable under the EU treaty for the proper implementation of the budget. Two of its departments are mainly responsible for overseeing the cohesion policy spending; namely, the Directorates General for *Regional Policy* and for *Employment, Social Affairs and Equal Opportunities*. The objectives and priorities for the use of funds are laid down in individual operational programmes at national or regional level, negotiated between the European Commission and each member state and formally approved by the commission. The programme authorities select the projects to attain objectives set and to

Table 2.1 Differences between 2007–2013 and 2014–2020 and between the programming periods 2007–2013 and 2014–2020

	2007–2013	2014–2020
Scope	Support for enterprises, urban development, energy efficiency and renewable energies in building sector	Support for all thematic objectives covered under a programme
Set-up	Voluntary gap analysis for enterprises and at the level of holding fund	Compulsory ex ante assessment
Implementation options	Financial instruments at national or regional level – tailor made only	Financial instruments at national, regional level, transnational or cross-border level: Tailor-made OR off-the-shelf OR MA loans/guarantees; contribution to EU level instruments
Payments	Possibility to declare to the commission 100 per cent of the amount paid to fund – not linked to disbursements to final recipients	Phased payments linked to disbursements to final recipients; national co-financing which is expected to be paid can be included in the request for the interim payment
Management costs and fees, interest, resources returned, legacy	Legal basis set out in successive amendments of the regulations and recommendations/interpretations set out in three COCOF notes	Full provisions set out from outset in basic, delegated and implementing acts
Reporting	Compulsory reporting only from 2011 onwards, on a limited range of indicators	Compulsory reporting from the outset on a range of indicators linked to the financial regulation
Scope	Support for all revenue generating investments under the RDP	Support for all revenue generating investments under the RDP
Set-up	Ex ante assessment only for guarantee funds	Compulsory ex ante assessment for any FI
Implementation options	Financial instruments at national or regional level – tailor made only Only loans, guarantees and venture capital	Financial instruments at national, regional level, transnational or cross-border level: Fund of funds; tailor-made OR off-the-shelf OR MA loans/guarantees; contribution to EU level instruments
Final recipients	Indirect access to the FI – access only for those with grant applications under a RDP measure selected by paying agencies	Direct access to the FI – any final recipient that fulfils the eligibility and selection criteria without the need to submit an application to the paying agency
Payments	Possibility to declare to the commission 100 per cent of the amount paid to fund – not linked to disbursements to final recipients	Phased payments linked to disbursements to final recipients
Management costs and fees, interest, resources returned, legacy	General legal basis set in the implementing rules	Full provisions set out from outset in basic, delegated and implementing acts
Reporting	No compulsory reporting – part of the general annual reporting on the programme's implementation	Compulsory reporting from the outset, on a range of indicators linked to the financial regulation

Source: Authors' elaboration.

which the funds contribute. Throughout the period, the member state regularly declares the programme expenditure to the commission, and the commission later reimburses the agreed EU contribution. As previously examined, the beneficiaries have until the end of 2015 to complete projects and present the expenditure. The programme authorities then present the final expenditure claim and the programme is closed with a final payment to the member state.[21] The funding of projects under an operational programme, as seen before, is subject to certain terms and conditions, laid down partly at EU and partly at member state level. These rules are established to ensure value for money, proper management of programmes and consistency with community policies.

These rules set out criteria for selecting the projects, assessment of cost benefits and earnings potential of the projects, competitive tendering, economic, social and environmental impact assessment and compliance with the EU legislation on state aid, if applicable. Moreover, the legislation imposes an indication of the location and type of the activities co-financed, the period during which the expenditure can be incurred, the minimum proportion of spending that is required on projects serving EU priorities such as innovation, job creation and environment, cost categories, restricted/excluded activities and, finally, the retention of supporting documents over minimum periods for audit and publicity purposes.[22]

Under the decentralised and shared management system, the member states have primary responsibility for the control of programme expenditure, while the European Commission performs a supervisory role over the national systems. The dissemination of information among all subjects involved is another key element to implement a proper management and control system, as it helps prevent problems and encourage compliance. A multilevel control system is put in place: it is integrated on the basis of clearly defined responsibilities for the various actors, established standards for the work required and reporting systems and feedback mechanisms so that each level of control builds on the preceding one, with a view to reducing the burden, in particular the beneficiaries. The different levels of control must be independent from one another in order to perform their functions properly. In the member states there are three levels of control, and the corresponding whose bodies in each programme are as follows (Figure 2.1):

- *The managing authority*: represents the first level of control and has the key responsibility for making sure that the programme is effectively and correctly implemented. It must ensure that the operations

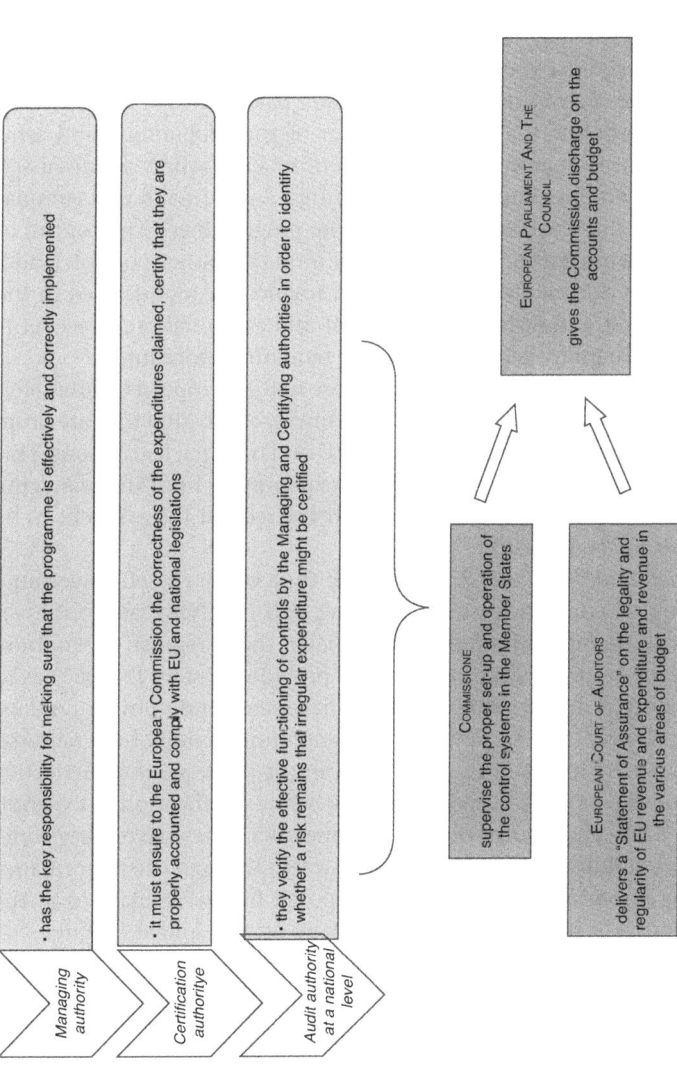

Figure 2.1 Control process.
Source: Authors' elaboration.

selected for the programme comply with the criteria established by the European Commission; it must advise the beneficiaries on what they have to do to meet the terms and conditions of funding; it must put in place and manage internal controls to check that the expenditure presented by the beneficiaries is regular. In addition, it must correct irregular expenditure found by withdrawing it from payment claims and recovering any grant already paid from the beneficiaries; it must monitor the implementation of the programme and send the commission annual reports on performance, which are discussed with the commission at annual meetings, and a final report summarising the implementation of the entire programme.[23] The control of the managing authority may take the form of on-the-spot visits, desk checks on documents such as lists of invoices or reports used in the programme, interviews with the staff and examination of accounts and documentary records relating to tendering procedures.

- *The certification authority*: it must ensure to the European Commission the correctness of the expenditures claimed, certify that they are properly accounted for and comply with EU and national legislations. This authority receives the statements of expenditure from the managing authority before they are included in the request for payment to be sent to the commission.[24]
- *The audit authority at a national level*: they verify the effective functioning of controls by the managing and certifying authorities in order to identify whether a risk remains that irregular expenditure might be certified. Accordingly, they provide constant feedback as to the effective functioning of the management and control systems. Audits by EU bodies examine the overall functioning of the national control systems. Audits, however, cannot make up for ineffective first-level controls or lack of checking before certification of expenditure.[25] The audit authorities in the member states have a key function in building up assurance in the system through the performance of the important responsibilities imposed by the regulations at the beginning of the period, during implementation and at closure.

At EU level, the role of the commission is to supervise the proper set-up and operation of the control systems in the member states by means of

- the compliance assessment procedure, approval of audit strategies and scrutiny of annual control reports and audit opinions;
- carrying out audits on the member states to gain assurance that the systems are working effectively; the EU Commission focuses on the

reliability of the work of the audit authorities to provide this assurance through their annual control reports and audit opinions;
- monitoring information reported by member states on irregularities and recoveries of unduly paid funds;
- providing formal guidance to establish benchmarks and spread good practices; regulatory and control issues are discussed in the management committee composed of representatives of the European Commission and the member states (the Coordination Committee of the Funds, COCOF), in the technical working group of the ESF Advisory Committee and in technical meetings with the audit authorities;
- checking at the programme closure that the funding for the programme is properly justified.[26]

In addition, once a year the European Court of Auditors delivers a "statement of assurance" on the legality and regularity of EU revenue and expenditure and revenue in the various areas of budget. The assessments are based on audits carried out by the court in the member states and the commission, including a statistical sampling of 180 projects of member states.[27]

Finally, the European Parliament and the Council scrutinise the use of EU funds in the annual discharge procedure, which lasts from November to April, at the end of which the parliament gives the commission discharge on the accounts and budget.[28]

Assurance on the effectiveness of the control systems in preventing, detecting and correcting irregularities is built up throughout the whole programming period. In the negotiations on the operational programmes, the European Commission ensures that programme authorities are properly designated, and any problems found with the systems in previous period are adequately addressed. After programme approval, the compliance assessment procedure gives assurance on the satisfactory set-up of monitoring systems before any expenditure is reimbursed. Within 12 months from programme approval, a national audit body – often the audit authority – has to issue a certificate of compliance with regard to the internal control systems for the programme. The European Commission looks at the compliance assessment report and opinion to make sure it is consistent and reliable. Only after any necessary corrective measures have been taken and the commission is satisfied that the control system fully meets the regulatory requirements will it start to reimburse expenditure for the programme. At the beginning of the programme period, the commission also examines and approves the audit strategy submitted by the audit authority within nine months of programme adoption.[29] As previously mentioned, the European

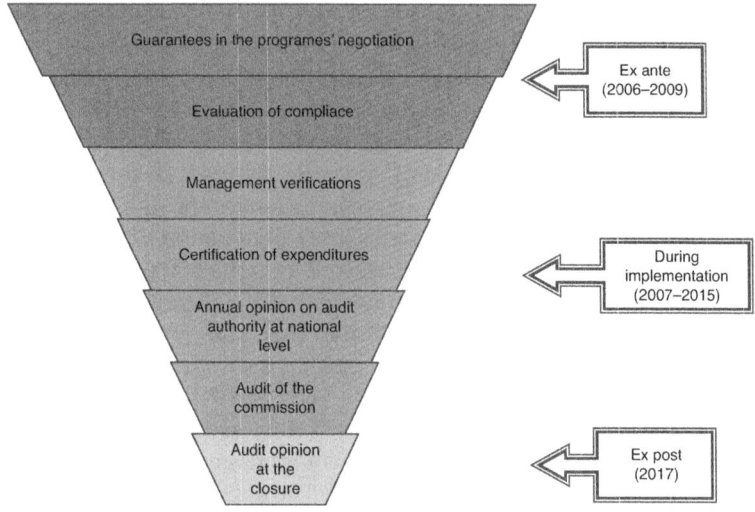

Figure 2.2 The monitoring process: phases
Source: Authors' elaboration on EU, "The Control System for cohesion policy", 2009.

Commission must examine also the reports prepared by the certification and audit authorities during the programming period.

Finally, at the end of the programme period, the audit authority issues an opinion on the accuracy and compliance with the rules of the expenditure declared from the programme in the final statement of expenditure; in addition, in its closure report, the audit authority gives details of the actions taken to improve systems and correct any irregular expenditure. The European Commission carefully scrutinises all closure declarations and, if needed, asks for more information or the performance of more audit work.

Figure 2.2 summarises the monitoring phases in the programming process. It is necessary to point out that the correction of any discrepancies lies in the responsibility of the member states, which must inform, every three months, the European Anti-Fraud Office of all irregularities[30] related to EU funds exceeding €10,000.

2.4 Structural funds and microfinance

The European structural funds can be an effective mechanism to provide access to finance for small and microenterprises. As confirmed by a study carried out by the European Microfinance Network,[31] microfinance is a financial instrument which can be supported by at least two structural funds: the European Social Fund (ESF) and the European Regional Development Fund (ERDF).

Since several years ago, at least at EU level, microfinance has gained growing recognition, as it represents a cost-effective tool for social inclusion on the one hand and for regional economic growth on the other. Supporting the setting up or developing of a microbusiness costs only a fraction of unemployment and health benefits paid out and activates excluded people's potential to become again active members of their communities. In the national action plans for social inclusion (NAPs),[32] however, microfinance is most often not mentioned at all. If it is, it is not translated into the EFS operational programmes. The ERDF operational programmes instead tend to focus on funding for SMEs. During periods of crisis, national and regional policies tend to give priority to employment rather than self-employment initiatives; they tend to prefer small-, medium- and large-sized companies to microenterprises. Especially in the current crisis context, public policies specifically focus on requalification, training and advice for (former) employees of large enterprises rather than on establishing and developing microbusiness. It is therefore necessary to systematically integrate microfinance as a basic social and financial service into the national action plans and the structural funds' operational programmes. Moreover, microfinance, self-employment and microentrepreneurship should become policy priorities in the field of social exclusion and economic growth.

Microentrepreneurship and self-employment have proven a way to activate the labour market. Some individuals, in particular ESF beneficiaries (unemployed, immigrants, women, people 50 and up, young people), have a hard time finding a job but would be very good entrepreneurs. Supporting them in the creation of businesses is not just a way to save on unemployment or welfare benefits. In this sense, according to the Europe 2020 strategy, entrepreneurship is a key element to achieve smart, sustainable and inclusive growth. As mentioned in Chapter 1, the EC, therefore, encourages the member states to implement measures to promote entrepreneurship and self-employment initiatives by facilitating access to finance. Several programmes are available at EU level to support access to finance for small enterprises, such as CIP and JEREMIE, in addition to other programmes specifically designed for microfinance, such as JASMINE (Joint Action to Support Microfinance Institutions), EPPA (European Parliament Preparatory Action) and PROGRESS Microfinance (Programme for Employment and Social Solidarity). In addition to the above initiatives aimed at facilitating inclusion in the labour market, the EU has provided a specific form of support, both at regional and/or national level, represented by the use of financial engineering instruments under the structural funds (ESF and ERDF), both through direct grants and the JEREMIE programme. If on the one hand the ERDF resources are mainly used to support enterprises (mostly SMEs), urban development, energy efficiency and the use of renewable energy sources, on the other hand the ESF is used to promote self-employment, microenterprises and the creation of start-ups.[33]

More generally, the ESF aims to increase employment, promote entrepreneurship and improve social inclusion by favouring equal opportunities and non-discrimination as well as ensuring mobility and permanent education in Europe, in light with the Lisbon strategy and the integrated guidelines for economic growth and job creation.

2.5 Implementing a microfinance programme through the structural funds

Within the decision-making process for the structural funds, the managing authorities are invited to submit their national reform programmes (NRP)[34] in the month of April every year, while they must also publish the National Strategic Reference Frameworks (NSRF) and the relevant operational programmes (OPs) in the first year of the programming period. The member states must use these documents to explain how they intend to integrate the EU objectives and priority guidelines in their respective national policies. The national reform programmes (NRP) are an important tool to implement the Europe 2020 strategy and monitor the expected results.

In several EU countries and regions, the managing authorities have already put in place microcredit programmes and schemes in accordance with the ESF operational programmes.

In Sardinia, the Fondo Microcredito (Microcredit Fund) was established in December 2009 and provided with a budget allocation of €30 million by the ESF,[35] subsequently increased by €20 million. The programme's objective is to improve access to the labour market, create jobs and support SMEs and self-employment initiatives. This fund was created as the economic study highlighted critical unemployment levels, especially among women, and a tighter access to credit than in other regions in Italy. Moreover, numerous pilot projects had previously shown a strong demand for microcredit. Under this programme, loans up to €25,000 are granted to enterprises (not to single individuals) in different priority areas, such as retail, manufacturing business, social and personal services, tourism and ICT.

The correct management of the financial instruments co-funded by the EU structural funds lie in the responsibility of the managing authorities. The latter are active at national or regional level; they can be, for instance, the Ministry of Labour or a regional government body. When a microfinance programme is activated, several ministries can work in collaboration with the managing authority. Each ministry is vested with specific and clear responsibilities and carries out its functions according to different political perspectives (sometimes in compliance with different regulations). It is therefore essential to combine tasks and expertise between different government organisations and merge their practices using a variety of approaches. Moreover, the microfinance sector (specifically, microcredit) is regulated by different national regulatory frameworks, in particular by legislation on the provision of credit, consumer protection law and tax legislation.[36] The legislation of the member states on different compartments of microfinance and microcredit may therefore greatly impact the activation and management process of microfinance programmes.

In order to implement and manage a successful microfinance programme, the managing authority needs to possess global expertise: political, technical, legal skills and assessment of potential areas of risk. With the aims of aligning all actors, implementing an integrated initiative[37] and combining all the skills needed, most countries decided to create a steering committee or task force entrusted with the task of setting up the fund. This committee connects the interested parties to a central level (within a ministry or a plurality of ministries) and other actors involved. Such a practice proved effective in rationalising the process under several aspects; in fact, it allowed concentrating a variety of functions in one single entity and facilitated policy implementation.[38]

Once the decision on the creation of the fund has been made and the main actors have been involved, the next stage should consist in the preparation of a business plan, which must include a financial plan (EU financing and national and/or regional co-financing), the interested parties, activities to be carried out, processes, quality and quantity objectives and indicators of the microcredit fund, such as provision of credit, beneficiaries (e.g., ESF's priority groups), loan terms and conditions and exit plans. The financial engineering instruments funded by structural funds can be set up both as independent legal entities, governed by agreements between co-financing partners or shareholders, or as a separate block of finance within a financial institution. Once they have been established in both forms, they are regulated by specific regulations and other applicable documents and operate in accordance with the industrial plan or a specific document agreed upon with the managing authority or the holding fund.[39] Terms and conditions for the operational programme contributions to the financial engineering instruments are set out in a funding agreement, which must be signed by the authorised representative of the financial instrument and the member state or the managing authority. As a part of the decision-making process, the latter should evaluate whether to implement the financial engineering action through a holding fund or direct contributions from the operational programme to the financial engineering instrument.

The fund holder or managing entity shall manage the funds provided by the ESF and the ERDF. This subject may consist of a public, regional, national or European financial intermediary. Theoretically, all public financial intermediaries may become fund operators, including those organisations already involved in the management of ERDF or ESF instruments.

As part of the decision-making process, the member states or managing authorities shall evaluate whether to implement the financial engineering operations through public contracts, in compliance with the legislation on public procurements, or through direct contributions. In general, the managing authorities organise a tendering procedure for the appointment of fund managers. However, regional or national organisations, such as development banks with fund managing expertise, may be designated as fund managers without the need for contract award procedures. In this case, regulatory or administrative provisions compatible with the EU treaty shall be applied in order to confer to the entity at issue exclusive management rights on the fund for the operations included in the programming period 2007–2013.[40]

The provision of direct contributions to experienced in-house managers has different advantages:

- Efficiency: lower control and administrative costs during programme selection and management phase.
- Reliability: a regional/national entity ensures compliance with the objectives of regional/national planning, transparent information flows and immediate controls.

In the event that a regional or national entity is chosen, the latter should have proven financial management expertise and skills (related to projects co-financed by the EU), sound knowledge of legislation and procedures, commitment to supporting regional development objectives and a strong result-oriented policy. State members or the managing authorities may also decide to implement the programme by awarding a contract directly to the European Investment Bank or the European Investment Fund, thanks to their particular legal status of EU organisations created under the EU treaty. Another option is to rely on institutions which collaborate as fund co-managers, such as regional financial institutions willing to use the EIF contributions.[41]

Once selected, the member state or the managing authority shall sign a funding agreement with the fund manager/operator. These contracts must ensure correct implementation of the strategy – including objectives, areas of intervention and final recipients/beneficiaries to be supported according to the operational programme – through a consistent investment plan, products and expected objectives to be achieved through the financial engineering instruments. The funding agreements should also include a performance-based remuneration system for the fund managers. Moreover, the funding agreements must include a set of regulations, covenants and procedures that must be followed by all interested parties with regard to the financial support granted by the operational programme.[42] The financial intermediaries can be chosen by way of either public procurement or direct appointment by fund managers. Their choice should be based on the political-legal framework and the specific requirements of the microcredit/microfinance programmes to be implemented.

The design of a microfinance programme involves also additional phases than those above described (creation of partnerships, implementation of specific products, communication and marketing, risk management, compliance with the code of conduct, etc.), which are all essential for its success. In the future, one of the main challenges for microfinance programmes lies in achieving self-sustainability and independence from public aid. ESF contributions, in fact, offer the opportunity to strengthen the capacity of the financial intermediaries to test, adapt and standardise credit procedures so as to gain a greater degree of independence in the future.

2.5.1 Some examples in Europe

No doubt, the financing of microfinance programmes represents a critical issue. Financial sustainability is hard to achieve, especially for those microfinance organisations in Europe working with beneficiaries who are excluded from the traditional banking system.

In France, the organisation France Initiative used the ERDF Regional Funds to fund equity and management costs of its own finance platforms.[43] France Initiative is a network of associations offering honour loans (guarantee-free and interest-free loans), which currently coordinates 230 platforms.[44] Active since 1985, it supported over 17,000 start-ups, creating or maintaining over 37,000 jobs. It generated a volume of €166 million of honour loans with a repayment rate of 98 per cent.[45] The loans' average amount is €8,150, and they are destined for unemployed individuals, young people and women. The enterprises supported have an average of 2.2 employees each. Resources are provided by local government authorities, banks and companies, customers, public entities and international funds. In 2011, €315 million dedicated to credit were financed by the regional councils (22.7 per cent), the European Funds (ERDF and LEADER+;[46] 7.2 per cent) and savings and loans banks, companies and other private contributors. Besides financing the honour loans, the European Funds provided financial support to business support services for entrepreneurs, in particular during the start-up phase of companies, with a 7 per cent share of the total budget.[47]

In England and Scotland, the ERDF and ESF made possible the creation of several funds providing loans to microenterprises, including groups of particularly vulnerable individuals. For instance, Principe Scottish Youth Trust Business PSYBT used the ERDF funds for the implementation of its combined "credit and grant" programme dedicated to young entrepreneurs in need of financial inclusion.[48]

Likewise, the First Enterprise Business Agency was received funds from the ERDF to support its activities supporting immigrant entrepreneurs and ethnic minorities.[49]

In Finland, the ERDF supports investments by Finnvera; specifically, investments in working capital, loans to enterprises, microcredit, loans to female entrepreneurs and other credit with environmental purposes. Moreover, Finnvera provides ERDF-backed guarantees.[50]

In Portugal, ERDF and ESF were used to create a fund for microenterprises by a network of commercial banks that cover the entire national territory (RIME project, budget allocation: €20 million). Established 1995, RIME aimed to develop local entrepreneurship potential, promote the creation of jobs and tackle adverse economic conditions. RIME provided important contributions to investments and the creation of jobs as well as low-interest loans to microenterprises (crafts, local services and rural tourism), in particular those created by young entrepreneurs in densely

Table 2.2 Use of ERDF and ESF for microfinance programmes

Country	Fund	Use
France	ERDF	to finance honour loan platforms
United Kingdom	ERDF and ESF	funds to youth, immigrants and ethnic minorities
Finland	ERDF	investments in Finnvera
Portugal	ERDF and ESF	RIME project, loans for microenterprises

Source: Authors' elaboration.

populated areas. Between 1994 and 1999, 18,479 jobs were created, of which 9,919 benefit women.[51] However, in the most critical regions, such as the Lima Valley (North Region), the programme saw a very low number of applicants. This was due to a lack of local infrastructure, red tape, low education of the potential beneficiaries and poor information on the support services for the submission of the applications.[52]

Notes

1. Although this chapter was prepared jointly by the authors, Sections 2.1 and 2.2 were written by Giorgio Centurelli, while Section 2.3 and 2.5 was written by Pasqualina Porretta and Section 2.4 was written by Fabrizio Santoboni.
2. EU (1992), Treaty of Maastricht on European Union, https://www.ecb.europa.eu/ecb/legal/pdf/maastricht_en.pdf.
3. European Commission (2004), Annex of the commission regulation (EC) no. 448/2004 of 10 March 2004 – Rule no. 8: Venture capital and loan funds and Rule no. 9: Guarantee funds, http://ec.europa.eu/regional_policy/sources/docoffic/official/regulation/content/en/02_pdf/00_9_4_expend2_en.pdf.
4. European Commission (2000), Commission regulation laying down detailed rules for the implementation of council regulation (EC) no. 1260/1999 as regards eligibility of expenditure of operations co-financed by the structural funds, *Official Journal of the European Communities*, http://ec.europa.eu/regional_policy/sources/docoffic/official/regulation/pdf/reg_elig_en.pdf.
5. European Commission (1999), Council regulation laying down general provisions on the structural funds, *Official Journal of the European Communities*, http://eur-lex.europa.eu/legal-content/EN/TXT/PDF/?uri=CELEX:31999R1260&rid=5.
6. European Commission (2004), Commission regulation amending regulation (EC) no. 1685/2000 laying down detailed rules for the implementation of council regulation (EC) no. 1260/1999 as regards the eligibility of expenditure of operations co-financed by the structural funds and withdrawing regulation (EC) no. 1145/2003, *Official Journal of the European Communities*, http://eur-lex.europa.eu/legal-content/EN/TXT/PDF/?uri=CELEX:32004R0448&rid=4.

7. European Commission (2004), Commission regulation amending regulation (EC) no. 1685/2000 laying down detailed rules for the implementation of council regulation (EC) no. 1260/1999 as regards the eligibility of expenditure of operations co-financed by the structural funds and withdrawing regulation (EC) no. 1145/2003, *Official Journal of the European Communities*, http://eur-lex.europa.eu/legal-content/EN/TXT/PDF/?uri=CELEX:32004R0448&rid=4 – Rule no. 9 – 1 General rule.
8. European Commission (2004), Setting out rules for the implementation of council regulation (EC) no. 1083/2006 laying down general provisions on the European Regional Development Fund, the European Social Fund and the Cohesion Fund and of regulation (EC) no. 1080/2006 of the European Parliament and of the Council on the European Regional Development Fund, http://eur-lex.europa.eu/legal-content/EN/TXT/PDF/?uri=CELEX:32006R1828&from=IT.
9. Council regulation (EC) (2006), Laying down general provisions on the European Regional Development Fund, the European Social Fund and the Cohesion Fund and repealing regulation (EC) no. 1260/1999, http://eur-lex.europa.eu/legal-content/EN/TXT/PDF/?uri=CELEX:02006R1083-20131221&rid=1.
10. European Parliament and Council (2006), On the European Regional Development Fund and repealing regulation (EC) no. 1783/1999, http://eur-lex.europa.eu/legal-content/EN/TXT/PDF/?uri=CELEX:02006R1080-20100618&qid=1404848626582&from=EN.
11. http://eur-lex.europa.eu/legal-content/EN/TXT/PDF/?uri=CELEX:32006R1081&from=IT.
12. As part of free competition within the EU domestic market and, specifically, in light of public services opened up to competition from the private and voluntary sector, member states sometimes intervene by using their own resources to support certain businesses or protect some of their domestic sectors. By supporting some companies to the detriment of the competitors, state aid can distort competition. State aid is prohibited by the treaty on the Functioning of the European Union. Yet a number of exceptions exist and authorise those aid measures justified by the need of protecting objectives of common interest, i.e., aid directed to services of general economic interest, provided that they do not distort the competition to an extent contrary to the common interest.
13. European Commission (2014), Fact sheets, Financial Instruments in Cohesion Policy 2014–2020, http://ec.europa.eu/regional_policy/sources/docgener/informat/2014/financial_instruments_en.pdf.
14. European Commission (2011), Communication from the commission to the European Parliament and the Council: a framework for the next generation of innovative financial instruments – the EU equity and debt platforms, COM(2011), 662 final of 19.10.2011, 19, http://ec.europa.eu/economy_finance/financial_operations/investment/europe_2020/documents/com2011_662_en.pdf.
15. European Parliament and Council (2011), Amending council regulation (EC) no. 1083/2006 as regards repayable assistance, financial engineering and certain provisions related to the statement of expenditures, http://eur-lex.europa.eu/LexUriServ/LexUriServ.do?uri=OJ:L:2011:337:0001:0004:EN:PDF.
16. Ibid.

17. Communication from the commission to the European Parliament and the Council. A framework for the next generation of innovative financial instruments: the EU equity and debt platforms – Final COM (2011) 662 of 19.10.2011, http://ec.europa.eu/economy_finance/financial_operations/investment/europe_2020/documents/com2011_662_en.pdf.
18. European Parliament and Council (2013) laying down common provisions on the European Regional Development Fund, the European Social Fund, the Cohesion Fund, the European Agricultural Fund for Rural Development and the European Maritime and Fisheries Fund and laying down general provisions on the European Regional Development Fund, the European Social Fund, the Cohesion Fund and the European Maritime and Fisheries Fund and repealing council regulation (EC) no. 1083/2006, http://eur-lex.europa.eu/LexUriServ/LexUriServ.do?uri=OJ:L:2013:347:0320:0469:EN:PDF.
19. European Commission (2014), Financial instruments in ESIF programmes 2014–2020: a short reference guide for managing authorities, http://ec.europa.eu/regional_policy/thefunds/fin_inst/pdf/fl_esif_2014_2020.pdf.
20. EU (2009), "The control system for Cohesion Policy. How it works in the 2007–13 budget period", http://ec.europa.eu/regional_policy/sources/docgener/presenta/audit2009/audit2009_en.pdf.
21. Ibid.
22. Ibid.
23. Ibid.
24. Ibid.
25. Ibid.
26. Ibid.
27. Ibid.
28. The discussion on the discharge is based on the annual report of the EU Court of Auditors as well as the EC special reports and opinions.
29. Ibid.
30. Typical irregularities are lack of supporting documents (e.g., time records of staff, invoices or overhead allocation keys) that should be kept for the purposes of the audit trail, to facilitate controls, non-deduction of revenue from project expenditure, inclusion of ineligible expenditure such as recoverable VAT and breaches of tendering requirements.
31. Brigitte Maas and Stefanie Lämmermann (2012), "Designing microfinance operations in the EU. A manual on how to build and implement microfinance support programmes using the ESF", http://www.microfinancegateway.org/sites/default/files/mfg-en-toolkit-designing-microfinance-operations-in-the-eu-a-manual-on-how-to-build-and-implement-microfinance-support-programmes-using-the-esf-2013.pdf.
32. The NAP for social inclusion is an instrument which, every two years, "provides the creation and development of a strategic plan to tackle any form of social exclusion and marginalisation at EU level".
33. Brigitte Maas and Stefanie Lämmermann (2012), "Designing microfinance operations in the EU. A manual on how to build and implement microfinance support programmes using the ESF", http://www.microfinancegateway.org/sites/default/files/mfg-en-toolkit-designing-microfinance-operations-in-the-eu-a-manual-on-how-to-build-and-implement-microfinance-support-programmes-using-the-esf-2013.pdf.

34. "The 2012 National Reform Programme (NRP) represents the main component of the 'European Semester', the annual cycle dedicated to the coordination of the economic and budget policies, and constitutes a key moment in the coordination between EU policies and national policies. The NRP aims to provide an overview on the reforms implemented following the recommendations adopted by the EU for the previous year, illustrating their scope, compliance with the European Union guidelines and their expected impact. Moreover, the NRP presents an agenda of interventions planned for the months ahead, to define the action plan through which Italy intends to achieve the objectives defined at European level", http://www.politicheeuropee.it.
35. ESF, Priority axis 3 on social inclusion.
36. Leone P. and Porretta P. (2014), "Microcredit guarantee funds in the Mediterranean. A comparative analysis", Palgrave Studies in Impact Finance, Palgrave Macmillan.
37. In Italy, for example, several actors were involved by the Lombardy Regional Administration in the implementation of the microfinance fund through JEREMIE, directed at strengthening the cooperative sector. Besides the ESF managing authority, the following actors were involved: Finlombarda (the regional financial entity entrusted with fund management), other regional directorates with responsibilities and functions in the cooperative system (DG for Family and Social Solidarity and DG for Enterprises and Industry, Crafts, Housing and Cooperation), the financial intermediaries, the cooperatives and the Ministry of Labour. All these organisations (apart from the ministry) were involved in a series of informal meetings to verify the economic and administrative feasibility of the project. Following the start-up phase, a steering committee was created to monitor the correct and effective management of the programme.
38. Brigitte Maas and Stefanie Lämmermann (2012), "Designing microfinance operations in the EU. A manual on how to build and implement microfinance support programmes using the ESF", http://www.microfinancegateway.org/sites/default/files/mfg-en-toolkit-designing-microfinance-operations-in-the-eu-a-manual-on-how-to-build-and-implement-microfinance-support-programmes-using-the-esf-2013.pdf.
39. COCOF_10-0014-04-EN.
40. Directive no. 2004/18/EC, art. 18.
41. http://www.eif.org/what_we_do/jeremie/faq/index.htm#What%20is%20the%20role%20of%20a%20Fund%20Holder.
42. COCOF_10-0014-04-EN.
43. EMN (2009), "COPIE 2 Access to Finance Baseline Study", http://www.emnconference.org/archives/news_summer-2009_en.html#paragraphe14.
44. http://www.initiative-france.fr/.
45. http://www.european-microfinance.org.
46. Liaison entre actions de développement de l'économie rurale (link between actions to develop the real economy), supports locally designed rural development projects aimed at revitalising the territory and the creation of jobs. In other words, its objective is to promote "an integrated, endogenous and sustainable development of rural areas".

47. France Initiative (2012), "Rapport annuel 2011", http://www.banque-france.fr/fileadmin/user_upload/banque_de_france/publications/Rapport-annuel-2011-Observatoire-de-la-Micro-finance.pdf.
48. EMN (2009), "COPIE 2 Access to Finance Baseline Study", http://www.emnconference.org/archives/news_summer-2009_en.html#paragraphe14.
49. Ibid.
50. Ibid.
51. http://www.europarl.europa.eu/meetdocs/committees/rett/20010619/439210EN.pdf.
52. INAISE (1997), "Financial instruments of the social economy (FISE) in Europe and their impact on job creation", and M. N. O. Roca (2000), "Financial instruments of the social economy (FISE) in Europe and their impact on job creation".

Except where otherwise noted, this work is licensed under a Creative Commons Attribution 3.0 Unported License. To view a copy of this license, visit http://creativecommons.org/licenses/by/3.0/

OPEN

3
EU Financial Engineering and Microfinance Non-financial Service: A Case Study

Maria Claudia Costantini, Maria Doiciu, Stefanie Lämmermann, Andrea Nardone and Giovanni Nicola Pes

3.1 The ESF and the credit access of microenterprises

3.1.1 The problem of access to credit for microenterprises

Small and medium-sized enterprises (SMEs) represent 99.8 per cent of the total number of enterprises in Europe and play a key role in terms of economic development and creation of jobs, by accounting for 57.6 per cent of added value in EU-27 and more than two thirds of jobs created in the private sector (Table 3.1). Over 90 per cent of European businesses are microenterprises with less than ten employees, whose importance is particularly significant in South European countries such as Italy, Spain and Portugal.[1]

While large businesses have ready access to equity capital markets to support their investment projects, SMEs – and, in particular, microenterprises – cannot access them and, therefore, are heavily reliant on bank lending: in 2013, bank lending (or other forms of financing such as leasing and factoring) represented the only source of funding for 54 per cent of micro, small and medium-sized enterprises in the European Union, and 75 per cent of them used at least one form of debt financing.[2] On the other side, equity financing was little used, only by 5 per cent of the EU enterprises in 2013, in particular by SMEs with a stock market listing and those with a turnover exceeding €50 million, but also by the so-called gazelles, that is, SMEs less than five years old which have grown at over 20 per cent per annum. As we underline in the previous chapters, promoting access to credit for microenterprises and SMEs is one of the key priorities of the European Union strategy for growth.[3] Moreover, the European Commission itself, in its communication

Table 3.1 Enterprises, employees and added value, EU-27, 2012

	Micro enterprises	Small enterprises	Medium-sized enterprises	Total SMEs	Large enterprises	Total
Number	18,783,480	1,349,730	222,628	20,355,839	43,454	29,399,291
%	92.1	6.6	1.1	99.8	0.2	100
Number of employees						
Number	37,484,458	26,704,352	22,615,906	86,814,717	43,787,013	130,601,730
%	28.7	20.5	17.3	66.5	33.5	100
Added value at factor cost						
Million €	1,242,72	1,076,388	1,076,270	3,395,383	2,495,926	5,891,309
%	21.1	18.3	18.3	57.6	42.4	100

Source: Authors' elaboration on Eurostat, National Statistical Offices data, DIW, DIW econ, London Economics.

"Europe 2020",[4] points out that the recent economic crisis has almost halved the potential for growth of these enterprises, forcing them to resize their investment plans, due both to sluggish demand and lack of funding (credit crunch). In particular, the sovereign debt crisis resulted in a severe shortage of funds available on the markets for European banks as well as reduced opportunities to access credit for households and businesses alike, many of which – especially microenterprises – have seen their creditworthiness fall lower.[5]

Recent quantitative surveys[6] highlight that although restrictions on the supply of credit are showing signs of gradual attenuation, the bank policies, especially towards smaller enterprises, are still influenced by the perception of high credit risk; as a result, such enterprises are still struggling to access credit. The feedback received from entrepreneurs on cases of loan refusal confirms the SMEs negative perception on the possibility of obtaining external funding. In particular, about one third of the SMEs participating in the survey claim not to be able to get the full credit amount needed to implement their investments in 2013, and 7 per cent of them (mainly micro start-ups) did not even apply for a loan as they were positive that their applications would be rejected.

All SMEs managers who participated in the survey were asked to evaluate a pre-supplied list of seven potential problems[7] that their companies might be currently facing and to choose among the most pressing issues on the list. Fifteen per cent of the EU SMEs regard access to credit as the second most pressing problem, preceded only by finding customers (Chart 3.1). However, there was a lot of variation across countries with regard to the evaluation of SMEs for access to finance. In fact, while France, the

Chart 3.1 Main criticalities perceived by European SMEs, 2013 (percentage values)
Source: Authors' elaboration on EC (2013), SMEs Access to Finance survey.

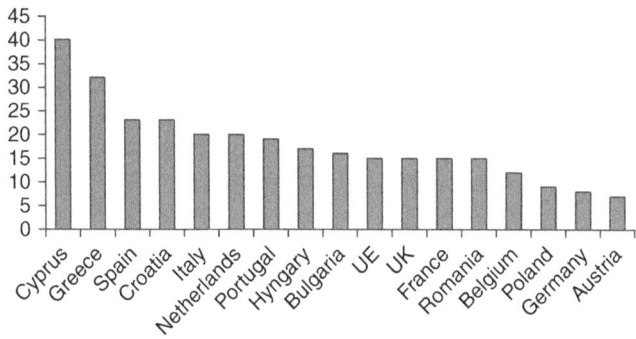

Chart 3.2 European SMEs regarding access to credit as the most pressing problem, 2013 (percentage values)
Source: Authors' elaboration on EC (2013), SMEs Access to Finance survey.

United Kingdom and Romania are levelled around the average percentage of 15 per cent, the figures become 32 per cent in Greece, 23 per cent in Spain, 20 per cent in Italy, Ireland and the Netherlands and then decrease to 9 per cent in Poland and 8 per cent in Germany (percentage values for the main European countries are indicated in Chart 3.2).

Recent data provided by the Bank Lending Survey[8] on the bank loan performance in the EU area in the first quarter of 2014 do not show significant changes in the restrictive policy adopted by EU banks in the provision of credit, which continues to be affected by the perception of high credit risk, especially towards smaller and microenterprises. However, the results of other econometric surveys[9] indicate that the difficulties met by SMEs and microenterprises as well as young businesses to access external financing cannot be totally related to risk perception, as these issues may persist even in cases of financial performance equal to that of medium-sized and large companies. According to these studies, the European bank credit market is characterised by a number of imperfections that are likely to originate from a series of information asymmetries: on one side, banks are not prone to lend if they are unable to obtain sufficient financial information on the profitability of investments by enterprises; on the other, enterprises are discouraged from applying for loans due to a lack of information on sources of financing and, often, also because they perceive a lack of willingness to lend by the banks.

3.1.2 European Social Fund and access to credit of microenterprises

The problem of access to credit for SMEs and microenterprises is at the centre of the EU policies for growth, employment and social inclusion. To solve it, the European Commission has activated a broad range of programmes and allocated resources to be provided by the funds directly managed by the commission itself (e.g., the COSME programme and progress microfinance for the microcredit sector) and by the structural funds managed by the individual state members and regions. Among the latter, the European Regional Development Fund (ERDF) undoubtedly plays a key role in the provision of financial support to enterprises, as it is specifically dedicated to financing investments made by enterprises, but also the European Social Fund (ESF), within the framework of its social inclusion objectives, which allows activating specific measures to access credit (and microcredit) within the regional operational programmes, especially for disadvantaged subjects who are willing to start or consolidate microenterprises or self-employment initiatives.

As is known, the essential objective of the European Social Fund is to "promote high levels of employment and job quality, improve access to labour market, support the geographical and occupational mobility of workers and facilitate their adaptation to industrial change and changes in production systems needed for sustainable development, encourage a high level of education and training for all and support the transition from education to employment for young people".[10]

The ESF, therefore, "benefits people, including disadvantaged people, such as the long-term unemployed, people with disabilities, migrants, ethnic minorities, marginalised communities and people of all ages facing poverty and social exclusion. The ESF also provides support to workers, enterprises, including actors in the social community and entrepreneurs, as well as to systems and structures with a view to facilitating their adaptation to new challenges, including reducing skill mismatches and promoting good governance, social progress, and the implementation of reforms, in particular in the fields of employment, education, training and social policies".[11]

It is quite a broad mission, which expressly includes support to SMEs and microenterprises also through the "use of financial instruments, including microcredit and guarantee funds"[12] according to art. 37 of EU regulation no. 1303/2013.[13] This policy to support SMEs and microenterprises, as well as all other measures co-financed by the ESF, refers to 4 out of 11 thematic objectives (TOs) identified by art. 9 of the aforementioned regulation no. 1303/2013 to implement the EU strategy for smart, sustainable and inclusive growth. In particular, the following:

- TO no. 8: *"Promoting sustainable and quality employment and supporting labour mobility"*;
- TO no. 9: *"Promoting social inclusion, combating poverty and any discrimination"*;
- TO no. 10: *"Investing in education, training and vocational training for skills and lifelong learning"*;
- TO no. 11: *"Enhancing institutional capacity of public authorities and stakeholders and efficient public administration"*.

For each of these objectives, art. 3 of EU regulation no. 1304/2013 of the Social European Fund, provides for an articulated series of investment priorities (see Box 3.1).

Box 3.1 Thematic objectives and investments priorities of the European Social Fund *(EU regulation no. 1304 of 17 December 2013, art. 3)*

"Promoting sustainable and quality employment and supporting labour mobility" (TO no. 8), by facilitating:

- Access to employment for job-seekers and inactive people, including the long-term unemployed and people far from the labour market, also through local employment initiatives and support for labour mobility.
- Sustainable integration into the labour market of young people, in particular those not in employment, education or training, including young people at risk of social exclusion and young people from marginalised communities, including through the implementation of the Youth Guarantee.
- Self-employment, entrepreneurship and business creation including innovative micro, small and medium-sized enterprises.
- Equality between men and women in all areas, including in access to employment, career progression, reconciliation of work and private life and promotion of equal pay for equal work.
- Adaptation of workers, enterprises and entrepreneurs to change.

- Active and healthy ageing.
- Modernisation of labour market institutions, such as public and private employment services, and improving the matching of labour market needs, including through actions that enhance transnational labour mobility as well as through mobility schemes and better cooperation between institutions and relevant stakeholders.

"Promote social inclusion, combating poverty and any discrimination" (TO no. 9), by facilitating:

- Active inclusion, including with a view to promoting equal opportunities and active participation, and improving employability.
- Socio-economic integration of marginalised communities such as the Roma.
- Combating all forms of discrimination and promoting equal opportunities.
- Enhancing access to affordable, sustainable and high-quality services, including health-care and social services of general interest.
- Promoting social entrepreneurship and vocational integration in social enterprises and the social and solidarity economy in order to facilitate access to employment.
- Community-led local development strategies.

"Investing in education, training and vocational training for skills and lifelong learning" (TO no. 19):

- Red ucing and preventing early-school leaving and promoting equal access to good quality early-childhood, primary and secondary education including formal, non-formal and informal learning pathways for reintegration into education and training.
- Improving the quality and efficiency of, and access to, tertiary and equivalent education with a view to increasing participation and attainment levels, especially for disadvantaged groups.
- Enhancing equal access to lifelong learning, for all age groups in form, non-formal and informal settings, upgrading the knowledge, skills and competences of the workforce, and promoting flexible learning pathways including through career guidance and validation of acquired competencies.
- Improving the market labour relevance of education and training systems, facilitating the transition from education to work, and strengthening vocational education and training systems and their quality, including through mechanisms for skills anticipation, adaptation of curricula and the establishment and development of work-based learning systems.

"Enhancing institutional capacity of public authorities and stakeholders and efficient Public Administration" (TO no. 11):

- Investment in institutional capacity and in the efficiency of public administrations and public services at the national, regional and local levels with a view to reforms, better regulation and good governance.
- Capacity building of all stakeholders delivering education, lifelong learning, training, employment and social policies, including through sectorial and territorial pacts to mobilise for reform at national, regional and local level.

As you can see, in light of the above objectives, the support provided to enterprises to facilitate access to credit is part of a broader vision targeting social inclusion, training, education and increased employment opportunities for disadvantaged groups, such as young people, women, long-term unemployed individuals and migrants. These objectives have been adopted by a number of EU member states within their ESF regional operational programmes (PORs) within the programming period 2007–2013, with the aim of creating microcredit funds to support certain categories of disadvantaged subjects as identified by the aforementioned EU regulations. According to surveys carried out at a European level, which are referred to herein as well, Italy seems to be one of the most active EU countries in this field, as it included specific microcredit measures within its ESF regional operational programmes. In particular, the central and southern Italian regions included revolving or guarantee funds co-financed by the European Social Fund, which will continue to operate also in the current programming period 2014–2020. Below you can find a summary of such measures, their objectives and operational methods.

Box 3.2 For ESF Italy 2007–2013 providing from microcredit measures

REGION ABRUZZO

Objectives: To support local microenterprises and self-employment by financing start-ups and promoting new investments and/or the consolidation of existing businesses, for all those subjects, whether individuals or legal entities, who are unable to access traditional credit services due to personal and/or objective reasons.
Beneficiaries: Existing microenterprises or being formed and self-employed workers.
Financial instrument: Revolving fund for the provision of unsecured loans.
Financial conditions: Maximum loan amount is €10,000 for individuals and €25,000 for legal entities; maximum duration 60 months; 1 per cent interest rate.

REGION CAMPANIA

Objectives: To support start-ups and implementation of new investments for existing enterprises, including spin-offs, for categories of subjects who struggle to access traditional credit and are affected by disadvantaged conditions.
Beneficiaries: Individuals willing to start new microenterprises, existing microenterprises or companies being formed (including spin-offs), enterprises operating in the service sector (social associations and cooperatives), whether existing or being formed.

Financial instrument: Revolving fund for the provision of unsecured loans.
Financial conditions: Maximum loan amount is €25,000; maximum duration is 60 months; interest-free.

REGION APULIA

Objectives: To support access to small-amount loans to promote a regional development model based on high human capital intensity and low environmental impact, rewarding enterprises created by young people and women and supporting innovative and sustainable conversion of traditional businesses.
Beneficiaries: Existing microenterprises.
Financial instrument: Revolving fund for the provision of unsecured loans.
Financial conditions: Maximum loan amount is €25,000; maximum duration is 60 months; interest rate equal to 70 per cent of the EU reference rate.

REGION BASILICATA

Objectives: To promote an innovative and integrated action to support local microenterprises, cooperatives and unemployed/inactive subjects and create new enterprises, through a support and guarantee fund co-financed by the ESF with the aim of facilitating access to credit for microenterprises and support new entrepreneurs, including initiatives started by disadvantaged subjects, by way of the following: (a) provision of low-interest loans; (b) provision of guarantees.
Beneficiaries: Non-bankable subjects who set up enterprises, social enterprises and self-employed workers.
Financial instrument: Support and guarantee fund.
Financial conditions: Maximum loan amount is €25,000; maximum duration is 60 months; interest-free.

REGION CALABRIA

Objectives: To promote microcredit programmes as an instrument to fight poverty and social exclusion in order to develop participation and solidarity initiatives to support disadvantaged groups; to support employment through self-employment initiatives and the creation of microenterprises; to support initiatives aimed at enhancing local development potential.
Beneficiaries: Disadvantaged workers, disabled workers, immigrants, inmates, alcohol and drug addicts.
Financial instrument: Guarantee fund and interest-subsidy fund.
Financial conditions: Maximum loan amount is €25,000; maximum duration is 60 months; fixed interest rate negotiated with the banks. The fund guarantees 80 per cent of the loans and provides 100 per cent interest subsidy.

> **REGION SARDINIA**
>
> *Objectives*: To support start-ups or the implementation of new investments in existing businesses, for categories of subjects who struggle to access credit and are affected by disadvantaged conditions.
> *Beneficiaries*: Workers over 50 years old, young unemployed or inactive workers, off-workers, unemployed or inactive workers, women, migrants, single-parent families, new entrepreneurs.
> *Financial instrument*: Revolving fund for the provision of unsecured loans.
> *Financial conditions*: Maximum loan amount is €25,000; maximum duration is 60 months; interest-free.
>
> *Source*: Authors' elaboration.

3.2 The ESF and access to credit for microenterprises: a case study from Germany

During the last two decades a strong microcredit sector has developed in Germany. Small microcredit pilot projects already emerged in the 1990s and early 2000. Around 2005 the sector came to a consolidation; finally, from 2010 on it was rolled out on a nationwide level. In each of these phases, ESF funding played a pivotal role, especially for developing, testing and implementing new products, tools and processes. It is fair to say that the German microcredit sector would not exist today without support from ESF. The following paragraph highlights the role that ESF played in the development of microcredit in Germany.

3.2.1 History of microfinance in Germany

The pilot phase (2000–2004)

Already in the 1990s some scattered microcredit initiatives were set up around Germany (such as *Goldrausch*, providing microloans to women).[14] From the year 2000 on, more and more local and regional business support organisations realised that their clients faced difficulties in accessing finance for setting up or developing their small enterprise, especially entrepreneurs starting out of unemployment. These organisations therefore developed microcredit operations in addition to their consulting and training activities. Organisations such as *Enigma* (Hamburg),[15] *Verbund Enterprise* (Brandenburg),[16] *EXZET* (Stuttgart)[17] and *KIZ* (Offenbach)[18] created first pilot microcredit programmes in cooperation with different banks and with financial support from German public bodies such as the Federal Employment Agency, foundations as well as EU funds, notably ESF. In the pilot phase (2000–2004) so-called development partnerships were established in the frame of the ESF EQUAL programme in order to develop a one-stop-shop system for solo entrepreneurs in Germany, including financial support. In this context, a range of studies analysing and comparing the microfinance experience of existing pilot projects was carried out. Knowledge about microfinance practice in other EU countries was brought in, too. By doing so, microcredit was lifted to the attention of the German public, highlighting its main characteristics and success factors such as unbureaucratic procedures, flexibility, alternative guarantees, step loan provision and additional business support. Starting from the idea of making available easy access to capital, *Deutsches Mikrofinanz Institut* (DMI),[19] a nationwide microfinance network was created in April 2004. The first project of the association was to conduct a "test run" in order to develop a range of microfinance products and methods. First, about 10 members actively joined this pilot phase. Up to 30 other members assisted them voluntarily through collaboration and membership fees. Based on this support structure it was possible to reach a joint start of microfinance at different locations and trigger joint learning processes for the benefit of all involved actors. DMI, in close cooperation with the ethical-ecological bank GLS, developed a microfinance cooperation model for Germany and in June 2004 it was decided to set up the first microfinance fund. At first, capital was injected by GLS Bank and 80 private persons close to GLS. Thus, at the end of 2004, €500,000 were made available for microloan disbursement through the GLS Microfinance Fund.

The consolidation phase (2005–2009)

In the second EQUAL funding period the microfinance cooperation model was consolidated. The model is based on the cooperation of four different partners:

- So-called microfinance institutions (MFIs: business counselling companies, start-up centres, regional business initiatives and so on) carry out the client support, from the first contact till full repayment of the loan. The MFIs administer the loan securities, are responsible for constant monitoring of the loans and take over a substantial part of the risk.
- Due to German banking law a cooperating bank distributes the microloans upon the MFIs' recommendation (low risk and high scale).
- A guarantee fund covers 100 per cent of the risk for the bank.
- The supervising organisation assures the quality of the microloan operations through training, accreditation and benchmarking of the MFIs.

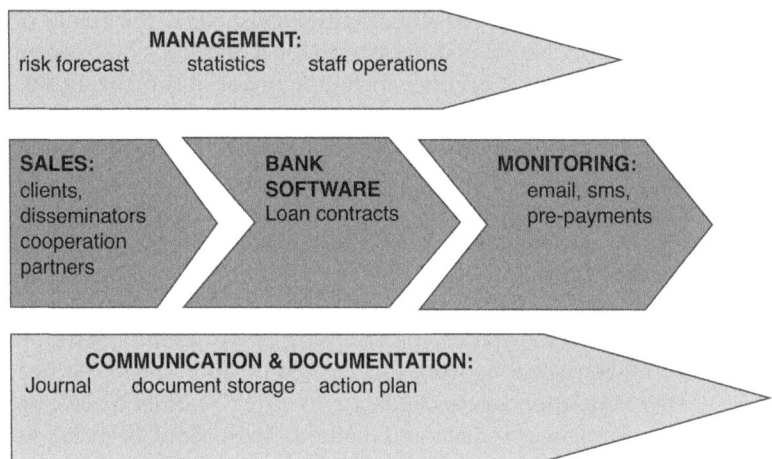

Figure 3.1 Overview of DMI MIS Inthepro
Source: Authors' elaboration.

In 2006, the Federal Ministry of Labour and Social Affairs, the Federal Ministry of Economy and Technology and the federal development bank KfW joined as investors of the microfinance fund established in 2004. They topped up the fund with €2 million and the fund was renamed Mikrofinanzfonds Deutschland (Microfinance Fund Germany).

In order to monitor and manage the loans the DMI network developed a sophisticated client monitoring and risk management system called *Inthepro* with initial funding from EQUAL (Figure 3.1). Inthepro maps the whole credit process, from the first contact until full repayment of the loan. It enables the MFIs to carry out a partly automatised, detailed client monitoring procedure; this is completed by a risk management and benchmarking system that classifies all outstanding loans into specific risk categories. Through monthly benchmarking the system ensures quality management and early-warning for MFIs as well as higher-level bodies.

Then, in autumn 2007, DMI launched Projekt 5000 (Project 5000 – Microfinance as an instrument to solve sociopolitical problems), a nationwide campaign with the aim of scaling up microfinance by developing a growth strategy and linking practitioners and supporters of microfinance. The project would end once the 5,000th microloan handed out. It was at the beginning of 2010 that this project received real impetus.

Roll-out (2010–today)

In January 2010, based on a study about access to finance for microenterprises and self-employed people, the Federal Ministry of Labour and Social Affairs and the Federal Ministry of Economy and Technology decided to start a new programme with a similar set-up as in 2004–2006: Mikrokreditfonds Deutschland (Microcredit Fund Germany). In total, €100 million were provided as a guarantee fund, 60 per cent coming from national European Social Fund and 40 per cent from the German government. The aim of the fund was to sustainably establish a nationwide offer of microcredits in Germany and disburse 15,000 microloans until 2015. The fund considerably improved the operating environment for MFIs.

MFIs active under the fund need accreditation from DMI and have to cover up to 20 per cent of the defaults (first loss). In return they receive a gratification payment (depending on the repaid loan volumes) and a (decreasing) item fee for each loan handed out, which the MFIs can use to cover part of their institution building costs. Besides, in the first two years of operation of the microcredit fund, from 2010 to 2012, the DMI network led a microcredit project in the frame of the large-scale ESF programme IDA: Integration durch Austausch (Integration through exchange). The project enabled the sector to scale up its know-how through exchange visits with other European countries as well as studies and pilot projects on topics such as processing cost, sustainability, transparency, outreach to target groups, risk management, scoring models and quality labels (EU Code of Good Conduct for Microcredit Provision). Through meetings, workshops and conferences, the lessons learnt on a Europe-wide level were shared with over 100 German microfinance practitioners from 40 MFIs as well as representatives from the banking sector, political actors and administrators. The German Mikrokreditfonds is today celebrated as great success all over Europe. From 2010 to 2013 the MFIs supported more than 16,500 German microentrepreneurs through loans. Unfortunately, since 2013 the microfinance activity has declined. The reasons are manifold. The system turned out to be complex, and too many incentives had been given for quick growth, while the experience and knowledge of the DMI network was neglected. Since 2013, the MFIs have had to cope with high lack of planning reliability due to several interruptions of the Mikrokreditfonds programme.

Appraisal of ESF support for microcredit in Germany

Microcredit aims at supporting disadvantaged people who wish to set up or develop a business; it is therefore an important instrument of labour

Table 3.2 Loan volumes since 2005 (preliminary numbers)

Period	Loans	Euro	MFIs
2005	12	106,050.00	5
2006	38	265,535.00	7
2007	89	562,694.00	9
2008	119	788,560.00	12
2009	287	1,962,461.00	12
2010	1,748	9,807,770.00	42
2011	4,869	29,720,551.00	57
2012	5,520	33,700,000.00	60
2013 (Preliminary numbers)	4,520	30,198,120.00	42
Total	17,202	107,111,741.00	

Source: Authors' elaboration.

market policy. The ESF, as stressed in Chapter 2, is Europe's main instrument for supporting jobs, helping people get better jobs and ensuring fairer job opportunities for all EU citizens. It is therefore exactly the right funding instrument when it comes to supporting microcredit in Europe. The German microcredit sector has benefited from ESF funding in several ways. First of all, within the framework of the EU community initiative EQUAL (2002–2007), standardised microlending processes were designed as well as products and tools adapted to the needs of the clients. These were subsequently tested and implemented by MFIs in different regions and for different target groups. They build the basis of what constitutes the German microfinance sector today. Secondly, ESF gave an important input to controlling and supervising the high quality of the microloan provision, through the development of the DMI Inthepro software and accreditation system. The DMI accreditation and training system has been acknowledged as good practice in microfinance in Europe. Moreover, with Inthepro, a powerful management information system now exists. It enables the MFIs to actively support their clients in the loan repayment while holding the cost as low as possible, and provides the possibility of comparison and mutual learning amongst all MFIs. Finally, ESF has shown its usefulness as a financial engineering instrument in Germany. Although the German experience has made clear that several parameters need to be adapted for such a programme to be successful and sustainable over time, a strong microcredit sector has emerged, with devoted MFIs who face the harsh reality in their everyday work – clients who cannot get finance, either from private nor public promotional banks, and who urgently need microfinance to establish their business. More than 17,000 entrepreneurs have received an average microcredit of around €6,000 under the various, national microfinance funds since 2005; in Germany 33 per cent of them are women, and 35 per cent have migrant background. Based on the assumption that one microloan creates or maintains two jobs, this means that microcredit has saved nearly 35,000 jobs in the last ten years in Germany. There is strong demand for a microcredit in Germany. Much still needs to be done in order to completely close the funding gap for small enterprises and self-employed people. Although much has been achieved, further ESF-funding is needed in order to back MFIs when it comes to developing their products and services and successfully reach out to their target groups.

3.3 Microfinance and non-financial services: the European resources to sustain non-financial services

The EU has long committed itself in strengthening the skills of existing entrepreneurs, new entrepreneurs and potential entrepreneurs. In 2006, within the project *DG Enterprise and Industry*, the European Commission entrusted a group of experts with the task of analysing the best practices of management capacity building in order to develop and support the competitiveness of the European SMEs. In its final report (EC, 2006, p. 29),[20] the group of experts proposed a set of 16 recommendations, aimed at all actors involved.

In particular, the following recommendations were directed to business support providers:

I. Promote courses and programmes to help assess enterprises' competitive positioning and directly impacting their profitability.
II. Make sure that all phases of the enterprise life cycle are covered.
III. Promote alliances with bigger companies.
IV. Facilitate the creation of networks and promote their use.
V. Schedule training so that small business managers can actually attend.
VI. Make good use of opportunities offered by e-learning.
VII. Business support service providers need to improve the marketing of their services.

While the recommendations directed to business and trade associations and individual entrepreneurs were as follows:

VIII. Identify and acquire information or knowledge matching the specific needs of the businesses.
IX. Identify useful courses and attend some (no excuses), business associations should contribute to assess the quality and relevance of the training offered.
X. Businesses need to be aware that they may gain additional knowledge through means other than courses and consultants – with an added bonus: it can be cheaper.

In 2007, the European Commission, in the *Communication from the Commission to the Council, the European Parliament, the European Economic and Social Committee and the Committee of the Regions of 13 November 2007 – a European initiative for the development of microcredit in support of growth and employment* (EC, 2007),[21] stressed the importance of microcredit both with regard to the implementation of strategies that may favour growth and the creation of jobs and the promotion of social integration. In this perspective, in its 2007 communication the European Commission recommended EU institutions and the single member countries to carry out measures supporting microcredit through the following directories:

1. Improve the legal framework and institutional environment of the member countries.
2. Change the background conditions and promote a business-friendly environment.
3. Promote the dissemination of best practices, including training.
4. Increase capitals available to the microcredit providers.

In particular, the commission stressed the necessity of "increasing the chances of success of new microenterprises through training, tutoring and development of business support services" (EC, 2007, p. 9).[22] Access to credit is definitely a major issue for new entrepreneurs and, generally, for all those subjects excluded from the traditional lending circuits, although not the only one. In fact, due to the complexity of the European entrepreneurial system, it is now necessary to provide the new entrepreneurs with skills and know-how they often lack. "Training, mentoring or coaching the new entrepreneurs are essential to improve the enterprise's chances of success" (EC, 2007, p. 8).[23]

However, in order to offer such services to microentrepreneurs, the microfinance providers must carefully analyse their financial sustainability and feasibility. The costs of such services, in fact, are unlikely to be borne by the commercial bank sector and the existing experiences at European level (such as the experiences in Italy and France) have highlighted the importance of the public and non-profit sectors in the promotion of non-financial services connected with microcredit.

The aforementioned communication already emphasised that a greater use of the resources provided by the FESR, the FSE (European Social Fund) and the FEASR (European Agriculture Fund for Rural Development) would be desirable to promote the business support services (EC, 2007, p. 8, 27).[24] A further step away from their centralisation is represented by the adoption of the Small Business Act (EC, 2008)[25] by the European Commission in June 2008 within the broader Action Plan 2020 for enterprises.

The Small Business Act called on all EU member countries to step up and promote a business-friendly environment for the development and growth of the SMEs through the application of ten basic principles, which are meant to address, from an operational point of view, the differences between American and European SMEs in terms of growth and productivity. In particular, principle no. 4, entitled "Turning principles into policy action", states that "the EU and Member States should create a healthy environment where entrepreneurs and family businesses can thrive and entrepreneurship is rewarded. They need to care for future entrepreneurs better, in particular by fostering entrepreneurial interest and talent, particularly among young people and women, and by simplifying the conditions for business transfers" (EC, 2008, p. 5).[26]

In order to translate these principles into practice, the European Commission committed its efforts:

- to promote an entrepreneurial culture and facilitating exchanges of best practices in entrepreneurship education;
- to launch the European SME Week in 2009 – an umbrella for many campaign-type events that will take place throughout Europe;
- to activate the Erasmus for Young Entrepreneurs initiative in 2008, which aims to promote exchanges of experiences and training by giving nascent entrepreneurs the possibility to learn from experienced host entrepreneurs and improve their language skills;
- to establish a EU network of female entrepreneurship ambassadors, promote mentoring schemes to inspire women to set up their own businesses and promote entrepreneurship among women graduates (EC, 2008, p. 6).[27]

The European Commission has focused its attention on non-financial services; in fact, member states are invited to:

- stimulate innovative and entrepreneurial mindsets among young people by introducing entrepreneurship as a key subject in school curricula, particularly in general secondary schools, and ensure that it is correctly reflected in the teaching material;
- ensure that the importance of entrepreneurship is correctly reflected in teachers' training;
- step up cooperation with the business community in order to develop systematic strategies for entrepreneurship education at all levels;
- provide mentoring and support for business transfers;
- provide mentoring and support for female entrepreneurs;
- provide mentoring and support for immigrants who wish to become entrepreneurs (EC, 2008, p. 6).[28]

To encourage entrepreneurship, besides reducing bureaucratic, fiscal and administrative barriers, the European Commission invites the member countries to implement a long-term strategy entrusting non-financial services with a central role. To create and stimulate entrepreneurial culture, therefore, it is necessary to start from the new generations by implementing stable programmes and measures that may facilitate the creation of knowledge and skills. At the same time, it is absolutely imperative and necessary to implement mentoring and support services for some specific target groups, such as women and immigrates, who may be involved in the creation of start-ups, to improve their living conditions, fight economic and social vulnerability, support the entrepreneurial community in developing a systematic strategy that may facilitates a permanent and continuous development at all levels as well as the transition of entrepreneurial skills and activities between different generations.

3.4 The new European plans

The current economic-financial crisis gripping the whole continent prompted the European Union to provide a response in terms of economic policy. As we have previously observed, the European Commission emphasised (and still does) the importance of non-financial services as a tool to support the growth and development of businesses; the role of entrepreneurship as a drive for economic growth and the creation of jobs. In particular, the SMEs represent the most important source of new jobs; according to the figures released by the European Commission, in fact, they account for the creation of over 4 million new jobs (EC, 2013, p. 4).[29]

In the *Entrepreneurship 2020 Action Plan*, the commission remarks that propensity to entrepreneurship greatly varies among the various EU member countries, due to a variety of factors, such as difficulty to access credit, red tapes and burdensome administrative procedures, difficulties to relocate companies, fear of sanctions in the event of bankruptcy, poor knowledge of the structure of small and medium-sized enterprises, inadequate measures to support them, an educational system that does not provide the basic knowledge and background to start and develop an entrepreneurial career.

Within the same action plan, the European Commission detects a widespread tendency in the current market context to ignore, or not acknowledge in the right way, the entrepreneurial efforts and initiatives as well as a lack of rewards for successful entrepreneurs (EC, 2013, p. 4).[30]

The Entrepreneurship 2020 Action Plan emphasises three areas of immediate action:

1. Entrepreneurship education and training aimed at supporting the creation and development of businesses.
2. Strengthening of the market conditions for the benefit of entrepreneurs, removing all structural obstacles and providing them with support during the most important phases of the enterprise life cycle.
3. Reignite the entrepreneurship culture in Europe: foster and raise a new generation of entrepreneurs.

The first action (Table 3.3) moves from the premise that entrepreneurship represents a key subject within the European education framework (EP and EC, 2006).[31] The action plan puts a particular emphasis on entrepreneurial education of young people as a fundamental instrument to promote that cultural change needed to support economic growth. Some authors (Jenner, 2012, p. 27)[32] stressed out that young people who receive an entrepreneurship-oriented education are more bound to develop not only a higher knowledge of the business world but also additional skills and attitudes to operate in this sector, including creativity, a spirit of entrepreneurship, tenacity, teamwork, responsibility and superior risk-assessment capacity.

Table 3.3 Main actions recommended by the European Commission to the member countries: action no. 1 – entrepreneurship education and training

Scope	Actions to be undertaken
Action 1 Entrepreneurship education and training aimed at supporting the enterprise creation and development	– Ensure that "entrepreneurship"-related subjects and teachings are included in the curricula of primary, secondary, vocational, higher and post-degree education by the end of 2015. – Offer students at least one opportunity to have an entrepreneurial experience before they complete their compulsory education cycle. – Boost entrepreneurship training for young people and adults alike within the educational system, by using the resources provided by EU structural funds, in particular those of the European Social Fund and resources for training available within the European Agricultural Fund for Rural Development. Entrepreneurship training must be regarded as an alternative option for all those who are in school or engaged in a working or training activity. – Promote entrepreneurship learning modules for young people who participate in the Youth Guarantee national programmes.

Source: Authors' elaboration data on European Commission (2013), *Entrepreneurship 2020 Action Plan – reigniting the entrepreneurial spirit in Europe*, http://ec.europa.eu/enterprise/policies/sme/entrepreneurship-2020/index_en.htm, accessed 7 July 2014.

Besides the programmes included in the compulsory education cycle, the action plan highlights the need of using multiple methods to provide youth with the above knowledge and skills; among them, formal and informal education and volunteering. The action should not just target the new generations but involve a variety of other subjects. In this perspective, a particularly relevant role should be played by partnerships and strategic alliances with other subjects. Entrepreneurial skills, in fact, can be effectively supported and taught only through the collaboration of academic institutions, business incubators, business networks and mobility opportunities within the project. To promote such a culture, in June 2013 the European Commission prepared a guidebook on entrepreneurship education specifically dedicated to educators (EC, 2013).[33] In addition to developing a number of pan-European initiatives to strengthen its policies, the commission invites all EU member countries to stimulate education to entrepreneurship at all levels, targeting both the young and adults, through the use of structural funds such as FSE and FESR.

Table 3.4 Main actions recommended by the European Commission: action 2 – strengthening the entrepreneurial environment

Scope	Actions to be undertaken	
Action 2 Strengthen the environmental conditions for entrepreneurs; remove current structural obstacles; give support in the crucial phases of the enterprise life cycle	At European level – Support to the Enterprise Europe Network – Develop integrated support systems through capacity building actions	Calls on member countries to – Make use of the FEASR to support start-ups – Support business clusters, networks and cooperation activities

Source: Authors' elaboration data on European Commission (2013), *Entrepreneurship 2020 Action Plan – reigniting the entrepreneurial spirit in Europe*, http://ec.europa.eu/enterprise/policies/sme/entrepreneurship-2020/index_en.htm, data accessed 7 July 2014.

The second action, related to the creation of a business-friendly environment where enterprises may be created and thrive, refers to six areas of action (Table 3.4):

- Access to funding;
- Support to entrepreneurs during the key phases of enterprise life cycle and growth;
- Activate new business opportunities in the digital age;
- Transfers of companies;
- Bankruptcy and second chances for honest entrepreneurs;
- Easing regulatory burdens.

Taking into consideration the second area of intervention, related to support for the crucial phases of the enterprise life cycle, the 2020 action plan highlights that 50 per cent of new enterprises go bust in the first five years of life, often due to the absence of a business-friendly *ecosystem* that may facilitate their development and growth (EC, 2013, p. 10).[34]

In this regard, business support services could step in and play a role in supporting such companies, which may benefit from their experience. Starting from the assumption that enterprises and entrepreneurs – of all levels and size – need support and advice to deal with new regulations, energy efficiency and recycle requirements, investments for product development, it is absolutely mandatory to promote holistic programmes suitable to combine key elements such as training, tutoring and creation of networks with other similar companies, suppliers and potential customers. To this end, the commission intends to strengthen – through direct-management funds – the partnership of the Enterprise Europe network at a pan-European level in order to provide effective assistance, support businesses and facilitate the access to the single market, and also help the single member countries to develop integrated support systems through the implementation of capacity building actions suitable to involve all the interested stakeholders (EC, 2013, p. 12).[35] At the same time though, the commission calls on all member countries to make full use of the newly introduced support options for start-ups within the FEASR, according to a model aimed at the creation of general systems that may favour professional exchanges between entrepreneurs and visits to farms, also providing support to business clusters, networks and cooperation programmes in the agricultural sector, forestry, food industry and non-agricultural rural enterprises (EC, 2013, p. 14).[36]

The third area of action identified by the commission to promote change in the business culture concerns the cultural perception of entrepreneurs by the community, their role in the society and the involvement of specific groups in the business world, such as women, the elderly, migrants, unemployed individuals and young people, all categories that are poorly represented in the population of entrepreneurs. With regard to specific groups and their role in entrepreneurship, measures aimed at ensuring greater participation and supporting their active role in this area should be based on a support integrated system that, in addition to financial backing, includes also training programmes designed and offered in partnership with education and training providers, schools, youth organisations, business counsellors, financial institutions and all those subjects providing assistance and guidance. With regard to women, who represent a large pool of potential entrepreneurs in Europe, in recent years the commission has implemented a number of measures and programmes to support enterprises created by women and raise awareness (the European network of female entrepreneurship ambassadors) on the necessity of correcting gender imbalances of publicly listed companies.

In line with its previous years, the commission (EC, 2013, p. 14)[37] will create an online platform meant to involve all aspects of tutoring, counselling, training and the creation of business networks for the benefit of female entrepreneurs. Moreover, the commission calls on all the EU member countries to design and implement national strategies to support female entrepreneurship aimed at increasing the number of enterprises led by women and implement conciliation policies (Table 3.5).

Table 3.5 Main actions recommended by the European Commission: action no. 3 – reigniting the entrepreneurial spirit in Europe through the involvement of specific groups (women)

Actions to be undertaken to support women	
At European level	Calls on member countries to
– Strengthen the European network of female entrepreneurship ambassadors – Correct gender imbalances in publicly-listed companies – Online platform on tutoring, counselling, training and creation of business networks	– Design and implement national strategies to support female entrepreneurship aimed at increasing the number of enterprises led by women – Support and extend the existing networks of female entrepreneurship ambassadors and mentors – Implement policies promoting a more balanced relationship between business and private life (through FEASR, FSE, FESR)

Source: Authors' elaboration data on European Commission (2013), *Entrepreneurship 2020 Action Plan – reigniting the entrepreneurial spirit in Europe*, http://ec.europa.eu/enterprise/policies/sme/entrepreneurship-2020/index_en.htm, data accessed 7 July 2014.

As for the elderly, the commission highlights that longer life spans imply also the possibility that some elderly may want to start a business for the first time. It is therefore necessary to design a complete range of services to support this choice. The action of the commission will be focused on the exchange of best practices also through programmes of reciprocal and intergenerational tutoring. The commission calls on the member countries to invite senior entrepreneurs to transfer their know-how and skills to those with no business experience so as to create new integrated groups (Table 3.6).

As for immigrant entrepreneurs, the commission stresses the importance of strengthening their entrepreneurial role and potential. However, as observed by a number of specific studies on the issue (Rath and Swagerman, 2011, p. 40),[38] enterprises created by immigrants are more likely to fail than others due to lack of information, knowledge and language barriers. According to the commission, therefore, it is necessary to remove all regulatory obstacles and, at the same time, facilitate their access to information, training and business networks, in particular in densely-populated areas by migrants (Table 3.7).

As for the unemployment issue, in particular that affecting young people and aggravated by the current economic crisis, the commission

Table 3.6 Main actions recommended by the European Commission: action no. 3 – reigniting the entrepreneurial spirit in Europe through the involvement of specific groups (senior entrepreneurs)

Actions to be undertaken to support the elderly

At European level	Calls on member countries to
– Promote exchange of good practices. – Support through programmes of reciprocal and intergenerational assistance.	– Encourage senior entrepreneurs to transfer their know-how and skills to young and other entrepreneurs who do not have business experience so as to create integrated groups

Source: Authors' elaboration data on European Commission (2013), *Entrepreneurship 2020 Action Plan – reigniting the entrepreneurial spirit in Europe*, http://ec.europa.eu/enterprise/policies/sme/entrepreneurship-2020/index_en.htm, data accessed 7 July 2014.

Table 3.7 Main actions recommended by the European Commission: action no. 3 – reigniting the entrepreneurial spirit in Europe through the involvement of specific groups (immigrants)

Actions to be undertaken to support immigrants

At European level	Calls on member countries to
	– Remove regulatory obstacles to encourage the creation of enterprises by immigrant entrepreneurs – Facilitate access to information, training and business networks

Source: Authors' elaboration data on European Commission (2013), *Entrepreneurship 2020 Action Plan – reigniting the entrepreneurial spirit in Europe*, http://ec.europa.eu/enterprise/policies/sme/entrepreneurship-2020/index_en.htm, accessed 7 July 2014.

highlights the importance of promoting and fostering business support measures in order to encourage the creation of new companies as a solution to escape the vicious circle of unemployment[39] (Table 3.8). According to the European Commission (EC, 2013, p. 28),[40] all programmes to support the creation of businesses should indicate information and contacts of business support and counselling services as well as those of tutoring and assistance providers. These services may include the teaching of specific skills and be administered through informal (mentors) or formal methods (courses). This support should be provided in close cooperation with business services, support providers and loan providers.

Table 3.8 Main actions recommended by the European Commission: action no. 3 – reigniting the entrepreneurial spirit in Europe through the involvement of specific groups (youth)

Actions to be undertaken to support youth	
At European level Calls on member countries to	
	– Link public employment services with business support services and microloans providers
	– Design training programmes for entrepreneurship dedicated to unemployed young people and articulate them in distinct phases; start programmes on the labour market to provide financial support to unemployed individuals for the creation of start-ups
	– Design and manage entrepreneurship educational programmes dedicated to unemployed individuals to facilitate their reintegration into the labour market as entrepreneurs through the training and education system

Source: Authors' elaboration data on European Commission (2013), *Entrepreneurship 2020 Action Plan – reigniting the entrepreneurial spirit in Europe*, http://ec.europa.eu/enterprise/policies/sme/entrepreneurship-2020/index_en.htm, accessed 7 July 2014.

The goal is to help the unemployed to succeed in the transition from unemployment to self-employment, increase the sustainability of their companies and provide specific support to groups that may request additional resources, such as young people or those who cannot be reached through the traditional channels to support businesses.

According to the commission, particular attention should be given to those groups having more potential, such as young people, women and unemployed subjects with professional skills, who can be guided towards self-employment initiatives through forms of tutoring (Table 3.9). For this reason, the commission will start a number of specific programmes (EASI,[41] Progress,[42] the Youth Guarantee,[43] etc.). At the same time, the member countries shall carry on their initiatives at multiple levels (EC, 2013, p. 26).[44]

It should be noted that when the commission refers to specific programmes for entrepreneurship, the business support services (counselling, training and qualification, tutoring and access to credit) should be activated for each phase of the enterprise life cycle (planning, start-up, consolidation and growth). Moreover, the above programmes must necessarily be implemented in partnership with youth organisations, organisations working with women, elderly and immigrants, business consultants and existing financial institutions.

Table 3.9 Main actions recommended by the European Commission: action no. 3 – reigniting the entrepreneurial spirit in Europe through the involvement of specific groups (unemployed individuals)

Actions to be undertaken to support unemployed individuals	
At European level	Calls on member countries to
Start specific programmes (EASI, Progress, Youth Guarantee, etc.)	– Link public employment services with business support services and microloans providers – Design entrepreneurship training programmes dedicated to unemployed young people and articulate them in distinct phases – Start programmes on the labour market to provide financial support to unemployed individuals for the creation of start-ups – Design and manage entrepreneurship educational programmes dedicated to unemployed individuals to facilitate their reintegration into the labour market as entrepreneurs through the training and education system

Source: Authors' elaboration data on European Commission (2013), *Entrepreneurship 2020 Action Plan – reigniting the entrepreneurial spirit in Europe*, http://ec.europa.eu/enterprise/policies/sme/entrepreneurship-2020/index_en.htm, accessed 7 July 2014.

3.5   Non-financial services: advantages and operational features

The term "business development services" (BDS) is used by the European Micro-finance Network (2011)[45] to refer to all services needed to support the development of enterprises; within the microcredit system, they are considered additional services to financial products.

Awareness of supporting the provision of financial resources with such services has considerably increased in recent years, in particular in European countries. In fact, the operators realised that microcredit programmes and initiatives can have greater social and economic impact if supported by non-financial services. The interest for these services is justified also by the high number of small and microenterprises operating in Europe as well as by the social and economic background of those willing to start microenterprises. In fact, it is important to keep in mind that the beneficiaries of the microcredit programmes are, generally, disadvantaged individuals who often do not possess the technical skills (managerial, financial, organisational skills, etc.) required to successfully start a microenterprise. As previously seen, business development services play a particularly relevant role within the European economic system, which – given its bureaucratic requirements and complex fiscal, regulatory and accounting systems – does not facilitate the birth and survival of microenterprises and self-employment initiatives. With regard to microcredit for businesses (as well as social microcredit), support services may greatly increase the efficacy of any microfinance measure. Microcredit operators, through their support services, can make available to entrepreneurs instruments and skills to support them during the start-up phase of their companies.

To determine which measures fall in the category of non-financial services, we can start from the definition of BDS found in the *Guiding Principles for Donor Intervention* of the *Committee of Donor Agencies for Small Enterprise Development* (2001, p. 11):[46] "BDS are services that improve the performance of the enterprise, its access to markets, and its ability to compete (...). This includes a wide array of business services both strategic and operational (...) aimed at individual enterprises".[47]

While operational services cover those areas needed to run daily operations (information, accounting, regulatory and fiscal management), strategic services regard medium and long-term issues related to the market or competitiveness. These services range from information on markets to training, technical assistance and counselling for entrepreneurs.

A second definition of non-financial services include all those services, provided either formally or informally, that meet the needs of small and medium-sized enterprises other than financial services. They may include: counselling, training, marketing, transportation, connections, information, communication and so on (Gibson, 2001).[48]

BDSs may be divided into three categories, each one with its own relevance within a specific type of enterprises:

1. *Client development service*: Raising awareness among clients of their basic business or (personal) financial situation. Generally aimed at preventing harmful situations (e.g., overindebtedness, unhealthy environments). Clients are in survival mode and generally not willing to pay for these services.
2. *Entrepreneurship development services*: Helping individuals to start their own business and raising awareness on entrepreneurship as a career choice, plus basic business skills training. Clients seek to set up a business as a conscious choice, not so much out of necessity.
3. *Business Development Service*: Supporting existing small-sized businesses to improve their operations, with services ranging from business counselling to technical skills training and linking entrepreneurs to markets.

3.5.1 Types of non-financial services

The data collected in a survey carried out by Fondazione Risorsa Donna for the International Year of the microcredit in Mediterranean countries (Corsi, 2008),[49] show a positive correlation between the integrated approach to microcredit (provision of loans combined with BDS) and return rate.

Moreover, empirical research has shown that in those countries where it is not possible to compare different approaches to microfinance (Corsi, 2008),[50] the best results in terms of social and economic women's *empowerment* seem to be those obtained by MFIs supporting the provision of credit and savings instruments with non-financial services (integrated approach). Integrated programmes lead on average to a positive impact in terms of *empowerment* for 76 per cent of the women interviewed, while institutions providing just microcredit achieve 62 per cent of positive results; it is, therefore, clear the importance of providing non-financial services in order to positively impact the *empowerment*.

Non-financial services may be of different types, as we will see below, but they need to meet some criteria:[51]

- They must meet customer needs and requirements as well as new types of businesses and new methods of doing business that are emerging in the market.
- They must be accessible to their customers.
- They must ensure a link between financial and non-financial services, but costs must be kept separate.
- They must be convenient for customers.

Depending on the contexts and the programmes in which they are provided, non-financial services may be structured in different ways and be present in various degrees within the microcredit supply chain. According to the *Dictionary of Micro-finance* (Santangelo, 2013),[52] the following are the main non-financial services:

- Guidance to loans;
- Business start-up;
- Business management support;
- Financial education;
- Advice on debt.

Some microcredit providers may include among them also approach and information on their services (Nardone and Costantini, 2011),[53] tutoring, training, coaching and post-credit monitoring. In particular cases, where customers are represented by specific groups, non-financial services may include also linguistic literacy, IT literacy, specific initiatives aimed at women's empowerment and the provision of essential goods (basic health-care services, education for children, food supply).

Approach and information constitute the first qualified and professional contact with the "opportunities" offered by community institutions to enter the labour market and access an articulated microcredit path. Within the approach and information activity, operators act as interfaces between the potential beneficiaries and the physical space where information is disseminated. During this phase, the providers carry out an initial screening process of potential customers.

During the orientation phase (Nardone and Costantini, 2011),[54] the providers perform an initial assessment of customer needs, requirements and skills. Orientation allows examining issues and resources available to users (both material and immaterial resources) as well as verifying the feasibility of the business projects. The orientation phase includes the possibility of assessing skills and capacities. This is a tool allowing to identify and reconstruct the set of skills and capacities possessed by the customers, enhancing also the mechanisms that govern and support their acquisition. The focus is put also on the so-called implicit skills (those skills and capacities acquired through actual experiences but not managed through structural communication flows) so as to make them spendable on the labour market.

The skills assessment phase is a person-centred process: potential entrepreneurs are required to put in place their own projects and, through the evaluation, make the necessary adjustments in their future choices. It consists of individual meetings where interests, motivations, skills and potential are examined in order to identify a business development plan. At the same time, a loan orientation service is provided (Santangelo, 2013, p. 761),[55] which consists in identifying the most appropriate loans for the borrowers in terms of amount granted, return times and type of financial product.

During the orientation phase, a further screening of the potential customers is performed. The orientation, in fact, can be used to direct users towards other processes or types of loans that better suit their profiles, as emerged from the interviews. Business start-up services include tutoring, pre-assessment and training.

In the tutoring service, the final recipients are assisted in the development of their business projects by the non-financial services providers, which offer an initial counselling on opportunities and criticalities detected. Tutors act as facilitators for the fulfilment of administrative and fiscal obligations, preparation of business plans, assistance for the preparation of documents, document transmission and accompanying service to the banks or microcredit providers.

The pre-assessment service provides for an analysis of:

- the business idea;
- skills (including potential skills) and attitude of the potential recipients;
- the appropriateness of the requests;
- customer reliability.

Training activities focus especially on financial and management issues and their goal is to improve the entrepreneurs' *skills on economic-operational-financial issues*. This phase includes those training activities that may involve the preparation of business plans; business operational and management issues; budget and accounting; short language courses for immigrants; IT literacy sessions for disadvantaged groups.

The courses may consist of multiple levels of specialisation but are essential for all those who approach the entrepreneurial activity for the first time. In the phase following the start-up, entrepreneurs may be assisted through the provision of specific services, such as mentoring, technical assistance, training, tutoring and financial monitoring. Mentoring consists in a path where new entrepreneurs are coached by senior entrepreneurs, with the aim of transferring experiences made by the latter in similar or identical business sectors. This activity is even more effective if the mentor is a former microcredit recipient. To strengthen the skills of the new entrepreneurs and support them in the most delicate phase of their enterprises – generally the first three years – it is necessary to envisage the provision of special technical support services to be offered at offices/branches (on request) on business operating management areas, such as tax and fiscal assistance, marketing, IT, access to funding sources.

Training in the phase following the start-up covers mainly financial and management issues, aimed at improving the entrepreneurs' economic-operating-financial skills. Here, possible areas of teaching are as follows: business development services, commercial marketing, financial literacy, financial and accounting management. Following the disbursement of the loans and the start-up phase of the companies, end-users are equally assisted, for a period of at least three years, through the tutoring activity. The aim here is to detect any difficulties and problems

Table 3.10 Non-financial services in the different phases of the enterprise life cycle

Enterprise life-cycle	Non-financial services	Definition
Concept	Approach and information	Communication to the target clientele on local opportunities to enter the labour market
Concept	Orientation	Initial assessment of skills and capacities Loan orientation
Design	Tutoring	End-users are assisted in the development of their business ideas through initial counselling on the opportunities and difficulties detected
Design	Pre-assessment	Analysis of business ideas, skills (including potential skills) and attitude of the potential end-users Analysis of appropriateness of the requests and reliability of the applicants
Design	Training	Acquisition of economic-operational-financial skills Preparation of business plan Financial, linguistic, IT literacy Operating and management aspects of the microenterprises
Start-up	Mentoring	Mentoring by "senior" entrepreneurs to transfer experiences
Start up (in the first three years of the enterprise)	Technical support	Special support for all matters related to operational management
Start-up	Training	Aimed at improving financial and management skills
Start-up (in the first three years of the enterprise)	Tutoring	Aimed at detecting financial and management issues affecting the enterprises
Start up (in the first five years of the enterprise)	Financial monitoring	Verification of loan repayment
Start-up	Networking	Creation of the cultural and operating context to facilitate the survival of enterprises through local networks

Source: Authors' elaboration.

that may arise in due course and affect loan repayments and the survival of companies. Tutoring takes place through periodic visits or telephone interviews to the beneficiaries. Finally, financial monitoring ensures timely verification of the loan repayments for their whole duration. This activity must be performed periodically (once a month) and carried out in collaboration with the lenders (banks).

Networking represents a non-financial service transversal to the stages preceding and following the disbursement of the loans. It consists in the creation of local networks of public institutions, training providers, schools, businesses, chambers of commerce, employers' organisations, microfinance institutions, business service centres, operators, and the like. The objective here is to create a healthy cultural and operational context needed to promote entrepreneurship and facilitate the survival of businesses.

3.5.2 Who funds the non-financial services?

We have mentioned the importance of the BDS as essential instruments for start-ups. However, the main problem faced by microfinance institutions and those microcredit providers is to identify who can fund and support their operations. Such services, in fact, have a cost in terms of human and financial resources.

A survey (Lämmermann and Ribbink, 2011)[56] carried out by the European Microfinance Network[57] at a European level showed different models (Lobbezoo, 2012)[58] of provision of financial services and financial support in Europe (Table 3.11). As previously seen, the European Commission invited all member countries to make use of the financial resources provided by the structural funds to support these services (EC, 2013),[59] in particular the European Social Fund.

3.6 Partnerships in delivery financial and BDSS services to the microcredit beneficiaries in Romania

Microfinance activities specifically targeting microentrepreneurial activities started in Romania around 20 years ago (1992–1995), when the first international microfinance organisations launched entrepreneurship development and microfinance projects in Romania. At the end of the project phase, the microfinance activities were transferred to the NGOs/foundations established to ensure continuation and sustainability of the interventions. During 2004–2009, due to the changes in the legal framework for microcredit provision, the NGOs registered as non-bank

Table 3.11 Methods of provision of non-financial services and financial support

	Delivery and payment model	Executor	Examples	Combination with microcredit
Fully subsidised	Government pays for the services to clients	Professional coaches	Social security agency Netherlands (BBZ system)	Yes but not necessary
Partly subsidised	Voucher scheme with discounts up to 90%	Professional coaches	Gründer coaching Germany	MFIs refer clients to Gründer coaching
	Token contribution by entrepreneurs per activity or for the whole programme, cost paid by local government and partners	Professional coaches	Enterprise development programmes in the Netherlands (Wijk in Bedrijf, IkStartSmart)	Sometimes but with different trajectory
Fully commercial	Full contribution by entrepreneurs sometimes based on outcome of the process	Professional coaches	Romanian private sector provider (ROMCOM) Professional coaches (all countries)	Not necessary
Volunteer services	Organisational cost paid by government, EU, other sponsors or MFI	Volunteer coaches	Foundations of (former) entrepreneurs (Ondernemersklank bord, the Netherlands, Micro-mentor in the US)	Independent from microcredit
	Small contribution by entrepreneurs or fully free		MFIs like Qredits in the Netherlands with Qoachpool, ADIE in France and the Prince's Trust in the UK	Mandatory as part of the loan agreement

Source: Authors' elaboration on data in M. Lobbezoo (2012), *Volunteer versus paid coaches within microfinance initiatives: what do we actually know about effectiveness?*, European Micro-finance Network eRB III, pp. 8–12.

financial institutions (NBFIs) and transferred their financial portfolio to the newly established entities, becoming majority owners of the NBFIs.

According to the EMN's MF survey 2010–2011, the Romanian microfinance sector ranks fifth in the European Union in terms of value and number of business microloans disbursed,[60] a position maintained during 2012–2013. The Romanian MFIs were among the most active participants and beneficiaries of the EU-funded financial instruments Progress Microfinance and JASMINE-TA program during 2009–2013 and subscribed to comply with the clauses of the European Code of Good Conduct of Microcredit Provision (EUCoGC).

A specific approach to deliver BDS to the microcredit clients is developed by the Romanian MFIs mainly due to a specific legal framework requirement; therefore the only activity authorised to be developed by the non-bank financial institutions (NBFIs) is financial activity. In the current legal context, the BDSS are provided by NBFIs' partners, consulting and training firms and/or NGOs specialising in entrepreneurship development or the foundations which are the major shareholders of the NBFIs.

3.6.1 Case study 1. Partnership in the delivery of integrated financial and business development services: FAER NBFI and FAER Foundation

FAER Romania[61] is currently one of the medium-size MFIs specialising in financial and non-financial services for rural agribusiness. It consists of FAER IFN (NBFI), provider of microcredits, and FAER Foundation, which provides BDSS and other non-financial services, mainly community development services, to the FAER NBFI's microcredit clients and to the communities where its clients are located.

The financial resources needed to provide BDSS and other non-financial services are the profit of the financial operations, donations and EU structural funds for entrepreneurship and human resource development as additional funds that co-finance the services provided to the FAER NBFI's microcredit clients and to the potential clients within the communities where the MFI is operating.

The project Entrepreneurship from Ideas to Success, implemented during 2019–2011, with financial support from EC structural funds and the Romanian government, has had as overall objective to encourage sustainable development by promoting entrepreneurship among small businesses and potential entrepreneurs, including young people who want to start a business in small Romanian towns. The project activities were designed to facilitate the entrepreneurs' active role in community life, helping them to initiate, develop and better manage their microbusiness and individual enterprises (sole entrepreneurs, legally registered professionals, family business, registered small farmers, etc.) contributing to jobs creation, job maintenance and self-employment.

The project contributed to the objectives of Romania's human resource development strategy at three levels: entrepreneurship promotion, enhancement of training and business performance management culture through a network of four business information and advisory centres, advice and assistance and an e-learning platform to facilitate the continuity and multiplication of project's results.

During the two years of project implementation, according to the project's report,[62] the following results were achieved:

- 1,560 participants (ca 700 women) attended the information sessions, business courses, business development advice sessions and exchange visits organised within the project;
- 32 trainers/business advisors were trained and certified;
- a network of four business information and advisory centres to support entrepreneurship was created and 100 MSMEs assisted and received advisory services;
- 50 start-ups were assisted to register their legal operational entity;
- 50 investment and development project proposals submitted by the targeted beneficiaries were funded.

3.6.2 Case study 2. Partnership in the delivery of integrated financial and BDS services: RoCredit-NBFI and Eurom business consulting company

In order to fulfil its mission and enhance the impact of financial services, the BDS services provided to its clients are delivered in partnership with specialised business training and consulting providers. The BDS services – for example, financial education and business training and consulting – are delivered to RoCredit's beneficiaries by RoCredit loan officers and business consultants/trainers of Eurom Consultancy and Studies SRL. RoCredit microfinance institution was founded in January 2007 by Romanian investors as an NBFI. The funders' initial contribution was the start-up capital of the MFI. In March 2007 RoCredit was certified and licensed by the Romanian Central Bank as a non-bank financial institution. Currently RoCredit has a gross loan portfolio of €15 million and 1,300 active clients served through a network of 11 offices located in Transylvania and Muntenia regions. It is currently the third largest MFI in Romania in terms of GLP, registered in the special registry (for large NBFI) of NBR. The targeted beneficiaries of RoCredit are sole traders, self-employed and micro- and small enterprises which carry out their activity in urban or rural areas, not bankable business in the development phase, having as main field of activity production, services, trade, farmers owning a small semi-subsistence farm with low income. RoCredit offers a large range of financial products to the targeted beneficiaries, from short-term working capital credit lines or credit lines secured by promissory note to medium-term working capital credits and investment credits, guarantee and financial products designed to co-finance investments of the EU structural funds beneficiaries. Eurom Consultancy and Studies SRL[63] was established in 2002 as a private consulting company with a major portfolio of clients and assignments in the area of SMEs access to finance and microfinance, including:

- business consulting to SMEs and entrepreneurs looking for finance and financial institutions with social inclusion mission: MFIs, credit unions;
- training programs for MSMEs and potential entrepreneurs on various topics from financial literature to investment project's appraisal;
- research and studies, technical assistance to financial services providers: MFIs performance assessment; feasibility studies and TA for financial instruments; revolving microcredit schemes; guarantee funds for SMEs, equity investments in SMEs; grant scheme for local/regional development and rural development.

Eurom was a member of the European Microfinance Network's board of directors as vice-president for central and eastern Europe between 2006 and 2010, coordinated and led the EMN's Legal and Regulatory Working Group and during 2007–2013 partnered EMN in the implementation of JASMINE help desk and JASMINE workshops.

Eurom contributed, along other key stakeholders of the MF sector in Europe, to the development of the European Code of Good Conduct for Microcredit Provision.[64]

Brief description of the BDS services

"*Client first*" is an innovative initiative that combines financial services: microcredits for investments in productive asset and equipment acquisition with tailored business development support services (BDSS) for clients and potential clients: microenterprises, farmers, start-up entrepreneurs located in rural areas and small towns of Romania.

Context: The microenterprises represent 89.3 per cent of the Romanian private sector in the years 2009–2012 in the context of the financial crisis, the tendency of microenterprises and sole traders of reducing the investments in productive assets, aimed to develop production/services base, due to lack of appropriate resources is preventing their development, growth and graduation into small and medium enterprises.

According to the RoCredit's 2010–2011 annual portfolio report, 95 per cent of the loans are extended to microenterprises. Analysing the percentage of microcredits used to purchase productive assets or for investments in improving the productive premises, it was observed the high rate of applications rejected (35 per cent), compared to the working capital loan applications.

Therefore, RoCredit in partnership with Eurom initiated in 2012 a pilot project aimed to increase the microcredit portfolio for productive assets acquisition, improve its quality and to diminish the applications' rejection rate.

First phase

The BDSS pilot project consists in organising "project clinics" (workshops) for RoCredit clients and potential clients for the assessment of the feasibility of the client's investment proposal using an financial analysis and forecasting tool developed as MS Excel application; following positive result of the proposal's appraisal, the provision of the loan was made with characteristics that match the investment specifics – for example, loan period, grace period. The monitoring of the client's investment proposal implementation and assessment of the beneficiary performance during the loan period was performed by the RoCredit loan officers.

So far funded from its own resources and benefiting from the program Entrepreneurship from Idea to Success, an EU-funded project, 11 clinics were organised in Pitesti and Bistrita RoCredit's branches (2 of 14 branches of RoCredit) for 58 entrepreneurs. A project clinic consists of a one-hour presentation of the investment's assessment methodology, followed by one-to-one working sessions. The beneficiary and the Eurom consultant are assessing and computing the input data of the investment, calculation of the investment project indicators for up to five years and interpretation of the investment's indicators, forecasted P&L and cash flow.

Based on the analysis the client may decide on n investment's opportunity, the size, the implementation schedule of the investment, and it will get guidance from RoCredit's credit officers in the selection of the appropriate financial product from RoCredit offer that will fit to the investment characteristics and potential for reimbursement; for example, value of the loan, loan period, grace period (for interest), repayment schedule. The project's first-phase results were positive, the investment loan portfolio in the two branches increased by 30 per cent, the investment application rejection rate decreased by 50 per cent and the quality of the portfolio improved.

Second phase

In October 2012, the training for the RoCredit's credit officers in assessment of investment project's feasibility and utilisation of the assessment tool was introduced in the curriculum of the JASMINE TA program and delivered to all RoCredit's credit officers, branch managers and risk management department staff. The investment indicators NPV (net present value) and IRR (internal rate of return) were introduced in the loan risk-assessment procedure.

Third phase (ongoing)

Project clinics are organised in each Rocredit branch with the assistance of Eurom consultants; impact indicators are collected, analysed and reported each quarter in order to improve the efficiency of the business development services delivery and its effectiveness on client performance.

In this perspective, it's important to underline the innovative open-door approach of the BDSS in partnership. Clients and potential clients are invited to participate to the event organised in the brunch office special organised and equipped to host up to ten participants. The business development services are not extended exclusively to the RoCredit's clients but to potential clients as well: start-ups, young entrepreneurs, potential entrepreneurs currently unemployed, minorities, and so on. It is not exclusively a marketing tool to promote RoCredit's financial offer but mainly a customised business service aimed to assist the client in the development of its business.

The innovative methodology and assessment tools used are described below:

- *Presentation*: The project's assessment tool is presented by the consultant or credit officer using a PowerPoint presentation and the video projector; handouts of the presentation are available. After the project's assessment tool presentation by the consultant or credit officer, the beneficiary becomes the main "actor" of the show.

- *Financial analysis and forecasting tool*, developed as MS Excel application, is designed based on UNIDO's SME's investment projects' feasibility assessment methodology, in constant prices (inflation influence is ignored).
- *Compilation of analysis's input data* is based on the info provided by the beneficiary therefore confidentiality of beneficiary data and info is ensured by signing and confidentiality agreement. The input data consist of
    - value and items of the investment and their depreciation period;
    - products/services resulted after the project implementation: quantity and current unit price; estimated production capacity utilisation within the analysis period (five years);
    - costs related to the production/services: labour costs, raw materials, administrative costs, marketing, taxes and so on;
    - working capital needs, based on the characteristics of the products/services;
    - financial inputs: beneficiary's own financial resources, loan, grant, equity investment.
- *Transfer of the input data*: After compilation of the input data, the transfer to the tool is provided by the consultant or the credit officer.
- *Outputs from the forecasting tool* are obtained instantaneously:
    - forecasted investment project's balance sheet, P&L and cash flow;
    - forecasted investment project's indicators: profitability indicators and break-even, liquidity and coverage indicators and investment indicators NPV and IRR;
    - graphical representation of the main indicators.
- *Interpretation and fallow up*: At the end of the session the client receives not only the know-how to interpret the investment performance indicators as its sensitivity towards market potential changes during the investment phase but the printed forecasts of the project's balance sheet, P&L and cash flow of its own investment project idea, as well as clear guidance to selecting a suitable financial product.

What differentiates the "client first" BDSS services from the current consulting services provided by RoCredit to its clients is the focus on clients' and potential clients' specific and long-term needs, the capacity building component in beneficiary's self-assessment of the investment project feasibility, the improvement of the internal risk appraisal techniques for loan applications with an investment component.

What differentiates the "client first" BDSS services from other BDSS services in the market is the establishment on a solid base of long-term partnership in development, one based on trust and fairness between the BDSS and financial services providers and the beneficiaries.

Sustainability

At the EU level, the eastern European MFIs are considered and labelled as more commercially than socially oriented. The efforts the main Romania MFIs, RoCredit included, are making to chance the "commercial label" consist in targeting and serving the non-bankable entrepreneurs, increasing transparency, providing innovative business development services and support to the clients, and fully implementing the European Code of Good Conduct for microcredit provision. Within the last three years 55 per cent of the annual profit was reinvested by RoCredit in development and outreach co-financed by EU-funded programs and/or through partnerships with BDSS providers, investment in training and development of staff, new products and services, MIS and in the market development ensured the continuous growth of the organisation.

Sustainability of the "client first" initiative

In the initial stage, due to the positive impact, the board of administration decided the "client first" BDSS to be further developed within the partnership agreement signed in January 2013 with Eurom.

In 2013–2014 the estimated number of "client first" clinics organised is 40 in all branches located in four Romanian economic regions with an estimated 300 participants, entrepreneurs and potential entrepreneurs, 20 per cent of RoCredit active clients, at least 200 projects assisted to be financed and implemented successfully.

The "client first" methodology and approach will be extended to all RoCredit current financial products for microentrepreneurs; the internal loan application risk-assessment procedures will include the investment indicators along with the liquidity and financial coverage indicators. Impact indicators and case studies of successfully implemented investment/development projects alongside the "client first" clinics are planned to be the main marketing instruments of the MFI within the following years. Subject of availability of resources the "client first" investment project feasibility assessment tool will be further develop in an online assessment tool, posted on the RoCredit website, available for all clients and potential clients of the MFI.

Impact

The aim of the "client first" initiative is to redesign the BDSS, having in mind that the client-focused mission of the MFIs has to be translated and implemented not only through the financial products designed to meet the client's needs but through non-financial services as well; the client's interest and benefit should become the first priority; the MFI benefit should follow in the second position. Therefore impact indicators, qualitative and quantitative, financial and non-financial, were developed to assess the efficiency and effectiveness of the initiative. The pilot phase's impact indicators' outputs and results/outcomes obtained and targets for 2014 are in Table 3.12.

The "client first" initiative, as presented, does not address only the issues specific to the MFI – for example, high rejection rate of loan applications for investment, credit officers' lack of knowledge in assessing the feasibility of the investment projects, PAR and so on. It addresses a general issue of the MFIs' targeted beneficiaries: start-ups and micro-enterprises, potential entrepreneurs, lack of knowledge, clear guidance and appropriate financial resources to implement their business idea or development plan. The "open-door approach", the "innovative methodology" partnership with a business consulting firm, specialising in services related to SMEs access to finance, the targeted beneficiaries; current and potential clients, and never the less, the cost effectiveness of the initiative recommend it to be adopted by the other Romanian MFIs in the first stage. Transformed in an online investment project feasibility assessment tool, assisted on line by the consultants and the credit officers of the MFIs, will make it more accessible, less time and resources consuming and therefore more efficient. Adapted to the specifics of each country legal fiscal regime for entrepreneurship activities and micro enterprises, the tool can be replicated in the neighbouring Eastern European countries, where the MFIs' targeted beneficiaries are facing the same growth difficulties, as well as in other countries where the MFIs are targeting the start-ups and non-bankable clients. The positive results of the pilot phase recommended the initiative to be expanded, the lessons that will be learned from this challenging experience will be subject to case studies and presentations to the microfinance events organised in Romania and in Europe, with the support of the EMN working groups: IT and Social impact, the Client first initiative will be promoted among the European MF providers.

Table 3.12 Impact indicators' outputs and results/outcomes obtained and targets for 2014

Quantitative indicators	Results/outcomes obtained – pilot /2012–2013	Targets 2014	Assessment tool used
Number of project clinics	11 located in 2 branches; outreach 2 economic regions	40 located in 14 branches; outreach 4 economic regions	Training/consulting event reports
Number of participants/beneficiaries	Total 55 30 women entrepreneurs 42 young (<35 years old)	Total 300 >50% women entr. <50% young entr.	Participants questionnaire, event report
Number of projects analysed	45 projects analyses	90% of participants are submitting projects to analysis	Event report
Number of loan appl. with investment component submitted	40 – credit application	>80% – credit application	Branch activity report
Number of loan application approved and financed	32 – loans extended	>80% – loans extended	Branch activity report 80% approval rate
% of satisfied beneficiaries – Relevance and utility of the BDS – Quality of training and training materials – Organisation and efficiency	75% – excellent 15% – very good 10% – good	75% – excellent 15% – very good 10% – good	Event beneficiaries evaluation questionnaire Event report
Portfolio at risk for the loans extended to BDS beneficiaries	3.5%	3%	Pilot project monitoring report, three times lower than RoCredit 2012 PAR
Investment implemented according to the initial plan (±10%)	70%	70%	Monitoring reports/questionnaires, telephone interviews, site visits
Profitability indicators compared with the forecasts (±10%)	NA– financial data 2012 available in March 2013	70%	Monitoring reports/questionnaires, telephone interviews
Liquidity indicators compared with the forecasts (±10%)	NA– financial data 2012 available in March 2013	70%	Monitoring reports/questionnaires, telephone interviews

Source: Authors' elaboration of RoCredit presentation to the EMN workshop on BDSS, EMN Conference Stockholm 2012.

Notes

1. Although this chapter was prepared jointly by the authors, §3.1 was written by Giovanni Nicola Pes, §3.2 by Stefanie Lämmermann, §§3.3 and 3.4 by Andrea Nardone, §§3.5, 3.5.1 and 3.5.2 by Maria Claudia Costantini and §3.6 by Maria Doiciu.
2. European Commission (2013), *2013 SMEs' access to finance survey, analytical report*, 14 November, pp. 6ff.
3. See esp. "Europe 20" and "Small Business Act".
4. COM 2020 of 3 March 2010: "Europe 2020, a strategy for smart, sustainable and inclusive growth".
5. In 2011, the European Central Bank (ECB) started to adopt a number of specific measures that are partly reducing the risk that a reduction of bank assets might result in a direct contraction of the economic activity. Lately, the decisions adopted by the ECB Governing Council in June 2014 – which established, among other things, that, starting September 2014, the amount of funds granted to each bank shall be proportional to the volume of loans that the bank itself granted to the economic system – should further loose monetary restrictions and support the provision of credit.
6. Survey jointly carried out by the European Commission and the European Central Bank by administering a specific questionnaire to the EU-28 SMEs, in the period August-October 2013. The survey results are indicated in "SMEs Access to Finance survey, Analytical Report", 14 November 2013.
7. The pre-coded list included the following potential problems: finding customers, access to credit, availability of experienced and qualified personnel, regulation, competition, cost of production or labour, other.
8. This survey, which terminated on 8 April 2014, was participated also by eight of the main bank groups in Italy. The results for our country can be found on the website: www.bancaditalia.it, while those for the Euro area at: www.ecb.int.
9. EC elaboration of ECB survey results on Amadeus and EFIGE data, in "European Competitiveness Report 2014 – Helping firms grow", Commission Staff Working Document SWD (2014) 6319 final, pp. 15ff.
10. See EU regulation no. 1304 of the European Parliament and Council of 17 December 2013, on the European Social Fund, art. 2, paragraph 1.
11. See EU regulation no. 1304 of the European Parliament and Council of 17 December 2013, on the European Social Fund, art. 2, paragraph 3.
12. See EU regulation no. 1304 of the European Parliament and Council of 17 December 2013, on the European Social Fund, art. 15.
13. Art. 37 of the aforementioned regulation states that "Where financial instruments support financing to enterprises, including SMEs, such support shall target the establishment of new enterprises, early-stage capital, that is, seed capital and start-up capital, expansion capital and capital for the strengthening of the general activities of an enterprise, or the realisation of new projects, penetration of new markets or new developments by existing enterprises, without prejudice to applicable Union State aid rules, and in accordance with the Fund-specific rules. Such support may include investment in both tangible and intangible assets as well as working capital within the limits of applicable Union State aid rules and with a view to stimulating the private sector as a supplier of funding to enterprises. It may also include

the costs of transfer of proprietary rights in enterprises provided that such transfers take place between independent investors".
14. http://www.goldrausch-ev.de/.
15. http://www.wasistgarage.de/.
16. http://www.microlending-news.de/artikel/enterprise.htm.
17. http://www.exzet.de/index.html.
18. http://www.kiz.de/.
19. http://www.mikrofinanz.net/.
20. European Commission – DG Enterprise and Industry (2006), *Management capacity building – final report of the expert group*, p. 29, http://ec.europa.eu/enterprise/policies/sme/files/support_measures/mcb/mcb_en.pdf, accessed 7 July 2014.
21. European Commission (2007), Communication from the Commission to the Council, the European Parliament, the European Economic and Social Committee and the Committee of the Regions, *A European initiative for the development of microcredit in support of growth and employment*, http://eur-lex.europa.eu/LexUriServ/LexUriServ.do?uri=COM:2007:0708:FIN:en:PDF, accessed 7 July 2014.
22. European Commission (2007), Communication from the Commission to the Council, the European Parliament, the European Economic and Social Committee and the Committee of the Regions, *A European initiative for the development of microcredit in support of growth and employment*, p. 9, http://eur-lex.europa.eu/LexUriServ/LexUriServ.do?uri=COM:2007:0708:FIN:en:PDF, accessed 7 July 2014.
23. European Commission (2007), Communication from the Commission to the Council, the European Parliament, the European Economic and Social Committee and the Committee of the Regions, *A European initiative for the development of microcredit in support of growth and employment*, p. 8, http://eur-lex.europa.eu/LexUriServ/LexUriServ.do?uri=COM:2007:0708:FIN:en:PDF, accessed 7 July 2014.
24. European Commission (2007), Communication from the Commission to the Council, the European Parliament, the European Economic and Social Committee and the Committee of the Regions, *A European initiative for the development of microcredit in support of growth and employment*, p. 8, 27, http://eur-lex.europa.eu/LexUriServ/LexUriServ.do?uri=COM:2007:0708:FIN:en:PDF, accessed 7 July 2014.
25. European Commission (2008), Think small first. A "small business act" for Europe, http://ec.europa.eu/enterprise/policies/sme/documents/sba/index_en.htm, accessed 7 July 2014.
26. European Commission (2008), Think small first. A "small business act" for Europe, p. 5, http://ec.europa.eu/enterprise/policies/sme/documents/sba/index_en.htm, accessed 7 July 2014.
27. European Commission (2008), Think small first. A "small business act" for Europe, p. 6, http://ec.europa.eu/enterprise/policies/sme/documents/sba/index_en.htm, accessed 7 July 2014.
28. Ibid.
29. European Commission (2013), *Entrepreneurship 2020 Action Plan – reigniting the entrepreneurial spirit in Europe*, p. 4, http://ec.europa.eu/enterprise/policies/sme/entrepreneurship-2020/index_en.htm, accessed 7 July 2014.

30. Ibid.
31. European Parliament, European Council (2006), *Recommendation of the European Parliament and of the Council of 18 December 2006 on key competences for lifelong learning*, Official Journal of the European Union, L394/10, http://eur-lex.europa.eu/LexUriServ/LexUriServ.do?uri= OJ:L:2006:394: 0010:0018: en: PDF. accessed 7 July 2014.
32. Jenner C. (2012), Business and education: powerful social innovation partners, *Stanford Social Innovation Review*, August, p. 27; European Commission (2012), *Rethinking Education: Investing in skills for better socio-economic outcomes*, http://ec.europa.eu/digital-agenda/en/news/communication-rethinking-education, accessed 7 July 2014; OECD, European Union (2012), Policy brief on youth entrepreneurs, Brussels.
33. European Commission – DG Enterprise and Industry (2013). *Entrepreneurship education: a guide for educators*, http://ec.europa.eu/enterprise/policies/sme/promoting-entrepreneurship/files/education/entredu-manual-fv_en.pdf, accessed 7 July 2014.
34. European Commission (2013), *Entrepreneurship 2020 Action Plan – reigniting the entrepreneurial spirit in Europe*, COM (2012) 795 final, p. 10, http://ec.europa.eu/enterprise/policies/sme/entrepreneurship-2020/index_en.htm, accessed 7 July 2014.
35. European Commission (2013), *Entrepreneurship 2020 Action Plan – Reigniting the entrepreneurial spirit in Europe*, COM (2012) 795 final, p. 12, http://eurlex.europa.eu/LexUriServ/LexUriServ.do?uri=COM:2012:0795:FIN:IT:PDF, accessed 7 July 2014.
36. European Commission (2013), *Entrepreneurship 2020 Action Plan – Reigniting the entrepreneurial spirit in Europe*, COM (2012) 795 final, p. 14, http://eurlex.europa.eu/LexUriServ/LexUriServ.do?uri=COM:2012:0795:FIN:IT:PDF, accessed 7 July 2014.
37. Ibid.
38. Rath, J. and Swagerman A. (2011), *Promoting ethnic entrepreneurship in European cities*, European Foundation for the Improvement of Living and Working Conditions, Publications Office of the European Union, Luxembourg, p. 40. http://www.eurofound.europa.eu/pubdocs/2011/38/en/2/EF1138EN.pdf, accessed 7 July 2014.
39. As indicated in the Policy Brief on Youth Entrepreneurship in Europe (EC, 2012), there are very few programmes to support the creation of businesses specifically targeting unemployed youth.
40. European Commission (2013), *Entrepreneurship 2020 Action Plan – reigniting the entrepreneurial spirit in Europe*, p. 28, http://ec.europa.eu/enterprise/policies/sme/entrepreneurship-2020 /index_en.htm, accessed 7 July 2014.
41. With regard to social solidarity, the European Parliament and Council reached a political agreement on the EU programme for employment and social innovation that goes under the name of EASI. Along with the European Social Fund, the Fund for the European Aid for the most Deprived and the European Globalisation Adjustment Fund, EASI constitutes the fourth pillar of the EU initiative to promote employment and social inclusion within the broader Action 2014–2020. The EASI will provide support to the member countries to design and implement social and employment reforms, both at a national and regional and local level through a number of policies meant

to coordinate, identify, analyse and share the best practices. EASI integrates and extends the coverage of three existing programmes:
- Progress (Programme for Employment and Social Solidarity);
- EURES (European Employment Services);
- European Progress Micro-finance Facility.

In the latter, the combination of microfinance and social entrepreneurship will be oriented towards the facilitation to credit access for entrepreneurs, especially those who struggle to reach the traditional credit market, and for social enterprises. The support to the development of social enterprises is the true innovative aspect of this axis, compared to the current Progress of microfinanced that kick-started in 2010, to which is added also a greater support to microcredit providers through the funds granted to the capacity building actions promoted by these subjects. http://ec.europa.eu/social/main.jsp?catId=1081, accessed 7 July 2014.

42. http://ec.europa.eu/social/main.jsp?catId=327.
43. http://www.youth-guarantee.eu/, accessed 7 July 2014.
44. European Commission (2013), *Entrepreneurship 2020 Action Plan – reigniting the entrepreneurial spirit in Europe*, p. 26, http://ec.europa.eu/enterprise/policies/sme/entrepreneurship-2020 /index_en.htm, accessed 7 July 2014.
45. Lämmermann S. and Ribbink G. (2011), *Micro-finance and business. Development services in Europe. What can we learn from the South?*, European Micro-finance Network.
46. Committee of Donor Agencies for Small Enterprise Development (2001), Business development services for small enterprises. Guiding principles for donor intervention, February, Washington, Donor Committee, p. 11.
47. Committee of Donor Agencies for Small Enterprise Development (2001), Business development services for small enterprises. Guiding principles for donor intervention, February, Washington, Donor Committee, p. 11.
48. Gibson A. (2001), Principles of good practice in business development services, in Levitsky and Mikkelsen, *Micro and small enterprises in Latin America*, London, IADB, ITDG.
49. Corsi M. (2008), *Women and micro-finance. A look at the Mediterranean countries*, Rome, Aracne. This study covered microfinance institutions from the following countries: Albania, Bosnia and Herzegovina, Croatia, Egypt, France, Italy, Jordan, Kosovo, Lebanon, Morocco, Spain and Tunisia.
50. The literature refers to integrated and minimalist approaches to define different models of microfinance existing in different countries worldwide. So we have MFIs that, through an integrated approach provide their customers with financial and non-financial services (such as social mediation, creation of groups, leadership development services for businesses, training on commercial marketing and social services, education, health-care services and food education). The MFIs adopting a minimalist approach provide only financial services, namely credit and savings. In Corsi M. (2008), *Women and micro-finance: a look at the Mediterranean countries*, Rome, Aracne, p. 32.
51. Lämmermann S. and Ribbink G. (2011), *Micro-finance and business. Development services in Europe. What can we learn from the South?*, European Micro-finance Network, p. 7.
52. Santangelo, F. (2013), Financial services, in Pizzo G. and Tagliavini G. *Dictionary of micro-finance, types of micro-credit*, Rome, Carocci.

53. Nardone A. and Costantini M. C. C. (2011), *BDS for inclusion: the case of Fondazione Risorsa Donna*, European Micro-finance Network electronic Research Bulletin, Brussels, III, pp. 4–7.
54. Nardone A. and Costantini M. C. C. (2011), *BDS for inclusion: the case of Fondazione Risorsa Donna*, European Micro-finance Network electronic Research Bulletin, Brussels, III, pp. 4–7.
55. Santangelo, F. (2013), Financial services, in Pizzo G. and Tagliavini G., *Dictionary of micro-finance, types of micro-credit*, Rome, Carocci, p. 761.
56. Lämmermann S. and Ribbink G. (2011), *Microfinance and business. Development services in Europe. What can we learn from the South?*, European Micro-finance Network, p. 34.
57. The European Micro-finance Network is the main European network created in 2003 to promote microfinance and fight against social and financial exclusion in the European Union. The EMN is active in promoting microenterprises and self-employment initiatives, thanks to the support of its members and their lobbying activity, and raises awareness on the need to create business-friendly regulatory frameworks that favour the development of microfinance in Europe. Its main activities are the capacity building actions of its members, information exchange, networking, advocacy at European level, text publication and dissemination, project implementation. www.european-microfinance.org.
58. Lobbezoo M. (2012), Volunteer versus paid coaches within micro-finance initiatives: What do we actually know about effectiveness?, European Microfinance Network eRB III, pp. 8–12.
59. European Commission (2013), *Entrepreneurship 2020 Action Plan – reigniting the entrepreneurial spirit in Europe*, COM (2012) 795 final, Brussels, http://ec.europa.eu/enterprise/policies/sme/entrepreneurship-2020/index_en.htm.
60. EMN: Overview of the microcredit sector in the European Union 2010–2011, Romanian rank the fifth after Germany, France, Spain and Poland.
61. http://www.faer.ro.
62. http://www.antreprenoriat.faer.ro/.
63. www.eurom-consultancy.ro.
64. The EUCoGC provides a set of standards in terms of management, governance, risk management, reporting, and customer and investors relations that are common to the microcredit sector in the European Union. These standards are for the benefit of customers, investors, funders, owners and partner organisations. The code is primarily designed to cover non-bank microcredit providers which provide loans up to €25,000 to microentrepreneurs.

Except where otherwise noted, this work is licensed under a Creative Commons Attribution 3.0 Unported License. To view a copy of this license, visit http://creativecommons.org/licenses/by/3.0/

OPEN

4
Microfinance and Capacity Building in the EU Policy

Alessandro Cardente, Perrine Lantoine, Fulvio Pellegrini, Giovanni Nicola Pes, Pasqualina Porretta, Paolo Rita and Fabrizio Santoboni

4.1 Microcredit in the new EU programmes: the role of the Italian National Agency for Microcredit and the Capacity Building project

4.1.1 Microcredit in the new EU programmes

Microfinance instruments, in particular microcredit, play a key role in the implementation of the European strategies to support entrepreneurship, employment, social and financial inclusion.[1,2] These instruments, in fact, can support start-ups through the provision of microloans characterised by simplified administrative procedures and absence of collateral requirements, offering to socially excluded and disadvantaged subjects an opportunity to ensure dignified living conditions for themselves and their households. The economic crisis that has hit the European economy in recent years resulted in high social costs that call for the adoption of specific measures to support the weakest segments of the population as well as effectively contribute to the economic recovery through the creation of new development opportunities. Today, individuals at risk are not just those outside the labour market due to disadvantaged conditions, but also other numerous subjects – young people, women, immigrants, off-workers, those ejected from the labour market – who, although in possession of professional skills, are unable to enter (or re-enter) the labour market due to a scarce demand for jobs by enterprises and the impossibility to access credit. In this context, the European Commission regards microcredit as a key instrument to fight unemployment and combat the new forms of poverty, to promote access to credit and, more generally, to financial services, a necessary condition to fully participate in the social and economic life of the community. A strong expansion of microcredit is, therefore, one of the relevant strategic objectives at European level, also in light of the sheer and growing number of financially excluded subjects. Such need is made even more impellent by the current financial and economic crisis, also because subjects who join new areas of poverty and marginalisation do not represent an appealing market for financial institutions, due to limited profitability, low income and high risk. One of the first EC documents expressly dedicated to microcredit is the communication of 13 November 2007, entitled "European initiative for the development of microcredit to support economic growth and employment", which identifies four priority fields:

(a) improving the legal and institutional environment in the member states;
(b) further changing the climate in favour of entrepreneurship;
(c) promoting the spread of best practices, particularly in relation to training;
(d) providing additional financial capital for microcredit institutions.

As a first step to implement this programme, the European Commission and the European Investment Bank (EIB) took joint action to support microfinance institutions in 2008: JASMINE (Joint Action to Support Microfinance Institutions in Europe), which provides orientation services and financing to non-banking microfinance institutions. In addition, with the EC communication of 3 June 2009, entitled "A shared commitment for employment", the commission stressed the need to offer new opportunities to unemployed individuals and the possibility to create enterprises for some of the most disadvantaged groups in Europe, who struggle to access the traditional credit market. Besides the existing instruments, the commission called for the implementation of specific action to further strengthen economic and social cohesion through the enhancement of the activities carried out by the EIB, the European Investment Fund (EIF) and other international financial institutions, without prejudice to the measures implemented by member states. Consequently, the EC solicited the use of a new European instrument (the microfinance instrument) in order to leverage microfinance to reach out to groups at particular risk and further support the development of enterprises, social economy and microenterprises. This tool helps support those organisations engaged in the social economy working with people excluded from the social reintegration process by helping them develop the minimum necessary skills to commit to a long-term entrepreneurial project. Moreover, a microfinance instrument at a European level can maximise the support provided by international financial institutions and avoid a dispersed approach, thus increasing the availability of microloans in all member states. Actions supported by this instrument, starting from the previous EU programming periods, are consistent and complementary with other EU policies, including the former Competitiveness and Innovation programme (CIP), the new programme for the competitiveness of enterprises and SMEs 2014–2020 (COSME), JASMINE, the European Agricultural Fund for Rural Development (EAFRD), the European Social Fund (ESF) and JEREMIE (Joint European Resources for Micro to Medium Enterprises Initiative).

The European Instrument of Microfinance Progress (Progress Microfinance), created in 2010, increases the availability of microloans for the creation or development of small businesses. Although not directly financed by entrepreneurs, Progress Microfinance allows microcredit intermediaries operating in the EU (public and private banks, non-banking microfinancial institutions, non-profit microcredit providers) to increase their loan volume by providing guarantees to cover the risk of loss and making available further funds for the provision of microloans. This instrument can be used by those willing to start self-employment initiatives or create/develop a microenterprise, especially in the social economy sector, unemployed individuals, those ejected from the labour market, young people, women and, more generally, all those who struggle to access credit.

4.1.2 The role of the Italian National Agency for Microcredit in the Capacity Building project

As for the Italian scenario, the Italian National Agency for Microcredit is the public entity, created pursuant to law no. 81 of 11 March 2006, entrusted with the role of promoting microcredit as an instrument to combat poverty and identify measures for the development of financial initiatives aimed at the creation of microenterprises for the benefit of subjects affected by poverty and social exclusion through integrated measures aimed at mitigating the effects of the economic crisis on human capital while protecting the capacity to act and the professional skills of individuals and ensuring social and labour inclusion through access to microcredit. Following different pieces of legislation over time, today the agency is engaged in a number of initiatives aimed at promoting and coordinating microcredit and microfinance measures or programmes to be implemented at national and European level. Specifically, the agency:

- acts as the coordinating entity at national level and is entrusted with promotion, guidance, assessment and monitoring of the microfinancial instruments promoted by the European Union, as well as the microfinance activities co-financed by the EU funds (law no. 106 of 12 July 2011, art. 1 paragraph 4bis);
- monitors and assesses all microcredit and microfinance schemes implemented in Italy (Directive of the President of the Council of Ministers of 2 July 2010, published in the Official Gazette no. 220 of 20 September 2010);
- promotes, continues and supports microcredit and microfinance programmes dedicated to the social and economy development of the country, as well as those dedicated to developing countries and economies in transition (microfinance for cooperation), in collaboration with the Ministry of Foreign Affairs (law no. 244 of 24 December 2007, art. 2, paragraphs 185–187).

With regard to its operations, therefore, the activities carried out by the agency can be divided into two operational macroareas: one related to microcredit projects and the other one revolving around instrumental and ancillary services related to the single projects and the microcredit market.

The agency is also engaged in the implementation of the EU programmes JEREMIE, Progress micro-finance and JASMINE, dedicated to the development of microfinance in Europe, in particular playing a contact point role at national level for the programme Progress (EU decision no. 283/2010 of the European Parliament and Council). In this context, the agency supports microfinance operators in the process of accessing EU funds, overcoming issues related to their size and the difficulty of achieving full sustainability. At European level, it advocates the adoption by the commission of legislation that includes business development actions (training, technical assistance, tutoring) in the definition of microcredit. As for its projects, the agency has signed a number of agreements with the Ministry of Labour and Social Policies, as well as with the Department for Public Service, to implement the following projects to be co-financed by the European Social Fund:

- Project "Monitoring the labour policies integration with policies of social development of production systems in the microcredit and microfinance sector" (ongoing);

- Project "Microcredit and Employment Services – system action for the promotion and creation of innovative operating methods aimed at promoting self-employment and microentrepreneurship at employment service points" (ongoing);
- Project "A.MI.CI – Access to Microcredit for Immigrant Citizens" (ended 2011);
- Project "*Capacity Building* on financial instruments – definition and experimentation of new skills and tools for efficient programme management, training programme dedicated to the Public Administration" (regions involved in the former convergence programme; ended 30 November 2014).

Strengthening institutional capacity for the planning and management of microcredit and microfinance schemes to support development policies represents one of the most relevant activities of the agency, as this is a pressing need perceived also within the institutional and socio-economic contexts of the so-called advanced economies. The relevant *capacity building* approach calls for the involvement of an extended number of actors in the design and implementation phases of strategies for growth, one of the thematic objectives of the structural funds programming period 2014–2020, in compliance with the Europe 2020 plan.

In fact, the reform measures adopted in Italy in the last twenty years and aimed at improving the efficiency of the public administration (PA), were not enough to fill all the gaps and, consequently, this situation ended up affecting the socio-economic systems of the weakest regions, in particular those located in Southern Italy. As indicated by the draft partnership agreement for 2014–2020, "The weaknesses of the Public Administration are evident also with regard to cohesion policy management: difficulties in implementing the planning for the 2007–2013 period show excessively slow administrative improvements. The measures to strengthen the administrative capacity already implemented in the previous programming periods, despite offering some important experimentation, in general showed poor effectiveness in promoting a substantial and long-lasting change. Several factors can be pointed out as the reasons behind such delay, including an approach mostly based on the adoption of legislative measures that failed to take in proper consideration the existing skills and expertise within the Public Administration and, therefore, did nothing to strengthen them and promote an organisational change". In general, also according to some international indicators (*governance indicators* of the World Bank and *European Quality of Government Index*), there is no clear strategy in place to overcome the weaknesses of the Italian administrative system, in particular those related to the effectiveness of the measures co-financed by the EU funds. From the Italian National Agency for Microcredit point of view, capacity building should be a transversal principle to be applied to all strategic planning so as to allow identifying, for each area of intervention, the most suitable mechanisms to improve the administrative capacity of the subjects and structures entrusted with the implementation of the policies. This inevitably entails a complete revision of the public administration organisational model at all levels, including planning, programming and management processes. In this perspective, the exploitation of the additional contribution provided by the structural funds to support the capacity building action is a key factor to drive positive change in the direction proposed. Obviously, optimising the effectiveness of such actions requires an approach able to link the measures promoted by the public administration with the requirements of the underlying social, economic and institutional environment. In other words, to implement successful public policies for socio-economic development through microcredit, it is imperative to build a basic analytical framework, a tool to investigate the reference socio-economic contexts and their needs; the public administration must undergo a comprehensive "restructuring" process according to a competence-based redesign, including the provision of specific skills and expertise. These considerations have been discussed in the preliminary institutional debate for the elaboration of the 2014–2020 programmes, not just with regard to the regional administrations involved in the former convergence programme – the recipients of the capacity building measures activated by the Italian National Agency for Microcredit in the programming period 2007–2013 – but also other institutions operating on the national territory. The European Commission, in its observations on the draft partnership agreement, suggested, among other things, a start to work on the strategy for developing institutional and administrative skills by addressing the critical points first and, in a transversal logic, implementing the general strengthening of the structures entrusted with fund management, with specific focus on a network-type approach and effective use of the partnership. With regard to the capacity building for the public administration, the criticalities identified by the agency can be summarised as follows:

(a) lack of specific know-how on microcredit;
(b) lack of adequate coordination between different operational centres and levels.

The strengthening of the public administration, therefore, necessarily entails the building of specific skills at different levels, from central to local government authorities, through a variety of dedicated functions and coordination centres. To this end, the capacity building action promoted by the agency aims to invest in the training of the PA personnel through the creation of vertical and horizontal information networks, helping harmonise them and disseminating a technical language that should be shared and used by all the public administration staff involved in planning, designing and management of microfinance activities. This would allow the public administration to strengthen its capacity to interact with the actors operating on the territory. Such is the direction taken by the Italian National Agency for Microcredit, which revolves around the necessity to provide all actors and structures involved in the management of microcredit funds 2014–2020 with key skills and expertise to ensure effective planning, based on defined and measurable results. The agency is committed to creating the conditions for the implementation of microfinance projects dedicated to improving the skills of the public administration personnel and the stakeholders so as to lay the conditions to fully exploit the opportunity offered by the new structural fund framework, namely investing resources through the use of financial engineering instruments in accordance with policies promoting employment and social inclusion.

4.2 Microleasing, microinsurance, social housing: the new frontiers for European microfinance

Microleasing, microinsurance and housing microfinance are part of that group of microfinance products and services specifically designed for a target of subjects (microenterprises or individuals) who find themselves in difficult social and economic conditions and struggle to access the traditional banking circuit.[3] Microfinance supply, not just limited to microcredit, represents an important innovation within the policies promoting financial inclusion, with the involvement of market operators (financial intermediaries and non-profit organisations) as well as public entities entrusted with the implementation of policies for welfare and territorial development (ministries, regional administrations, local government authorities). Although a common opinion trend regards microfinance as a typical feature of developing countries (see, e.g., the enormous success of microinsurance in countries such as India and Bangladesh), developed economies too have seen in recent years a growing popularity of products/services such as microleasing, microinsurance, microsavings and housing microfinance, which are implemented according to a modern integrated approach, based on the cooperation of a plurality of public and private subjects. The developed economies have testified the first successful applications of this type of "organised microfinance".

Among the most consolidated experiences in Europe, we must mention France, where the Banque de France systematically monitors the sector through a specific "microfinance observatory", whose reports are published every two years;[4] this institution promoted a number of qualified conferences on the sector, that is, the meeting organised in Paris in July 2011, to provide a contribution to the G20 policies dedicated to financial inclusion.[5] In particular, the discussion highlighted the need for extending the range of microfinance instruments by offering a greater number of diversified products and services (microcredit, microdeposits, microsavings, microinsurance, microleasing, payment services) in order to meet the increasing needs and requirements of microenterprises that struggle to access traditional credit or by other subjects in conditions of economic distress. Moreover, besides the supply of financial services/products, the debate stressed the need for the microfinance institutions to be physically close to the beneficiaries, to activate personal relationships, to seek an operational flexible model, to introduce non-financial services supporting microfinance and, mostly, to include microfinance instruments in policies aimed at fighting social and financial exclusion in order to implement a sustainable growth model.

These are also the guidelines followed by the *Capacity Building project*[6] promoted by the Italian National Agency for Microcredit and involving the regions of the former convergence objective, a project co-financed by the European Social Fund. After an initial phase dedicated to the strengthening of the regional microcredit skills, the project focused on the analysis of other microfinance products – specifically microinsurance, microleasing and housing microfinance. Such instruments were comprehensively debated by the natural beneficiaries of the projects, the regional government administrations and the stakeholders, as well as by a number of academics and market operators. The choice of focusing specifically on the three aforementioned microfinance instruments originates from the fact that these instruments are regarded as the most suitable to support the investment plans of the microenterprises (in case of microinsurance and microleasing) or the need to restore/refurbish housing in case of families/individuals affected by harsh living conditions (in case of the housing microfinance), whose activation is based on the involvement of the partnership networks built within the Capacity Building project, also for the purpose of using the resources provided by the structural funds in the programming period 2014–2020. The microfinance sector obviously includes also other products/services, such as microsavings, remittances, payment services and transfer of funds, microventure capital,[7] which are not examined herein. The Italian National Agency for Microcredit has activated a number of workshops with market operators and academics[8] (2014) to start a public debate on the main issues on microinsurance, microleasing and housing microfinance, and to prepare specific operational proposals for the microfinance sector within the programming period 2014–2020 of the EU structural funds. Below you can find the main considerations that emerged from such debates, in particular during the workshop of 7 April 2014 (see Box 4.1).

Box 4.1 Capacity Building project: initial considerations on microleasing, microinsurance, housing microfinance

Microinsurance

In the absence of a specific national regulatory framework providing a univocal definition, "The Italian legislation does not provide, to this date, a univocal definition of microinsurance, as this instrument, unlike microcredit, is not regulated. In fact, while useful regulatory references on microcredit can be found in the provisions of art. 111 of the Consolidated Banking Law, the Insurance Code does not provide any on microinsurance", the phenomenon of microinsurance follows the international guidelines issued by the International Association of Insurance Supervisors (IAIS, 2007), "Issues in regulation and supervision of micro-insurance", June, p. 10. The document can be read at www.irsa.it/get_file.php?id=14420. According to the IAIS, "micro-insurance should not be regarded as a different activity from standard insurance services, except for the reduced amount of premium to be paid, reduced coverage and type of recipients, who are qualified as low-income subjects". For any other aspects, the IAIS does not differentiate it from the traditional insurance business. Following is the literal definition of microinsurance provided by the IAIS: "Micro-insurance is insurance that is accessed by low-income population, provided by a variety of different entities, but run in accordance with generally accepted insurance practices (which should include the Insurance Core Principles). Importantly this means that the risk insured under a micro-insurance policy is managed based on insurance principles and funded by premiums. The micro-insurance activity itself should therefore fall within the purview of the relevant domestic insurance regulator/supervisor or any other competent body under the national laws of any jurisdiction". For further consideration on this matter, see F. Santoboni, paragraph 4.4. If microinsurance, like microcredit, caters to subjects "excluded" from the traditional financial circuits, its potential recipients are "micro-entrepreneurs struggling to access credit, including immigrants, fresh graduates, young people willing to start a business, but also subjects engaged in household activities, who would greatly benefit from an insurance policy, as it would help them corroborate their own businesses". On the supply side, instead, subjects involved in this business are "the traditional insurance companies, including those having a greater commitment to mutual purposes. And then banks, one of the subjects involved in the provision of micro-credit, and, obviously, micro-finance institutions. In principle, if micro-insurance is to be regulated by the same framework applicable to traditional insurance policies, its distribution channels must necessarily coincide with those indicated by the Insurance and Reinsurance Brokers Registry". As for the microinsurance products, in principle, no restrictions are envisaged for their content and scope. First of all, we must consider accident and liability policies, which could be particularly useful, for instance, in case of immigrant microentrepreneurs. After all, we already have insurance policies on the market that, in some cases, can be considered as "eligible" guarantees, therefore perfectly valid for asset allocation deduction purposes. Moreover, there are other policies that, despite failing to meet the eligibility requirements, "would sensibly reduce the chance of default of micro-enterprises and are worth to be considered for creditworthiness assessment purposes, as they would allow borrowers to access credit under more favourable terms and conditions" (F. Santoboni, Adjunct Professor of Economy and Management of Insurance Companies at the Sapienza University of Rome). In particular, CPI (creditor protection insurance) policies are specific products suitable to support loans, as well as other types of insurance contracts, which, as a matter of fact, reduce the general risk profile of a given subject, including property policies, liability policies, business interruption policies and others. These are all obviously tailor-made agreements, designed according to the risk profiles of the enterprises, depending on the sectors where they operate.

One of the critical issues here is represented by the low level of financial and insurance literacy among microentrepreneurs. Another weakness is the necessity of reaching a "critical threshold" of "microinsured" subjects, for both technical reasons and the profit margins of the companies. Finally, the reduction of the enterprises' default rate related to insurance coverage at the moment does not translate into improved conditions for access to credit. "When entrepreneurs enter into insurance policies, their profiles become less risky; so, it is hard to understand why they would not benefit from the virtuous relationship between insurance coverage, credit risk and access to credit. In principle, such relation should translate into increased creditworthiness" (Santoboni).

A number of important studies (e.g., a recent survey carried out by ANIA) have highlighted a strong bond between credit and insurance, meaning that small and medium-sized enterprises that enjoy insurance coverage "benefit also from improved access to credit" (F. Palermo, FeBAF, Federation of Banks, Insurance and Financial Companies. In addition, insurance companies can market and sell their microinsurance products also by offering a free check-up on the enterprises' risk or a form of consulting to plan customer insurance needs and requirements.

One of the strengths of microinsurance is the possibility for the recipients to enjoy national and EU subsidies aimed at lowering the amount of the premium upon signing of the contracts. With regard to this aspect, insurance companies have already a practical experience related to the use of EU funds, specifically with regard to Italian Legislative decree no. 102 of 2004, which allocates EU resources to the agricultural sector by referring to "hail risk". In this case, the state covers up to 80 per cent of the insurance premium, while the remaining 20 per cent must be paid by the insured farmers, as "the aim here is to avoid the so-called moral hazard: if the recipient knows that another subject is covering a risk on his behalf, he will not keep a pro-active conduct to mitigate risk effects. This is to say that when an insurance company decides to enter a market, it must have a competitive advantage; here, the competitive advantage is given not by the EU contributions, as their interest lies in having the premium before the risk, but in the advantage in terms of portfolio stability. If the insurer does not have enough money to ensure risks, the consequent damages will affect not just its business but the whole community of insured subjects that entered into agreements with it, therefore, producing a damage for the entire community". The example of micropolicies against hail risk, mainly entered by the so-called defence associations on behalf of a plurality of farmers, is particularly significant also because it highlights the advantages offered by collective signing. This method, in particular, "allows the insurer to optimize costs and completely cut the brokerage costs it would bear if negotiating the policies with several small farmers on an individual-basis". In fact, low returns on a single product may limit, or in some cases scrap off, the incentive for insurance companies to enter the microinsurance market, although "this downside can be bypassed through the signing of collective policies, which substantially reduce the costs that otherwise insurance companies would meet" (P. Negri, ANIA), http://www.ania.it/it/index.html.

Among the main critical aspects of the sector is "the lack of a specific regulation on micro-insurance, similar to the micro-credit; this is a limiting aspect which creates uncertainties and difficulties to the operators" (Palermo). Moreover, the insurance companies "need to access a number of data, which should be shared among all those engaged into the micro-insurance business: this could definitely make their life easier during the risk assessment phase" (Santoboni); the problem here, in fact, "is to have a defined reference context, where insurance companies are able to access information and data that today they cannot consult" (Negri). Insurance companies, in fact, cannot rely on instruments similar to those used by banks (credit rating, scoring) to evaluate the risk profile of their potential customers and this is why it is increasingly important to have other subjects able to carry out such analysis on their behalf. "Insurance companies build their range of insurance products through a preliminary risk analysis that allows them to operate in relatively safe conditions. If such activity could be carried out by third parties able to ensure the validity of the operations, this would result in a clear advantage for the insurance providers. Here, for instance, we should focus on the role that could be played by the volunteering associations operating on the territory" (Negri).

There is definitely a widespread interest, both among market operators and insurance academics, in the possibility of defining a package of micropolicies aimed at facilitating financial inclusion of certain target subjects. To this end, therefore, we must keep in account the following factors, which are deemed essential for the development of the microinsurance sector:

1. It is necessary to optimise: (a) administrative costs related to the policies; (b) settlement costs when damages occur; (c) brokerage costs. In fact, in a potential future microinsurance market, administrative and settlement costs related to the policies (adequacy assessment, privacy statement, statements related to IVASS supervision) would be the same as those of standard policies (Negri), http://microcreditoitalia.org/images/pdf/programma-07042014.pdf.
2. It is advisable to use collective signing of policies, which would allow reaching out to a greater number of subjects in a timely manner as well as optimising the aforementioned costs (Negri; Santoboni).
3. Insurance companies must be allowed to access comprehensive and detailed information that would enable them to thoroughly evaluate customer risk and creditworthiness during the preliminary assessment phase (Negri; Santoboni). It is recommended that such evaluations be carried out by qualified third parties, as this would result in important cost savings for the insurance providers (Negri).
4. Most critical points, both on the supply and demand side, can be overcome through a microinsurance/microcredit integrated approach suitable to combine the technical features of micropolicies with those of the microloans (Palermo).
5. Increased financial training and literacy is needed, along with greater awareness of the entrepreneurs on the risks associated to their businesses; this would translate into improved creditworthiness and, possibly, cheaper premium amounts (Santoboni; Palermo).

Microleasing

As with microinsurance, so too microleasing does not enjoy a regulatory framework that allows identification of characteristics that differentiate it from standard leasing, except for the limited amount of operations and the reference target – namely microentrepreneurs most often. Referring to the two classic types of leasing – financial leasing and operational leasing – microleasing mainly falls under the former, which allows redeeming the goods at the end of the contractual period and always involves the intervention of a financial intermediary.

Microleasing and microcredit can be regarded as the two main forms for financing the productive investments of enterprises, the difference between them being the acquisition methods of the goods: in case of leasing, in fact, the lessor remains the owner of the leased goods, while the lessee may opt, upon termination of the contract, to purchase them at market value or renew the contract. Microleasing offers the chance also to microentrepreneurs to invest without the need of using their own capital or debt capital, because the basic concept of leasing lies in the separation between ownership of goods and their possession for economic purposes. In addition, leasing offers to henterprises great financial, operational-management and fiscal advantages; in particular, the last are assuming growing importance in Italy thanks to the modifications and simplified procedures introduced by the law for stability of 2014. Law no. 147, of 27 December 2013, published in the Official Gazette of the Republic of Italy, no. 302, of 27 December 2013. On this topic, see Assilea (2014), "Guide to new fiscal provisions for leasing 2014 – the calculation model for the leasing fiscal advantages", January, pp. 7ff.

With regard to microleasing, a first aspect to be clarified is that this product "essentially caters to the so-called entrepreneurial finance, which is constituted by micro-entrepreneurs (artisans, farmers, etc.), rather than the social micro-finance, represented by households and individuals affected by social and economic vulnerable conditions".

As for microleasing's technical and operational features, another issue concerns the redemption option that can be exercised by the lessee upon termination of the contract: "It is an option that can be exercised by the end-recipients, even if the European Commission stated that, in order to be able to enjoy State Aid, the leasing contract must necessarily provide for the redemption of goods. This is why in the notices issued by regional administrations such requirement is often mandatory and this represents a contradiction with the basic principle of leasing. The issue was solved by the Italian Tax and Revenue Agency with Resolution No. 4/E of 2009, which indicated that the appendix of the leasing contract must provide for the commitment of the Lessee, as of now, to redeem the leased goods upon termination of the financial leasing contract" (Palermo).

Another issue raised by the leasing operators relates to the fact that the regional administrations and business associations must establish some guidelines to facilitate the success of microleasing. Such guidelines should also clarify the above-mentioned issues related to the redemption of goods, delivery and testing date, which coincides with the actual date of effectiveness of the leasing contract (Palermo).

More generally, we can observe that any microleasing programme, in order to succeed, must be structured since the beginning through the provision of different kinds of instruments designed according to individual cases and regions, including guarantee funds, revolving funds and grants for payment of leasing instalments. The first issue to be addressed is "how to provide a strong guarantee similar to that offered by the central guarantee funds for the SMEs in terms of coverage percentage: a guarantee that may allow also the credit guarantee consortia to issue counter-guarantee and, in turn, transfer the guarantees upon first request" (Guenzi, Unicredit Leasing; Grillo, Alba Leasing). The second product to be carefully examined, mainly used by leasing companies, is the revolving fund. In this case, "The regional administrations should provide resources at subsidized rate to the leasing companies, and the latter must immediately transfer them to the beneficiary enterprises" (Guenzi). The third product is the contributions for payment of leasing instalments, which is not regarded as a priority by the leasing companies, but can be a useful tool to support enterprises. "These contributions, anyway, should not exceed 15% and should not be paid in a single solution, in order to avoid recovery problems in case of default" (Guenzi).

As for possible development of microleasing, we should take into account the following considerations coming from the market operators:

- Leasing companies can carry out low-amount operations for the microenterprises, but they must always operate in terms of costs, expenses and profit and, as such, assess the sustainability of such operations, which entail a number of administrative and management costs (Grillo).
- Regional administrations should act in two ways: first of all, by providing information and tutoring services to microentrepreneurs, so that the latter can operate according to valid criteria recognised by the lenders; in addition, by granting public guarantees (Grillo).
- In order to avoid situations of scarce demand for microleasing products, they should be designed so as to be fully manageable by operators. To this end, it is necessary to organise more opportunities for discussion with all the stakeholders, like those coordinated by the Italian National Agency for Microcredit (Palermo; Grillo).

Housing microfinance

The microfinance products described so far are characterised by a high degree of social responsibility, as microinsurance, microleasing and housing microfinance must be supported by non-financial services such as coaching, training, monitoring and tutoring, including those financial education services needed to ensure a successful exit process of the beneficiaries from conditions of financial exclusion. The recipients can be individuals willing to start an enterprise or a self-employed activity but also weak, underserved subjects: immigrants, unemployed individuals, young people and others.

It is therefore necessary to think of microfinance in terms of an integrated approach based on the collaboration of public and private entities, including enhanced relationships between the public administration and the banking and financial system in order to verify the concrete opportunity to develop specific products within the operational programmes co-financed by the EU structural funds in the programming period 2014–2020. Besides the technical peculiarities of the instruments, a new and sensible microfinance culture must be encouraged and actively promoted with the aim of offering "integrated packages", where microcredit, microinsurance and microleasing products are simultaneously present. All this entails the collaboration of the interested parties: institutional policymakers, microcredit and microfinance promoters, banking and financial intermediaries, fund managing authorities and non-financial service providers.

Source: Authors' elaboration.

4.3 Microleasing: introduction and Capacity Building project issues

In common business practice, "microleasing" generally refers to the leasing of capital goods directed at low-income microentrepreneurs and characterised by small loans (usually not exceeding €25,000, the same amount provided by microcredit). Financial leasing is a contractual arrangement between two parties, which allows one party (the lessee) to use an asset owned by the other (the lessor) in exchange for specified periodic payments. The lessee uses the asset and pays rental to the lessor, who legally owns it (Gallardo, 1997). Microleasing is thus the leasing of assets to the poor to alleviate poverty by enabling those usually unable to access productive assets to generate income. In the main, there are two types of leasing: financial leasing (after the period of leasing, the asset is owned by the lessee) and operational leasing (after the period of leasing, the asset returns to the lessor; Deelen et al., 2003; Goldberg, 2008). Narrowing down the study to the community countries,[9] it should be noted that, to date, there is no empiric evidence of the development of this financial instrument, in terms of volume of activated contracts, investments, categories of recipients and business sectors involved. This is due both to a lack of specific legislation on microleasing, which does not allow for an objective identification of the phenomenon, and to the scarce availability of scientific studies and specific statistical analysis carried out by research centres and market operators on this subject. Also, the latest international studies on microfinance confirm this conclusion; furthermore, they all highlight the necessity of starting in-depth studies on microleasing. See, for instance, the Report 2012[10] by the EPPI Centre,[11] *The Evidence for Policy and Practice Information and Co-ordinating Centre*, on effects generated by microcredit, microleasing and microsavings on financial inclusion of vulnerable subjects, in particular women. This report shows ample evidence of the difficulties and issues that the study's authors met in acquiring information and data on microleasing:

> We also used a number of different search terms and so were surprised that we did not identify any relevant studies, let alone good quality ones – none of the 84 studies identified from screening and subject to critical appraisal were about micro-leasing.[12] We suspect that leasing is an old practice which has only relatively recently been regarded as a micro-finance product and requires services providers to have specific asset management skills. We therefore came to the conclusion that micro-leasing has only recently been included in the group of micro-finance products and that it did not enjoy the same visibility and attention that micro-credit and micro-savings had in the last twenty years; as such, it has not been subject to the same evaluative scrutiny. Despite the lack of evidence, the theory suggests that micro-leasing

may constitute a more effective measure than micro-credit, because lending someone a productive asset such as a bicycle or a market stall rings the borrower one step closer to engaging in economic opportunities than lending someone money. There is therefore an imperative for rigorous research in this area.[13]

The lack of a specific literature on microleasing does not, therefore, indicate a scarce interest for this opportunity by European microenterprises; the operational practice, in fact, shows frequent leasing operations characterised by small amounts to the benefit of small-size businesses and this context certainly includes a consistent number of entrepreneurs who represent the natural recipients of microleasing products.[14] According to the results of an in-depth survey carried out at European level by Oxford Economics on behalf of Leaseurope (the European federation of the leasing companies)[15] in July 2011, European SMEs' use of the leasing is quite widespread, especially in those countries, like Italy, where SMEs – in particular the microenterprises – represent almost the total of existing enterprises[16] and, therefore, play a key role in the economy in terms of added value and employment. The survey covered around 3,000 small and medium-sized enterprises engaged in nine different areas of business, from eight European countries (France, Germany, Italy, Holland, Poland, United Kingdom, Spain, Sweden) which, in 2011, represented as a whole 83 per cent of the European economy and 78 per cent of the leasing market in Europe.

According to the survey outcomes, leasing is, after equity and bank loans (regardless of their duration), the third most widespread form of financing among European SMEs, mainly microenterprises. This is followed, in order of importance, by bank loans with a duration of over three years, bank overdraft, commercial credit, bank loans with duration of less than three years, private equity/venture capital and factoring. Moreover, the survey shows that in the period 2010–2011, more than 40 per cent of European SMEs resorted to leasing and, through this instrument, were able to invest in production capacity for an amount of approximately €110 billion. The manufacturing sector plays a prominent role in the group of leasing customers; it is the most capital-intensive one and the one in which instrumental machinery has strategic importance for the leasing activity.[17]

According to the above figures, there seems to be a strong preference for the use of leasing also by microenterprises, which represent the bulk of the SME universe. Moreover, the leasing contract offers also some interesting advantages to small enterprises, both in financial terms and for their operational/management and fiscal aspects. In fact,

(a) from a financial standpoint:
- it allows using the good without tying up the sum needed to buy it;
- it allows funding the entire cost of the good (including VAT);
- it does not affect the creditworthiness of the lessee;

(b) from an operational/management standpoint:
- it provides enterprises with fast and simple access to finance;
- it allows for the opportunity to obtain substantial discounts on the cost of the goods leased thanks to the lump sum payment by the leasing company to the supplier;
- it is a flexible instrument which can be custom-tailored to specific needs and requirements: duration of the contract, frequency and amount of the lease payments, redemption value of the good, provision of additional services, such as technical support, insurance and maintenance;
- it provides for the possibility to purchase the good at the end of the contract according to the terms and conditions set therein;

(c) from a fiscal standpoint:
- it allows deducting the lease payments (both principal and interest);
- it allows splitting the VAT in the periodic payments;
- it may allow, under certain conditions, for an accelerated depreciation compared to the regular depreciation tables, through the deductibility of the periodic lease payments throughout the duration of the contract.

With regard to microfinance, we should consider that a vast number of microentrepreneurs saw their options to access traditional bank loans sensibly reduced, mainly due to the effects of the financial crisis that occurred in recent years; the same occurred for credit supplied by other financial intermediaries, such as leasing companies; many of them, thus, ended up in that grey zone that goes by the name of financial exclusion. All subjects involved in microfinance – policymakers, public administrations, market operators, non-profit organisations, academic and scientific institutions – should therefore develop specific micro-leasing products to promote the growth of the most vulnerable enterprises, using them as tools to promote financial inclusion and stimulate manufacturing production and the creation of jobs.

These issues were addressed in Italy by the National Body for Microcredit, which, within the Capacity Building project, kicked off a number of initiatives to promote research projects aimed at designing microfinance products/services, such as microleasing. The studies received positive feedback and indications on the opportunity to start projects for the development of microleasing instruments that may facilitate financial inclusion of those microentrepreneurs unable to access traditional bank loans. In particular, all stakeholders acknowledged the importance of the role played by the National Body for Microcredit to act as a stimulus to solve the issues at stake. Among such issues, the following were specifically raised:

(a) the need for specific microleasing regulations, if not at legislative level, at least in terms of guidelines and operational standards set out by professional associations, to be published in the bulletins of the regional government administrations;
(b) the need to activate training programmes, technical assistance, monitoring and coaching initiatives dedicated to the microenterprises using microleasing; these kinds of activities should also be promoted by policymakers through the involvement of specialised operators;
(c) regional government administrations should create guarantee funds or revolving funds to support microleasing, in order to make this market more attractive to financial intermediaries.

The public administration, in fact, can play a substantial role in terms of stimulating design and development of microleasing products, by leveraging on the operational programmes co-financed by the EU structural funds to promote incentives for investments made through financial leasing, even in conjunction with other financial engineering instruments. In this regard, the creation of guarantee funds or revolving funds financed by national resources represents a best practice for the microleasing and the microcredit alike:

- It can guarantee funds, by reducing the risk of credit operations, often playing a fundamental role in the implementation of microfinance programmes and, in many cases, allow financiers to charge the beneficiaries a lower price; moreover, they improve the sustainability of microfinance programmes and have a positive impact on the capacity to provide financial services to those segments of the population excluded from the traditional banking circuit (*outreach*).
- With the revolving funds, the public administration (central government or regional government administrations) can provide operators

with a fund to be used for microleasing operations on concessional terms and with the obligation to transfer this benefit directly to the beneficiary enterprises. In this case, the latter are offered a rate equal to the weighted average between the subsidised funding rate (often equal to zero) and the ordinary lending rate. In addition, revolving funds are self-sustaining instruments as returns from the leasing payments and will accumulate and then be reinvested in other microleasing activities.

Another topic of discussion is the risk assessment to be performed by the leasing companies on the lessee. This type of risk is usually covered by the title on the property of the goods, which remains with the leasing company for the entire duration of the contract and is transferred to the lessee only if and when the latter decides to exercise the redemption option. However, as financial leasing is basically an asset-based lending, it requires that in any case the lessor carefully assess not just the customer credit risk but also the risk connected to the technical and economic obsolescence of the goods on the market. Despite being one of the traditional forms of creditworthiness assessment, if the customer risk assessment is applied to microcredit, it might be affected by some issues related to lack of sufficient data on the credit history of the potential beneficiaries. In this perspective, it would be advisable for leasing companies interested in entering this market to adopt a portfolio management policy which takes into account also the social and economic context of the beneficiaries and provides for flexible lease payment schedules according to customers' income.

However, information asymmetries might potentially complicate the risk-assessment process to be carried out by the financing subjects, due to difficulties to assess businesses, their reference market and their cost structures. A key factor here, just as in the case of microcredit, could be the provision of so-called non-financial services, which allow for an initial screening of the applications submitted to the leasing companies, accompanied then by monitoring and coaching services for the beneficiary enterprises. The provision of such services may prove key to ensure the successful implementation of microleasing schemes, as already experimented with in the microcredit programmes, provided that the subjects entrusted with their provision (whether public or private entities) are carefully selected through clear and transparent tendering procedures and meet highly specialised standards and requirements. These subjects, in fact, are called to implement a number of communication, information, training, technical assistance and coaching actions aimed at increasing the level of financial and economic inclusion of the beneficiaries as well as their ability to repay. Just think about, for instance, the importance of the so-called BDS (Business Development Service), which is intended to support the microentrepreneurs during the seeding or start-up phases of their businesses and fill any gaps in terms of professional, financial, economic and technical expertise. These services, therefore, play a highly strategic role, as their objective is to help entrepreneurs develop medium- to long-term planning in financial, management, marketing and operational areas, which are essential to support the daily operations of any business.

As for the above, microleasing can represent an important tool to encourage the development of local productive systems; microentrepreneurs who do not possess the financial means to purchase the goods used in their production may be able to get hold of these assets by way of microleasing agreements without acquiring ownership. In this perspective, microleasing can be regarded as an instrument promoting social and financial inclusion and facilitating the redistribution of resources within a given economic system. Ultimately, microleasing can be either an alternative to microcredit or a complementary tool to be used in conjunction with the latter; it can be used by enterprises that need to make investments exceeding the microcredit limits and were deemed unreliable by the banks. However, as previously mentioned, at the moment there are no experiences that testify with certainty the impact of microleasing on the economic and financial situations of microentrepreneurs (especially the most vulnerable of them) entering microleasing agreements. This is also due to the fact that, in general, it is extremely difficult to isolate the effects that microfinancial instruments (including microleasing) may produce on the economy as a whole as well as on the individual beneficiaries, although a number of authors tried to systematically measure them (Dowla, 2004; Heyn, 2001; Pinder, 2001). Ultimately, the success of any microleasing scheme lies in a savvy policy of portfolio composition, knowledge of customers and constant monitoring and supervision of the evolution of the microleasing contracts.

4.4 Microinsurance: a solution just for the "developing countries"?

4.4.1 Introduction

Low-income individuals living in risky environments are vulnerable and exposed to numerous perils. These can be related to their life cycle or to economic, political and social issues or consist of natural disasters like floods or climate changes (Radermacher and Brinkmann, 2011, p. 63). The poor are more vulnerable to risks than the rest of the population, and they are also the least able to cope when a crisis does occur. Furthermore, poverty and vulnerability happen to reinforce each other in an escalating downward spiral (Churchill, 2007, p. 401). In addition, low-income individuals face numerous further risks as they usually lack access to formal risk-coping solutions, including "conventional" insurance products. As a result, it becomes extremely difficult for such households to manage unforeseen expenditure or loss of income, a situation that renders them highly vulnerable to life, health and financial shocks (Swiss Re, 2010, p. 4). For these reasons, in recent years microinsurance – or insurance for the poor – has been receiving an increasing amount of attention from policymakers and researchers due to its potential to assist in alleviating poverty. However, on a practical basis, successful provision of microinsurance products is often hindered by a variety of obstacles, including relatively high administrative costs and limited financial literacy and education among the target population. From this perspective, policymakers around the globe have considered a number of initiatives intended to stimulate the creation of a robust and sustainable insurance industry (Biener et al., 2014, p. 21). Generally, when we speak of microinsurance the obvious reference is constituted by experiences as represented by specific contributions in literature or reports compiled by organisations involved in the microfinance sector, mostly active in North African countries as well as in South America and South-East Asia. The common trait of such experiences is represented by the provision of specific insurance policies designed for and tailored upon the needs and requirements of the target clientele – consisting of both low-income individuals and legal entities – that are unable to access the "conventional" insurance market. On the other hand, microinsurance differs from the latter in the type of subjects involved in the design and marketing of its products as well as in the limited amount of premiums paid and, consequently, the coverage provided. Following the experiments carried out in such contexts, in light of what has already happened in the microfinance and microcredit industry, it seems that the time is now ripe to start thinking how to adapt the experiences carried out in the aforementioned financially and economically "disadvantaged" countries to more advanced contexts, catering to the requirements and needs of an increasing number of subjects, who, de facto, are being excluded from the "traditional" insurance market, through the development of a number of proper instruments suitable to meet their necessities. All this, in particular, with a priority eye on EU member or candidate countries, although the same considerations and patterns may also apply to other "developed" socio-economic contexts. Moving from this perspective, the present chapter aims to analyse the main features of microinsurance in the countries where it was originally developed and then gradually succeeded while trying to indicate some aspects worth examining in order to apply such solutions within economic and financial systems characterised by a greater degree of "sophistication" and in which a relevant amount of demand for insurance coverage is not met, a situation that could generate ample business opportunities for insurance providers. The remainder of the chapter is structured as follows. Section 4.4.2, which starts with an overview of the most important contributions on the matter from academics, researchers, regulatory and supervisory authorities and operators, aims to provide a complete and exhaustive definition of the concept of microinsurance. Section 4.4.3 considers the demand and supply dynamics in the microinsurance sector. Section 4.4.4 describes the main microinsurance products and their distribution channels. Section 4.4.5 examines strengths and criticalities related to the potential application of microinsurance solutions to more "advanced" contexts. Finally, Section 4.4.6 wraps up our study.

4.4.2 Microinsurance: definition, literature and regulatory profiles

In recent years, the microfinance movement has grown more and more demand-oriented and diversified its offer by introducing new product lines, such as savings and insurance products, mostly catering to low-income groups (Arun and Bendig, 2010, p. 2). Like some traditional insurance products, microinsurance is suitable to cover different risks, such as life, health, farming and property. The prefix "micro-" is normally added to specify that this type of insurance targets poor segments of the population, usually residing in developing countries. Given the specificity of target groups, limited benefit packages are made available in order to keep premiums affordable; in other words, micro-premiums are paid for microcoverage (Radermacher and Brinkmann, 2011, p. 64). The very expression "microinsurance" echoes the well-known microcredit phenomenon. Both, in fact, have a specific focus on low-income households in the developing world. Moreover, they were designed to tackle a number of market imperfections that are deemed to perpetuate poverty. The concept of microinsurance, though, proves to be even more complex than microcredit. Firstly, because it implies the payment of a regular premium against an uncertain payout. Secondly, it is mostly conceived as individual contracts, where some parties benefit from compensation while others do not. Finally, microinsurance is far from being homogeneous, as it includes a wide variety of risks and takes a lot of different forms (De Bock and Gelade, 2012, p. 2).

Microinsurance is widely debated by academics, multinational organisations, national governments, public institutions, financial intermediaries, sector operators, non-governmental organisations (NGOs), and the like. Its analysis covers different areas, from the examination of operational solutions aimed at starting and/or developing microinsurance programmes (Churchill, 2007) to the acknowledgment of the prominent role played by microinsurance in providing, along with other microfinance products and solutions, complete management solutions for different types of risks faced by individuals and companies alike (Arun and Bendig, 2010), up to the analysis of the ethical objectives pursued by such initiatives (Radermacher and Brinkmann, 2011). However, while taking into consideration a variety of aspects, including, in particular, regulatory issues (Biener et al., 2014; IAIS, 2007, 2010, 2012; Chatterjee, 2012), demand/supply dynamics (Eling et al., 2014; Liu et al., 2013; Arun et al., 2012; Dercon et al., 2012; De Bock and Gelade, 2012; Arun and Bendig, 2010; Cohen et al., 2005; Churchill et al., 2003; Churchill, 2002), the distribution channels of microinsurance products and the variety of contractual forms offered (Sheth, 2014; Prashad et al., 2013; Clarke and Dercon, 2009), the common thread that holds together the numerous contributions developed over the years is represented by the fact that all such microinsurance programmes were developed and implemented in developing countries; no traces are found of similar experiences in more "advanced and developed" socioeconomic systems. Since the primary objective of this study is precisely to reduce the "information gap" before addressing the problem of how to apply the aforementioned microinsurance programmes to advanced economies, the first necessary step is to analyse the scope of this particular form of insurance. Of course, any time new activities are started, two types of obstacles usually arise: regulatory barriers and operational issues. Obviously, such need becomes even more compelling when the new activities are suitable to produce effects within the financial markets or in those social or economic areas deemed particularly "sensitive" by national governments and where the priority is the protection of the fundamental rights of the public (Santoboni and Vincioni, 2002, p. 32; Proietti et al., 2006, p. 6). From this perspective, considering that the regulation of any market can either promote or halt its development (Biener et al., 2014, p. 21), the first necessary step involves, then, taking a look at the current state of regulation of the microinsurance sector. The first useful reference goes to the provisions of a document jointly prepared by the IAIS (International Association of Insurance Supervisors) and the CGAP Working Group on Microinsurance (CGAP WG MI) in 2007, where, among other things, it is stated that "'micro-insurance' means different things for different supervisors. In most jurisdictions, micro-insurance is not considered as a separate type of insurance and just viewed as insurance available in small sums. This could be cited as one of the reasons for non-development of a separate set of rules for micro-insurance in many jurisdictions. There are many ways in which micro-insurance can be explained, for example:

- risk-pooling instruments for the protection for low-income households;
- insurance with small benefits;
- insurance involving low levels of premium;
- insurance for persons working in the informal economy, etc."[18]

From this initial definition, a further document prepared by the IAIS in 2012 (which substantially confirms what the 2007 paper already anticipated) defines microinsurance "as insurance that is accessed by low-income population, provided by a variety of different entities, but run in accordance with generally accepted insurance practices (which include the ICPs – Insurance Core Principles). Importantly, this means that the risk insured under a micro-insurance policy is managed based on insurance principles and funded by premiums. Premiums can be privately or publicly funded, or a combination of both. The micro-insurance activity itself should therefore fall within the purview of the relevant domestic insurance supervisor."[19]

According to the above statements, there seem to be no apparent obstacles, either from an operational or a regulatory point of view, to implementation of such programmes also in contexts other than those in which they were originally designed and developed, as microinsurance is clearly regarded as an activity that must be run and managed in accordance with the same management and regulatory principles applicable to the traditional insurance business. In addition, no substantial differences from the conventional insurance model are envisaged or highlighted, including with regard to the type of products and clientele targeted by microinsurance (low-income individuals). Table 4.1 highlights the key distinguishing features of microinsurance compared to conventional insurance.

Table 4.1 Microinsurance vs conventional insurance

Insurance value chain	Microinsurance	Conventional insurance
Target market	• Low-income individuals • Emerging markets • Extremely limited insurance awareness/knowledge • Socially responsible culture	• High and medium income individuals • Developed markets • Market is largely aware of insurance benefits • Corporate, profit-maximising business culture
Product design	• Simple product designed with easy-to-understand features	• Multiple coverage and features
Premium collection	• Generally door-to-door premium collection weekly or monthly	• Premium collection: annual or semi-annual
Premium calculation	• Generally community or group pricing • Limited actuarial data • In case of individual pricing, often higher premium due to risk level of policyholders and lack of competition on supply side	• Risk-based pricing driven by multiple parameters • Good data quality
Marketing and distribution	• Innovative distribution with multiple tie-ups • Often sold by unlicensed intermediaries • Usually sold as combined product through microfinance institutions	• Sold by licensed intermediaries • Employs conventional channels, including agents, bank, Internet • Insurance sold by licensed and supervised insurers and intermediaries
Underwriting	• Simple underwriting practices (often non-screening) • Low premium levels • Small sum assured • Simple, easy-to-understand policy document • Minimal or no exclusions	• Comprehensive underwriting • Large sum assured • Complex policy document • Complex language with multiple exclusions, terms and conditions
Administration	• Irregular premium payments, by cash or bundled with other products	• Regular payments paid by cheque, direct bank debit, credit card
Claims handing	• Simple and quick claims turnaround process • Limited documentation	• Comprehensive process; detailed documentation
Asset management	• As per regulatory norms or investment rules of the risk carrier	• As per regulatory norms or investment rules of the risk carrier

Source: Authors' elaboration on McCord and Churchill (2005), p. 57; IAIS (2007), p. 12; Swiss Re (2010), p. 3; McCord (2012), p. 12.

Starting from the above considerations, the following paragraphs try to provide a description of the most important features of microinsurance as well as their potential forms should they be applied to "developed" countries.

4.4.3 Microinsurance: subjects involved

Provision of microinsurance

In order to achieve efficient functioning of the insurance market, a combination of the following should take place: customers and insurance providers need to come together and understand risks and insurance requirements, provide product information, enrol in insurance programs, make payments of premiums, advise, assess and settle claims and deal with other administrative processes in a cost-effective and economically viable way, consistent with market needs (IAIS, 2010, p. 10). From this perspective, insurance undertakings must always identify the best operating solutions, considering the "reciprocal relationship" existing between distribution, customers and insurance services/products; in other words, the development of any strategy to approach the market must inevitably be based on a consistent relationship between such elements. As expressly provided by the IAIS (2007, p. 24), microinsurance products can be provided by a variety of subjects. Here, in fact, we can identify three different categories of microinsurance providers (Table 4.2):

(a) organisations regulated and licensed under the insurance law (insurers);
(b) organisations regulated and/or licensed under other kinds of law (formal entities under laws other than the insurance law);
(c) informal schemes (entirely unregistered and under no legal setting).

It is clear that only providers of the first type are suitable to provide microinsurance products/services in the more advanced socio-economic systems, as they are subject to specific regulatory provisions that are not applicable to the other two categories.

4.4.4 Demand for microinsurance

Generally, individuals, households, and commercial enterprises (in particular, micro and small enterprises) are exposed to a number of risks that can be summarised in the following list, which identifies three main types: pure risk; speculative risk; demographic risk.

Table 4.2 Insurance providers according to their legal status

Organisations regulated and licensed under the insurance law (insurers)	Organisations regulated and/or licensed under any other law (formal entities under laws other than the insurance law)	Informal schemes (entirely unregistered and under no legal setting)
• Commercial insurers (joint stock companies) • Cooperative or mutual insurers (member-based) Some jurisdictions exempt certain insurers from being supervised even though they do insurance business	• Funeral societies or associations • Cooperatives under the cooperatives authority • Mutuals under the mutual authority or under other laws • Health insurance schemes or health providers under health authority • Insurance offered through post office under the postal authority • Non-governmental organisations (NGOs)	• Funeral parlours or unregistered death benefit associations • Informal groups and community associations

Source: Authors' elaboration on IAIS data (2007), p. 24.

Pure risk is the possibility of the occurrence of a future unfavourable event of random nature that, if it occurs, may result in damage. On the other hand, speculative risk refers to an uncertain future event that may result in adverse (in terms of loss or damage) or positive (in terms of profit) effects; this category is typical of financial risks. Finally, the definition of demographic risk covers future events related to the human life cycle (in particular, death or survival). Of course, any subject – whether a physical individual or legal entity – is exposed to a variety of risks that represent, so to speak, a "unique" situation that differentiates him or her from other individuals or entities (Santoboni, 2012, p. 11). As most of these subjects often lack proper financial-insurance literacy as well as, more frequently, the economic resources to identify and manage such risks, their needs and requirements in terms of safety can be met through the pooling and transfer of risk offered by insurance services. As a result, access to insurance represents a key issue to facilitate the economic well-being, in particular for the benefit of those subjects with limited resources available to protect themselves from adversity. At the same time, those subjects lacking proper means may be more exposed to specific vulnerable situations. However, in practice, several markets are characterised by challenges and obstacles that limit access to insurance, particularly for the most vulnerable subjects, including low-income segments of the population and small enterprises (IAIS, 2010, p. 10). These subjects are, de facto, excluded from the "formal" financial markets and generally consist of low-income individuals with irregular income streams, often self-employed or employed in informal enterprises. They are likely to live in high-density urban areas or in remote rural zones that lack proper infrastructures such as roads, markets and access to water and electricity services. They often have low levels of education and financial literacy and in some cases do not even possess a national identity card or certificate of their health status (IAIS, 2007, p. 30).

Considering the typical profile of the excluded subjects in the developing countries, now, conversely, the question is who falls into that category in those countries boasting more advanced economic and financial systems? First of all, they would surely include all those individuals and legal entities that, especially after the economic crisis that started in 2008, fail to access any type of traditional financial and insurance service: the wide pool of immigrants (Magnoni et al., 2010), who now represent a considerable percentage of the population residing in the developed countries; women – such as housewives – willing to start small businesses; unemployed young people having no chance of turning self-employed or starting their own business (Porretta and Santoboni, 2014); subjects who had problems with drugs or with the law and are willing to start new personal or business careers and, mostly, microentrepreneurs, who play a key role in the development and growth of the economy in several European countries, as they represent their backbone in terms of turnover, generation of wealth and employment. With regard to the last, it should be pointed out that microinsurance represents an undeniable advantage for any enterprise, as it helps outsource business-related risks. Secondly, personal insurance allows entrepreneurs to use microcredit solely for their business. In fact, as highlighted by Hamid et al. (2011), improved health conditions lead to higher productivity and reduced expenditure on health care. If households are insured against health risk, they are likely to invest more in their business because they do not need to hold highly liquid assets for precautionary purposes (Ashta, 2013, p. 2). From this perspective, the economic growth of these countries is also dependent on the capacity/possibility of microentrepreneurs to exploit potential business opportunities to their fullest, provided that they are allowed to access credit and proper insurance coverage (Santoboni and Arcadi, 2011).

4.4.5 Microinsurance: products and distribution channels

Microinsurance offers a viable alternative to the traditional insurance system to low-income individuals, households, and commercial enterprises, as it gives them an opportunity to manage their risks (Swiss Re, 2010, p. 1). In recent years, a number of innovative products have been specifically designed for the developing world (Clarke and Dercon, 2009, p. 6). However, though the array of microinsurance products on offer is wide, in many case they are limited to some forms of life and health microinsurance (IAIS, 2007, p. 17). Like all types of insurance, microinsurance policyholders make regular premium payments proportionate to the likelihood and cost of the risk involved. However, microinsurance is more than a simply downscaled "formal" insurance; it is a type of formal insurance tailored to a clientele with vastly different income and risk profiles than those involved in traditional insurance schemes indeed. To create viable microinsurance programmes requires innovation in designing suitable products and services in terms of coverage, timeliness, accessibility and affordability. Achieving the most appropriate design of such products requires an understanding of both the microinsurance demand and supply dynamics as well as its products, with regard to both formal and informal instruments (Cohen et al., 2005, pp. 319–320).

In order to identify the types of products most in demand in developing countries, we should firstly refer to the types of risks that individuals and legal entities residing in those countries are mostly exposed to. From this perspective, health-related risks naturally represent the biggest source of concern for low-income families and microentrepreneurs, as accidents and disabilities, such as illnesses, may result in high expenditure for medical treatment as well as indirect costs, including income loss. However, other types of risks are worth considering, too, including the following:

- *Life-cycle risks*: death or permanent disability of household heads or entrepreneurs can further aggravate the poor conditions of their families or enterprises. In addition, many low-income households and microenterprises appear also ill equipped to face major life cycle events such as old-age and retirement.
- *Financial risks*: such as crop spoilage, lower market prices for products, death of livestock or loss of business assets may significantly impact the earnings of low-income families and microenterprises.

- *Disaster-related risks*: events such as earthquakes, tsunamis, storms and floods may result not just in a great deal of human losses but also in relevant damages to property, assets and economic activities that affect the livelihood of low-income individuals (Swiss Re, 2010, p. 4).

Several microinsurance products and instruments are available to tackle and manage such types of risks faced by low-income subjects, whose scope and range is almost as varied as that provided by the so-called commercial insurance system. Microinsurance can be offered as a single-risk product, or several types of coverage can be bundled into composite products, including instruments underwritten by different risk carriers (Churchill, 2007, p. 402). However, in normal business practice the products most in demand are:

- credit life insurance: these policies are generally combined with other microcredit products allowing subjects to regularly pay their creditors not only in the event of death or injury, which prevent them from generating income, but also in case of job loss;
- health insurance: these policies offer protection to individuals against
  (a) events that cause objectively discernible injuries, resulting in death, permanent or temporary disabilities;
  (b) situations of need arising from illness, such as the necessity to undergo medical treatment or surgery or, generally, any situation where the insurers need to access health-care services;
- funeral insurance: an insurance policy where the benefit is used to cover funeral expenses; the benefit can be in the form of a funeral service, a cash benefit that can be used to help pay for a funeral, or a combination of the two (Hougaard and Chamberlain, 2012, p. 217);
- assets insurance: these policies allow protecting the assets of households or entrepreneurs (e.g., homes, business assets and so on);
- agriculture insurance: as microinsurance was initially created and developed mostly in rural contexts where agriculture represents one of the main activities, this kind of policy protects households and microentrepreneurs against a variety of events (mainly climate-related) that may affect their yearly crops and jeopardise the profits from agricultural activity.

Here it is clear that were microinsurance solutions to be implemented in the economies of the developed countries, theoretically all the above types of insurance policies would be applicable and marketable in their own reference markets. First of all, liability insurance policies, health insurance policies, accident insurance policies, not to mention funerary expenses policies, could be particularly useful for immigrants, including immigrants engaged in entrepreneurship.

Moreover, some insurance policies, defined as eligible guarantees (unfunded ones) by the Basel Committee in the Credit Risk Mitigation rules, can be used to reduce the banks' capital requirements and, consequently, facilitate access to credit for the applicants. Then there are other policies that do not "make life easier" for the banks in terms of recovering their credit but help by considerably reducing the risk of default by enterprises (or microenterprises); they would be worthy of greater consideration to assess and determine creditworthiness, allowing thus access to credit in more advantageous terms and conditions for the applicants. Whereas in "developing countries" we have women working on their weaving looms, which represent the necessary tools of their trade, in "developed" countries microentrepreneurs may rely on machinery to carry out their work and, therefore, generate profits. If the machinery breaks down, such profits obviously cannot be generated any more and, theoretically, also their capacity to return the credit obtained is halted. Hence, proper insurance coverage could help these subjects achieve their objectives in terms of loan repayments. In particular, loans can be supported by specific products, such as credit protection insurance policies (CPI); this, without omitting the importance of other types of insurance contracts, which, de facto, reduce the general risk profile of the subjects insured; the latter include liability insurance policies, so-called business interruption policies, etc. These are all tailor-made instruments designed for the needs and risks associated with the enterprises according to their areas and sectors of activity. As for the distribution channels, microinsurance products can be marketed to their target clientele in different ways. Here too, we should distinguish between "developing" and "developed" countries. In the former, customers often live geographically far from where insurance services are available and may migrate seasonally in search of work. For this reason, sales and servicing result very challenging. Access to microinsurance products, therefore, can be achieved through different distribution channels: "traditional" channels (agents and brokers), banks, microfinance institutions (MFIs), non-government institutions, direct marketing (e.g., call centres), direct mail (e.g., mail lists purchased from other mass-service providers), retailers (e.g., supermarkets, clothing stores, pawnshops, furniture and electronic goods stores and corner shops), alternative direct sales entities (e.g., electricity, gas, landlines and mobile telecommunications companies) and technology-based distribution (e.g., mobile phones and Internet providers; see Smith et al., 2011; Prashad, 2013). Delivery could also be supported via community-based schemes or groups and credit unions, as well as innovative mass-based distributors such as retail shops, post office outlets, religious associations and trade unions. Not only are these alternative outlets potentially bound to overcome geographic barriers, but they also have the capacity to reach customers in a more cost-effective fashion, leveraging on infrastructure and overcoming issues of mistrust (IAIS, 2012, p. 10). Looking at the "developed" countries instead, as the supply of microinsurance products must necessarily follow the regulatory framework designed to govern the "conventional" insurance sector, it is clear that microinsurance policies can be distributed only by the aforementioned regulated subjects; namely only those expressly recognised by the reference legislation: agents, brokers, banks and other authorised insurance intermediaries and direct sales (including phone and online sales).

4.4.6 Microinsurance in the developed countries: strengths and weaknesses

In some contexts, conventional insurance services are oriented to serve some areas of the market but look poorly equipped to cater to other customers, such as workers operating in the informal sector, those characterised by highly variable and unreliable income and those with particularly low income or segments of the population who see conventional insurance as only for wealthy people (IAIS, 2010, p. 11). From this perspective, it appears that development of microinsurance solutions could represent a key risk management solution for this pool of subjects in demand for insurance and whose needs are not met by the traditional/conventional insurance circuit. However, prior to experimenting with new initiatives, it is imperative to perform a preventive analysis of the costs and benefits associated with them. In this sense, considering that an increasing number of insurance providers based in developed countries are trying to penetrate new markets in developing countries through specific microinsurance products and channels, what could be the advantages and disadvantages of starting microinsurance programmes and initiatives also in more advanced economies?

As for the strengths, the following are identified:

- Use of the same target clientele of microcredit and/or microfinance programmes. Basically, since the potential recipients of microinsurance

and microfinance products are the same, microinsurance policies could enjoy particular advantages during the placement phase.
- Limited amount of premiums: generally, premiums paid against the signing of microinsurance policies are of modest size and, therefore, affordable also by subjects who are generally excluded from the "conventional" insurance system.
- Reduction of risk of default of the insured subjects: as these subjects are exposed to risk to a lesser degree, they are also likely to be better equipped to face adverse events that may affect their personal life and/or business. As already seen, such circumstance should lead to improved conditions to access credit.
- Possibility to check up risk profiles and provide assistance in planning insurance needs: customers entering insurance/microinsurance policies should also benefit from "insurance risk management" services. In other words, the subjects selling the microinsurance products should go beyond their role of providers, offering also assistance and advice services to individuals and microentrepreneurs alike.
- Promoting and raising awareness of potential risk areas to which subjects are exposed: this aspect is strictly related to the previous bullet point, as the possibility of enjoying a check-up service on potential risks generally allows customers to improve the planning of their insurance needs and, consequently, make the most appropriate choices according to their risk profile.
- High "social" return for all subjects involved: the dissemination of microinsurance solutions could result in positive effects for all stakeholders (customers and providers; the general public, the numerous public actors, such as governments, policymakers, regulators/supervisors; etc.) involved in this sector.
- Presence of partial/total incentives to enter into such contracts: possible public contributions/subsidies for the payment of the premiums, provided by central and/or local government authorities; this aspect could be the key to trigger the full-scale development of this insurance model also in developed countries.

In particular, with regard to the last considerations, it must be pointed out that in several countries where microinsurance is widespread, the state – as the risk manager of last resort and guarantor of a basic level of social protection for all – may determinate that there is a need to sponsor access to microinsurance for the benefit of the most underprivileged subjects through redistributive practices. From this perspective, it is possible to identify three different ways for funding microinsurance:

(a) premiums may be fully paid by the policyholders (privately funded);
(b) premiums may be partially paid by the state (hybrid schemes and publicly funded);
(c) premiums may be paid by other components of the community, such as formal sector employers (cross-subsidies through the contributions paid to statutory social security schemes).

Since some microinsurance risks are, by their nature, social security-oriented, governments should determine the scope and level of a minimum guaranteed package of social security for all and organise access to it through legislative and regulatory means. Microinsurance could then be used by national governments to deliver this social protection package and thereby extend social security to uncovered segments of the population (IAIS, 2007, pp. 14–15).

While these are the undeniable strengths associated with microinsurance, conversely, the presence of several weak points cannot go unmentioned:

- provision of limited guarantees: of course, limited premium amounts can only go hand by hand with limited insurance coverage;
- need of reaching a critical threshold of the insurance pool, both for technical and economic reasons (profit): this critical element is connected with:
   (a) lack of technical data to determine the tariffs: from an operational standpoint, this is probably the greatest obstacle that might discourage insurance providers from entering the microinsurance market; companies should, therefore, resort to alternative methods to assess the risk profiles of microinsurance clients: from this perspective, a number of data should combined and shared (in order to determine "reasonable" tariffs) by all subjects involved during the start-up phase of the microinsurance programmes;
   (b) low economic returns from individual products: the fact that every policy is associated with a premium of limited amount often discourages potential microinsurance providers from entering this market;

- low levels of financial/social security/insurance literacy: the desired population target is, in most cases, characterised by poor knowledge of the risks to which individuals and/or microentrepreneurs are exposed; this circumstance often affects the choice of the most suitable products/solutions for the timely management of said risks;
- a reduced default rate related to insurance policies still does not translate, from an operational point of view, to improved conditions to access credit; however, as we have already seen, the practice has highlighted a number of synergic efforts characterised by the combination of microfinance products backed and/or supported by microinsurance policies (Santoboni et al., 2012a, 2012b); as a confirmation of this, the IAIS itself (2007) duly stressed that any time microinsurance customers were able to access microcredit, they proved to be reliable borrowers and were generally able to honour their obligations.

4.4.7 Some conclusions on microinsurance

The economic crisis that has gripped the developed countries in recent years has contributed to exacerbating a number of chronic issues that have long characterised their social and economic systems, in particular those related to the gap between a limited number of wealthy individuals and growing sectors of the population that struggle to make ends meet and fail to secure a minimum level of subsistence. From this perspective, with an eye on a number of some consolidated microfinance and microcredit experiences, this study represents a first attempt to affirm microinsurance not simply as a phenomenon catering exclusively to the most vulnerable strata (or the totality, in some cases) of the population, often far away (not only geographically) from the "developed" countries, but also as an "alternative" form of providing insurance services, which, following proper operational and regulatory adjustments, could be applied also to advanced economies in order to meet the demand and needs of those subjects traditionally excluded from the "conventional" insurance circuit. Obviously, several obstacles may hinder the full-scale development of this new model of providing insurance. As already mentioned, first of all there are regulatory obstacles, which may considerably prevent potential microinsurance providers from entering this market; to this must be added operational hurdles, including strictly technical problems (e.g., the creation of pools of insurers allowing for an effective management of the risks undertaken) as well as strategic issues (assessing, e.g., the opportunity – besides the mere economic convenience – of entering the microinsurance business), commercial (e.g., the selection of products and distribution channels) and organisational issues. Yet although aware of the existence of the above obstacles, the authors believe that interrupting an already started trend and moving backwards would definitely lead to giving up all the undeniable "social" returns as well as the other advantages offered by microinsurance – for the benefit of all the stakeholders involved, on both the demand and supply sides.

4.5 Social housing: introduction and the Capacity Building project issues

4.5.1 New developments of housing policies in the European Union

The European Parliament Resolution of 11 June 2013 on Social Housing in the European Union (2012/2293(INI)) is the reference document establishing the foundations for a new strategic plan for the housing policies of EU member states.[20] This plan aims to integrate the existing national policies on the matter by establishing a common quality framework, which should include:

- policies for equal social housing opportunities;
- social inclusion policies;
- policies for the promotion of citizenship and non-discrimination;
- local development policies.

According to the resolution, access to decent and adequate housing is one of the fundamental rights of EU citizens and represents a key tool to achieve justice and social cohesion. From this point of view, investment in affordable housing is a precondition for enhanced labour mobility[21] and increased employment opportunities, in an effort to meet the growing demand for affordable homes of ample segments of the EU population who struggle to cope with the severe economic crisis that continues to entangle the whole continent with its harshly negative effects. A social housing policy is an integral part of services of general economic interest by helping to meet housing needs, facilitate access to property, improve existing living space and adapt housing to the family situation and resources of the occupiers. More and more people are being affected by the current economic and social crisis; for many of them access to housing represents the minimum prerequisite to access citizenship rights. Specifically, we refer here to young people, multi-individual families, students and young people starting their careers, young unemployed couples and people with disabilities. Among the most vulnerable categories are single-female-adult-headed families with children, women with low incomes, women with poorly paid jobs, migrant women, widows with dependent children and women who are victims of domestic violence. Relying only, as has often been the case in recent years, on a combination of market forces and financial austerity measures to rebalance such a critical picture is likely to aggravate a situation which is already spinning out of control. Moreover, cuts in housing benefits and social services, the growing taxation of social housing providers and the selling off of parts of national social housing stocks have all contributed to fragmentation and weakening of housing schemes aimed at promoting fair, equal and social housing, for in many countries their weight is minimal. The financial crisis and the persistent and recurrent property bubbles have further tightened the conditions for accessing the housing market, hitting hard, and mostly, at the middle class, especially in those European countries, like Italy, where the number of government-owned residential and social housing units is low and, conversely, there is a high percentage (over 70 per cent) of first-home owners. An increase in the number of forced evictions[22] and the persistent reluctance of the local banks to step in a socially responsible manner to provide financial support to growing sectors of the society for their housing needs is currently putting a strain on governments struggling to find adequate and, mostly, long-lasting solutions to the issue. The European Parliament, therefore, calls on all member states, through its resolution, to take action and increase the consistency and integration of financial instruments used in the past and develop new financial tools in order to tackle this serious situation. Innovative, multilevel housing policies are called upon to harmonise and integrate national policies on different levels and areas of intervention, including state aid, structural funds, policies for savings and energy-efficiency improvement, fight against poverty and social exclusion, health-care policies.

In this perspective, the aforementioned act encourages tenants, landlords and their most representative associations to actively participate in defining housing strategies, calling for their involvement in the decision-making process. In addition, the following are encouraged:

- use of the structural fund resources to support energy efficiency and renewable energy projects in social housing, which must be affordable, as well as sustainable and integrated urban development projects;

- new integrated development instruments ("community-led local development" and integrated territorial investments) are needed for the promotion of strategies to support residential housing, where social housing providers, authorities[23] and tenants can play an essential role;
- innovative use of the resources provided by the European Social Fund (ESF) to invest in training, creation of jobs and professional requalification, in particular for those "green" professions, such as those related to replacement and/or reconversion of heating systems in buildings.

Finally, the following aspects are stressed:

- potential advantages originating from incentives to be used for the installation of energy-efficiency systems and the generation of renewable microenergy in social housing;[24]
- the advantages of the fight against energy poverty (reduction of domestic energy consumption for heating due to high costs, deterioration of living conditions in the buildings, etc.) related to the health of occupiers (e.g., respiratory and cardiovascular diseases, allergies, asthma, carbon monoxide intoxication, mental illness).

In short, the aforementioned resolution incorporates and properly outlines a number of guidelines on social policies in Europe, sheds light on some important future developments and, mostly, pushes for increased integration between policies, programmes, stakeholders and financial instruments; integration is actually regarded as the key aspect to ensure the efficacy of these measures. That being said, policy integration at a European level is undermined by the variety of different national housing policies, which are characterised by specific connotations and peculiarities, starting from the different welfare systems in place in each country. Generally, the consistency of social housing, that is, housing dedicated to the weakest segments of the population, can be measured by looking at the percentage of social rented houses owned and managed by the state on the total rental housing.[25] Also, there is little doubt that the new policies emerging from the economic crisis are characterised by a strong use of public resources for social housing. They instead show a preference for programmes and interventions where public actors assume the role of activator, promoter and partner of public–private partnerships and the last-resort supporter of measures aimed at mitigating the risk of losing access to decent and adequate housing.

4.5.2 Social housing and housing microfinance

In these paragraphs we analyse the peculiarities of another instrument of microfinance: social housing. Although not expressly mentioned in the aforementioned EU resolution, the set of actions supporting the provision of buildings for social purposes is commonly called social housing.[26] However, it is not easy to formulate a univocal definition[27] of this expression, and this is also the reason why, in our opinion, no specific reference can be found in the above resolution. In a nutshell, the following are common features of social housing in the EU member countries:

- the concept of general interest intrinsically connected to social housing schemes;
- the objective of increasing the supply of affordable homes for a number of target beneficiaries;
- relative vulnerability of the target subjects.

Apart from these common factors, the different national systems show no significant homogeneity in methods of access to (1) housing, (2) construction land ownership, (3) rental systems, (4) methods to access finance for the target population. This makes the national experiences extremely different from one another and characterised by different general performances and a mix of instruments in place. With regard to its most widespread forms of social housing, the expression may basically refer to two different types of interventions.

The first type includes activities carried out by public and private actors and generally refers to subsidised housing related to assistance to alleviate the payment of interests for the purchase of real estate property, tax incentives, supplements or special grants for long-term acquisition of land ownership and implementation of low-cost public services. The second type, the more traditional, refers to housing tenure owned and managed by the state, which, through incentives and other forms of aid, builds directly a number of social rent homes, homes built by cooperative providers or through a combination of public/private partnerships.[28] Both concepts are characterised by the absence of for-profit actions and the possibility of long-term rents in order to recover investment as well as operational costs for ordinary and extraordinary maintenance.

According to these definitions, the following fall under the category of social housing:

- houses built thanks to support and intervention of the state that today are deteriorated and need maintenance and/or restoration in order to improve the quality of both living spaces and their energy performance; most of them are state-owned;
- houses built by private or public–private partnerships with highly diversified levels as for types, products and forms of ownership;[29] this housing group too is often in bad need of refurbishment/retrofit. In these cases, most interventions tend to focus especially on energy efficiency of buildings and/or houses, as it is one of the main factors driving up costs.

In light of the foregoing, there is no doubt that social housing is a useful tool, albeit not the only one, to address the above issues and include that set of interventions that go by the name of housing policies. Housing policies promoting social inclusion, in fact, are not limited to the supply of adequate and affordable housing to low-income individuals at risk of poverty and/or social exclusion, although such interventions are fully justified and needed. In recent years, housing policies developed in different European countries, in fact, have combined social housing interventions with a variety of ordinary measures at various levels, including the following:

- measures to facilitate access to credit for the purchase of homes at subsidised costs;
- self-construction and small maintenance interventions to improve quality of housing;
- measures to support the payment of arrears for people struggling with their housing costs and/or at risk of eviction;
- supplements to meet domestic energy cost or rents for temporary homes for a limited period of time for homeless families;
- measures to improve habitability and safety of houses occupied by elderly and disabled people (home automation);
- measures for the supply of temporary dwellings for the homeless.

The above measures are urgently needed and justified also in light of the following:

- the gravity of the current economic crisis and the fact that access to decent housing is considered one of the fundamental rights under the EU rights, equality and citizenship programme;

- a worrisome increase in the number of potential recipients of housing measures, including middle class, which are at risk of poverty and/or losing the full use of their dwellings;
- strongly diversified and fragmented target groups, each one carrying issues related both to the need for decent and adequate housing and lack of subsistence income (of which rent is often the largest portion);
- continuous and growing situations where poor housing conditions are worsened by a reduction of domestic energy consumption, which call for measures to support and improve the health of tenants;
- strong correlation between urban regeneration policies, housing needs and policies aimed at improving urban energy performance as a basis for local development and the creation of a new model of "urban living".

In light of such premises and given the extreme variability and extent of the demand for affordable housing as a primary citizenship right, today housing policies in the EU member states tend to be divided into:

- *preventive policies*, characterised by measures and interventions preventing the risk of losing housing. These economic support measures prevent the beneficiaries from entering circuits of real economic hardship and poverty as well as the relevant social risks (eviction, decay, diseases, social isolation);
- *policies for repairing and improving*, characterised by interventions aimed at increasing the quality of living spaces and restoring standard living conditions, thus reducing the existing housing problems.[30] This group includes those interventions that improve energy performance and the provision of basic services and utilities, both for single houses or entire buildings;
- *expansive policies*, characterised by long-lasting interventions promoted by the state and private subjects (including public–private partnerships) aiming at increasing the supply of social housing (with subsidised costs and rents);
- *inclusive policies*, focusing on particularly vulnerable subjects (elderly, disabled, single mother supporting children, immigrants, young couples, Roma, etc.).[31]

These categories can help us identify some of the possible features of the interventions as well as the main differences between the instruments currently in use. In any case, they are not meant to set any interpretative limits. Actually, they should be regarded as opportunities to introduce innovative measures that may lead to integrated and modular interventions relying on instruments characterised by greater flexibility and customisation. Such instruments are currently being introduced by social housing policies and for social inclusion purposes, as they enrich and complement each other.

In fact, in light of the persistent economic crisis and a consolidated trend where the state and local government administrations are consistently reducing social housing measures,[32] the issue of social housing cannot be effectively addressed and solved only through the use of long-term and expansive instruments. On the contrary, short-term measures are definitely needed to tackle and combat social exclusion and create conditions to maintain long-term ownership and full habitability of dwellings, for the benefit of a wide spectrum of beneficiaries who struggle to cope with rising housing costs. This picture, therefore, calls for systematic use of forms of assistance, to be negotiated between public and private actors, that focus on reuse, improvement of living spaces and energy performance in buildings in an effort to mitigate the risk of losing houses due to occupants' low income. In particular, these short- to medium-term policies aimed at social inclusion:

- coverage of financial needs of individuals (for purchase, refurbishment, energy efficiency, maintenance and habitability of houses) supported by guarantees provided by public entities to the financial intermediaries;
- state aid measures (also in partnership with private subjects) for the improvement of urban living conditions through the use of certain financial opportunities and instruments at a local, regional, national and European level (e.g., national and regional plans, European Social Fund, European Regional Development Fund).

represent, in general, two aspects to be considered to effectively promote housing investments in the next two years of the programming period. As for long-term policies, in particular those termed expansion policies, we believe that governments need to carefully assess the options at stake, also in light of future developments of the current economic crisis, which is likely to significantly drive and shape the political agenda. Anyway, what instruments are available to facilitate development of interventions to support broader and more articulated housing policies aiming at social inclusion?

Elsewhere in this volume, we have closely analysed a number of measures designed to promote social inclusion and local economic and social development through the activation of forms of assistance for disadvantaged subjects. Most European experiences described in so far revolve around the use of microfinance instruments and, in particular, microcredit through the creation of guarantee funds or European programmes, such as Progress or JEREMIE, to support enterprises; also, in collaboration with qualified national and European financial intermediaries. However, in addition to microcredit for enterprises, other forms of support are spreading thanks to the use of financial instruments such as microinsurance, microleasing and microcredit, dedicated to some categories of disadvantaged beneficiaries (tenants and small landlords) within the aforementioned housing policies. This is an innovative approach, which finds its historical references, just like in the case of microcredit to support enterprises, in programmes already tested in various developing countries around the world under the name of housing microfinance. The typical housing microfinance schemes of the last 30 years[33] provided financial support to instruments directly implemented and managed by households and/or specific target groups with the assistance of financial providers (non-financial services) and according to their living standards. Such measures consisted in the construction of buildings or part of them, modification of living spaces through improvements of their habitability, control and development of urban areas characterised by rapid and forced urbanisation or reconstruction of housing stock hit by wars and/or natural disasters.[34] Typical examples would be the expansion of floor space due to new households' needs (birth of new children), improvement of toilets or the general quality of dwellings (statics, structure, minimal safety conditions, etc.). These interventions were made possible by:

- the presence of free skills to the household that can support the self-builder;
- the possibility of using/acquiring low-cost expertise at the local level;
- the technical characteristics of the interventions, which generally do not entail strong technology criticalities;
- the substantial absence of stringent general housing regulations;
- the implementation of interventions in low-density rural and/or urban areas.

The microfinance instruments already developed in the late 1990s by global financial institutions and banks met the needs and requirements of a number of recipients in a flexible, effective and efficient manner by strengthening the use of housing microfinance in several geographic areas worldwide through the provision of specific financial services targeting specific categories of beneficiaries with limited financial means or at risk of poverty. These experiences, which include a variety of situations and phenomena that cannot always be included under the aforementioned types, share the trait of support being provided to improve living and housing conditions in developing countries, often within broader financial and aid programmes aimed at improving and developing the economies and societies of entire geographic areas. Such developments were also made possible thanks to the resources provided by specialised financial entities and organisations, including NGOs. Although it is hard to automatically transfer such experiences to the European context and, more specifically, to EU member countries, given the strong peculiarities of the developing countries where they were first applied, these schemes, with a few exceptions characterised by excessively "pauperist" connotations in countries where such experiences were first consolidated, have shown the strength, versatility and effectiveness of microfinance products applied to general housing.[35]

4.5.3 The Capacity Building project. Social microcredit to support local housing policies: new instruments for social inclusion

The Capacity Building project is trying to identifying, in a testing phase (types of recipients, types of interventions to be financed, repayment methods, types of financiers), innovative instruments and schemes to support housing policies. It seems possible to successfully implement these interventions also in urban and metropolitan areas, starting from a clear definition of the objectives in terms of social inclusion of the beneficiaries. The pilot project launched through the Capacity Building project, implemented in Italy by the National Microcredit Authority, proposed a reconfiguration of the existing housing microfinance tools. The instrument chosen is the social microcredit,[36] in accordance with the national legislation and supporting the social and housing inclusion of the recipients, within broader innovative policies for social housing[37] that are currently being activated. Such instruments are naturally integrated with other tools characterised by a broader scope, such as those financed by the EU structural funds to promote energy efficiency of buildings and urban regeneration,[38] as well as those funded by the national funds under the house plan approved in 2014.[39] As already highlighted, the Capacity Building project aims to boost the administrative expertise of the Italian regions already involved in the former programme Objective Convergence. Regional administrations receive training to develop organisational skills aimed at improving their use of innovative financial engineering instruments. The instrument used for this kind of intervention is social microcredit,[40] that is, financing in the form of personal loans supported by a public guarantee fund, which according to certain eligibility requirements of the recipients and specific repayment terms and conditions, may allow some categories of vulnerable subjects to cope with sudden housing conditions that may, if not appropriately addressed and solved, lead to poor living conditions and social exclusion.

Below is a summary of the main characteristics of the project on housing (Table 4.3).

The Capacity Building project includes also support to a number of specific operational activities summarised by the table below (Table 4.4).

The diversity and complexity of the various forms of intervention under this platform are the result of in-depth discussion which involved the main stakeholders of social housing policies at national and local level, such as regional administrations and municipalities of the largest metropolitan areas in the regions involved in the project, the main

Table 4.3 Capacity Building project: main characteristics for housing

Purpose of the intervention	• Provide funds, through social microcredit supported by guarantee funds, for interventions aimed at improving housing conditions in order to facilitate social inclusion of disadvantaged individuals in metropolitan areas
Specific objectives	• Promote urban regeneration, that is, limited refurbishments aimed at improving quality of living spaces and energy efficiency of buildings
	• Facilitate the provision of loans for landlords and tenants in order to prevent risk of social exclusion
End beneficiaries	• Homeowners gripped by poor housing conditions and social and economic instability
	• Tenants of private and public housing in poor housing conditions and social and economic instability
Financial instrument	• Guarantee fund created by regions (or municipalities) to support social microcredit (max. €10,000) provided by banks affiliated with the public entities (regions, municipalities)

Source: Authors' elaboration.

Table 4.4 Operational proposals of the Capacity Building project

Recipients	Activities that can be directly supported by social microcredit
Homeowners in poor material, social and economic conditions[a]	– Payment of a (limited) number of mortgage rates to prevent risk of insolvency for the creditor banks – Small refurbishment work of properties needed to ensure decent hygienic and sanitary conditions for the habitability of houses – Expenditure for retrofitting of electric, plumbing, heating systems, etc. – Improvement of energy efficiency in houses/buildings (replacement of doors and windows, installation of photovoltaic systems, etc.) – Building renovation – Interventions to remove asbestos from old, privately owned residential and commercial buildings
Tenants in poor economic and social conditions[b]	– Payment of a limited number of rent arrears to avoid eviction – Coverage of the costs arising from damages caused by tenants – Coverage of defaulted monthly instalments – Refurbishment work agreed with property owners, to be deducted from the rents accordingly – Advances on safety deposits to rent of new apartments to avoid eviction and/or advance payments of the first monthly rents – Support to the payment of rent for temporary housing (max. 18 months) in case of eviction while awaiting new housing
Tenants of private and public housing in poor economic and social conditions	– Payment of a limited number of rent arrears to avoid eviction – Support to the payment of rent for temporary housing (max. 18 months) in case of eviction while awaiting new housing – Advances on safety deposits to rent new apartments to avoid eviction and/or advance payments of the first monthly rents

[a]Conditions and terms to access the benefits will be outlined later.
[b]Supporting the rights of private property owners who rented their property or are willing to do so under the agreed rental scheme.
Source: Authors' elaboration.

cooperative organisations that do not own or manage public housing stock[41] (Federcasa), non-profit organisations (Lega Cooperative Abitanti,[42] Federabitazioni) and the most representative tenant associations (SUNIA)[43] and small homeowners' organisations (UPPI).[44] To these must be added a number of technical partners who train operators and provide adequate technological expertise, such as various architect associations, the National Board of Architects and national technical partners, such as Casa Clima, specialising in energy-efficiency work. As for the financial operators, the project involves commercial banks and the network of microcredit operators already involved in previous activities aimed at developing microcredit programmes to support enterprises. This platform is being discussed and examined in order to activate pilot projects within the programming period 2014–2020 as soon as possible.

4.5.4 Possible developments within the programming period 2014–2020: the Italian case

In Italy, the Ministry of Infrastructures and Transport, through its directorate-general for housing policies, is working to promote a national programme which should promote a policy to harmonise opportunities offered through the Italia partnership agreement and its thematic objectives. This is the national plan for residential housing, in process of being finalised, whose objectives are as follows:

- to reduce housing problems;
- to maximise use of buildings;
- to ensure safety of buildings;
- to reduce building energy consumption and management costs;
- to regenerate urban spaces;
- to prevent social insecurity and disintegration;
- to facilitate the development of cohesive communities and solidarity among residents.

The plan aims to intervene, within a series of opportunities offered by the thematic objectives of the partnership agreements, by providing for adequate synergies with other interested ministries (Ministry of Economy, Ministry of Labour, Ministry of Health). Besides thematic objectives 4[45] and 5,[46] within the broader framework to support technological innovation under thematic objective 1, such interventions shall focus on implementation of the provisions under thematic objective 9, *Social inclusion and fight against poverty* (*promote social inclusion, fight any form of poverty and discrimination*). More specifically, this thematic objective provides for the activation of a number of measures within the housing policy that target the weakest segments of the population. Such interventions intend to:

- build social housing for social inclusion purposes dedicated to specific targets: immigrants and refugees, individuals in emergency conditions due to eviction or family issues, etc. (*ERDF, ESF*);

- build social housing provided with shared facilities; for instance, dedicated to elderly or single mothers with dependent children (*ERDF*, *ESF*);
- develop housing solutions within an integration plan between social and health-care services and generally dedicated to independent living (housing lead) (*ERDF*, *ESF*);
- create or strengthen networks for housing policies, social services, health and employment services between local government authorities and also with private entities engaged in the provision of measures to fight marginalisation, in particular with regard to non-profit entities. (*ESF*);
- implement promotional services to support assisted housing within the pilot project aimed at experimenting innovative housing and social models, targeting the needs and requirements of specific target subjects;
- promote measures to support costs of living (energy poverty, innocent arrears);
- support infrastructural interventions aimed at improving living conditions for individuals with disabilities and serious limitations of their independence (e.g., elderly assisted with the use of ambient assisted living technology);
- tighten the requirements of the registry of social housing beneficiaries to tackle frauds, improve management processes and facilitate actual access to social housing for the most disadvantaged groups.[47]

It is clear that the platform developed by the Capacity Building project fits consistently and creatively with this scenario, as it intends to support and implement schemes and measures by way of the resources provided by the EU structural funds. It should also be noted that these instruments can be combined with local synergies and the interventions provided under the *National Operational Programme Metropolitan Cities*, which has among its objectives the implementation of urban regeneration measures aimed at facilitating the social inclusion of residents. The regional administrations and the metropolitan municipalities can play a relevant role in the creation of financial engineering instruments and use their growing expertise to combine experiences and skills to fully assess housing needs and requirements, identification of range of beneficiaries and eligibility criteria. Such will be some of the areas to be addressed by the Capacity Building project.

4.6 Housing microcredit: the French case

4.6.1 Introduction

In 2013, the Caisses d'Epargne launched a pilot programme to develop housing microcredits; namely, personal loans for disadvantaged owner-occupiers to help them finance their refurbishment work. Its three objectives are to fight energy poverty, combat insalubrity and adapt housing to the needs of people with disabilities. At the end of July 2014, the Caisses d'Epargne had provided 220 housing microcredits, in close collaboration with regional actors involved in improving housing conditions for vulnerable groups. Although housing microcredit is still at an early development stage, current experimentation opens new scenarios, discussions and collaboration between banks, NGOs and public authorities. It also illustrates the flexibility of personal microcredit as a tool to promote social inclusion.

4.6.2 Context of the experimentation

General overview of personal microcredit in France

France is a pioneer in developing personal microcredit on a large scale. Since the implementation of a national guarantee fund in 2005, the number of microcredits provided and actors involved in the supply chain have significantly increased. In 2013, around 13,000 personal microcredits were provided, of which more than 30 per cent were by the Caisses d'Epargne.[48] Personal microcredit is defined by French law as a loan dedicated to finance social inclusion projects for the benefit of individuals, excluded from mainstream banks, who can take advantage of customised coaching provided by a social partner. Although in 2005 it was exclusively a tool dedicated to employment policy, all social purposes are now eligible under the programme, including housing.[49] The loan amounts vary between €300 and €5,000, with a 50 per cent public guarantee. Following eight years of rapid growth, personal microcredit has now entered a new development phase in France. Recent trends show increased synergies with the traditional banking sector, the emergence of new types of stakeholders and experimentation focusing on specific social needs. Housing microcredit is an emblematic example of this diversification.

Within this national scheme, the Caisses d'Epargne have developed their own microcredit programme. They operate through a network of associations called Parcours Confiance.[50] Its mission is to provide access to finance to people excluded from the mainstream banking circuit. It is also a "laboratory" of social and financial innovation, which allows Caisses d'Epargne to propose financial engineering instruments to respond to unmet social needs. The underlying philosophy of Parcours Confiance is to assess vulnerable clients' creditworthiness through customised tools and in-depth budget and social analysis, whereas nowadays, conversely, most banks rely on highly computerised processes, using automated credit scoring. This is made possible by establishing close ties with its social partners (non-profit organisations, social workers, etc.), which pre-select the applications and bring in their social inclusion expertise. Prior to the interventions, the social workers ensure that available welfare benefits are activated; according to a "subsidiarity" principle, microcredit should not replace any available forms of social aid. A typical process would unroll in any of the following ways: a partner identifies a financing need; a young man is offered a job but cannot accept it unless he buys a car as he lives far away; a woman wants to move to another home as she has troubles with her partner; a family has to face an unexpected death and struggles to pay the funeral expenses. Parcours Confiance steps in, assesses creditworthiness and decides whether to finance the project or not. In case of refusal, a viable alternative solution is proposed. On the other hand, if the loan is granted, Parcours Confiance closely monitors the reimbursement process in order to prevent any difficulties the client could face.

Parcours Confiance employs a total of 70 managers and loan officers. It relies on Caisses d'Epargne IT for credit management (release of funds, credit monitoring, etc.) but uses also its own dedicated software, which includes information generally not available in banking databases: partners, in-depth budget analysis, social performance (possibly to monitor project completion) and so on.

Energy poverty: a rising problem

The activity of Caisses d'Epargne in the housing microcredit sector finds its roots in the increased solicitations by local partners, mainly with regard to energy poverty. Energy poverty refers to households who are unable to afford to keep the home warm at reasonable cost. It is a major and growing issue in Europe, as many people struggle to pay their energy bills due to low income. This can result in unpaid energy bills, or arrears, self-disconnecting, disease linked to the cold, dampness and/or mould. Those most likely to fall into the energy poverty spiral are found in social housing but also increasingly amongst poor owner-occupiers, in particular in rural areas. The latter are often left out of public energy-efficiency programmes, although they represent a large part of the population. It is estimated, in fact, that around 300,000 homes in France are in the hands of low-income owner-occupiers.[51] Since 2012, the French public authorities have implemented a national policy to tackle energy poverty, in which financial support can be channelled towards vulnerable groups, namely low-income owner-occupiers. This national programme led to the creation of networks of non-profit or public institutions that are able to mobilise social, administrative and technical engineering to carry out a global diagnosis of the specific housing needs and ensure complete support in all phases of refitting. However, despite public support low-income households often find it hard to finalise the financing of the refitting that would end or alleviate energy poverty; finding an adequate source of financing can be an insurmountable obstacle indeed. In order to tackle this issue, a local savings bank, Caisse d'Epargne Bretagne Pays de Loire, initiated some pilot projects with local partners active in social housing. After successful testing, all Caisses d'Epargne got involved, with different levels of maturity.

4.6.3 Main characteristics of housing microcredit

Target group

As for traditional personal microcredit, eligible clients consist of financially excluded individuals; that is, people who cannot access credit from mainstream banks: low-income subjects (people on welfare, working poor); people without credit history (immigrants, young people, etc.) or bad credit history; people affected by social difficulties (divorce, illness, isolation, Roma community, etc.); labour-related difficulties (unemployment, precariousness, etc.); difficulty using financial services (financial illiteracy, etc.). More precisely, housing microcredit targets owners-occupiers. This is the main difference from traditional personal microcredit: the former represents a marginal part of the Caisses d'Epargne's microcredit portfolio. Another difference is that the clients' average income and reimbursement capacity is slightly higher here, although they could not manage to fund the projects on their own nor access the mainstream credit distribution chain.

Amount, duration, cost

The amount and duration of microcredits had to be adapted to the new types of projects financed. Housing microcredit provides for loans in the maximum amount of €10,000, whereas other personal microcredits are limited to €5,000. The duration can be up to 72 months, which is longer than traditional personal microcredit. A specific agreement was negotiated between the FNCE and the national public bank Caisse des Dépôts et Consignations (CDC), which manages the national guarantee fund for personal microcredit. Following this agreement, housing microcredits are eligible for public guarantees even if the amount exceeds €5,000. More recently, the FNCE developed a new partnership with one of the major actors involved in the improvement of housing conditions in France, the Fondation Abbé Pierre. Through this new agreement, the Caisses d'Epargne will provide a new guarantee line for housing microcredits up to €25,000.

For these microcredits, the Caisses d'Epargne offers an affordable interest rate, around 3 per cent. For other microloans it charges a fixed interest rate. There are no – or very low – fees and the beneficiaries enjoy free technical assistance.

Eligible works

Eligible works for financing are interventions to improve energy efficiency (building insulation, boiler replacement, etc.), upgrade to legal standard (on-site sanitation, ventilation, electrical installations, etc.), reduction of unhealthy housing and refitting of housing to meet the needs of the disabled.

Credit assessment methodology: combining energy efficiency and financial expertise

Creditworthiness assessment had to be adapted, too. A traditional personal microcredit assessment would include a deep analysis of revenue and charges, along with an assessment of the customer's social situation, with a customised approach as described above. In the case of housing microcredit, the traditional assessment is completed by carrying out a housing condition diagnosis, which includes an evaluation of the minimum essential interventions to be executed. As for energy poverty microcredit, there is an assessment of the expected energy improvements. In other words, the loan officer analyses more profoundly the energy costs on the household's budget, according to the technical energy-efficiency diagnosis made by the partner. In case of households with an excessive energy bill, the cost of the interventions should be offset by the savings generated; in the event that households do not heat their homes because it is too costly, a strict budget must be followed, so that they can develop their reimbursement capacity. In all cases, strict and customised credit assessment is a necessary condition to avoid client overindebtedness.

4.6.4 A shared-value approach

Expected impacts

This experiment will have three kinds of impacts: for society, for the beneficiaries and for the Caisses d'Epargne. In fact, housing microcredit combines a "triple bottom line" approach (people, profit, planet), as it is an economic tool designed to generate both social and environmental value. A specific report will be prepared in order to analyse these impacts.

Environmental impact

Reducing energy consumption and dependency is a major objective for our societies. Meeting this challenge requires the implementation of major energy-efficiency programmes that take into account the private housing sector; namely, owner-occupiers. The strong increase in precariousness since the 2008 economic crisis, amongst owners especially, calls for new financial approaches.

Impact on the beneficiaries

Social exclusion combined with indecent, insalubrious and substandard housing has formidable consequences for families' daily life. Children

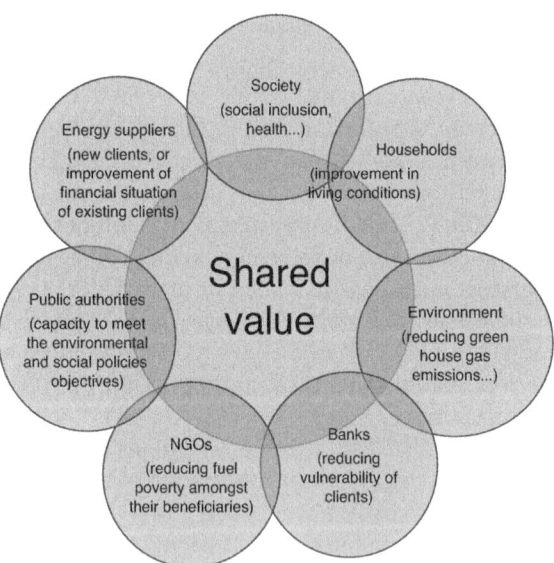

Figure 4.1 Shared-value approach
Source: Authors' elaboration.

are often the first victims of this situation, from a health standpoint (resurgence of illnesses such as tuberculosis or lead poisoning) but also in terms of educational and developmental progress (absenteeism, academic delays). Parents confined to such environments may experience helplessness, with consequent desocialisation processes or difficulties committing themselves to an active job search.

Financial impact

One of the main issues to be evaluated through this experiment is the actual loss ratio of this kind of microcredits. According to the first budget and asset data analysed, the loss ratio should be far lower for housing projects than in the case of loans for mobility or employment purposes.

Sustainability: a multistakeholder approach

The sustainability of the energy poverty microcredit model relies on a multistakeholder approach, where each actor contributes according to the potential advantage to be obtained. The objective is to control energy expenditure for the low-income households through contributions provided by a large pool of stakeholders.

4.6.5 Lessons learned: first insights

An important demand

The first months of programme experimentation confirmed that housing microcredit can provide an effective response to a growing need. Finding partners and eligible projects to be financed was relatively easy. The main challenge is to improve the efficiency of these new partnerships: combining financial, housing and social expertise requires specific know-how. That is why the programme took time to take off. Once partnerships are operational, the acceptance rate seems to be higher than for traditional personal microcredit: around 80 per cent of applications are accepted.

Clients' profile

Currently, most applicants are people over 50 years old. The oldest client is 93. In this case, age is the main reason why these subjects are excluded from credit. Other clients are households under the poverty line but that nonetheless manage to reimburse around €100 a month.

Types of projects

Housing microcredit was designed to respond to three types of needs: energy poverty, insalubrity and adaptation of housing to the needs of

Table 4.5 Contribution for different stakeholders

Actors involved	Contribution
National and local public authorities	Improving housing conditions is a major issue for policymakers, especially regarding energy efficiency, which is a major step for achieving a low-carbon economy and reducing energy spread within our societies. The social and environmental impacts expected justify the involvement of national and local public authorities. Public authorities' contribution consists in activating the national guarantee fund (50 per cent guarantee on microcredits) and support partners, which provide energy-efficiency diagnosis and subsidies that absorb part of the works' costs
Banks	The Caisse d'Epargne contributes by providing experienced staff to Parcours Confiance and by absorbing the credit management-related costs (back office, IT, etc.), for the microcredit is on its balance sheet. Backing the credit activity with a major local bank gives the possibility of pooling resources and reducing costs
Expert partners	Specialised social housing networks see microcredit as a way to diversify their financing tools for low-income households. In many cases, refurbishment projects would not be possible without microcredit
Clients	The clients' contribution consists in paying loan costs and interest

Source: Authors' elaboration.

the disabled. Alleviating energy poverty seems to be the main drive behind this type of microcredit; it is the business line which developed most rapidly. Reporting analysis highlights three broad types of needs, with different financial levels:

- energy-efficiency interventions: €16,000 on average, including €5,000 microcredit;
- work to make dwellings compliant with regulatory standards: €25,000 on average, including €7,000 microcredit;
- work to upgrade insalubrious housing: €30,000 on average, including €9,000 microcredit.

Some obstacles

Following early experiences, upgrade of insalubrious housing has proved to be quite prohibitive and hard to finance through microcredit.

In many cases, it is difficult to match the high level of work needed with the low reimbursement capacity of the borrowers. To really develop these financing schemes, new forms of financial supports should be found, whether private or public (guarantees, grants, etc.). Another issue is the lengthening of reimbursements, as borrowers, who are often at an advanced stage of life, can unexpectedly pass away or suffer from infirmity. In order to ensure the project's viability, financial security mechanisms, such as insurance subscriptions or third-party guarantees, should be developed for microcredits exceeding €10,000.

New stakeholders, mainly suppliers

One innovative aspect of this experiment is the partnership with new actors, such as energy suppliers. The objective is here to help households reduce their energy bill through increased energy efficiency. New stakeholders such as insurance companies or other suppliers may be interested in joining the pool of partners in the future.

Notes

1. Although the chapter has been prepared by the authors jointly, Sections 4.1 and 4.2 have been written by Giovanni Nicola Pes, whereas Section 4.3 by Paolo Rita, Sections 4.4.1–4.4.3, 4.4.5–4.4.7 were written by Fabrizio Santoboni, Section 4.4.4 by Pasqualina Porretta, Section 4.5.1, 4.5.2, 4.5.4 by Fulvio Pellegrini, Section 4.5.3 by Alessandro Cardente and Section 4.6 was written by Perrine Lantoine.
2. According to the definition provided by the UN, microfinance can refer to "loans, savings, insurance, remittance services, micro-loans and other financial products destined to low-income customers". According to another, more general, definition proposed by an Italian academic (Viganò, 2004), microfinance consists of the "promotion and dissemination of forms of financial intermediation dedicated to underserved customer sectors, which cannot be catered to through the traditional methods and channels, due to their size, low income or lack of financial education".
3. Ibid.
4. Banque de France (2012), "Rapport annuel de l'observatoire de la microfinance". Latest edition, Exercise 2012.
5. Banque de France (2011), "Colloque international sur la Microfinance", July.
6. http://www.microcreditoitalia.org/capacitybuilding/.
7. See, for example, Christine Poursat in "Dossier thématique: Diversification des produits", *Portail de la Microfinance*, January 2014. See also Marc Labie, Carolina Laureti and Ariane Szafarz, "Flexible products in micro-finance: overcoming the demand-supply mismatch", Centre Emile Bernheim (CEB) Research Institute in Management Sciences, Working Paper no. 13/044, December 2013.

8. In particular, we refer here to the workshop "Micro-finance and the new programming period 2014–2020", held in Rome in April 2014, which was attended by representatives of the regions involved in the convergence programme, the main bank, insurance and leasing associations (ABI, ANIA, Assilea), market operators, academics and politicians. The results of the workshop were published by the Italian National Agency for Microcredit (www.microcreditoitalia.org/capacitybuilding).
9. In developing countries (PVS) microleasing is more widespread than in European countries, esp. in rural areas.
10. Ruth Stewart et al. (2012), "Do micro-credit, micro-savings and micro-leasing serve as effective financial inclusion interventions enabling poor people, and especially women, to engage in meaningful economic opportunities in low- and middle-income countries? A systematic review of the evidence". EPPI, Centre – The Evidence for Policy and Practice Information and Coordinating Centre, http://r4d.dfid.gov.uk/pdf/outputs/systematicReviews/Microcredit2012StewartReport.pdf.
11. The EPPI-Centre (http://eppi.ioe.ac.uk) is part of the Social Sciences Research Unit of the Institute of Education, University of London. The centre develops methods for systematic reviews and abstracts, by carrying our reviews and providing orientation and training.
12. The 84 relevant studies took place in 33 different countries: Bangladesh, Bolivia, Bosnia and Herzegovina, Côte d'Ivoire, Ecuador, Egypt, El Salvador, Ethiopia, Ghana, Haiti, India, Indonesia, Kenya, Madagascar, Malawi, Mexico, Mongolia, Morocco, Nicaragua, Nigeria, Pakistan, Paraguay, Peru, Philippines, Syria, Tanzania, Thailand, Tunisia, Uganda, Uzbekistan, Vietnam, Zambia, Zimbabwe.
13. Ruth Stewart et al. (2012), pp. 100–101.
14. Within the classic division between microfinance "for enterprises" and "social" microfinance (according to art. 111 of the Unified Banking Act), microleasing is a definitely product dedicated to the former.
15. Oxford Economics (2011), "The use of leasing amongst European SMEs", Leaseurope, Brussels. Leaseurope, the European federation of leasing companies, represents 44 associations from 34 countries.
16. According to the applicable EU legislation (recommendation 2003/361/EC) of the European Commission of 6 May 2003 concerning the definition of microenterprises, small and medium-sized enterprises), a microenterprise is defined as an enterprise employing fewer than 50 persons and whose annual turnover and/or balance sheet total do not exceed €2 million. In the 25 country EU, around 23 million SMEs provide around 75 jobs and represent 99 per cent of the total number of enterprises. With specific regard to microenterprises, Italy is the European country where enterprises with less than ten employees play the most relevant role in terms of added value and employment: in 2010, the share of added value created by such enterprises in the country was equal to 33 per cent (around 14 points higher than the European average) and up to 50 per cent if we consider only tertiary and construction sectors. Bank of Italy (2013), Economic and Financial Issues, "Micro-enterprises in Italy: an introductory analysis", April, pp. 5–6.
17. See the declarations of the most prominent players in the international leasing sector in the article "Built to last" in *Leasing Life*, January 2012,

according to which, SMEs engaged in the manufacturing sector account for the highest number, almost a fifth of the total.
18. IAIS (2007), p. 10.
19. In this regard, it should be noted that the IAIS itself specifies that "micro-insurance does not include government social welfare as this is not funded by premiums relating to the risk, and benefits are not paid out of a pool of funds that is managed according to insurance and risk principles. For the same reason, it does not include emergency assistance provided by governments, for example, in case of natural disasters (floods, fires) in low-income townships. However, as a risk manager of last resort, the State may determine that there is a need to sponsor access to micro-insurance for the most underprivileged subjects through redistributive practices. There are cases where the State plays a stronger role in fully funding schemes, but these could only be considered micro-insurance if they are run according to insurance principles" IAIS (2012), pp. 11–12.
20. Housing policies are part of the policies for social services of general interest (SSGI). For a further elaboration on the concept of social housing, see European Commission (2010), *Second biennial report on social services of general interest*. Commission Staff Working Document, Brussels, 22 October 2010, SEC (2010) 1284 final.
21. In terms of increase in employment opportunities originating from the recovery of the social housing market.
22. The total forced evictions ordered in 2013 amount to 73,385. See Ministry of the Interior – School of the Administration of the Interior – General Statistics Office (2014), *Forced evictions in Italy: performance of eviction procedures in residential buildings 2013*, Statistics Notebook no. 1, Rome.
23. Social housing represents an integrated answer to sustainability. Today social housing involves around 25 million houses in Europe, half of which are characterised by energy consumption exceeding 150 kWh/m^2/year. To promote energy requalification of these buildings means first of all reducing CO_2 emissions as well as the poverty originating from high energy costs. In addition, these measures can also stimulate a more environmentally friendly and competitive economy. For further investigations on this issue, see Forcella D. (2013), *European green microfinance: a first look*, EMN Research 2013, Brussels.
24. These structural measures entail broad benefits in terms of energy savings and the possibility of a more equitable distribution of savings among tenants, social housing associations and owners, which could be invested to finance further modernisation and improvement of buildings. In this context, we should take into account the provisions introduced by EU directive 2012/27/ of the European Parliament and Council of 25 October 2012 on energy efficiency, amending directives 2009/125/EC and 2010/30/UE and cancelling directives 2004/8/EC and 2006/32/EC with regard to energy efficiency of buildings in the member states, including renovation of buildings, as the existing building stock represents the sector with the greatest potential for energy savings.
25. The situation is quite variegated: figures go from over 30 per cent in the Netherlands to 2 per cent in Spain, through a composite and different scenario across the EU member states, which can be explained only by referring to different welfare systems and historic developments. Moreover, the

same percentages, although similar, can be the results of different measures taken over time.
26. The most commonly accepted definition of social housing is the one provided by the Cecodhas Housing Europe – the European Federation of Public, Cooperative and Social Housing, which defines it as "the group of activities aimed at providing affordable housing, by way of precise allocation rules, to support households who struggle to access housing at market conditions, either because they are unable to access credit or because they are affected by particular issues". Dwellings built, sold or rented according to the principles of the free market, therefore, do not fall under the category of social housing. Government support to social housing may assume different forms, such as government-guaranteed loans, grants for the payment of interests on loans, guarantees or fiscal incentives. Public support may be provided by the central government and local government authorities to tenants or providers, to finance both the construction of new buildings and maintenance of existing buildings. Unlike other types of accommodation, social housing is typically assigned to the weakest and most vulnerable segments of the population, according to selection criteria established by central or local government authorities, which take into account income limits and/or implicit or explicit allocation mechanisms where points are assigned according to the social and economic status of the applicants, such as students, elderly, disabled, immigrants, etc. See http://www.housingeurope.eu/.
27. For a more articulated discussion on meaning and general characteristics of the forms of social housing in Europe, see Cechodhas (2011), *Housing Europe review 2012. The nuts and bolts of European and social housing systems*, Brussels and EC (2013), Directorate-General for Internal Policies, *Social housing in EU*, Brussels.
28. These are supported by public incentives and may result in a subsequent division of ownership between partners or maintain the property undivided.
29. These houses are mostly owned by cooperatives, social housing providers and private individuals who collaborate with the cooperatives/organisations for the maintenance of common spaces and activities.
30. This is the direction followed also by all urban regeneration interventions whose objective is to recover housing stocks, especially in urban centres, without extending building space and urban sprawl.
31. It goes without saying that all the aforementioned policies are aimed towards social inclusion. They explicitly refer to target groups characterised by poor conditions and severe social distress.
32. This group includes also government-owned houses already occupied but restored for the above purpose.
33. For a further insight, see http://www.habitat.org/housing_finance/best_practices.aspx; http://www.citiesalliance.org/. The definition accepted herein indicates housing microfinance as follows: *Housing micro-finance (HMF) is primarily the provision of unsecured microcredit, but may include other related financial services – such as access to savings, remittances, and micro-insurance – to meet the demand of low-income households to repair or improve their existing homes or build their own homes incrementally one loan at a time. These loans may also require mandatory savings or serialised assets and other collaterals. Credit*

assessment is similar to the cash flow analysis and character investigation processes applicable to unsecured small business loans to individual entrepreneurs. The process often includes documentation to verify residence, a list of building materials to be purchased or that have already been saved by the borrower, and an estimate for specialised labour. Character investigation may also include questions on the borrower's social capital to enhance the incremental building process: social networks, contacts with NGOs or building materials suppliers, and free skills available to the household that can support the self-builder. See http://www.hofinet.org, a specialised website connected with financial institutions under the World Bank.

34. See, for example, http://www.affordablehousinginstitute.org/?mtheme_portfolio=identifying-and-upgrading-in-ulaanbaatar, or Kihato M. (2013), *State of housing: micro-finance in Africa*, Centre for Affordable Housing Finance in Africa, Housing Finance Information Network, Philadelphia, USA.
35. Housing as a construction practice.
36. For a detailed reading, see Bank of Italy (2014), *Consolidated act on banking and construction laws*, updated version to Legislative Decree 4 March 2014, no. 53.
37. Social housing is regarded in Italy as a policy for the development of subsidised housing and access to decent and affordable housing by segments of the population that are currently excluded (also through the purchase of property). The Italian legislation (ministerial decree on infrastructures, 22 April 2008) provided a comprehensive and detailed definition of the term: "Definition of social housing for the purpose of exemption from notice requirements of State Aid, according to arts no. 87 and 88 of the del Treaty establishing the European Community", pursuant to art. 5 of law no. 9/2007, paragraph no. 2 of art. 1, "social housing", defines it as "housing tenure for residential use and permanently leased, which fulfils functions of general interest, in the protection of social cohesion and with the aim of reducing housing problems of disadvantaged individuals and households, who cannot afford house rentals on the free market. Social housing is a key element of the residential housing system constituted by the total of housing services aimed at the fulfilment of primary needs; Paragraph 3. The definition under paragraph No. 2 include houses built or recovered by public and private operators, by way of public grants or incentives – such as tax exemptions, allocation of areas or buildings, guarantee funds, planning facilitations – dedicated to temporary house rental for a period of at least eight years and to ownership as well; Paragraph 4. Social and residential housing is provided by public and private operators through the provision of houses to be leased, which must be allocated the largest part of available resources as well as support to facilitate home ownership, pursuing the integration of different sectors of the community and contributing to the improvement of the recipients' living conditions; Paragraph 5. As a service of general economic interest, social housing constitutes the additional planning standard to be ensured through free assignment of areas or dwellings, according to methods established by regional legislations". Art. 2, paragraph 7 "Social housing must be built in accordance with principles of environmental sustainability and energy savings, using, where applicable, alternative energy sources".

38. Including the interventions under the National Operational Programme for Metropolitan Cities, which will act on the same issues in collaboration with the regional operational programmes financed by the European Investment Fund and the European Regional Development Fund.
39. Law decree no. 47 of March 2014. This decree, known as House Plan or Lupi Decree, introduces new provisions on social housing. In light of the strong constraints in access housing affecting vulnerable segments of the population, this decree provides, among other measures, for the increase in financial provisions of a number of funds created as support instruments, partly similar to social microcredit. They are the solidarity fund for mortgages to buy first homes, the fund to access loans to buy first homes, the support fund for leased houses and the guarantee fund to cover the risk of default of unreliable tenants. For an in-depth insight on the Italian legislation on housing, please refer to the document prepared by the Chamber of Representatives, http://www.camera.it/temiap/temi17/Am0050.pdf.
40. It should be mentioned here that, unlike microcredit dedicated to microenterprises, the financial allocation of social microcredit amounts to just €10,000; this has some specific consequences and effects on the financial instruments and their use within broader schemes. For example, limits to the type of interventions to be financed and their scope.
41. Both in the form of undivided property (with the presence of tenants) and organisation of individual property divided among the members of the cooperatives providing social housing.
42. Federcasa, Federabitazione-Confcooperative and Legacoop Abitanti are members of the CECODHAS Housing Europe – the European Federation of Public, Cooperative and Social Housing. Established in 1988, it is a network of 42 national and regional federations gathering about 41,400 providers in 22 countries, which manages over 25 million homes, about 12 per cent of the existing dwellings in Europe. http://www.housingeurope.eu/.
43. http://www.sunia.it.
44. http://www.uppi.it.
45. Sustainable energy and quality of living (to promote the transition towards a low carbon economy in all sectors); improve energy efficiency for end users and promote smart energy; reduce energy consumption in residential and commercial buildings, public buildings or buildings open to the public.
46. Climate and environmental risks (promote adaptation to climate changes, risk prevention and management); risk prevention and mitigation and adaptation to climate changes.
47. *Partnership agreement 2014–2020*, Italy, Annex Expected Results. Actions, 7 April 2014.
48. Caisse des Dépôts et Consignations, *Bilan du microcrédit personnel au 4ème trimestre 2013* (February 2014).
49. Law no. 2010–737 of 1 July 2010 brought credit reform to completion: "Les prêts destinés à participer au financement de projets d'insertion accordés à des personnes physiques confrontées à des difficultés de financement, dont les capacités de remboursement de ces prêts sont jugées suffisantes par les prêteurs et qui bénéficient d'un accompagnement social. Ces prêts sont accordés afin de permettre l'accès, le maintien ou le retour à un emploi. L'inscription des personnes intéressées au fichier national recensant les

informations sur les incidents de paiement caractérisés liés aux crédits accordés aux personnes physiques pour des besoins non professionnels prévu à l'art. L. 333-4 du code de la consommation ne peut constituer en soi un motif de refus de ces prêts. Ces prêts peuvent également être accordés pour la réalisation de projets d'insertion sociale qui ne sont pas directement liés à un objectif professionnel".
50. www.parcours-confiance.fr.
51. The national public policy designed in 2010 for the 2010–2017 period identified 300,000 poor owner-occupiers facing fuel poverty, especially in rural areas ("plan de précarité énergétique", 26 January 2010, and "programme Habiter Mieux").

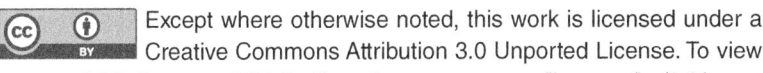 Except where otherwise noted, this work is licensed under a Creative Commons Attribution 3.0 Unported License. To view a copy of this license, visit http://creativecommons.org/licenses/by/3.0/

Part II
The Capacity Building Surveys: Results and Reflections

OPEN

5
Capacity Building Surveys

Riccardo Graziano, Pasqualina Porretta, Giovanni Nicola Pes, Cristiana Turchetti and Matteo Re

5.1 Methodological framework: aims, questionnaires

As underlined in the first chapter, the methodological approach of this research is based on two questionnaires on the managing authorities' capacity building in the microcredit sector and capacity building related to financial instruments within the new EU regulatory framework.[1] The previous chapter clarified the main guidelines of the EU cohesion policy, the key features and objectives of the EU structural funds and the possibility of using such funds to activate financial engineering instruments dedicated to the microfinance sector in general and specifically to microcredit.

An appropriate use of the structural funds requires programming, monitoring and reporting skills by the European managing authorities (MAs). It is therefore necessary to change the management methods of such funds, according to the following guidelines (see Figure 5.1):

- *Careful definition of the expected results according to the specific needs detected in the different territories*; the results must be measured through indicators of the impact produced by public intervention on the quality of living.
- *Compliance with project deadlines* by the subjects in charge.
- *Mobilised and adequately competent partnership with regard to the programmes to be implemented and the objectives set out* to be promptly involved in the decision-making process related to programming and implementation policies.
- *Information transparency and dissemination*, through a continuous and constructive exchange of information with the territories and the actors involved in the partnership process.

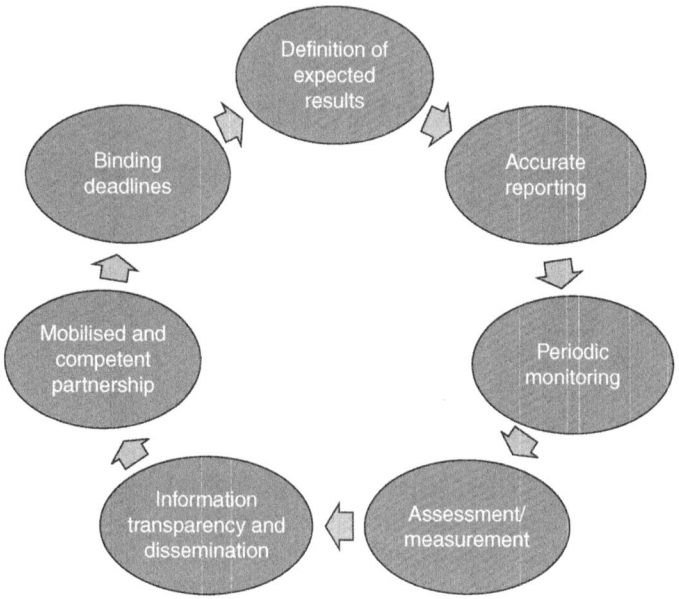

Figure 5.1 The management of structural funds: the main actions
Source: Authors' elaboration.

- *Assessment/measurement of the effects produced by the interventions* and how such effects take place through careful assessment of the social and economic benefits.
- Systematic monitoring of programmes carried out through field verification to ascertain the state of the art of the interventions carried out.
- *Careful reporting and continuous dialogue with EU authorities*; assistance and structured coaching of the national managing authorities with the relevant EU authorities with regard to the different thematic objectives/structural funds implemented.

In this perspective, the authors deemed useful to present here the results of two surveys dedicated to the MAs' general capacity building (first questionnaire) and their specific capacity building related to the microcredit/microfinance programmes (second questionnaire).

The first questionnaire (Figure 5.2), administered by the EIPA,[2] is divided into four key investigation areas: *analysis of the main results of the microcredit/microfinance programming activity, target group and other operational features, monitoring and reporting activities, regulatory framework for the microcredit/microfinance sector*. This first survey specifically aims to define

Figure 5.2 First questionnaire: investigation areas
Source: Authors' elaboration.

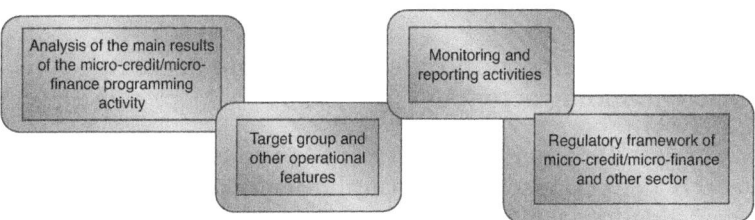

Figure 5.3 Second questionnaire: investigation areas
Source: Authors' elaboration.

the need for capacity building in relation to the new EU regulatory framework; identify what type of support may be more effective (exchange of personnel, shared practices and learning, online platform, peer-to-peer assistance); find out managing authorities available to share their experiences and good practices with others. The questionnaire will be sent to all managing authorities and certifying authorities of the member states.

The second questionnaire (Figure 5.3), administered by the Italian National Agency for Microcredit (Ente Nazionale per il Microcredito) within the Capacity Building project includes the following four investigation areas:

- *Analysis of the main results of the microcredit/microfinance programming activity*: number of microcredit projects activated, amount of loans granted, other results.
- *Target group and other operational features*: target group of the microcredit programme, average amount of loans, operators/institutions involved in the programme and their specific role, main guarantees required, etc.

- *Monitoring and reporting activities*: presence/absence of monitoring activity, reporting frequency, reporting methods, presence/absence of disclosure, websites, etc.
- *Regulatory framework for the microcredit/microfinance sector and others*: presence/absence of a specific regulatory framework for microfinance/microcredit, which undoubtedly influences the legal and institutional layout of the microcredit programmes and defines both the scope of operation and the technical and legal characteristics of the financial instruments used in different EU areas.

The following section illustrates the objectives and specific content of the investigation areas as well as the most significant results of the surveys. Each area of investigation was examined using only data collected through the questionnaires; no other sources were used.

5.2 The managing authorities' interest and needs in capacity building activities

To manage and implement ESI funds (European structural and investment funds) is a process that requires many different skills. Often, however, organisations face difficulties and have a hard time being efficient and effective. Indeed, on the basis that such difficulties are common in most of the member states, the European Commission decided to start a new project in order to tackle the problem and try to give appropriate tools to all those involved. The aim is to support intermediate bodies, enabling them to implement and manage European funds efficiently.

As highlighted by many studies carried out by the European Commission, the absorption level of European funds has been somehow low in certain parts of the European Union. Owing to the data provided in the study "A European fund for economic revival in crisis countries" (Marzinotto, 2011),[3] it is possible to view the amount of funds that each member state can exploit. The level of absorption is easily quantified, taking into account the amount of outstanding funds as a proportion of the single member states' GDP. This indicator draws a peculiar picture concerning the European Union and the unbalanced situation among member states. For example, in Greece the percentage of GDP of outstanding funds for the period 2007–2013 was 7 per cent (Marzinotto, 2011, p. 5), and in Portugal it was close to 9.5 per cent (Marzinotto, 2011, p. 5). Figure 5.1 provides data concerning the share of outstanding funds for the programming period 2007–2013 as a percentage of the total allocation of funds among member states. It is possible to see that for many different reasons – which are not the core of this study – there is underuse of the financial resources provided by the European Union. Ederveen et al. (2006)[4] points out that, for example, EU funds are more effective in an environment characterised by strong institutions (low corruption) and effective governance. This is not new in terms of environmental requirements for an effective way of pursuing certain goals. In fact, Charles Edquist gives a general definition of institutions strongly stressing their importance in an environment that can foster innovation and investments. "Many institutions are publicly created (such as laws and regulations) and therefore easy to modify by governments. However, others are created by private organizations, such as firm routines, and they are much more difficult to influence by government intervention" (Edquist, 2008, p. 14).[5]

Edquist's statement is very clear and useful for the purpose of this study. In fact, owing to this distinction between public and private institutions, it is possible to understand how easy it is, to a certain extent, to modify public institutions so as to make them more effective. This is very important for explaining why managing authorities have to have a very high skill level: they are part of institutions that are more likely to drive and influence the absorption of EU funds. Therefore, through their trustworthy feedback and suggestions, they can actually influence "public institutions", making the implementation of European funds easier for all the actors involved.

Nonetheless, in this scenario it is very hard to tell which can be the main problems in managing and implementing European funds correctly. However, among all possible causes slow absorption can be one problem for enhancing and ensuring a good level of training for intermediate bodies that are the channels for these funds. Therefore, DG Regio's[6] survey is very important for understanding the strengths and weaknesses of the organisations involved in the various processes of implementation, monitoring and evaluation.

5.3 The questionnaire: the investigation area

DG Regio structured the questionnaire in order to enable the member states' managing authorities to express their strengths and weaknesses clearly as regards all the relevant areas concerning the managing and implementation of EU funds. Considering that institutional and administrative capacity is considered essential for implementing EU funds effectively and efficiently, the survey aims at carrying out an in-depth analysis concerning where and how managing authorities can be supported. Thus, aiming at a better governance, the survey is very specific so as to clarify in which direction the European Commission's and member states' efforts should be channelled. Moreover, as stated earlier, an inefficient implementation and management of European funds leads to scarcity effects on the member states' real economy. Therefore, the need for a more effective capacity building strategy is almost obvious both in terms of a domestic administrative modernisation and technical assistance under ESI funds. In particular, a more effective targeting of technical assistance is needed in most member states. This entails a precise knowledge of the managing authorities' training needs. Therefore, this survey tries to investigate in which areas more effective training might be necessary. The starting point chosen concerns the thematic objective stated in art. 9[7] of the Common Provision Regulations. The provisions of art. 9 are quite general and common to many European funds. This occurs because the European Commission in its first proposal for these thematic objectives aimed at prioritising expenditure toward defined general objectives, such as

- strengthening research, technological development, innovation;
- enhancing access to and use and quality of ICT;
- enhancing the competitiveness of SMEs;
- supporting the shift towards a low-carbon economy in all sectors;
- promoting climate change adaptation, risk prevention and management;
- preserving and protecting the environment and promoting resource efficiency;
- promoting sustainable transport and removing bottlenecks in key network infrastructures;
- promoting sustainable and quality employment, supporting labour mobility;
- promoting social inclusion and combating poverty and discrimination;
- investing in education, training and vocational training for skills and lifelong learning;
- enhancing institutional capacity of public authorities.

Secondly, the ex ante conditionalities were assessed in terms of training needs. In fact, these are considered a key mechanism to ensure that member states can provide an appropriate policy, legal and administrative framework for the effectiveness of ESI funds. Many studies have clearly assessed how relevant it is to have the necessary capabilities for understanding and working out certain tasks (innovation, infrastructure and so forth). Therefore, it is necessary to have clear feedbacks from managing authorities regarding the ex ante conditionalities which they are able to fulfil. Should they not be able to, it is important to provide the assistance needed.

The general ex ante conditionalities concern

- *Antidiscrimination*: The existence of a mechanism which ensures effective implementation and application of directive 2000/78/EC of 27 November 2000 establishing a general framework for equal treatment in employment and occupation and directive 2000/43/EC of 29 June 2000 implementing the principle of equal treatment between persons irrespective of racial or ethnic origin.
- *Gender equality*: The existence of a strategy for the promotion of gender equality and a mechanism which ensures its effective implementation.
- *Disability*: The existence of a mechanism which ensures effective implementation and application of the UN Convention on the rights of persons with disabilities.
- *Public procurement*: The existence of arrangements for the effective application of EU public procurement law in the field of the CSF funds.
- *State aid*: The existence of arrangements for the effective application of EU state aid law in the field of the CSF funds.
- *Environmental legislation relating to environmental impact assessment (EIA) and strategic environmental assessment (SEA)*: The existence of arrangements for the effective application of union environmental legislation related to EIA and SEA.
- *Statistical system and result indicators*: The existence of a statistical basis necessary to undertake evaluations to assess the effectiveness and impact of the programs. The existence of a system of result indicators necessary to select actions which most effectively contribute to desired results, to monitor progress towards results and to undertake impact evaluation.

The last part of the survey was devoted to an in-depth assessment of training needs divided by topics. Therefore, for each "macro" topic – such as programming, management, implementation, evaluation and monitoring and financial management and control of the operational management – managing authorities were asked in which ambit they needed assistance or, if capable, whether they would provide such assistance to other actors involved in the process. This part is crucial for assessing the managing authorities' capabilities and for understanding if they would be able to deliver a good service to the final beneficiaries and the actors (i.e., SMEs) wanting to deal with European funds. The results of this survey enable to draw a general picture of the managing authorities' training needs. Moreover, it enables to address their lacks more effectively in terms of knowledge. The outcome of each part of the questionnaire will be further analysed in later sections.

5.4 The sample used

With the beginning of the new programming period and considering both the challenges and the problems faced during the previous one, DG Regio tried to understand which might be the lacks in terms of capabilities of the actors involved in the process of implementing, monitoring, auditing and certifying projects financed by European funds. The survey was sent to 500 representatives of managing authorities through unique links (i.e., links accessible only by the email address owner) in order to reach every region of each member state and understand, according to their practical experience in the field, to what extent and in which areas they would like to receive assistance.

Considering the nature of this survey and the specific questions asked concerning the actual level of capabilities owned by the organisation, only the employees aware of the internal capability level were able to reply consistently. Therefore, the level of knowledge required to answer the survey made the collection of responses rather difficult. To provide a better understanding of the results analysed in the following section, it is useful to consider some numbers. Hence, some data concerning DG Regio's survey are provided as follows: 410 email addresses, 130 surveys received before the deadline, return rate 31 per cent, 27 countries reached.

Considering that the survey examines specific topics, it is not surprising that of 410 unique email addresses, only 130 actually completed the survey. In fact, the information required was far beyond the awareness level expected from a common employee. Indeed, in most cases, all levels of the organisation were involved in an inner self-evaluating process. In this scenario, a higher return level could not be expected, precisely because of the amount of knowledge needed to assess in depth the skills owned. Managing authorities are usually very complex organisations, and to know inner strengths and weaknesses perfectly can be a difficult task that necessarily involves the entire organisation and requires quite a lot of time. Moreover, although English is nowadays very unlikely to be considered a "barrier", in this context it might have contributed to the low ratio of replies and discouraged some "recipients" from taking part in the survey.

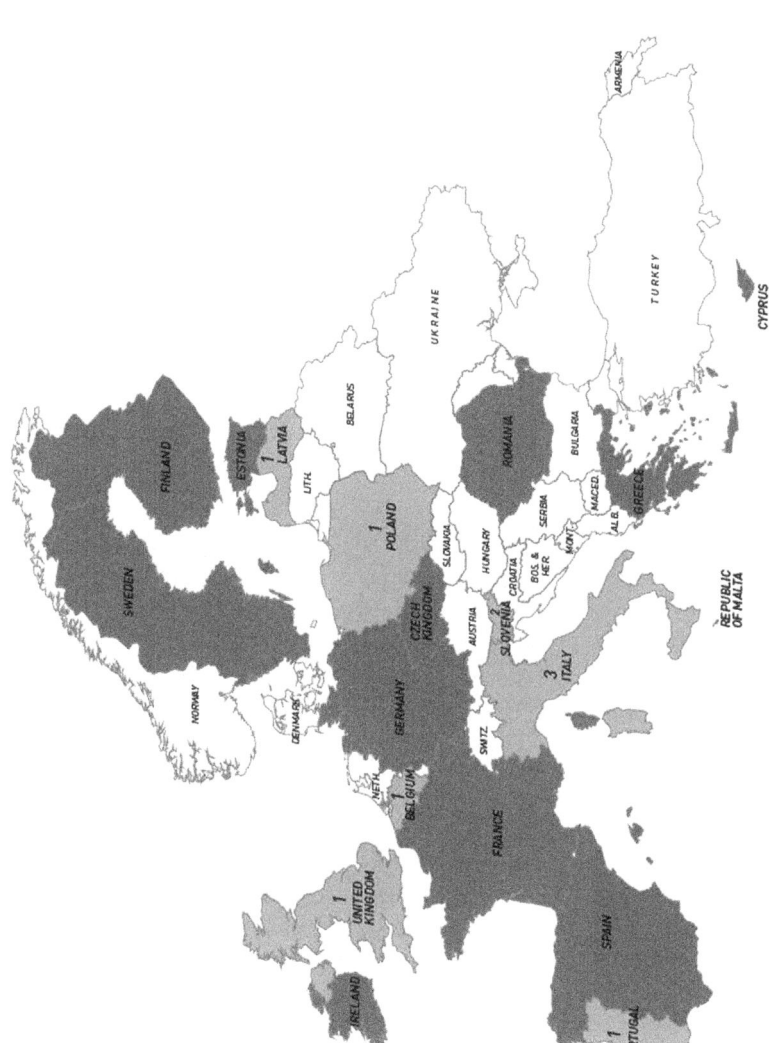

Figure 5.4 The sample used
Source: Author's elaboration.

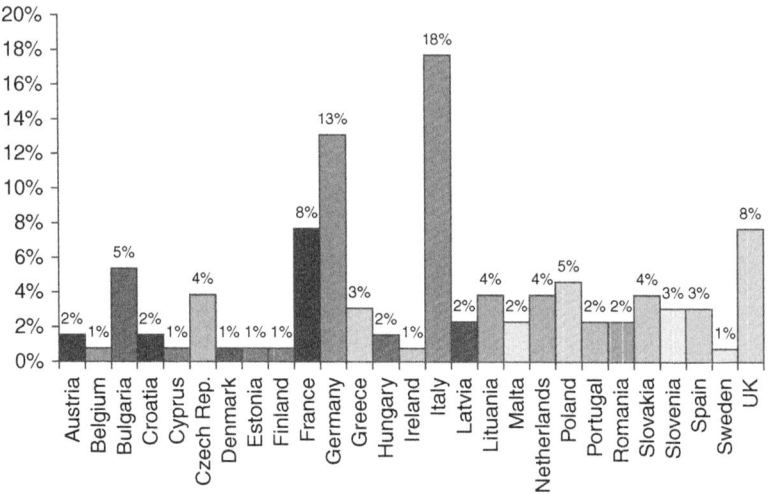

Chart 5.1 Geographical distribution of replies
Source: Authors' elaboration based on the survey's data.

Chart 5.1 represents the replies received per country. At an early stage, it is possible to see that Italy (18 per cent), Germany (13 per cent), together with the UK and France (both with the same number of replies), represent almost 50 per cent of the total. "The Managing Authority is usually either a strong central Ministry in the case of CSF and Objective 1 countries, or one of the line Ministries in the case of specific funds, OPs or ROPs" (2003, p. 68).[8]

In this context, the size of each country certainly played an important role in terms of number of replies. In fact, the managing authorities are regional organisations often embodied in the state's bureaus. Therefore, the high number of regions existing in the country can be the main reason for this disparity. However, despite the problems faced, the questionnaire produced enough data to draw interesting conclusions and especially provide a quite clear overview of managing authorities' training needs. Therefore, owing to this survey, it is possible to channel the European Commission's efforts more effectively in terms of training.

5.5 Main results

This section highlights the main outcomes. Thus, starting from the assessment of the training needs divided by thematic objectives – according to which managing authorities were asked in which areas they needed assistance – the results of the analysis develops toward ex ante conditionalities. The last part, instead, concerns very specific needs in terms of programming, management, implementation, evaluation and monitoring and financial management and control of the operational management.

5.5.1 Thematic objectives

Chart 5.2 represents the outcome of a general question concerning the thematic provisions stated in art. 9 of the Common Provision Regulations (CPR). As briefly described in Section 5.4, the CPR identifies eleven thematic objectives common to

- the European Regional Development Fund (ERDF);
- the European Social Fund (ESF);
- the Cohesion Fund (CF);
- the European Agricultural Fund for Rural Development (EAFRD);
- the European Maritime and Fisheries Fund (EMFF).

These different funds are established for pursuing common policy objectives, and their management is up to member states and the commission. Indeed, they represent one of the main sources of investments at EU level enabling member states to increase economic growth and sustainable development. "The Commission considers that they can be more effectively pursued if the five Funds are better coordinated to avoid overlaps and maximize synergies, integrated fully into the economic governance of the European Union, and contribute to the delivery of Europe 2020 by engaging national, regional and local stakeholders".[9]

The thematic objectives, as mentioned above, are definitely crucial for managing authorities and for the effective implementation of the resources available for the programming period 2014–2020. Therefore, an in-depth analysis of the results on this topic is crucial.

Chart 5.1 highlights the need for further assistance and training for all the thematic objectives. Especially in areas such as "Strengthening research, technological development innovation" and "Enhancing institutional capacity of public authorities", it is easy to notice that among the answers to the questions on the thematic objectives 46 per cent of the participants for the former and 52 per cent for the latter, respectively, indicated the need for assistance.

Another aspect on which it is important to focus attention concerns SMEs, more specifically "Enhancing the competitiveness of SMEs",

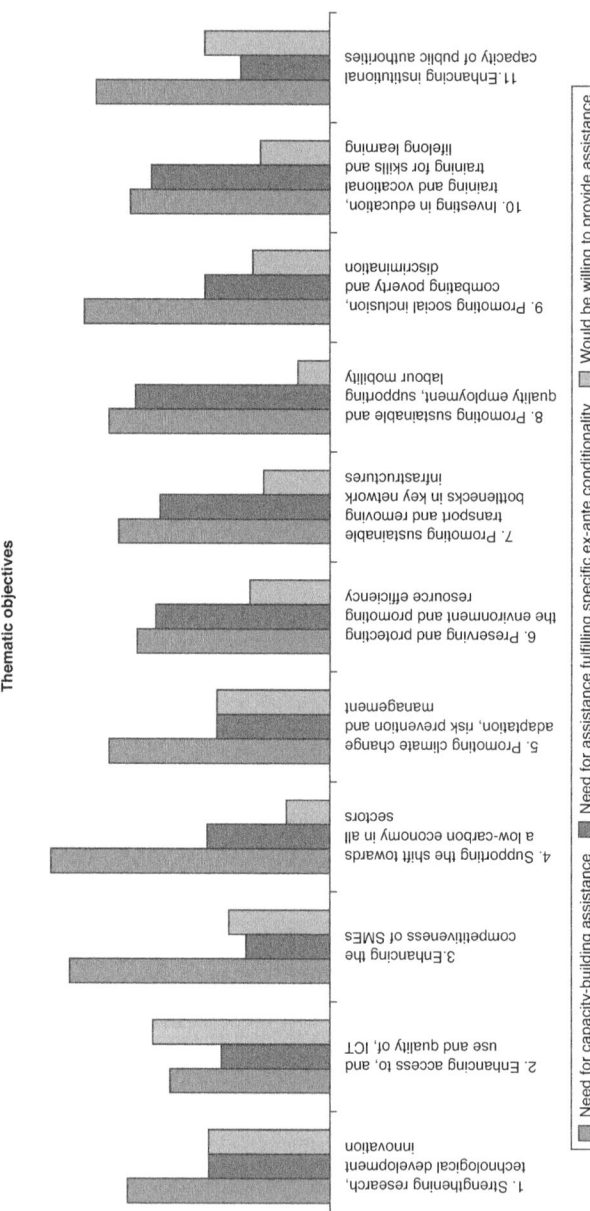

Chart 5.2 Thematic objectives

Source: Authors' elaboration based on the survey's data.

as well as "Supporting the shift towards a low-carbon economy in all sectors". The majority, 60 per cent and 63 per cent, respectively, indicated the need for assistance in these fields. This result highlights that the great majority of managing authorities does not think it has enough capabilities to achieve these important thematic objectives. This lack of capabilities can also be stressed by the fact that just 20 per cent of the organisations that answered this question consider themselves able to provide assistance to other organisations.

Nonetheless, the picture is not totally negative; in fact, regarding, for example, the thematic objective "Enhancing access to, and use and quality of, ICT", 40 per cent of the managing authorities replying that they would provide assistance. Hence, concerning the above-mentioned topic and some others, it is possible to find organisations capable of providing assistance; of course, to the extent of what they think about themselves. After focusing the attention on several specific aspects of the questionnaire, it is possible to adopt a general approach in order to have a broader picture of the results concerning the thematic objectives. Chart 5.1 highlights that in almost every topic taken into account, managing authorities are much more likely to ask for assistance instead of giving assistance. This means that there is a further need for training on thematic objectives. Therefore, the European Commission should consider this result as a "tip" for planning training more effectively in order to prepare the actors for the upcoming programming period and, in doing so, contribute to a higher absorption level in each member state.

5.5.2 Ex ante conditionalities

As suggested by the name itself, general ex ante conditionalities are criteria applicable to every sector and policy. The aim of the general ex ante conditionalities is to set up a balanced framework in which European funds can be implemented more efficiently. They concern antidiscrimination, gender equality, disability, public procurement, state aid, environmental impact assessment, statistical systems and result indicators.

As shown in Chart 5.3, the situation regarding ex ante conditionalities is slightly clearer compared with Chart 5.2. In fact, while in the thematic objectives' area there is a widespread need for assistance, concerning the general ex ante conditionalities it is possible to identify the specific topics that require more attention. For example, as regards antidiscrimination, gender equality and disability conditionality, it is possible to observe that roughly 60 per cent of the participants that

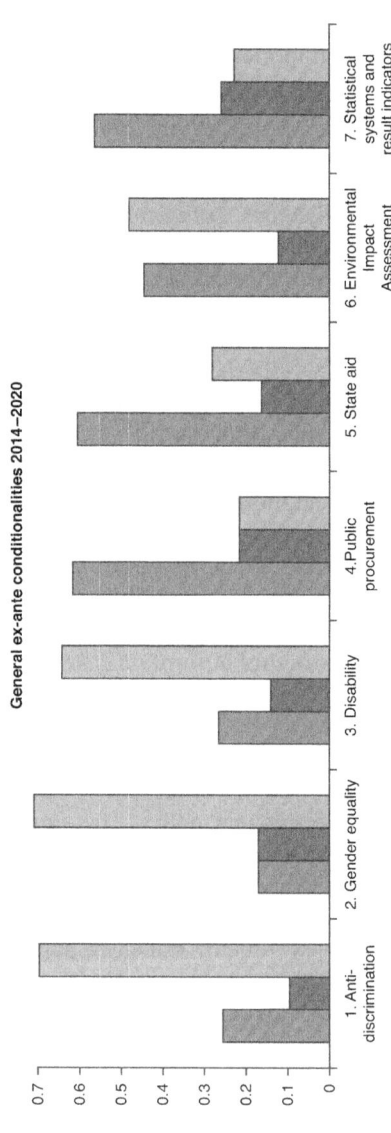

Chart 5.3 Ex ante conditionalities

answered this question marked "no need" for assistance. It is therefore correct to say that the majority of the managing authorities are quite confident on these topics. Nevertheless, this is not the only aspect that can be inferred from Chart 5.3. In fact, from observing this figure, it is also clear that in the case of topics such as public procurement (with 60 per cent of the total responses for need for capacity building assistance), state aid (with 58 per cent) and statistical systems (with 54 per cent), managing authorities expressed a general tendency of need for assistance.

5.5.3 Programming

As discussed earlier, the managing authorities' needs for assistance were analysed. In order to better understand the relevance of this topic, it may be useful to start with a consideration: "As well as being a core principle, Programming is a key management tool. Conducted on a multi-annual basis, it involves the determination of objectives to be achieved against the background of an analysis of the socio-economic context, and the identification of Priorities and Measures capable of converting these objectives into forms of intervention, or projects, that will deliver the outcomes desired" (Herta Tödtling-Schönhofer [ÖIR], Pat Colgan [ÖIR], Haris Martinos [LRDP], Begona Sanches [IDOM], 2003, p. 13).[10] In this regard, the participants were asked on what basis they chose the thematic objectives for whose tasks they needed assistance the most.

The first graph on programming (Chart 5.4) shows clear data highlighting recipients' general propensity toward need for assistance on programming. The data collected are as follows:

- Setting up financial instruments (implementing modalities): 91 per cent of total responses state "need for assistance".
- Developing and implementing strategies and plans in relation to the e-Cohesion: 81 per cent of total responses state "need for assistance".
- Establishing a performance framework: almost 93 per cent marked "need for assistance".
- All tasks related to programming: in this case, almost 64 per cent of the total responses stated "need for assistance".

Chart 5.5 highlights that managing authorities, at least those that answered this question, need help in managing this task. However, this is not a bad result. In fact, now it is possible for the European Commission

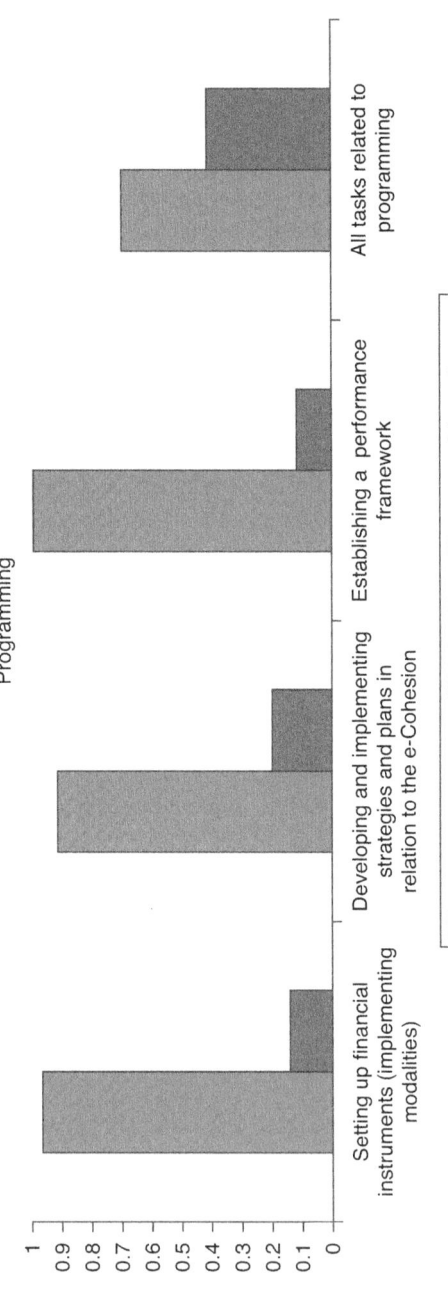

Chart 5.4 Programming, management, implementation, evaluation and monitoring and financial management and control of the operational management

Source: Authors' elaboration based on the survey's data.

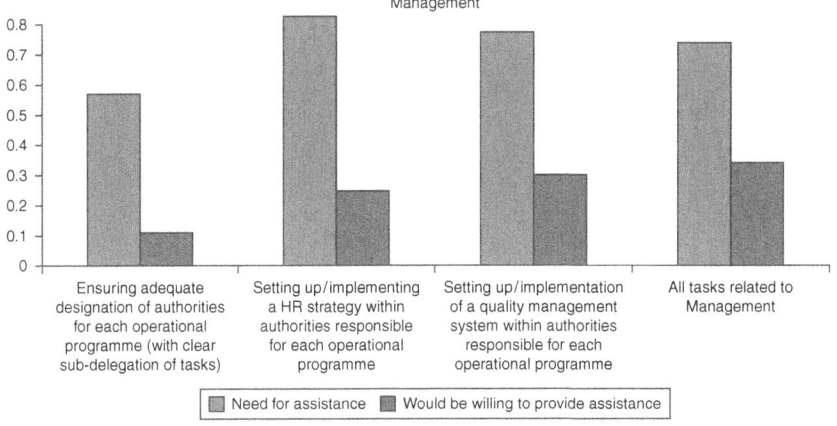

Chart 5.5 Management
Source: Authors' elaboration based on the survey's data.

to address the lack of capabilities that make managing authorities feel dubious or unable to provide assistance as regards a more effective and efficient "programming".

5.5.4 Management

Chart 5.6 confirms the general trend discussed above but with slightly different data. In fact, as regards the choices "Setting up/implementing a HR strategy within authorities responsible for each operational program" and "Setting up/implementation of a quality management system within authorities responsible for each operational program", it is possible to observe that for the former, almost 74 per cent of those that replied to this question marked "need for assistance", and almost 80 per cent did the same for the latter. As regards "Ensuring adequate designation of authorities for each operational programme (with clear subdelegation of tasks)", it is possible to observe that almost 53 per cent chose "need for assistance", while 47 per cent stated they were able to provide assistance. Therefore, in this respect it is necessary to increase the level of capabilities of managing authorities, even if not to the same extent as regards the programming task.

Chart 5.6 provides data on implementation; in other words, it shows whether managing authorities think they are capable of implementing European funds or need assistance. This task can be considered the one

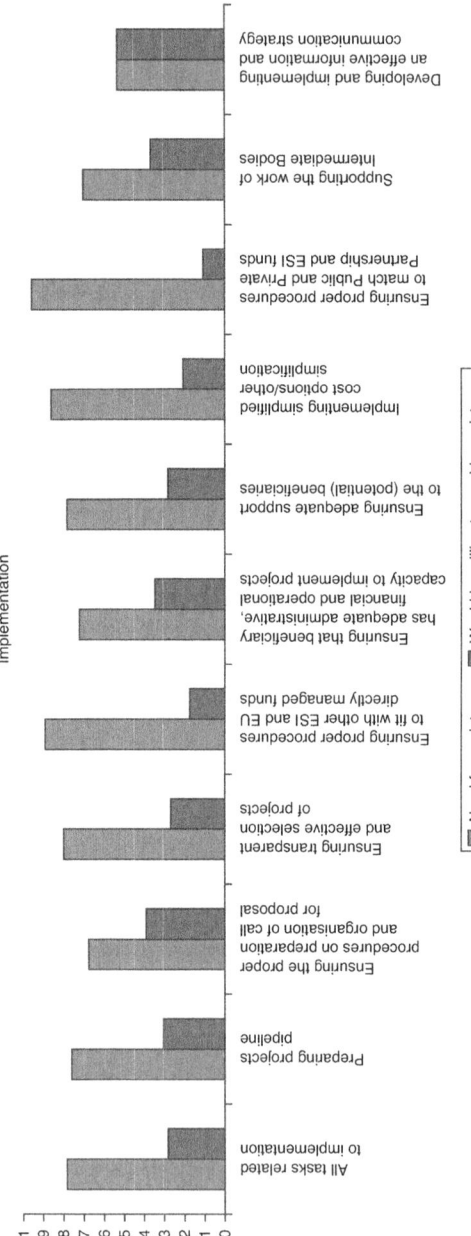

Chart 5.6 Implementation
Source: Authors' elaboration based on the survey's data.

that influences most directly the absorption of ESI funds; therefore each response deserves to be analysed.

- *Preparing projects pipeline*: concerning this topic, 75 per cent of the total responses stated "need assistance".
- *Ensuring the proper procedures on preparation and organisation of call for proposal*: here 72 per cent of the participants replied "need assistance".
- *Ensuring transparent and effective selection of projects*: also in this case, 64 per cent marked "need assistance".
- *Ensuring proper procedures to fit with other ESI and EU directly managed funds*: as regards the effective coordination with other direct funds, 85 per cent of repliers marked "need assistance"..
- *Ensuring that beneficiary has adequate administrative, financial and operational capacity to implement projects*: not to the same extent as other replies, but also here the majority of respondents (68 per cent) answered "need assistance".
- *Ensuring adequate support to the (potential) beneficiaries*: concerning the support to beneficiaries, almost 75 per cent marked "need assistance".
- *Implementing simplified cost options/other simplification*: in this case, 82 per cent of the participants replied "need assistance".
- *Ensuring proper procedures to match public and private partnership and ESI funds*: 92 per cent, in this case.
- *Supporting the work of intermediate bodies*: also concerning this topic, 66 per cent of the total responses stated "need assistance".
- *Developing and implementing an effective information and communication strategy*: this topic is the only one within the implementation task where the situation is balanced; 50 per cent chose "need assistance" and the other 50 per cent "would be willing to provide assistance".

Implementation is one of the most important tasks that positively or negatively affects the level of absorption and the actual "use" of European funds; nonetheless, in this field, managing authorities show a deep need for assistance in order to implement, plan and coordinate ESI funds.

5.5.5 Evaluation and monitoring

"Feedback complements the use of strategic objectives and decentralized implementation processes. Feedback systems should be improved to produce consistent monitoring and evaluation systems, which include transnational thematic evaluations by the Commission. Strict financial control would also become more important" (Lang et al., 1998, p. 5).[11] The European Commission's approach is based on the collection of data and feedback in order to modify and enhance how the European funds are managed and implemented. In this light, evaluation and monitoring have acquired increasing value across the years. Nonetheless, Chart 5.7 reflects a further need for training. Especially for topics such as "Setting up a system to gather reliable financial and statistical information on implementation" and "Drawing up an evaluation plan and executing evaluations, including evaluations to assess effectiveness, efficiency and impact of a programme", it is possible to see that both – the former with 88 per cent and the latter with 66 per cent – express an important need for additional assistance. These data are very important because the improvement of the effectiveness of ESI funds goes hand in hand with data collection and feedback. Therefore, it is necessary to respond to a request for assistance in order to have progress in the European funds framework.

5.5.6 Financial management and control of the operational management

Chart 5.8 represents the outcome of the task related to "financial management and control of the operational management". In this case, it is possible to see how the opinions collected are different for each area. In fact, as shown in the graph, in areas such as "Putting in place effective and proportionate anti-fraud measures", the majority (90 per cent of those that replied) needs assistance, and in areas connected to "all tasks related to financial management and control of the Operational management", 77 per cent of the people who replied pointed out an overall need for assistance. While these results can be easily interpreted because of the strong consensus of the need for assistance expressed by the recipients, the situation is quite different for other tasks; some of the recipients would like to receive assistance, but some others would like to offer it. In fact, it is possible to see how – for example, in the task "Ensuring proper procedures for administrative verifications and treatment of application for reimbursement, authorization of payments, and on-the-spot verifications" – 64 per cent of participants stated they would provide assistance. By adopting this option, they assume they are capable enough to fulfil this task and eventually provide assistance to external actors. Also, concerning "Monitoring the results of the management verifications and audit results", the data show how the situation is quite balanced, and thus, by creating an efficient network, managing authorities would be able to support each other in carrying out this task.

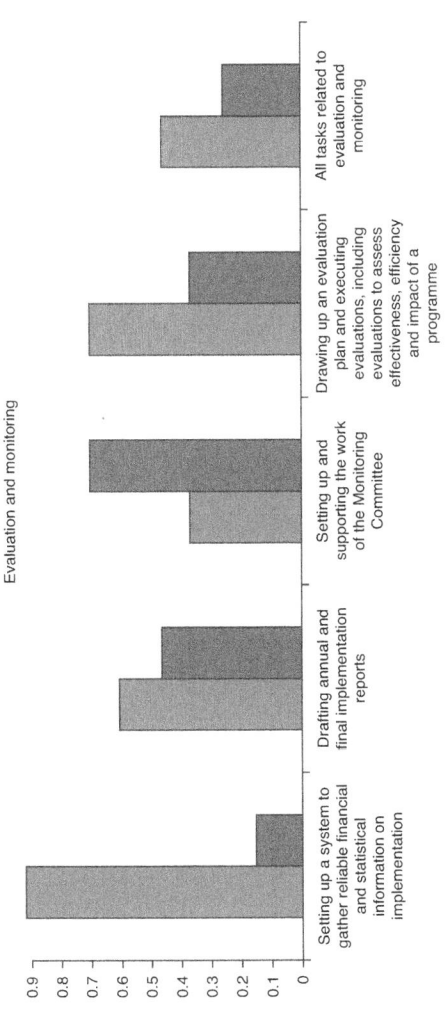

Chart 5.7 Evaluation and monitoring

Source: Authors' elaboration based on the survey's data.

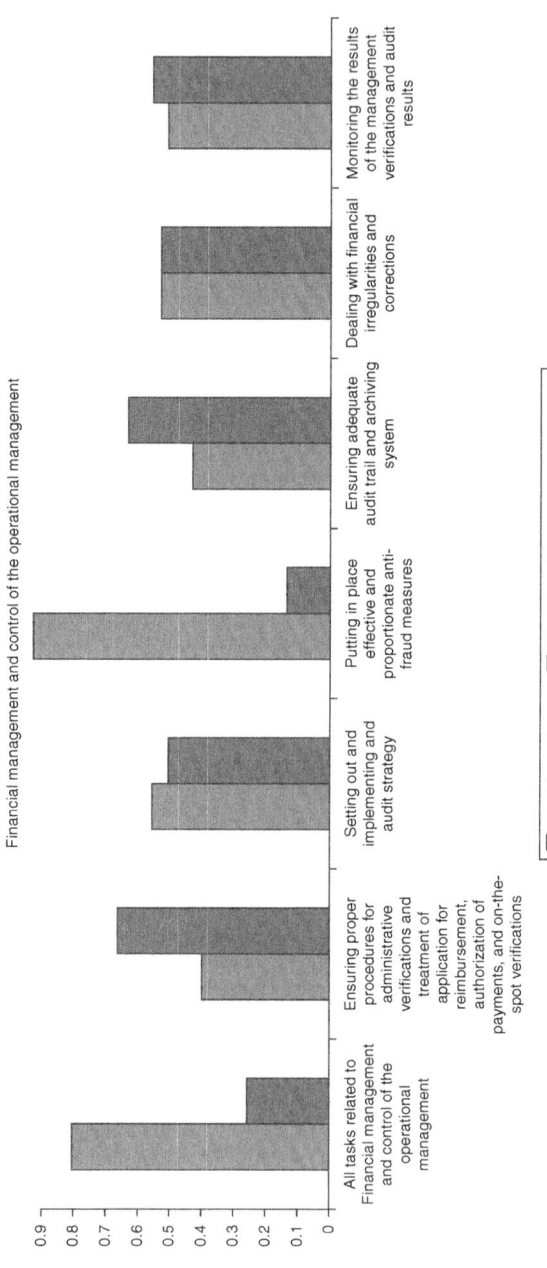

Chart 5.8 Financial management and control of the operational management

Source: Authors' elaboration based on the survey's data.

5.6 Conclusions on first survey

It is difficult to assess the training needs of intermediate bodies. It is even more difficult when taking into account that often these organisations are within bigger public administrative bodies. Indeed, this scenario makes the inner self-assessment process rather slow and hard to pursue. Nonetheless, the survey – carried out by DG Regio – produced very clear and important results for channelling the European Commission's training efforts more effectively. The theory according to which a highly skilled and independent bureaucracy is crucial for driving the economy toward innovation and therefore economic growth[12] can further clarify, if necessary, the relevance of this study and the importance of the capability level of intermediate bodies. Indeed, these are the most important actors for an efficient and effective implementation of public funds; therefore, for enhancing the impact on the real economy, the starting point can actually be training. The DG Regio survey does its part by highlighting the managing authorities' need for assistance, in other words training, throughout the EU. Owing to the data collected, it is possible for the commission to know how to fill the knowledge and capabilities gaps and make the EU's intermediate bodies able to fulfil the challenges put in place by the new programming period 2014–2020 and face the eurozone's still stagnant economic condition.

5.7 Second survey: aims, investigation areas and sample used

While the first questionnaire focused on the MAs' general capacity building in Europe, with the second questionnaire the Italian National Agency for Microcredit, within the Capacity Building project, sought to acquire information on the specific capacity building of the EU member countries in the microfinance sector for the following reasons:

- The microfinance sector is playing an increasingly strategic role following the economic slowdown and crisis that gripped several European countries and produced a growing number of financially excluded subjects (socially excluded as well).[13]
- The EU cohesion policy stresses the need for smart, sustainable and inclusive growth of population targets who struggle to be actively part of their social and economic contexts as well as the MAs' necessity to establish clear, transparent and measurable objectives.

The workgroup of the Capacity Building project of the Italian National Agency for Microcredit decided to verify the state of the art of the MAs' capacity building in terms of programming, monitoring, measurement/assessment of activity in the microfinance/microcredit programmes. In this perspective, the workgroup designed a questionnaire that started from a few key questions: "Did the MAs carry out measuring and monitoring activities on the micro-finance programmes? Do they own data on projects activated, loan amounts, etc.? What are the target beneficiaries of the programmes? Is there a regulatory framework on the micro-credit and micro-finance sector?" These questions constituted the guidelines used by the workgroup to elaborate the four investigation areas presented herein (see Section 5.1): *(1) analysis of the main results of the microcredit/microfinance programming activity; (2) target group and other operational features; (3) monitoring and reporting activities; (4) regulatory framework of microcredit/microfinance sector and others.* The questionnaire was prepared following meetings and discussions on the topics analysed by making use of all expertise and skills developed in the microfinance sector; the questionnaire underwent a preliminary testing phase in order to tweak and improve the questions; then it was sent by mail to the recipients, and they were contacted by phone to complete it – all over a period of two months. According to a precise choice of the workgroup, the questionnaire collected data related to the period 2011–2013.

The questionnaire was sent to the following countries: Belgium, Cyprus, Estonia, Finland, France, Germany, Greece, Ireland, Italy, Latvia, Malta, Poland, Portugal, United Kingdom, Czech Republic, Romania, Slovenia, Spain, Sweden. In some cases, multiple MAs were contacted within the same country, for instance Italy, where the questionnaire was sent to the four regions involved in the former convergence programme (Campania, Calabria, Apulia, Sicily). The questionnaire was administered by contacting the recipients by email and telephone. The response rate has been very low (see Figure 5.4); this does not allow us to infer statistically valid and solid observations on the topics investigated but only to lay down some preliminary considerations. The scarce number of questionnaires filled (just nine) is also the result of an objective difficulty of the MAs to find the required data and, most likely, also a sign of their poor reporting and monitoring activity on the microfinance programmes implemented.

These preliminary findings lead us to consider this questionnaire a work in progress to be sent again to the MAs in a few years, when hopefully the cohesion policy will prompt the member states to put greater attention to monitoring and measuring the social and economic impact produced by the funds provided by the European Commission. Likewise, the member states will hopefully focus on their reporting activity as well as on measuring and assessing results achieved.

However, this second empirical analysis provided an opportunity to reflect on the weaknesses of the structural funds management methods of the member states.

5.8 The main results of the survey: first considerations

This section highlights the main outcomes of the second survey; more precisely, it offers some reflections on the items analysed within the reference period (2011–2013) and the four investigation areas. Not all questions contained in the questionnaire were processed and presented in the tables below; we focused only on the ones that received the most answers.

5.8.1 Analysis of the main results of the microcredit/ microfinance programming activity

According to the nine questionnaires available, we can observe a growing number of microcredit programmes activated in the period investigated (Table 5.1); some of the countries that returned the completed questionnaire claimed that they did not activate any specific programme dedicated to the microcredit/microfinance sector in the three-year period analysed.

Table 5.2 shows instead that the total amounts of the loans granted under these programmes vary considerably from one country to another; for each one of these, the capacity building workgroup showed not just the total amount of loans granted (economic additionality) but also other results worth mentioning. The answers to this question are integrally presented in Table 5.3, which shows that the answer sought was often not provided. The main reason most likely lies in a lack of monitoring on the projects and programmes activated that could measure their social and economic impact. This is one of the criticalities specifically addressed by the new EU cohesion policy, which regards monitoring, measuring and reporting as some of the most strategic and critical phases of the entire programming activity.

The workgroup tried also to use the questionnaire to get an understanding of the type of microcredit programmes activated in the three-year period (entrepreneurial microcredit/social microcredit) as well as the beneficiary target groups of the microcredit/microfinance programmes.

Table 5.1 Programmes activated

How many microcredit/microfinance programmes have been implemented by your institution during the last three years (2011–2013)?	2011	2012	2013
Belgium	n/a	n/a	n/a
Italy (Sicily)		1	1
Italy (Campania)		1	1
Italy (Apulia)		1	1
Latvia	1: Microlending programme 1: Latvian Swiss microlending programme		1: Latvian Swiss microlending programme
Poland	n/a	n/a	2
Portugal	1: Azorean Scheme Support for microcredit based on banking loans	1: Azorean Scheme Support for microcredit based on banking loans	7: Azorean Scheme Support for microcredit based on banking loans
Slovenia (Maribor)	n/a	n/a	n/a
Slovenia (Ljubljana)	n/a	n/a	n/a
Wales	1: Delivery of JEREMIE microfund	2: Delivery of JEREMIE microfund Launch of Wales Micro-Business Loan Fund	2: Delivery of JEREMIE microfund Delivery of Wales Micro-Business Loan Fund
Total	4	6	15

Source: Authors' elaboration based on the survey's data.

Most MAs that were administered the questionnaires declared that 80 per cent of the programmes activated are entrepreneurial microcredit, and 60 per cent of them seem to be dedicated to bankable subjects. Some MAs clearly say that they have no clue about the bankability of the subjects financed: "We do not monitor and do not have any evidence whether enterprises are in a position to get the bank loans or not".

Table 5.2 Total amount of programmes activated

What is the total loan amount related to the microcredit/microfinance programmes disbursed in each of the last 3 years (2011–2013)?	2011	2012	2013
Belgium	n/a	n/a	n/a
Italy (Sicily)		1,554,281.00	Monitoring as of 30 June 2013. The total amount of loans disbursed including those granted in 2012 is 1,887,001.00
Italy (Campania)	n/a	n/a	9,516,190.90
Italy (Apulia)			365,167.45
Latvia	1,313,000	3,662,000	1,962,000
	n/a	n/a	n/a
Poland	n/a	n/a	Around €1 million
Portugal	27,611	59,361	112,178
Slovenia (Maribor)	5,000,000	n/a	n/a
Slovenia (Ljubljana)	n/a	n/a	n/a
Wales	496,995	95,613	1,988,282

Source: Authors' elaboration based on the survey's data.

Table 5.3 Other main results

What are the main results of your microcredit/microfinance programmes that you could highlight?	
Belgium	n/a
Italy (Sicily)	According to the 2012 results, the instrument of social microcredit pursuant to art. 25 of regional law no. 6/2009, as subsequently modified and amended, mainly met the need to support household expenditure for life projects aimed at developing and/or improving their social and economic conditions and to implement measures ensuring access to credit for households as well as the provision of decent housing with the minimum facilities to ensure dignified living
Italy (Campania)	Results cannot be evaluated at the moment

(*Continued*)

Table 5.3 (Continued)

What are the main results of your microcredit/microfinance programmes that you could highlight?	
Italy (Apulia)	The Microcredit Fund for Enterprises of the Region Apulia is provided under the Multiannual Operational Programme of Implementation of the PO FSE 2007–2013 (Axis II "Employability") with the objective to ensure access to credit to non-bankable subjects who have good investment ideas. 324 preliminary applications were completed online. They generated a total request for funding amounting to €7,194,940.68. The average loan requested per application is €22,206.60. 426 preliminary applications are being processed on the Apulia System (Sistema Puglia) portal. As of 31 December 2013, the first 315 applications submitted were checked for eligibility purposes, with the following outcome: 82 applications cannot be processed; 233 applications can be processed Out of the 233 applications that can be processed, for 169 of them interviews were held and requests for loan were formalised. Out of these applications, 90 were accepted, 33 were not accepted, and 27 applicants dropped their requests. Currently, 22 applications are being examined. Decisions to grant loans were approved for 90 enterprises. Total loan amount granted so far amounts to €365,167.45 for 16 enterprises
Latvia	Improved access to finance (both for investment and current assets) for microbusinesses, especially in rural areas; approximately 2,000 safeguarded or newly created jobs

Poland	1. The SEE Support Programme (the programme has been activated in March 2013):
	   – 51 loans granted to Social Economy Enterprises (SEE)
	   – Executed 17% of allocation of the SEE Support Programme
	   – Loans granted under 5 separate loan funds covering the whole area of Poland and loans granted directly to SEEs
	2. The start-ups support project:
	   – The project has been implemented for 6 months so far
	3. Loan funds for start-ups were established (start-up support project financed by national public funds).

Portugal	Allows for access to credit, creation of self-employment activities, development of personal projects, financial survival of families
Slovenia (Maribor)	Total of 212 micro and small enterprises supported
Slovenia (Ljubljana)	We did not have a financial instrument like microloans; with regard to financial engineering instruments, we implemented interest rate subsidies, guarantees and a joint venture scheme (repayable aid) through financial engineering instruments
Wales	n/a

Source: Authors' elaboration based on the survey's data.

Table 5.4 Target of the microcredit programmes

Years	Unemployed or people on welfare	Women	Young people (18–30 years old)
2011	X, X	X	X
2012	X	X	X
2013	X, X, X	X	X

Source: Authors' elaboration based on the survey's data.

Most microcredit/microfinance programmes activated in the 2011–2013 period were dedicated to unemployed individuals or people on welfare, women or young people, as shown by Table 5.4.

During the research, we also tried to investigate the kind of networks the MAs implemented for activation of the programmes; so we asked them to indicate what other institutions (banks, credit guarantee schemes, other financial corporations, etc.) were involved and the roles they played in the programme. The Latvian MA pointed out that "In both the previous and the current Micro-lending Programme, the bank is directly involved, with the exclusion of any other institutions". Generally, the most mentioned subjects were public regional financial companies and banking intermediaries. Companies/institutions providing non-financial services were never mentioned, probably due to scarce awareness that such services are strictly complementary to provision of credit.

Generally, the microcredit/microfinance programmes were activated to provide personal guarantees to support loans or, alternatively, guarantees required for loan disbursement purposes; in just one case (microloans for micro and small enterprises: Slovene-Ljubljana Programme) two bills were required, and in another one the publicly financed fund to cover the first loss of an operation was activated for small business enterprises (Slovene-Maribor).

Question 12 was aimed at identifying the financing methods of the microcredit programmes activated. Table 5.5 shows the clear reliance of these programmes on public funds – a peculiar yet common occurrence in the microcredit sector.

A few interesting answers were provided on features of the programmes that the MAs would like to change; some of them, in fact, pointed out a need for "more promotion of entrepreneurship, more entrepreneurship training in order to provide the skills needed to create a business".

Table 5.5 Financing methods

Mark with an X the financing method for each program	Programme name (write the year of execution in brackets)	Private and public funds	Structural funds (specify)	Other (specify)
Belgium	n/a			
Italy (Sicily)	Microcredit for families pursuant to art. 25 of the regional law no. 6/2009 as subsequently modified and amended (period 2012–2013)			
Italy (Campania)	ESF Microcredit Fund (2012)		ESF	
	ESF Microcredit Fund (2013)		ESF	
Italy (Apulia)	Microcredit for Enterprises of the Region Apulia (2012/2013)		ESF	
Latvia	Microlending programme	X		
	Latvian Swiss microlending programme	X		
Poland	The SEE Support Programme (2020)		ESF	
	The start-ups support project (2023)			
Portugal	Azorean scheme support for microcredit based on banking loans 2006–2013	X		
Slovenia (Maribor)	Microloans for micro and small enterprises (2013)		X (for the coverage of first loss)	
Slovenia (Ljubljana)	ERDF (2007–2013)	X	X	
Wales	JEREMIE micro fund	X	X (JEREMIE)	
	Wales Micro-Business Loan Fund			

Source: Authors' elaboration based on the survey's data.

5.8.2 Monitoring and reporting activities

All the MAs that filled the questionnaire claimed that they monitored and controlled the programmes activated, although such statements seem to collide with a clear lack of data on the social and economic impact of such programmes as requested by the questionnaire.

The question "describe how often the report is carried out as well as recording methods and data" was answered quite differently by the various MAs contacted (see Table 5.6); as a matter of fact, the table seems to indicate that the MAs are willing to monitor the activities only for the purpose of complying with the EU authorities, instead of considering it one of the strengths of the programmes. In particular, the Latvian MA pointed out that "the report contains both description of the progress and statistics of the microloans awarded (including regional dimension, branches, etc.), as well as detailed information on actual management costs (as these costs are fully covered by public funds)"; similarly, the Polish MA stated that "the report contains quantitative data concerning: loans, disbursements, borrowers, applications, state of a bank account, information and promotion, amortisation, vindication".

Almost all the MAs analysed activated a website dedicated to their microcredit/microfinance programme; in some cases though, such websites provided scarce information on the programme's details (Table 5.7).

5.8.3 Regulatory framework of microcredit/microfinance sector and other

Question 16 was aimed at understanding whether, in the MAs' opinion, their microcredit/microfinance programmes were or were not useful to tackle the current economic-financial crisis. Almost all MAs came up with a positive answer; the Welsh MA pointed out that "All applications for investment received by Finance Wales are from Welsh SMEs with growth aspirations, either from start-up business or existing companies. They approach Finance Wales if they have been unable to source the funding from traditional private sector sources. Finance Wales provides the 'gap' funding, as a result of the applicant being considered too high risk for the private sector or due to a lack of available security. As a result of the economic crisis the banks' appetite for risk has further diminished, increasing the need for Finance Wales provision. The businesses supported are looking to grow and safeguard and create local jobs". At the same time, the Latvian MA explained that in their opinion, "Every kind of micro-lending facilities, not only in the context of the crisis,

Table 5.6 Reporting activity: details

	Describe how often the report is carried out as well as recording methods and data
Belgium	
Italy (Sicily)	On a quarterly-basis
Italy (Campania)	Semi-annual periodic report sent to Igrue. Information is extracted from the MA database and sent on a specific format provided by the ministry
Italy (Apulia)	Semi-annual report containing the list of approved actions, including the following: loan amount, data on the enterprise supported (end beneficiary); list of unpaid instalments; loss to be absorbed by the fund; list of any amounts recovered; liquidity of the fund Semi-annual report monitoring financial and physical items including financial, physical and formal indicators as well as other information on the individual projects
Latvia	The project agreement requires submission of regular reports on a quarterly basis, as well as a yearly report at the beginning of each year. The reports contains both description of the progress and statistics of the microloans provided (including regional dimension, branches, etc.), as well as detailed information on actual management costs (as these costs are fully covered by public funds)
Poland	1. The SEE Support Programme: Reporting must be carried out at least on a quarterly basis through the web application form provided by the Polish Ministry for Infrastructure and Development; – quantitative data concerning loans, disbursements, borrowers, applications, state of a bank account, consulting, information and promotion, controlling, vindication 2. The start-ups support project: Reporting must be carried out at least on a quarterly basis using the Excel application form provided by the Ministry of Labour and Social Policy; – quantitative data concerning loans, disbursements, borrowers, applications, state of a bank account, information and promotion, amortisation, vindication
Portugal	Only statistical data
Slovenia (Maribor)	Reporting is carried out in accordance with the financial agreement with the Ministry of Economic Development and Technology: quarterly, yearly
Slovenia (Ljubljana)	We report to the EU Commission on the implementation of financial engineering instruments only on a quarterly-basis
Wales	Reporting required on a quarterly basis; reporting on investment performance and outputs

Source: Authors' elaboration based on the survey's data.

Table 5.7 Websites of the microcredit programmes activated

Italy (Sicily)	Microcredit for families start: 2012	http://pti.regione.sicilia.it/portal/page/portal/PIR_PORTALE/PIR_LaStrutturaRegionale/PIR_AssessoratoEconomia/PIR_Microcreditoperlefamigliesiciliane
Italy (Campania)	ESF Microcredit Fund (2012) ESF Microcredit Fund (2013)	http://microcreditofse.sviluppocampania.it/ http://microcreditofse.sviluppocampania.it/
Italy (Apulia)	Microcredit for Enterprises Region Apulia (2012/2013)	www.sistema.puglia.it/microcredito
Latvia		http://www.hipo.lv/lv/attistibas_programmas/mikrokreditesanas_programma http://www.swiss-contribution.admin.ch/latvia/en/Home/Projects/Approved_projects_in_detail?projectinfoID=201747#form2
Poland	The SEE Support Programme	www.bgk.com.pl/pes http://www.bgk.com.pl/43
	The start-ups support project EU financial instruments at BGK	www.bgk.com.pl/wsparcie-w-starcie http://www.bgk.com.pl/43
Portugal	Azorean scheme support for microcredit based on banking loans 2006–2013	http://www.azores.gov.pt/Portal/pt/entidades/vp-draic/textoTabela/Regime+de+apoio+ao+microcrédito+bancário.htm
Slovenia (Maribor)		www.podjetniskisklad.si
Slovenia (Ljubljana)	Slovenian Enterprise Fund (SEF) JEREMIE micro fund	www.podjetniskisklad.si
Wales	Wales Micro-Business Loan Fund	www.financewales.co.uk www.financewales.co.uk

Source: Authors' elaboration based on the survey's data.

is crucially important for the country. The current programme shows that there is a strong demand for micro-loans, especially in the countryside and smaller communities/ border regions. Implemented micro business projects provide jobs, create new ones, raise incomes for micro-enterprises and their families. Thus, these kinds of public support have positive economic as well as social effects". The Polish MA stated in the questionnaire that their programmes were aimed at supporting enterprises during the economic crisis. The SEE Support Programme's main goals are: support of SEE development (increasing incomes and/or skills of employees), creating a revolving financing system. The start-ups support project's main goals are youth entrepreneurship development and creation of new employment opportunities.

The MA from Slovenia (Maribor) indicated that "Micro-loans are dedicated to micro and small enterprises. The product prevents financial exclusion of micro and small enterprises. The eligible costs are: material investments and working capital". The MA from Ljubljana stated that the instruments activated were very helpful as they allowed SMEs to access financial sources and simplify the business environment. The MA from Sicily clarified that "The micro-credit programme for families under art. 25 of the Regional Law No. 6/2009, as subsequently amended and modified, is a useful instrument to prevent families facing economic difficulties from falling prey of loan sharks and usury".

The MA from Apulia provided a much more articulated answer to the question. In fact, it pointed out that "a significant obstacle hindering the economic development of our region lies in the difficulty to access credit for the local micro-enterprises, which, unlike their bigger competitors, are being affected by an increasingly scarcity of credit sources. In recent months, the problem has reached a critical point, to the extent of jeopardizing the very own existence of several businesses as well as generating severe impacts on their capability to retain their workers (for entrepreneurs and self-employed subjects alike). Even bigger is the impact on employment, with specific regard to youth. The impossibility to access credit, in fact, prevents companies from making new investments and, consequently, from hiring new workers. Demand for low-amount loans is high in the region, especially by small-sized businesses. An effective policy to support credit can help promote a new model of social and economic development in the region based on high human capital intensity and low environmental impact, with a specific focus on the role played by female and young entrepreneurs. Such policy will support entrepreneurship and the innovative and sustainable conversion of traditional activities, focusing on the human capital as the main productive factor".

We chose to quote the integral positions expressed by some of the MAs in the questionnaire as they provide the EU authorities with useful feedback for their future planning of activities.

Finally, we had the impression that the MAs contacted have poor knowledge or none at all of the regulatory framework on microcredit or microfinance, including aspects already covered by EU legislation (definition, eligible operators, eligibility requirements, etc.). Proof of this is that almost all of them did provide an answer when asked if there was a definition of microfinance and microcredit in their regulatory financial framework. The Welsh MA pointed out in the questionnaire that "There is no definition of microfinance or microcredit in the UK the Financial Conduct Authority. They, as well as other UK bodies including HMRC, define a 'micro-enterprise' as an enterprise that: employs fewer than ten persons; and has a turnover or annual balance sheet that does not exceed €2 million. An enterprise is any person engaged in an economic activity, including self-employed persons, family businesses, partnerships or associations".

On the same topic, the Latvian MA said: "The programmes implemented within the EU funds contain a definition of SMEs, including micro-enterprise, in accordance with Commission Regulation (EC) no. 800/2008 of 6 August 2008, declaring certain categories of aid compatible with the common market in compliance with arts 87 and 88 of the Treaty (general block exemption regulation)". However, there is no common definition for the terms "microfinance" and "microloans". Microfinancing is being implemented in accordance with the market practice. Likewise, there is no definition of the term "microcredit", although the programme regulations specify the maximum amount of the microloans.

5.9 Reflections on the second survey

Although not statistically solid, the second survey prompts some considerations on the current situation. It is clear that monitoring does not necessarily involve the production of a huge volume of documents and reports to comply with the EU authorities as normally happens; on the contrary, the monitoring phase should focus on and assess the impact of the use of structural funds over time. Using the ESF to fund several projects or using a great deal of EFS resources could be an alarming indicator if such resources are invested in harmful or useless projects;

claiming to have supported several companies to access credit is not the same thing as learning how to assess whether support is given to non-bankable or bankable subjects or not following their creditworthiness assessment (scoring/rating), the amount of the loans granted, their repayment terms and what kind of investments were supported through the loans and how many jobs they created.

For such purposes, it is necessary to build a monitoring system suitable to measure the programme's efficiency and use of public resources. From a methodological perspective, this translates into an integrated approach – from information to coaching – able to coordinate the efforts of all participants. This should be implemented in accordance with the objectives set within the Europe 2020 policy framework and reaffirmed by the European policy guidelines for the programming period 2014–2020, which encourage member states to devote public resources to economic development and social cohesion in a timely and efficient manner. Hence, the expected results in the surveyed countries need to be clearly defined and disseminated to both policymakers and end users in order to lead to a true open public debate. These recommendations are true for emerging countries as well as for the European sector, since our research has shown that the effectiveness and outreach of microcredit programmes in the latter is even more questionable. In any case, this is a delicate matter; it needs to be further investigated in order to substantially improve the policymakers' programming efforts.

In addition, the MAs must gain knowledge and use the financial instruments that can be activated thanks to the EU resources. Not just guarantees but also securitisation, microinsurance, housing microcredit, micro leasing, and the like. The programmes surveyed by this second survey provided loans through public financial entities or guarantees to support access to credit; the MAs must extend their range of products offered in accordance with the guidelines of the new programming period Europe 2020 and the needs of the market. In the current financial and economic crisis, it is necessary to adapt the products to the clientele in order to be able to best respond to their needs. This translates into a wider range of products, including customised tools. The MAs must develop and acquire specific skills dedicated to the financial instruments; the existing expertise has not always met the actual needs, and there has often been a lack of specific knowledge on financial instruments. The advantages of using such financial instruments have been repeatedly outlined in a number of reports, including Cowling (2010), ECA (2012), EC (2010, 2011, 2012a), EP (2012, 2012b), Michie and Wishlade (2011) and Ward (2012). The alleged advantages concern the following areas:

leverage effect; sustainability; capacity building; risk coverage; speeding up programme implementation; urban development. Such benefits must now be subjected to experiment by the operational practice, especially under the new programming period.

The MAs should also implement information systems on the programmes activated that could be easily accessed by the target beneficiaries. This would also improve their knowledge of the national regulatory frameworks on microfinance as well as the efficiency and effectiveness of EU resources; according to the few questionnaires completed, it seems that the MAs largely ignore the regulatory provisions in the microcredit/microfinance sector. In order to succeed, a specific programme dedicated to these sectors obviously entails the knowledge of their regulatory provisions. A definition of microcredit is shared by the EU member countries, but their regulatory frameworks do not include a definition of microfinance (the definition adopted by this research originates from business practice).

The European Commission, in fact, defines microcredit as any loan of €25,000 or less granted to a microenterprise (i.e., enterprises with fewer than ten employees whose annual turnover and/or balance sheet does not exceed €2,000,000). This limit has been adopted by several regulatory frameworks in Europe. "A European initiative for the development of micro-credit in support of growth and employment", published in November 2007 (COM (2007) 0708), encourages all member countries to adopt appropriate national, institutional, legal and commercial frameworks needed to promote a more favourable environment for the development of microcredit.

As is known, microcredit was born in Europe not only to tackle social exclusion and poverty but also to promote innovation and economic development by providing opportunities to access finance to subjects willing to unleash their entrepreneurial energies and spirit but excluded from the financial system.

However, there is no doubt that in order to develop the microfinance sector, regulators and governments in particular need to implement specific legislation and regulatory frameworks, consumer protection, and a solid financial infrastructure. In our opinion, any microfinance regulatory framework should ideally define and cover all microfinance activities (direct loans, mortgages, deposits, microinsurance, etc.), including the relevant specific risks and business practice, especially in markets where modern banking systems have not been developed yet. An accurate definition of the sector would certainly contribute to a more timely and proactive supervision (Leone and Porretta 2014).

Notes

1. Although the chapter was jointly prepared by the authors, Sections 5.2, 5.3 and 5.6 were written by Cristiana Turchetti, Sections 5.4 and 5.5 were written by Matteo Re, Sections 5.1, 5.7 and 5.8 were written by Pasqualina Porretta, Section 5.9 by Giovanni Nicola Pes and Riccardo Graziano.
2. www.eipa.nl/.
3. Marzinotto B. (2011) "A European Fund for Economic Revival in Crisis Countries". Retrieved at: http://www.bruegel.org/fileadmin/bruegel_files/Publications/Policy_Contributions/2011/PC_A_european_fund_for_Economic_revival_in_crisis_countries_BM.pdf, date accessed 9 May 2014. (BE) Belgium, (BG) Bulgaria, (CZ) Czech Republic, (DK) Denmark, (DE) Germany, (EE) Estonia, (IE) Ireland, (EL) Greece, (ES) Spain, (FR) France, (IT) Italy, (CY) Cyprus, (LV) Latvia, (LT) Lithuania, (LU) Luxembourg, (HU) Hungary, (MT) Malta, (NL) Netherlands, (AT) Austria, (PL) Poland, (PT) Portugal, (RO) Romania, (SI) Slovenia, (SK) Slovakia, (FI) Finland, (SE) Sweden, (UK) United Kingdom.
4. Ederveen S., Groot H. L. F. and Nahuis R. (2006) "Fertile soil for structural funds? A panel data analysis of the conditional effectiveness of European cohesion policy", *Kyklosvol*, 59(1), 17–42, 02.
5. Edquist C. (2008) "Identification of Policy Problems in Systems of Innovation through Diagnostic Analysis", http://www.cas.uio.no/research/0708innovation/Edquist_100608.pdf, date accessed 8 May 2014.
6. Directorate-General for Regional and Urban Policy. The mission of the European Commission's Directorate General (DG) for Regional and Urban Policy is to strengthen economic, social and territorial cohesion by reducing disparities between the levels of development of regions and countries of the European Union. In this way the policy contributes positively to the overall economic performance of the EU.
7. Art. 9: In order to contribute to the Union strategy for smart, sustainable and inclusive growth as well as the fund-specific missions pursuant to their treaty-based objectives, including economic, social and territorial cohesion, each ESI fund shall support the following thematic objectives: (1) strengthening research, technological development and innovation; (2) enhancing access to, and use and quality of, ICT; (3) enhancing the competitiveness of SMEs, of the agricultural sector (for the EAFRD) and of the fishery and aquaculture sector (for the EMFF); (4) supporting the shift towards a low-carbon economy in all sectors; (5) promoting climate change adaptation, risk prevention and management; (6) preserving and protecting the environment and promoting resource efficiency; (7) promoting sustainable transport and removing bottlenecks in key network infrastructures; (8) promoting sustainable and quality employment and supporting labour mobility; (9) promoting social inclusion, combating poverty and any discrimination; (10) investing in education, training and vocational training for skills and lifelong learning; (11) enhancing institutional capacity of public authorities and stakeholders and efficient public administration. Thematic objectives shall be translated into priorities that are specific to each of the ESI funds and are set out in the fund-specific rules.

8. European Commission (2003), Directorate General Regional Policy, http://ec.europa.eu/regional_policy/sources/docgener/studies/pdf/3cr/efficiency_methods_full.pdf, accessed 8 May 2014.
9. European Commission (2012), http://csdle.lex.unict.it/Archive/LW/Data%20reports%20and%20studies/Reports%20and%20%20communication%20from%20EU%20Commission/20120320-103800_SWD-61_2012_annexes_enpdf.pdf, accessed 9 May 2014.
10. Herta Tödtling-Schönhofer (ÖIR) Pat Colgan (ÖIR) Haris Martinos (LRDP) Begona Sanches (IDOM): "A Study of the Efficiency of the Implementation Methods for Structural Funds". Retrieved at: http://ec.europa.eu/regional_policy/sources/docgener/studies/pdf/3cr/efficiency_methods_sum.pdf.
11. Lang J., Naschold F. and Reissert B. (1998) Reforming the implementation of European structural funds: a next development step, *WZB Discussion Paper*, No. FS II 98–202.
12. For more information see Ziya Oni, "The logic of the developmental state".
13. With a few exceptions (Germany and Poland), several member states are still characterised by GDP figures and employment rates lower than the pre-crisis levels as well as unprecedented sovereign debt levels and reduced household incomes. Cohesion programmes for the programming period 2014–2020 shall, therefore, particularly emphasise the incentives for growth.

Except where otherwise noted, this work is licensed under a Creative Commons Attribution 3.0 Unported License. To view a copy of this license, visit http://creativecommons.org/licenses/by/3.0/

OPEN

Final Reflections

Gianfranco Verzaro

One of the most significant achievements of the Capacity Building project, which was finalised by the National Agency for Micro-credit, was to have identified new characteristics and issues of a sector, such as microfinance, which until the recent past was often associated with the simple offer of modest credit paid by not-for-profit institutions in favour of people or social groups who are particularly vulnerable.

From the analysis conducted in the course of the project – as well as from direct interactions with regional authorities, stakeholders, banking and financial intermediaries and numerous players within society – it became clear, in fact, that the target market for microcredit and microfinance presents somewhat different connotations today, due to the profound changes in recent years in relation to both the target beneficiary clientele and the range of microfinancial instruments that have been or will be activated. And this, as a direct result of the changes which have taken place in our society (consider, e.g., the massive immigration of individuals from developing countries) as well as the financial crisis which, in recent years, has given rise to new poverty and phenomena of financial exclusion even in areas which previously seemed to be immune.

On the supply side, we are today witnessing a differentiation in financing methods, from the moment that not-for-profit organisations were flanked by for-profit institutions, such as banks and financial intermediaries and, most recently, by new microcredit providers established in Italy under new specific legislation (the new art. 111, paragraph 1, of the Consolidated Banking Act), on whose operating norms the Banca d'Italia has opened a public consultation right in the days in which this volume goes to print.

Simultaneously, the expansion of the range of financial instruments offered to the traditional microcredit clientele has been confirmed; this has enabled a clear differentiation between the concepts of microcredit and of microfinance and has conferred greater definitive autonomy to microcredit. Today, microcredit is, admittedly, the first among a range of microfinance instruments – including microleasing, microinsurance, housing microfinance. But still newer instruments are emerging as concrete alternative or complementary possibilities to microcredit. And this is to the credit of the Capacity Building project, which first investigated them at the technical-scientific level and then, on the basis of in-depth comparisons with market players, proposed them to regional authorities who are responsible for operational programmes co-financed by structural funds, such as tools to support microenterprise and population groups who are the most disadvantaged.

Moreover, the evolution in the structure of the offer has enabled us to reach a larger audience of final recipients, due not only to the so-called poorest of the poor (a term borrowed from the experiences of developing countries and which, in Europe, should rather be referred to social-welfare policies) but to the broader category of people who are excluded from the financial system, primarily microentrepreneurs, who are no longer "trusted" by the banks because of their precarious economic-financial status, and aspiring entrepreneurs (young, unemployed, immigrants) who, while in possession of valid microenterprise or self-employment ideas, do not have access to bank credit due to a shortage or absolute lack of collateral.

In this context, the specific task of the Capacity Building project – namely, the reinforcement of public authority institutional capacities in the Italian regions of the former Convergence Objective with regard to structural funds resource programming intended for microcredit programmes – has enabled us to develop new ideas and valid methodologies even for the extension of the project to other Italian and European regions.

With the conclusion of the project, the present volume aims to provide deeper insight into the institutional capacity of the European managing authorities in relation to the planning, monitoring and evaluation of microcredit and microfinance programmes. A highly diversified framework has emerged which reveals that the field of microcredit and microfinance in Europe is still largely unexplored and, in any case, has vast potential for development.

One aspect which the Capacity Building project has been able to strongly highlight for the purposes of future development of microcredit is the need to strengthen the synergies between public authorities and territorial entities – in particular, financial intermediaries and not-for-profit organisations. It has been confirmed that establishing territorial networks for microcredit is a "winning" factor, since it gives added value to public planning through the development of ad hoc microfinancial instruments and the accompaniment of non-financial services for support, mentoring and monitoring.

In sum – and on the basis of the recommendations of this research – I believe that the results of the Capacity Building project will be promoted at the national and European level, having tables of discussion with the European Commission, regional authorities and market players, to arrive at new and more ambitious objectives already in the 2014–2020 programming period, through the strengthening of competences not only of public institutions but also of stakeholders. I consider, for example, the possibility of providing technical assistance to "regulators" of microcredit and microfinance, of developing a central credit register and a scoring model for microcredit, of strengthening the expertise of service providers accompanying measures for microcredit, also in view of a public system of certification, of the financing of networks, of encouraging the exchange of experiences between microcredit operators for the research of new technologies or the definition of new microfinance products and services and of training the staff of new microcredit intermediaries.

The processing of these basic themes can be effectively coordinated by the European Commission in close consultation with national authorities and supported by specialist organisations (e.g., the National Agency for Micro-credit in Italy) and with all stakeholders in the microfinance sector, such as financiers, investors, customers and organisations within the territory.

Except where otherwise noted, this work is licensed under a Creative Commons Attribution 3.0 Unported License. To view a copy of this license, visit http://creativecommons.org/licenses/by/3.0/

OPEN

Conclusions

Riccardo Graziano

Surveys conducted by the National Agency for Micro-credit for the fulfilment of this research, which represents the conclusive action of the project Capacity Building on Micro-credit Financial Instruments, allow us to focus on some issues that, starting from the Italian experience in ex-convergence regions, can form the basis for a future debate aimed at the development of the microfinance sector at both the national and European level.

It should be recognised, in fact, that in the course of the 2007–2013 planning cycle, Italy was the only country to adopt a complex project of capacity building aimed at strengthening the knowledge and various competences of the management staff of regional authorities and able to increase employment opportunities in the affected areas through the optimal use of so-called financial instruments, including, in the first place, microcredit.

It is also important to stress that the Capacity Building project has been a unique experience at the European level because, for the first time, it was intended to provide a direct and incisive response to the challenges encountered by the regional authorities, holders of operational programmes in construction, start-up and implementation of the financial instruments linked to the subjects of microcredit and microfinance and co-financed by resources from structural funds. One need only consider the problem of "underutilisation" of structural funds earmarked for development and employment policies or to the decrease in the supply of credit which, in these years of financial crisis, has heavily affected the business system and especially the smaller businesses.

It is also to help overcome these challenges that in the course of the Capacity Building project, a training proposal has been drawn up with a range of microcredit instruments capable of augmenting the operational tools available to public authorities whilst also strengthening the skills and knowledge of stakeholders on new financial engineering instruments.

In light of the activities carried out and the results obtained, there are good grounds to ensure that the Capacity Building project – around which synergies were created between regional authorities and key stakeholders competent in the field of credit, business, leasing, insurance and housing – can have a follow-up and because the wealth of relationships and knowledge created through the project will not be wasted but, on the contrary, valued throughout the country and, it is hoped, in the European countries that are closer to a microcredit model which, like our own, wants to maximise public–private synergies.

Therefore, we are demonstrating hereunder, in a necessarily brief way, the main items which, in our opinion, should characterise the future debate on the definition of an organic microfinancial policy that will have to be developed with the involvement of all stakeholders at the Italian and European level.

- *Strengthen institutional capacity*

The opportunity to strengthen the competences of public authorities in the fields of microcredit and microfinance is particularly felt not only in the regions of the convergence objective but also in the remaining regions of Italy, as has often been explicitly denoted to the National Agency for Micro-credit by qualified representatives of the banking and financial system.

- *Improve regional performance in the utilisation of structural funds*

Even in the presence of a significant acceleration in certified expenditure, the need to improve regional performance in the utilisation of structural funds is still evident, both for the closure of the 2007–2013 planning cycle and in the course of the new operational programmes 2014–2020 that sees, as noted, an even stronger regulatory framework of reference for financial engineering instruments. In this sense, the enhancement of public authority competences in the field of microcredit and microfinance can be a decisive action for the optimal utilisation of European resources.

- *Foster collaboration between public authorities and operators*

The Capacity Building project has facilitated the creation of a dialogue between public authorities and a number of operators in the various sectors of credit, leasing, insurance, and social housing. This dialogue must continue to be supported at the moment in which it translates into partnerships and concrete actions in favour of those sections of the population that are most disadvantaged.

- *Strengthen the competences of territorial operators*

Among the main achievements of the Capacity Building project, the strengthening of regional support networks for public authorities for the implementation of microcredit measures should be highlighted, in particular, through the strengthening of non-financial support services, mentoring and monitoring, as expressly provided for by Italian law.

The process leading to the formation of a virtuous partnership between public authorities and operators should be extended to the national level and appropriately enhanced through ad hoc training of operators, in accordance with the terms of the European Code of Conduct for microfinance operators, as well as a certification process for operators of non-financial services. Moreover, the need to strengthen operators through the development of skills which enable complementarity with public action is all the more necessary in view of the expansion of the range of financial products (microleasing, microinsurance) which may be activated and new policy areas (housing and green microfinance).

- *Continue the process of building an organic microcredit model*

The Capacity Building project has defined an organic microcredit model consistent with the specificity of the microcredit system in Italy, characterised by (1) government intervention through the allocation of financial resources for the activation of financial instruments; (2) the intervention of financiers (banks and microcredit operators) that should operate in market conditions in accordance with legislation on microcredit; and (3) the intervention of qualified territorial operators – since they are certified by a public entity – capable of interfacing with the public authority and with financiers for the pre-evaluation questions and the supply of other non-financial services, encouraging and thereby accelerating the delivery process of microfinance instruments. We must now continue to work on the information and on improvement of the microfinance culture so that this model can be fully implemented.

- *Strengthen the microfinance culture within public administration*

Microcredit constitutes, in the context of public policies, an innovative form of support for economic development and social inclusion, distinguishing itself from the traditional policies of financial incentivisation based on "spreading funds too thinly" and on outright grants. For these reasons, it is necessary to promote a microfinance culture also within the public administration, which favours the development of public programmes for microcredit capable of being not only indicators of the authorities' new responsibilities in the field of financial engineering but also effective mobilisation tools of organisational resources, human and finance, with a high social impact in the regions. This impact will become evident both through the improvement of the conditions of access to credit on the part of sections of the population historically excluded from such opportunities and, above all, through the effective realisation of projects capable of acting directly on the improvement of people's living conditions and having a significant social impact.

- *Enhance the concept of responsibility of the applicant*

A specific concept to develop is that linked to the need for the payment of a rate of interest on the part of the applicant, albeit in a fair and sustainable manner. The prediction of a rate of interest, in fact, in addition to increasing the degree of sustainability of the microcredit programme, has a pedagogical function, since it places responsibility on the applicants and helps to develop their skills for a more conscious use of money. The added value of microcredit, in fact, is in allowing access to financial resources that would otherwise be precluded but at the same time making it clear that microcredit is a loan which, as such, must be repaid.

- *Provide a scoring system for microcredit*

Lacking at the moment is a scoring system dedicated to the microcredit sector that is able to promote (1) the process of assessing the sustainability of projects of microentrepreneurship; (2) the assessment of the creditworthiness of microentrepreneurs; and (3) the process of financial inclusion. In the course of the Capacity Building project, the partners of the banking world have called for an effort at the system level to design and implement a credit scoring model targeted specifically at microcredit worthiness, within which even the added value of the accompanying non-financial services are rendered valuable. Such a system would enable, among other things, the creation of a "credit history" of microcredit applicants, thereby facilitating their paths of financial inclusion toward traditional channels of credit.

- *Structuring the basis for a microinsurance market in Italy*

As expressly shown to the National Agency for Micro-credit by representatives of the insurance sector, the need to design group insurance systems which will enable the microinsurance sector to optimise brokerage costs, recovery and liquidation of microinsurance policies is particularly felt.

In conclusion, we can state that the Capacity Building project has highlighted the need to boost the competences of public authorities in the field of microcredit and microfinance, even in regions that are not directly involved in the project itself. If, as we hope, the results of the project can be put to good use in the current 2014–2020 planning period, it will be possible to further improve regional performance in the utilisation of structural funds for the fulfilment of organic microcredit programmes which can also denote "good practice" for other territories in the European Union.

Except where otherwise noted, this work is licensed under a Creative Commons Attribution 3.0 Unported License. To view a copy of this license, visit http://creativecommons.org/licenses/by/3.0/

OPEN

Bibliography

Artola C. and Genre V. (2011) "Euro area SMEs under financial constraints: belief or reality?", *CESifo Working Paper: Monetary Policy and International Finance*, No. 3650.

Arun T. and Bendig M. (2010) "Risk management among the poor: the case of micro-financial services", *IZA Discussion Paper*, No. 5174, Bonn, September, 1–27.

Arun T., Bendig M. and Arun S. (2012) "Bequest motives and determinants of micro life insurance in Sri Lanka", *World Development*, 40(8), 1700–1711.

Ashta A. (2013) "Microfinance and microentrepreneurship: case studies in social innovation", *CEB Working Paper*, No. 13/046, 1–9.

Assilea (2014) "Guide to new fiscal provisions for leasing 2014 – the calculation model for the leasing fiscal advantages", January.

Atanasova C. and N. Wilson (2004) "Disequilibrium in the UK corporate loan market", *Journal of Banking and Finance*, 28, 595–614.

Avery R.B. and Samolyk K.A. (2004) "Bank consolidation and small business lending: the role of community banks", *Journal of Financial Services Research*, 25, 291–325.

Baily M., Neil E., Bartelsman J. and Haltiwanger J. (1996) "Downsizing and productivity growth: myth or reality?", *Small Business Economics*, 8(4), 259–278.

Baldini M. and Federici M. (2008) "The social housing in Europe", *CAP Paper*, No. 49, http://capp.unimo.it/pubbl/cappapers/Capp_p49.pdf.

Bank of Italy (2013) Economic and Financial Issues, *Micro-enterprises in Italy: an introductory analysis*, April, pp. 5–6.

Bank of Italy (2014) *Consolidated Act on banking and construction laws, updated version to Legislative Decree 4 March 2014*, No. 53.

Banque de France (2010) *Rapport annuel de l'Observatoire de la micro finance*, Banque de France, Paris, http://www.banque-france.fr/fileadmin/user_upload/banque_de_france/publications/rapport-annuel-2010-de-l-observatoire-de-la-microfinance.pdf.

Banque de France (2011) *Colloque international sur la Microfinance*, Banque de France, Paris, http://www.banque-france.fr/uploads/media/colloque-microfinance-2011.pdf.

Barricelli D. and Russo G. (2005) Think Micro First: *La micro-impresa di fronte alla sfida del terzo millennio: conoscenze, sapere politiche di sviluppo* (Micro-enterprises facing 21st century challenges: knowledge, know-how and development policies), Franco Angeli, Roma.

Becchetti L. and Trovato G. (2002) "The determinants of growth for small and medium sized firms. The role of the availability of external finance", *Small Business Economics*, 19, 291–306.

Beck T., Demirgüç-Kunt A., Laeven L. and Levine R. (2005) "Finance, firm size and growth", *World Bank Policy Research Working Paper*, No. 3485.

Beck T., Demirgüç-Kunt A., Laeven L. and Maksimovic V. (2006) "The determinants of financial obstacles", *Journal of International Money and Finance*, 25, 932–952.

Beck T., Demirgüç-Kunt A. and Maksimovic V. (2005) "Financial and legal constraint to growth: does firm size matter?", *Journal of Finance*, 25, 137–177.

Beck T., Demirgüç-Kunt A. and Martinez Perìa M.S. (2008) "Bank financing for SMEs around the world. Drivers, obstacles, business models, and lending practices", *Policy Research Working Paper*, No. 4785, November.

Berger A.N., Hasan I. and Klapper L.F. (2004) "Further evidence on the link between finance and growth: an international analysis of community banking and economic performance", *Journal of Financial Services Research*, 2, 169–202.

Berger A.N., Klapper L.F. and Udell G.F. (2001) "The ability of banks to lend to informal opaque business", *Journal of Banking and Finance*, 25, 2127–2167.

Berger A.N. and Udell G.F. (1998) "The economics of small business finance: the roles of private equity and debt markets in the financial growth cycle", *The Journal of Banking and Finance*, 22(6–8), 613–673.

Berger A.N. and Udell G.F. (2002) "Small business credit availability and relationship lending: the importance of bank organizational structure", *Economic Journal*, 112, 32–53.

Bhattacharya S. and Thakor A.V. (1993) "Contemporary banking theory", *Journal of Financial Intermediation*, 3, 2–50.

Biener C., Eling M. and Schmit J.T. (2014) "Regulation in microinsurance markets: principle, practice, and directions for future development", *World Development*, 58, 21–40.

Birch D. (1993) *Who's creating jobs?*, Cognetics, Cambridge.

Breglia M. (2013) *Social housing as a model of European welfare*, Rome, http://www.internews.biz/old/editoriale/SCENARI_IMMOBILIARI-SINTESI_STAMPA.pdf.

Bruhn-Leon B., Eriksson P.E. and Kraemer H. (2012) *Progress for Micro-finance in Europe*, European Investment Fund, http://www.eif.org/news_centre/publications/eif_wp_2012_13_microfinance.pdf.

Buca A. and Vermeulen P. (2012) "Corporate investment and bank-dependent borrowers during the recent financial crisis", *European Central Bank*, https://www.ecb.europa.eu/events/pdf/conferences/rolecred/Buca_Vermeulen.pdf?a6b52d39c73ba000a201e932ab65dc38.

Buera F.J. and Moll B. (2012) "Aggregate implications of a credit crunch", *National Bureau of Economic Research, Working Paper*, No. 17775.

Buildings Performance Institute Europe (2011) *Europe's buildings under the microscope*, Buildings Performance Institute Europe (BPIE), Brussel, http://www.bpie.eu/uploads/lib/document/attachment/21/LR_EU_B_under_microscope_study.pdf.

Bullier, A. and Milin, C., (2012) *Alternative financing schemes for energy efficiency in buildings*, http://www.managenergy.net/lib/documents/868/original_3-221-13_Bullier_-_Alternative_financing.pdf.

Cabral L.M.B. and Mata J. (2003) "On the evolution of the firm size distribution: facts and theory", *American Economic Review*, 93, 1075–1090, http://people.stern.nyu.edu/lcabral/publications/AER%202003.pdf.

Cafaggi F. (2011) *Contractual networks, inter-firm cooperation and economic growth*, Edward Elgar Publishing, UK.

Camagni, R. (2008) Financing of the public city, in Baioni, M. (ed.), *Building the public city*, Alinea, Florence, http://eugeniopari.files.wordpress.com/2008/09/il-finanziamento-della-citta-pubblica.pdf.

Cameron K.S. (1994) "Strategies for successful organizational downsizing", *Human Resource Management*, 33(2), 189–211, http://webuser.bus.umich.edu/cameronk/PDFs/Downsizing/Strat%20Successful%20Org%20Downsizing.pdf.
Canton E., Grilo I., Monteagudo J. and Van der Zwan P. (2010) "Investigating the perceptions of credit constraints in the European Union", *ERIM Report Series Reference*, No. ERS-2010-001-ORG, 2–14.
Caree M.A. and Klomp L. (1996) "Small business and job creation: a comment", *Small Business Economics*, 8, 317–322.
Carpenter R. and Petersen B.C. (2002) "Is the growth of small firms constrained by internal finance?", *Review of Economics and Statistics*, 84, 298–309.
Castelli P. and Modina M. (2010) I riflessi della crisi finanziaria sulla relazione banca impresa (The effects of the financial crisis on the bank-enterprise relationship), in Birindelli G.and M. Modina (eds), *Le evidenze di un'analisi territoriale alla luce della crisi finanziaria* (Feedback from the analysis of the territory following a financial crisis), Imprese Banche e Finanza, Franco Angeli Editore, 73–89.
Cechodhas (2011) *Housing Europe review 2012. The nuts and bolts of European and social housing systems*, Brussels, http://www.housingeurope.eu/resource-105/the-housing-europe-review-2012.
Chatterjee A. (2012) Access to insurance and financial-sector regulation, in Churchill C. and Matul M. (eds), *Protecting the poor: a microinsurance compendium*, Vol. II, International Labour Organization, Geneva.
Chittenden F., Hall G. and Hutchinson P. (1996) "Small firm growth, access to capital markets and financial structure: review of issues and an empirical investigation", *Small Business Economics*, 8(1), 59–67.
Christine Poursat (2014) "Dossier thématique: Diversification des produits", Portail de la Microfinance, January 2014, http://www.microfinancegateway.org/sites/default/files/mfg-fr-publications-diverses-diversification-offre-microfinance-03-2005-bim_0.pdf.
Churchill C.F. (2002) "Trying to understand the demand for microinsurance", *Journal of International Development*, 14, 381–387.
Churchill C.F. (2007) "Insuring the low-income market: challenges and solutions for commercial insurers", *Geneva Papers on Risk and Insurance*, 32(3), 401–412.
Churchill C.F., Liber D., McCord M.J. and Roth J. (2003) *Making insurance work for microfinance institutions. A technical guide to developing and delivering microinsurance*, ILO, Switzerland.
Clarke D. and Dercon S. (2009) "Insurance, credit and safety nets for the poor in a world of risk", United Nations, *DESA Working Paper*, No. 81, 1–16.
Cohen M., Mccord M.J. and Sebstad J. (2005) "Reducing vulnerability: demand for and supply of microinsurance in East Africa", *Journal of International Development*, 17(3), 319–325.
Cole R.A., Goldberg L.G. and White L.J. (2004) "Cookie-cutter versus character: the micro structure of small business by large and small banks", *Journal of Financial and Quantitative Analysis*, 39, 227–251.
Cole R.A. and Rebel A. (1998) "The importance of relationship to the availability of credit", *Journal of Banking and Finance*, 22, 629–670.
Coluzzi C., Ferrando A. and Martinez-Carrascal C. (2012) "Financing obstacles and growth: an analysis for Euro area non-financial firms", *The European Journal of Finance*, 1–18.

Commission of the European Communities (2003) *Commission Recommendation of 6 May 2003 concerning the definition of micro, small and medium-sized enterprises* (notified under document number C(2003) 1422), *Official Journal of the European Union*, http://eur-lex.europa.eu/legal-content/EN/TXT/PDF/?uri=CELEX:32003H0361&from=IT.

Commission of the European Communities (2006) *Communication from the Commission to the Council, the European parliament, the European Economic and Social Committee and the Committee of the Regions – Implementing the Community Lisbon Programme: Financing SME Growth – Adding European Value*, COM (2006) 349 final, http://eur-lex.europa.eu/legal-content/EN/TXT/PDF/?uri=CELEX:52006DC0349&qid=1403702569267&from=EN.

Commission of the European Communities (2007) *Communication from the Commission to the Council, the European Parliament, the European Economic and Social Committee and the Committee of the Regions – A European initiative for the development of micro-credit in support of growth and employment*, COM(2007) 708 final, http://eur-lex.europa.eu/legal-content/EN/TXT/PDF/?uri=CELEX:52007DC0708&qid=1403707249640&from=EN.

Committee of Donor Agencies for Small Entreprise Development (2001) *Business Development Services for Small Entreprises. Guiding Principles for Donor Intervention*, February, Washington, committee of donor agencies for small enterprise development Donor Committee, p. 11, http://www.enterprise-development.org/page/download?id=1291.

Cook P. and Nixson F. (2005) Finance and small and medium-sized enterprise development, in Green C.J., Kirkpatrick C.H. and Murinde V. (eds), *Finance and development: surveys of theory, evidence and policy*, Edward Elgar, UK.

Corsi M. (2008) *Donne e Microfinanza, uno sguardo ai paesi del Mediterraneo*, Aracne, Roma.

Cresme (2014) *Reuse 03 Building renovation, energy efficiency improvement, urban regeneration*, Rome, http://www.awn.it/AWN/Engine/RAServeFile.php/f/RAPPORTO_riuso03.pdf.

Cressy R.C. and Olofsson C. (1997) "European SME financing: an overview", *Small Business Economics*, 9(2), 87–96.

Dabrassi C. (1996) *Asimmetrie informative e mercati finanziari* (Information asymmetries and financial markets), Egea, Milano.

Dallago C. and Guglielmetti C. (2012) *The consequence of the international crisis on European SMEs. Vulnerability and resilience*, Routledge, Abingdon, Oxfordshire, 299 pp.

Daniels L. (1999) "The role of small enterprises in the household and national economy in Kenya: a significant contribution or a last resort?", *World Development*, 27(1), 55–65.

Davis S.J., Haltiwanger J. and Schu S. (1996) "Small business and job creation: dissecting the myth and reassessing the facts", *Small Business Economics*, 8, 297–315.

De Bock O. and Gelade W. (2012) "The demand for microinsurance: a literature review", *Microinsurance Innovation Facility, Research Paper*, No. 26, November, 1–30.

De la Torre T., Martinez Perìa M.S. and Schmuckler S.L. (2008) "Bank involvement with SMEs: beyond relationship banking", *Policy Research Working Paper*, No. 4649, June.

De Mitri S., De Socio A., Finaldi Russo P. and Nigro V. (2013) "Le microimprese in Italia: una prima analisi delle condizioni economiche e finanziarie (Micro-enterprises in Italy: a first analysis of economic and financial conditions)", *Quaderni di economia e finanza* (Occasional Papers), No. 162, Bank of Italy.

Deelen L., Dupleich M., Othieno L. and Wakelin O. (2003) *Leasing for small and micro enterprises. A guide for designing and managing leasing schemes in developing countries*, International Labour Organization, Geneva.

Dercon S., Gunning J.W., Zeitlin A. and Lombardini S. (2012) "The impact of a health insurance programme: evidence from a randomized controlled trial in Kenya", *Microinsurance Innovation Facility, Research Paper*, No. 24, November, 1–19.

Devereux M. and Schiantarelli F. (1989) "Investment, financial factors and cash flow: evidence from UK panel data", *NBER Working Papers*, No. 3116, September.

DFID (2000) *Eliminating world poverty: making globalisation work for the poor*, The Department for International Development, London, http://webarchive.nationalarchives.gov.uk/+/http://www.dfid.gov.uk/Documents/publications/whitepaper2000.pdf.

Dowgherty D. and Bowman E. (1995) "The effects of organizational downsizing on product innovation", *California Management Review*, 37, 28–44.

Dowla A.U. (2004) "Micro leasing: the Grameen bank experience", *Journal of Microfinance*, 6(2), Winter, 137–160.

Edwards T., Delbridge R. and Munday M. (2005) "Understanding innovation in small and medium-sized enterprises: a process manifest", *Technovation*, 25(10), 1119–1127.

EIP (2011) *Final evaluation of the entrepreneurship and innovation programme. Final Report March 2011*, http://ec.europa.eu/cip/files/docs/eip-final-evaluation-report_en.pdf.

Eling M., Pradhan S. and Schmit J.T. (2014) "The determinant of microinsurance demand", *Geneva Papers on Risk and Insurance, Issues and Practice*, 39(2), 224–263.

Erikkson P., Kraemer-Eis H. and Conforti A. (2011) "Microcredit as a tool of ethical financing for sustainable development", *APS Bank Publication*, 49–86.

European Central Bank (2014) *Survey on the access to finance of small and medium-sized enterprises in the Euro area – October 2013 to March 2014*, https://www.ecb.europa.eu/pub/pdf/other/accesstofinancesmallmediumsizedenterprises201404en.pdf?da920468528300ff549d8cc95522eb81.

European Commission (1999) Council Regulation – laying down general provisions on the Structural Funds, *Official Journal of the European Communities*, http://eur-lex.europa.eu/legal-content/EN/TXT/PDF/?uri=CELEX:31999R1260&rid=5.

European Commission (2000) Commission regulation – laying down detailed rules for the implementation of Council Regulation (EC) No 1260/1999 as regards eligibility of expenditure of operations co-financed by the Structural Funds, *Official Journal of the European Communities*, http://ec.europa.eu/regional_policy/sources/docoffic/official/regulation/pdf/reg_elig_en.pdf.

European Commission (2004) Commission regulation amending Regulation (EC) No 1685/2000 laying down detailed rules for the implementation of Council Regulation (EC) No 1260/1999 as regards the eligibility of expenditure of operations co-financed by the Structural Funds and withdrawing Regulation (EC) No 1145/2003, *Official Journal of the European Union,* http://eur-lex.europa.eu/legal-content/EN/TXT/PDF/?uri=CELEX:32004R0448&rid=4.

European Commission (2004) Annex of the Commission Regulation (EC) No. 448/2004 of 10 March 2004 amending Regulation (EC) No 1685/2000 laying down detailed rules for the implementation of Council Regulation (EC) No 1260/1999 as regards the eligibility of expenditure of operations co-financed by the Structural Funds and withdrawing Regulation (EC) No 1145/2003, *Official Journal of the European Union,* http://ec.europa.eu/regional_policy/sources/docoffic/official/regulation/content/en/02_pdf/00_9_4_expend2_en.pdf.

European Commission (2004) Setting out rules for the implementation of Council Regulation (EC) No 1083/2006 laying down general provisions on the European Regional Development Fund, the European Social Fund and the Cohesion Fund and of Regulation (EC) No 1080/2006 of the European Parliament and of the Council on the European Regional Development Fund, *Official Journal of the European Union,* http://eur-lex.europa.eu/legal-content/EN/TXT/PDF/?uri=CELEX:32006R1828&from=IT.

European Commission (2006) Council Regulation (EC) No 1083/2006 of 11 July 2006, laying down general provisions on the European Regional Development Fund, the European Social Fund and the Cohesion Fund and repealing Regulation (EC) No 1260/1999, http://eur-lex.europa.eu/legal-content/EN/TXT/PDF/?uri=CELEX:02006R1083-20131221&rid=1.

European Commission (2006) CIP Financial Instruments, Entrepreneurship and Innovation Programme, http://eur-lex.europa.eu/LexUriServ/LexUriServ.do?uri=OJ:L:2006:310:0015:0040:EN:PDF.

European Commission (2006) Regulation (EC) No 1081/2006 of the European Parliament and of the Council of 5 July 2006 on the European Social Fund and repealing Regulation (EC) No 1784/1999, *Official Journal of the European Union,* http://eur-lex.europa.eu/legal-content/EN/TXT/PDF/?uri=CELEX:32006R1081&from=IT.

European Commission, DG Enterprise and Industry (2006) *Management Capacity Building – Final Report of the Expert Group on Management Capacity Building,* p. 29, http://ec.europa.eu/enterprise/policies/sme/files/support_measures/mcb/mcb_en.pdf, data accessed 7 July 2014.

European Commission (2007) *Communication from the Commission to the Council, the European Parliament, the European Economic and Social Committee and the Committee of the Regions. A European initiative for the development of micro-credit in support of growth and employment,* http://eur-lex.europa.eu/legal-content/EN/TXT/PDF/?uri=CELEX:52007DC0708&rid=2.

European Commission (2008) *Think Small First. A Small Business Act for Europe,* http://eur-lex.europa.eu/LexUriServ/LexUriServ.do?uri=COM:2008:0394:FIN:EN:PDF, data accessed 7 July 2014.

European Commission (2010) *Internationalisation of European SMEs Final Report,* http://ec.europa.eu/enterprise/policies/sme/files/support_measures/internationalisation/internationalisation_sme_final_en.pdf.

European Commission (2010) *Europe 2020 – a strategy for smart, sustainable and inclusive growth,* http://eur-lex.europa.eu/legal-content/EN/TXT/PDF/?uri=CELEX:52010DC2020&from=EN.

European Commission (2010) Commission Staff Working Document – *Second Biennial Report on Social Services of General Interest*, SEC (2010) 1284 final, Brussels, http://ec.europa.eu/social/BlobServlet?docId=6221&langId=en.

European Commission (2011) *Communication from the Commission to the European Parliament and the Council – a framework for the next generation of innovative financial instruments – the EU equity and debt platforms*, COM(2011) 662 final, http://ec.europa.eu/economy_finance/financial_operations/investment/europe_2020/documents/com2011_662_en.pdf.

European Commission (2011) *Guidance Note on Financial Engineering Instruments under Article 44 of Council Regulation (EC) No 1083/2006*, http://ec.europa.eu/regional_policy/archive/funds/2007/jjj/doc/pdf/cocof_guidance_note3_en.pdf.

European Commission (2011) *European Code of Good Conduct for Microcredit Provision*, http://ec.europa.eu/enterprise/newsroom/cf/itemdetail.cfm?item_id=5479&lang=en.

European Commission (2011) *A roadmap for moving to a competitive low carbon economy in 2050*, COM (2011) 112 final, Brussels, http://eurlex.europa.eu/LexUriServ/LexUriServ.do?uri=COM:2011:0112:FIN:EN:DOC.

European Commission (2011) *Energy roadmap 2050*, COM (2011) 885 final, Brussels, http://eur-lex.europa.eu/legal-content/EN/TXT/PDF/?uri=CELEX:52011DC0885&from=EN.

European Commission (2011) *A framework for the next generation of innovative financial instruments – the EU equity and debt platforms*, COM (2011) 662, http://ec.europa.eu/economy_finance/financial_operations/investment/europe_2020/documents/com2011_662_en.pdf.

European Commission (2012) *Rethinking education: investing in skills for better socio-economic outcomes*, http://ec.europa.eu/digital-agenda/en/news/communication-rethinking-education, data accessed 7 July 2014.

European Commission (2012) *Financial instruments in cohesion policy*, SWD (2012) 36 final, Brussels, http://ec.europa.eu/regional_policy/sources/docoffic/official/communic/financial/financial_instruments_2012_en.pdf.

European Commission (2013) *Summary of data on the progress made in financing and implementing financial engineering instruments co-financed by Structural Funds*, http://ec.europa.eu/regional_policy/thefunds/instruments/doc/summary_data_fei_2012.pdf.

European Commission (2013) *A recovery on the horizon? Final annual report on European SMES 2012/2013*, http://ec.europa.eu/enterprise/policies/sme/facts-figures-analysis/performance-review/files/supporting-documents/2013/annual-report-smes-2013_en.pdf.

European Commission (2013) *2013 SMEs' access to finance survey – analytical report*, http://ec.europa.eu/enterprise/policies/finance/files/2013-safe-analytical-report_en.pdf.

European Commission (2013) *One out of three SMEs did not get the finance they needed in 2013*, Brussels, http://europa.eu/rapid/press-release_IP-13-1070_en.htm.

European Commission (2013) *Entrepreneurship & Innovation Programme Committee*, p. 7, http://ec.europa.eu/cip/files/cip/eip_performance_report_2007-2013_en.pdf.

European Commission (2013) *Summary of data on the progress made in financing and implementing financial engineering instruments co-financed by Structural Funds*, http://ec.europa.eu/regional_policy/thefunds/instruments/doc/summary_data_fei_2012.pdf.

European Commission (2013) *Entrepreneurship 2020 Action plan*, http://ec.europa.eu/enterprise/policies/sme/entrepreneurship-2020/index_en.htm, data accessed 7 July 2014.

European Commission (2013) *Entrepreneurship 2020 Action plan – reigniting the entrepreneurial spirit in Europe*, COM (2012) 795 final, http://eur-lex.europa.eu/LexUriServ/LexUriServ.do?uri=COM:2012:0795:FIN:EN:PDF, data accessed 7 July 2014, data accessed 7 July 2014.

European Commission (2013) *Entrepreneurship & Innovation Programme Commitee, EIP performance report*, http://ec.europa.eu/cip/files/cip/eip_performance_report_2007-2013_en.pdf.

European Commission (2013) *Green Paper – a 2030 framework for climate and energy policies*, COM(2013) 169 final, http://eur-lex.europa.eu/LexUriServ/LexUriServ.do?uri=COM:2013:0169:FIN:EN:PDF.

European Commission (2013) *Commission staff working document accompanying the document report from the Commission to the European Parliament and the Council. Financial support for energy efficiency in buildings*, COM(2013) 225 final, http://ec.europa.eu/energy/efficiency/buildings/doc/swd_2013_143_accomp_report_financing_ee_buildings.pdf.

European Commission (2013) *A 2030 framework for climate and energy policies*, COM (2013) 169 final, Brussels, http://eur-lex.europa.eu/legal-content/EN/TXT/PDF/?uri=CELEX:52013DC0169&from=EN.

European Commission – DG Enterprise and Industry (2013) *Entrepreneurship education: a guide for educators*, http://ec.europa.eu/enterprise/policies/sme/promoting-entrepreneurship/files/ education/entredu-manual-fv_en.pdf, data accessed 7 July 2014.

European Commission, European Investment Bank and European Bank (2013) *Jaspers Annual Report*, European Investment Bank, Luxembourg, http://www.jaspers-europa-info.org/attachments/article/161/JASPERS%20Annual%20Report%202013_en.pdf.

European Commission and Ipsos MORI (2013) *2013 SMEs' Access to Finance survey*, http://ec.europa.eu/enterprise/policies/finance/files/2013-safe-analytical-report_en.pdf.

European Commission (2014) *Factsheets – financial instruments in cohesion policy 2014–2020*, http://ec.europa.eu/regional_policy/sources/docgener/informat/2014/financial_instruments_en.pdf.

European Commission (2014) *Financial instruments in ESIF programmes 2014–2020 – a short reference guide for Managing Authorities*, http://ec.europa.eu/regional_policy/thefunds/fin_inst/pdf/fi_esif_2014_2020.pdf.

European Commission (2014) *European Competitiveness Report 2014 – helping firms grows*, http://ec.europa.eu/enterprise/policies/industrial-competitiveness/competitiveness-analysis/european-competitiveness-report/index_en.htm.

European Commission (2014) *Horizon 2020 Work Programme 2014–2015. 10. Secure, clean and efficient energy. Revised*, http://ec.europa.eu/research/participants/data/ref/h2020/wp/2014_2015/main/h2020-wp1415-energy_en.pdf.

European Commission (2014) *Financial instruments in the cohesion policy 2014–2020*, http://ec.europa.eu/regional_policy/sources/docgener/informat/2014/financial_instruments_en.pdf.

268 Bibliography

European Commission (2014) *Technical guidance. Financing the energy renovation of buildings with cohesion policy funding*, final report, Brussels, http://ec.europa.eu/regional_policy/newsroom/detail.cfm?id=1292&lang=en.

European Council (2006) Council Regulation (EC) No 1083/2006 of 11 July 2006 – laying down general provisions on the European Regional Development Fund, the European Social Fund and the Cohesion Fund and repealing Regulation (EC) No 1260/1999, *Official Journal of the European Union*, http://eur-lex.europa.eu/LexUriServ/LexUriServ.do?uri=OJ:L:2006:210:0025:0078:EN:PDF.

European Investment Bank (2008) *JESSICA – a new way of using EU funding to promote sustainable investments and growth in urban areas*, European Investment Bank, Luxembourg, http://www.eib.org/attachments/thematic/jessica_2008_en.pdf.

European Investment Bank (2012) *Energy focused urban development funds*, final report, http://ec.europa.eu/regional_policy/thefunds/instruments/doc/jessica/jessica_horizontal_study_energy_focused_ud_en.pdf.

European Investment Bank (2012) *JASPERS serving the European Union's cohesion policy*, European Investment Bank, Luxembourg, http://www.jaspers-europa-info.org/attachments/article/123/JASPERS%20brochure%202012.pdf.

European Investment Fund (2012) *JEREMIE – a new way of using EU Structural Funds to promote SME access to finance via Holding Funds*, European Investment Fund, Luxembourg, http://www.eif.org/news_centre/publications/Jeremie_leaflet_files/jeremie_leaflet_en.pdf.

European Investment Fund (2013) *Annual report 2013*, Imprimerie Centrale, Luxembourg, http://www.eif.org/news_centre/publications/eif_annual_report_2013.pdf.

European Microfinance Network (2009) *COPIE 2 access to finance baseline study*, http://www.cop-ie.eu/sites/default/files/TG_Access_to_Finance_baseline_study_finance_2009.pdf.

European Microfinance Network (2012) *Overview of the microcredit sector in the European Union*, http://www.european-microfinance.org/docs/emn_publications/emn_overview/1.overview2010-2011-final.pdf.

European Parliament (2001) Draft Report on the Commission's 11th Annual Report on the Structural Funds COM(2000) 698 – C5-0108/2001 – 2001/2057 (COS) – Committee on Regional Policy, Transport and Tourism, http://www.europarl.europa.eu/meetdocs/committees/rett/20010619/439210EN.pdf.

European Parliament (2013) Directorate-General for Internal Policies, *Social Housing in UE*, Brussels, http://www.europarl.europa.eu/RegData/etudes/note/join/2013/492469/IPOL-EMPL_NT(2013)492469_EN.pdf.

European Parliament (2013) *Resolution on social housing in the European Union* (2012/2293(INI)), http://www.europarl.europa.eu/sides/getDoc.do?pubRef=-//EP//TEXT+TA+P7-TA-2013-0246+0+DOC+XML+V0//EN.

European Parliament and European Council (2006) On the European Regional Development Fund and repealing Regulation (EC) No 1783/1999, http://eur-lex.europa.eu/legal-content/EN/TXT/PDF/?uri=CELEX:02006R1080-20100618&qid=1404848626582&from=EN.

European Parliament and European Council (2006) Recommendation of the European Parliament and of the Council of 18 December 2006 on key competences for lifelong learning, *Official Journal of the European Union*, L394/10, http://eur-lex.europa.eu/LexUriServ/LexUriServ.do?uri=OJ:L:2006:394:0010:0018:en:PDF, data accessed 7 July 2014.

European Parliament and European Council (2006) Decision No. 1639/2006/CE of the European Parliament and of the Council of 24 October 2006 establishing a Competitiveness and Innovation Framework Programme (2007 to 2013), *Official Journal of the European Union*, http://eur-lex.europa.eu/LexUriServ/LexUriServ.do?uri=OJ:L:2006:310:0015:0040:en:PDF.

European Parliament and European Council (2010) Directive 2009/28/EC of 23 April 2009 on the promotion of the use of energy from renewable sources and amending and subsequently repealing Directives 2001/77/EC and 2003/30/EC, *Official Journal of the European Union*, http://eur-lex.europa.eu/legal-content/EN/TXT/PDF/?uri=CELEX:32009L0028&from=EN.

European Parliament and European Council (2010) Directive 2010/31/EU of the European Parliament and of the Council of 19 May 2010 on energy performance of buildings, *Official Journal of the European Union*, http://eur-lex.europa.eu/LexUriServ/LexUriServ.do?uri=OJ:L:2010:153:0013:0035:EN:PDF.

European Parliament and European Council (2011) Amending Council Regulation (EC) No 1083/2006 as regards repayable assistance, financial engineering and certain provisions related to the statement of expenditure, *Official Journal of the European Union*, http://eur-lex.europa.eu/LexUriServ/LexUriServ.do?uri=OJ:L:2011:337:0001:0004:EN:PDF.

European Parliament and European Council (2012) Directive 2012/27/EU of the European Parliament and of the Council of 25 October 2012 on energy efficiency, amending Directives 2009/125/EC and 2010/30/EU and repealing Directives 2004/8/EC and 2006/32/EC, *Official Journal of the European Union*, http://eur-lex.europa.eu/LexUriServ/LexUriServ.do?uri=OJ:L:2012:315:0001:0056:EN:PDF.

European Parliament and European Council (2013) Regulation (EU) no 1287/2013 of the European Parliament and of the council of 11 December 2013 establishing a Programme for the Competitiveness of Enterprises and small and medium-sized enterprises (COSME) (2014–2020) and repealing Decision No 1639/2006/EC, *Official Journal of the European Union*, http://eur-lex.europa.eu/legal-content/EN/TXT/PDF/?uri=CELEX:32013R1287&qid=1401115426118&from=IT.

European Parliament and European Council (2013) Laying down common provisions on the European Regional Development Fund, the European Social Fund, the Cohesion Fund, the European Agricultural Fund for Rural Development and the European Maritime and Fisheries Fund and laying down general provisions on the European Regional Development Fund, the European Social Fund, the Cohesion Fund and the European Maritime and Fisheries Fund and repealing Council Regulation (EC) No 1083/2006, *Official Journal of the European Union*, http://eur-lex.europa.eu/LexUriServ/LexUriServ.do?uri=OJ:L:2013:347:0320:0469:EN:PDF.

European Parliament and European Council (2013) *Regulation (EU) no 1304/2013 of the European Parliament and of the Council of 17 December 2013 on the European Social Fund and repealing Council Regulation (EC) No 1081/2006*, http://eur-lex.europa.eu/legal-content/EN/TXT/PDF/?uri=CELEX:32013R1304&from=EN.

European PPP Expertise Center (2013) *European Regional Development Fund (ERDF) Investments in energy efficiency improvements and use of renewable energy in residential buildings 2007–2013*, http://www.eib.org/epec/ee/documents/factsheet-erdf-en.pdf.

European Union (1992) *Treaty of Maastricht on European Union*, https://www.ecb.europa.eu/ecb/legal/pdf/maastricht_en.pdf.

European Union (2004) Directive 2004/18/EC of the European Parliament and of the Council of 31 March 2004 on the coordination of procedures for the award of public works contracts, public supply contracts and public service contracts, *Official Journal of the European Union*, http://simap.europa.eu/docs/simap/nomenclature/32004l18en.pdf.

European Union (2009) *The control system for cohesion policy. How it works in the 2007–13 budget period*, http://ec.europa.eu/regional_policy/sources/docgener/presenta/audit2009/audit2009_en.pdf.

European Union (2010) Consolidated Versions of the Treaty on European Union and the Treaty on the Functioning of the European Union, *Official Journal of the European Union*, C 83, 30 March, http://eur-lex.europa.eu/legal-content/EN/TXT/PDF/?uri=OJ:C:2010:083:FULL&from=IT.

European Union (2010) *Internationalisation of European SMEs Final Report*, http://ec.europa.eu/enterprise/policies/sme/market-access/files/internationalisation_of_european_smes_final_en.pdf.

Fazzari S.M., Hubbard G.R. and Petersen B.C. (1988) "Financing constraints and corporate investments", *Brooking Papers on Economic Activity*, 1, 141–195.

Ferrando A. and Griesshaber N. (2011) "Financing obstacles among Euro area firms: who suffers most?", *ECB Working Paper*, No. 1293, January.

Ferrando A., Köhler-Ulbrich P. and Pál R. (2007) "Is the growth of Euro area small and medium-sized enterprises constrained by financing barriers?", *Industrial Policy and Economic Reform Papers*, No. 6, DG Enterprise and Industry.

Floyd D. and McManus J. (2005) "The role of SMEs in improving the competitive position of the European Union", *European Business Review*, 17(2), 144–150.

Forcella D. (2013) *European green micro-finance. A first look*, EMN Research, Brussels, http://www.european-microfinance.org/news.php?pg=28.

Gallardo J. (1997) "Leasing to support small businesses and microenterprises", *Policy Research Working Paper*, No. 1.

Gandolfi F. and Neck P. (2007) "Causes, implementation, and processes of downsizing", *Revista de Management Comparat Internaţional*, 8(4), December, 18–31.

Gibson A. (2001) Principles of good practice in business development services, in Levitsky and Mikkelsen (eds), *Micro & small entreprises in Latin America*, IADB, ITDG.

Goldberg M. (2008) *Microleasing: overcoming equipment financing barriers*, World Bank, Washington, https://openknowledge.worldbank.org/handle/10986/10265.

Green C.J. and Kirkpatrick C.H. (2002) "Finance and development: an overview of the issues", *Journal of International Development*, 14, 207–210.

Green C.J., Kirkpatrick C.H. and Murinde V. (2006) "Finance for small enterprise growth and poverty reduction in developing countries", *Journal of International Development*, 18(7), 1017–1030.

Gronum S., Verreynne M.L. and T. Kastelle (2012) "The role of networks in small and medium-sized enterprise innovation and firm performance", *Journal of Small Business Management*, 50(2), 257–282.

Grosh B. and Somolekae G.(1996) "Mighty oaks from little acorns: can microenterprise serve as the seedbed of industrialization?", *World Development*, 24, 1879–1890.

Guelpa F. (2005) "Crescita dell'impresa e complessità finanziaria" (Enterprise growth and financial complexity), *Economia e Politica Industriale*, XXXII(2), 35–54.

Hall G., Hutchinson P. and Michaelas N. (2004) "Determinants of the capital structures of European SMEs", *Journal of Business Finance & Accounting*, 31, 711–728.

Hamid S.A., Roberts J. and Mosley P. (2011) "Evaluating the health effects of micro health insurance placement: evidence from Bangladesh", *World Development*, 39(3), 399–411.

Hartaska V. (2005) "Governance and performance of micro-finance institutions in Central and Eastern Europe and the Newly Independent States", *World Development*, 33(10), 1627–1643.

Havers M. (1999) "Micro-enterprise and small business leasing – lessons from Pakistan", *Small Enterprise Development Journal*, 10(3).

Henrekson M. and Johansson D. (2010) "Gazelles as job creators: a survey and interpretation of the evidence", *Small Business Economics*, 35, 227–244.

Hessels J. and Parker S.C. (2013) "Constraints, internationalisation and growth: a cross-country analysis of European SMEs", *Journal of World Business*, 48(1), 137–148.

Heyn M. (2001) *Final Evaluation Report: MicroStart Mongolia*, UNDP, Ulaanbaatar, Mongolia.

Hillary R. (2004) "Environmental management systems and the smaller enterprise", *Journal of Cleaner Production*, 12(6), 561–569.

Hougaard C. and Chamberlain D. (2012) Funeral insurance, in C. Churchill and M. Matul (eds), *Protecting the poor: a microinsurance compendium*, Vol. II, International Labour Organization, Geneva.

Hutchinson J. and Xavier A. (2006) "Comparing the impact of credit constraints on the growth of SMEs in a transition country with an established market economy", *Small Business Economics*, 27, 169–179.

IAIS (2007) *Issues in regulation and supervision of microinsurance*, International Association of Insurance Supervisors, Basel, Switzerland.

IAIS (2010) *Issues paper on the regulation and supervision of mutuals*, Cooperatives and other Community-based Organisations in increasing access to Insurance Market, International Association of Insurance Supervisors, Basel, Switzerland.

IAIS (2011) *Insurance core principles, standards, guidance and assessment methodology*, International Association of Insurance Supervisors, Basel, Switzerland.

IAIS (2012) *Application paper on regulation and supervision supporting inclusive insurance markets*, International Association of Insurance Supervisors, Basel, Switzerland.

Istat (2013) *Census of housing*, http://dati-censimentopopolazione.istat.it.

Italian Parliament, Chamber of the Representatives (2013) *Housing policies*, March, http://www.camera.it/temiap/temi17/Am0050.pdf.

Iyer R., Peydró J.L., Da-Rocha-Lopes S. and Schoar A. (2013) "Interbank liquidity crunch and the firm credit crunch: evidence from the 2007–2009 crisis", *Review of Financial Studies*, 27(1), 347–372.

Jenner C. (2012) *Business and education: powerful social innovation partners*, Stanford Social Innovation Review, August, p. 27.

Keeble D. and Wilkinson F. (1999) "Collective learning and knowledge development in the evolution of regional clusters of high technology SMEs in Europe", *Regional Studies*, 33(4), 295–303.

Kihato M. (2013) *State of housing micro-finance in Africa: a report commissioned by the centre for affordable housing finance in Africa*, Housing Finance Information Network, Philadelphia, USA, http://www.housingfinanceafrica.org/wp-content/uploads/2013/01/State-of-Housing-Microfinance-in-Africa-FINAL-20-FEB-2013.pdf.

Klein N. (2014) "Small and medium size enterprises, credit supply shocks and economic recovery in Europe", *IMF Working Paper European Department*.

Kraemer-Eis H., Lang F. and Gvetadze S. (2013) *European small business finance outlook – December 2013*, European Investment Fund, http://www.eif.org/news_centre/publications/eif_wp_2013_18.pdf.

Kuman K.B., Rajan R.G. and Zingales L. (1999) *What determines firm size?*, University of Chicago, Mimeo, Graduate School of Business, 26–27.

Labie M., Laureti C. and Szafarz A. (2013) *Flexible products in micro-finance: overcoming the demand-supply mismatch*, Centre Emile Bernheim (CEB) Research Institute in Management Sciences, Working Paper No. 13/044, December, http://www.iap-socent.be/sites/default/files/SOCENT%20Pub%202013-08%20(wp13044).pdf.

Lämmermann S. and Ribbink G. (2011) *Microfinance and business. Development services in Europe. What can we learn from the South?*, European Microfinance Network, http://www.european-microfinance.org/docs/emn_publications/emn_research_papers/4.af-bds-handbook-lowres2.pdf.

Landi A. and Rigon A. (2006) *Finanza e sviluppo delle PMI in Europa* (Financing and development of the SMEs in Europe), Bancaria Editrice, Roma.

La Torre M. (2010) *Finanza Etica e Microfinanza*, in Enciclopedia del XXI secolo, 3°volume, Treccani, Rome.

La Torre M. and Mango F. (2012) Social lending in Europe: structures regulation and pricing models, in De Guevara Radoselovics, J.F. and Monsálvez, P.J. (eds), *Crisis, risk and stability in financial markets*, Series: Palgrave Macmillan Studies in Banking and Financial Institutions, Palgrave Macmillan, UK.

La Torre M. and Mango F. (2013) Microcredit securitization, in Falzon J. (ed.), *Bank performance, risk and securitisation*, Series: Palgrave Macmillan Studies in Banking and Financial Institutions, Palgrave Macmillan, UK.

La Torre M. and Vento G. (2006) *Microfinance*, Palgrave Macmillan, Basingstoke and New York.

Lega Ambiente (2013) *Energy efficiency in buildings: from promises to construction sites*, Rome, http://www.legambiente.it/sites/default/files/docs/efficienza_energetica_in_edilizia_doclegambiente-cnappc.pdf.

Lega Ambiente and Cresme (2014) *Municipal building regulations and the scenario of energy and environmental innovation in Italy, Report ONRE 2013*, Rome, http://www.legambiente.it/contenuti/dossier/rapporto-onre-2013-ediliziasostenibile-crescita.

Leone P. and Porretta P. (2014) *Microcredit guarantee funds in the mediterranean. A comparative analysis*, ISBN 9781137452986, Palgrave Studies in Impact Finance, Palgrave Macmillan, UK.

Leone P., Porretta P. and Leo S. (2013) "Guarantee funds in microfinance: a comparative analysis", *Journal of Applied Finance and Banking*, 3(6), 161–199.

Levy B. (1993) "Obstacles to developing indigenous small and medium-sized enterprises: an empirical assessment", *The World Bank Economic Review*, 7, 65–83.

Lewis W.A. (1955) *The theory of economic growth*, Allen and Unwin, London.
Liedholm C.E. and Mead D.C. (1999) *Small enterprises and economic development: the dynamics of micro and small enterprises*, Routledge Studies in Development Economics, Vol. 2, Routledge, London and New York.
Liu Y., Chen K., Hill R. and Xiao C. (2013) "Borrowing from the insurer: an empirical analysis of demand and impact of insurance in China", *Microinsurance Innovation Facility, Research Paper*, No. 34, July, 1–24.
Lobbezoo M. (2012) *Volunteer versus paid coaches within microfinance initiatives: what do we actually know about effectiveness?*, INHOLLAND University of Applied Science Research Group on Microfinance and Small Enterprise Development, 8–12, http://www.360responsibility.nl/nieuw/wp-content/uploads/2013/01/Report-Volunteer-versus-paid-coaching.pdf.
Love J.H. and Roper S. (2013) "SME innovation, exporting and growth – a review of existing evidence", *ERC White Paper*, 5.
Lukacs E. (2005) "The economic role of SMEs in world economy, especially in Europe", *European Negotiation Studies*, 4, 3–12.
Maas B. and Lämmermann S. (2012) *Designing microfinance operations in the EU. A manual on how to build and implement microfinance support programmes using the ESF*, ESF Agency Flanders, Brussel.
MacLean J.C. and Siegel J.M. (2007) *Financing mechanisms and public/private risk sharing instruments for financing small scale renewable energy equipment and projects*, UNDP http://www.energyandsecurity.com/images/SSRE_UNEP_Report__20August_2007.pdf.
Magnoni B., Lovoi A., Brown J. and Thornton R. (2010) *Risk across borders. A study of the potential of microinsurance products to help migrants cope with cross border risk*, Multilateral Investment Fund, September, 1–51, http://idbdocs.iadb.org/wsdocs/getDocument.aspx?DOCNUM=35550420.
Marino A., Bertoldi P., Rezessy S. and Boza-Kiss B. (2011) "A snapshot of the European energy service market in 2010 and policy recommendations to foster further market developments", *Energy Policy*, 39(10), October 2011, 6190–6198.
Massa S. and Testa S. (2008) "Innovation and SMEs: misaligned perspectives and goals among entrepreneurs, academics, and policy makers", *Technovation*, 28(7), 393–407.
McCord M.J. (2012) *Microinsurance product development for microfinance providers*, IFAD, Rome.
McCord M.J. and Churchill C. (2005) "Delta life Bangladesh", *CGAP Working Group on Microinsurance, Good and Bad Practices*, Case Study No. 7.
Ministry of Labour and Social Policies (2012) Policies for social housing in Italy, *Social Research Handbooks*, No. 22, Rome, http://www.lavoro.gov.it/AreaSociale/Inclusione/Documents/qrscasa.pdf.
Ministry of the Interior – School of the Administration of the Interior – General Statistics Office (2014) Evictions in Italy: performance of eviction procedures in residential buildings 2013, *Statistics Notebook*, No. 1, Rome, http://ssai.interno.it/download/allegati1/pubblicazionesfratti2013.pdf.
Mirabal N. and De Young R. (2005) "Downsizing as a strategic intervention", *Journal of American Academy of Business*, 6(1), 39–45.
Mkandawire T. (1999) Developmental states and small enterprises, in King K. and McGrath S. (eds), *Enterprise in Africa: new contexts, renewed challenges*, Edward Elgar, Cheltenham.

Morduch J. (1999) "The microfinance promise", *Journal of Economic Literature*, 37(4), 1569–1614.

Mosley P. and D. Hulme (1998) "Micro-enterprise finance: is there any conflict between growth and poverty alleviation?", *World Development*, 26(5), 783–790.

Myers S.C. (1984) "The capital structure puzzle", *Journal of Finance*, 39(1), 575–592.

Myers S.C. and Majluf N.S. (1984) "Corporate financing and investment decision: when firms have information that investors do not have", *Journal of Financial Economics*, 13, 187–221.

Nardone A. and Costantini M.C. (2011) "BDS for inclusion: the case of Fondazione Risorsa Donna", *European Microfinance Network electronic Research Bulletin, Brussels*, III, 4–7.

Nomisma (2011) *The housing situation in Italy. Report 2010*, Agra, Rome.

Nunes P.M., Gonçalves M. and Serrasqueiro Z. (2013) "The influence of age on SMEs' growth determinants: empirical evidence", *Journal Small Business Economics*, 40(2), 249–272.

Observatoire de la Microfinance (2011) *Rapport annuel 2011*, Banque de France, Paris, http://www.banque-france.fr/fileadmin/user_upload/banque_de_france/publications/Rapport-annuel-2011-Observatoire-de-la-Microfinance.pdf.

O'Donnell A., Gilmore A., Carson D. and Cummins D. (2002) "Competitive advantage in small to medium sized Enterprises", *Journal of Strategic Marketing*, 10(3), 205–223.

OECD (2012) *Financing SMEs and Entrepreneurs 2012: an OECD Scoreboard*, http://www.oecd.org/officialdocuments/publicdisplaydocumentpdf/?cote=CFE/SME%282012%2912/FINAL&docLanguage=En.

OECD (2013) *Fostering SMEs' participation in global markets: final report*, http://www.oecd.org/officialdocuments/publicdisplaydocumentpdf/?cote=CFE/SME%282012%296/FINAL&docLanguage=En.

OECD and European Union (2012) *Policy brief on youth entrepreneurship*, Publications Office of the European Union, Luxembourg, http://www.oecd.org/cfe/leed/Youth%20entrepreneurship%20policy%20brief%20EN_FINAL.pdf.

Ongena S. and Smith D.C. (2000) Bank relationship: a review, in Harker P.T. and Zenios S.A. (eds), *Performance of financial institutions, efficiency, innovation, regulation*, Cambridge University Press, Cambridge.

Otero M. (1999) "Bringing development back into micro-finance", *Journal of Micro-finance*, 1(1), 1–19.

Oxford Economics (2011) *The use of leasing amongst European SMEs*, Leaseurope, Brussels, http://www.leaseurope.org/uploads/documents/SME%20Support%20Pack%20for%20MA/Leaseurope%20SME%20Report%20Key%20Findings.pdf.

Pal R. and Ferrando A. (2010) "Financing constraints and firms' cash policy in the Euro area", *European Journal of Finance*, 16(2), 153–171.

Parkhe A., Wasserman S. and Ralston D.A. (2006) "New frontiers in network theory development", *Academy of Management Review*, 31(3), 560–568.

Petersen M.A. and Rajan R.G. (1994) "The benefits of lending relationship: evidence from small business data", *Journal of Finance*, 49, 3–37.

Pinder C. (2001) *SELFINA (Sero Lease and Finance Company) Tanzania*, www.enterprise-impact.org.uk/pdf/SELFINA.pdf.

Pissarides F. (1999) "Is lack of funds the main obstacle to growth? Ebrd's experience with small- and medium-sized businesses in central and eastern Europe", *Journal of Business Venturing*, 14(5–6), 519–539.

Porretta P. and Santoboni F. (2014) "Banks and young people in Italy: financial product, credit and other features", *Journal of Applied Finance & Banking*, 4(3), 115–139.

Poursat C. (2014) *Dossier thématique: Diversification des produits*, http://www.microfinancegateway.org/sites/default/files/mfg-fr-publications-diverses-diversification-offre-microfinance-03-2005-bim_0.pdf.

Prager R.A. and Wolken J.D. (2008) "The evolving relationship between community banks and small business: evidence from the survey of small business finance", *Finance and Economics Discussion Paper 2008–60, Boards of Governors of the Federal Reserves System*, 32–34.

Prasad S., Green C.J. and Murinde V. (2005) Company financing, capital structure and ownership: a survey and implications for developing countries, in Green C.J., Kirkpatrick C.H. and Murinde V. (eds), *Finance and development: surveys of theory, evidence and policy*, Edward Elgar, UK.

Prashad P., Saunders D. and Dalal A. (2013) "Mobile phones and microinsurance", *Microinsurance Innovation Facility, Research Paper*, No. 26, November, 1–41.

Proietti L., Santoboni F. and Vincioni A. (2006) "La vigilanza dei Sistemi finanziari nell'area del SEBC. Le recenti tendenze evolutive", *Banche e Banchieri*, 1, gennaio-febbraio, 5–23.

Radermacher R. and Brinkmann J. (2011) "Insurance for the poor? First thoughts about microinsurance business ethics", *Journal of Business Ethics*, 103(1), 63–76.

Rath J. and Swagerman A. (2011) *Promoting ethnic entrepreneurship in European cities*, European Foundation for the Improvement of Living and Working Conditions, Publications Office of the European Union, Luxembourg, p. 40, http://www.eurofound.europa.eu/pubdocs/2011/38/en/2/EF1138EN.pdf, data accessed 7 July 2014.

Reid G.C. (1996) "Financial structure and the growing small firms; theoretical underpinning and current evidence", *Small Business Economics*, 8(1), 1–7.

Rezessy S. and Bertoldi P. (2010) *Financing energy efficiency: forging the link between finance and project implementation*, Joint Research Centre of the European Commission, http://ec.europa.eu/energy/efficiency/doc/financing_energy_efficiency.pdf.

Ryan L. and Macky K.A. (1998) "Downsizing organizations: uses, outcomes and strategies", *Asia Pacific Journal of Human Resources*, 36(2), 29–45.

Santangelo, F. (2013) Servizi finanziari, in Pizzo G. and Tagliavini G. (eds), *Dizionario di microfinanza, le voci del microcredito*, Carocci, Roma.

Santoboni, F. (2012) *Manuale di gestione assicurativa. Intermediazione e produzione*, Cedam, Padova.

Santoboni F. and Arcadi V. (2011) "Le polizze assicurative nel processo di affidamento: nuove opportunità di accesso al credito per le imprese", *Rivista Bancaria*, 3, 25–56.

Santoboni F., Tomatis M. and Vincioni A. (2012a) "Polizze per le imprese ed accesso al credito in Italia: il punto di vista delle banche e delle compagnie di assicurazione", *Banca Impresa Società*, 1, 119–152.

Santoboni F., Vento G.A. and Porretta P. (2012b) "Corporate insurance and debt capacity: empirical evidence from Italy", *Journal of Governance and Regulation*, 1(4), 54–75.

Santoboni F. and Vincioni A. (2002) "La vigilanza nei sistemi finanziari in Europa. Analisi comparativa", *Rivista Bancaria*, 3, maggio-giugno, 31–62.

Sapelli G. (2009) Between urban and financial income: the city in fractals – "International Dialogues. Cities of the World", No. 10.

Scott J.A. (2004) "Small business and value of community financial institutions", *Journal of Financial Service Research*, 25, 207–230.

Sheth K. (2014) "The distributional consequences of micro health insurance: can a pro-poor program prove to be regressive?", *Microinsurance Innovation Facility, Research Paper*, No. 38, March, 1–29.

Smart Energy – *Europe II, Implementation Report 2012* (2013) http://ec.europa.eu/energy/intelligent/files/library/reports/iee-2-impl-report-2007-2012.pdf.

Smith A., Smit H. and Chamberlain D. (2011) "Beyond sales: new frontiers in microinsurance distribution", *Microinsurance Innovation Facility, Microinsurance Paper*, No. 8, April, 1–32.

Stewart R., Van Rooyen C., Korth M. et al. (2012) *Do micro-credit, micro-savings and micro-leasing serve as effective financial inclusion interventions enabling poor people, and especially women, to engage in meaningful economic opportunities in low- and middle-income countries? A systematic review of the evidence*. EPPI, Centre – The Evidence for Policy and Practice Information and Coordinating Centre, http://r4d.dfid.gov.uk/pdf/outputs/systematicReviews/Microcredit2012StewartReport.pdf.

Storey D. (1994) *Understanding the small business sector*, Routledge, London.

Swiss Re (2010) "Microinsurance. Risk protection for 4 billion people", *Sigma*, No. 6, Zurich, Switzerland.

Symeonidis G. (1996) "Innovation, firm size and market structure: schumpeterian hypotheses and some new themes", *OECD Economic Department Working Papers*, No. 161.

Ten Donkelaar, M. and Heinze, C., (2012) *Structural and cohesion funds for sustainable energy investments – technical input and best practices for managing authorities (and potential beneficiaries)*, SF Energy Invest, http://www.sfenergyinvest.eu/uploads/media/SFD2_2_Evaluation_SCF_financed_projects_final.pdf.

Van Maanen G. (2004) *Microcredit sound business or development instrument*, Oiko Credits, Voorburg, SGO Uitgeverij – Hoevelaken, Netherlands, http://www.microfinancegateway.org/sites/default/files/mfg-en-paper-microcredit-sound-business-or-development-instrument-sep-2004.pdf.

Varum C.A. and Rocha V.C. (2013) "Employment and SMEs during crises", *Small Business Economics*, 40(1), 9–25.

Viganò L. (a cura di) (2004) *Microfinanza in Europa*, Collana "Finanza e Sviluppo", Fondazione Giordano Dell'Amore, Giuffrè editore, Milano.

Vrande V.J., De Jong P.J., Vanhaverbeke W. and De Rochemont M. (2009) "Open innovation in SMEs: trends, motives and management challenges", *Technovation*, 29(6–7), 423–437.

Wagenvoort R. (2003a) "Are finance constraints hindering the growth of SME's in Europe?", *European Investment Bank Paper*, 7, 22–50.

Wagenvoort R. (2003b) "Bank survey evidence on 'Bank lending to SMEs in European Union'", *EIB Papers*, Economic and Financial Report 2003/01.

Website

ANIA Associazione Nazionale tra le Imprese Assicuratrici http://www.ania.it/it/index.html
Banca Italia www.bancaditalia.it
Breakdown by sector http://www.eib.org/projects/loans/sectors/index.htm?start=2013&end=2013
Competitiveness and Innovation Framework Programme (CIP) http://ec.europa.eu/cip/index_en.htm
Dipartimento Politiche Europee http://www.politicheeuropee.it/
Enterprise and Industry http://ec.europa.eu/enterprise/policies/finance/risk-capital/business-angels/index_en.htm
EPPI Centre http://eppi.ioe.ac.uk/cms/
EU Programme for Employment and Social Innovation (EaSI) http://ec.europa.eu/social/main.jsp?catId=1081
European Central Bank www.ecb.int
European Commission – Competitiveness and Innovation Framework Programme (CIP) http://ec.europa.eu/cip/index_en.htm
European Commission – COSME, EU Programme for the Competitiveness of Enterprises and Small and Medium-sized Enterprises (SMEs) http://ec.europa.eu/enterprise/initiatives/cosme/index_en.htm
European Commission, European Investment Bank and European Bank – JASPER: Joint Assistance to Support Projects in European Regions http://www.jaspers-europa-info.org/
European Commission – Financial Engineering http://ec.europa.eu/regional_policy/archive/themes/financial/index_en.htm
European Commission – JASMINE: Joint Action to Support Micro-finance Institutions in Europe http://ec.europa.eu/regional_policy/thefunds/instruments/jasmine_en.cfm
European Commission – JASPERS: Joint Assistance to Support Projects in European Regions http://ec.europa.eu/regional_policy/thefunds/instruments/jaspers_en.cfm
European Commission – State Aid: Commission Authorises Temporary Italian Interest Rate Subsidies for Green Products http://europa.eu/rapid/press-release_IP-09-1581_en.htm
European Investment Bank http://www.eib.org/
European Investment Bank – Finance Contracts Signed
European Investment Bank – Supporting Urban Development (JESSICA) http://www.bei.org/products/jessica/index.htm
European Investment Fund http://www.eif.org/
European Microfinance Network http://www.european-microfinance.org
Exzet http://www.exzet.de/index.html
Goldrausch-EV http://www.goldrausch-ev.de/
Housing Europe http://www.housingeurope.eu/
Initiative France http://www.initiative-france.fr/
Kiz http://www.kiz.de/
JASMINE: Joint Action to Support Microfinance Institutions http://www.eif.org/what_we_do/microfinance/JASMINE/

JASMINE: Joint Action to Support Micro-finance Institutions in Europe http://ec.europa.eu/regional_policy/thefunds/instruments/jasmine_en.cfm#2
Joint Assistance to Support Projects in European Regions (JASPERS) – Action Plan Cycle http://www.jaspers-europa-info.org/index.php/how-we-work.html
Microcredito Italia http://www.microcreditoitalia.org/index.php?lang=it
Microcredito Italia http://www.microcreditoitalia.org/capacitybuilding/
MicroFinanza Rating http://www.microfinanzarating.com/index.php?option=com_content&view=article&id=97&Itemid=167&lang=en
Microlending http://www.microlending-news.de/artikel/enterprise.htm
Mikrofinanz http://www.mikrofinanz.net/
Planet Rating http://www.planetrating.com/EN/who-are-we-a.html
Politiche Euripee http://www.politicheeuropee.it
Progress Program http://ec.europa.eu/social/main.jsp?catId=327
Small Business Act http://europa.eu/legislation_summaries/enterprise/business_environment/et0001_it.htm
SUNIA – Sindacato Unitario Nazionale Inquilini ed Assegnatari http://www.sunia.it
UPPI – Unione Piccoli Proprietari Immobiliari http://www.uppi.it
Wasistgarage http://www.wasistgarage.de/
http://www.eipa.nl/
http://www.eif.org/what_we_do/jeremie/faq/index.htm#What%20is%20the%20role%20of%20a%20Fund%20Holder
http://www.eif.org/what_we_do/jeremie/faq/index.htm#What%20is%20the%20role%20of%20a%20Fund%20Holder
Youth guarantee http://www.youth-guarantee.eu/

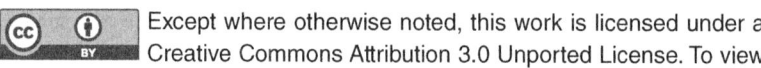 Except where otherwise noted, this work is licensed under a Creative Commons Attribution 3.0 Unported License. To view a copy of this license, visit http://creativecommons.org/licenses/by/3.0/

Index

A.MI.CI (Access to Microcredit for Immigrant Citizens), 152
antidiscriminalities, 219, 225, 226
Apulia, 109, 236, 238–40, 242, 244–6
asset stripping, 47, 70n40
audit authority, control process, 87, 88

bank borrowing, SMEs, 23–4
bank overdrafts, 29
Basel Committee in the Credit Risk Mitigation, 178
BDS (business development services)
　categories, 127
　client first initiative, 136, 139, 140, 141
　description of, 136–7
　first phase, 137–8
　impact of, 141, 142
　importance of, 167
　non-financial services, 126–7
　partnership in delivery of, 135–42
　second phase, 138
　sustainability, 140
　third phase, 138–40
Belgium, 104, 222, 236
Birch, David, 16, 68n8

Calabria, 109, 236
Campania, 108–9, 236, 238–9, 242, 244–5
Capacity Building project
　approach, 152
　characteristics for housing, 192
　future development of microcredit, 253–4
　housing microfinance, 161
　microfinancial policy, 256–9
　microinsurance, 156–9
　microleasing, 159–61
　microleasing issues, 161–7
　operational proposals, 193
　role of Italian National Agency for Microcredit, 150–4, 155
　social inclusion, 191–4
　training proposal, 255–6
Capacity Building surveys
　evaluation and monitoring, 231–2, 233
　ex ante conditionalities, 219, 225–7
　financial management, 232, 234
　financing methods, 242
　geographical distribution of replies, 221, 222
　implementation, 229–31
　main results of questionnaires, 222–34, 237–49
　management, 229–31
　managing authorities' interest and needs, 216–17
　methodological framework, 213–16
　monitoring and reporting, 243, 244
　operational management, 232, 234
　programming, 227–9, 237–41
　questionnaire investigation areas, 214–16, 217–35, 235–7
　reflections of, 235, 247–9
　regulatory framework of microcredit/microfinance, 243, 246–7
　samples used for, 220–2
　thematic objectives, 223–5
　websites of microcredit programmes, 245
CBS (Capacity Building Scheme), financial instrument, 45, 46, 49–51
CEB (Council of Europe Development Bank), 49–50, 51, 53–4, 56
centralised organisational model, entrepreneurs, 15–16
certification authority, control process, 87, 88
CF (Cohesion Fund), 51, 57, 71n46, 79, 98n8–9, 99n18, 223
CGAP Working Group on Microinsurance, 171

COCOF (Coordination Committee of the Funds), cohesion policy, 79–80, 85, 89
cohesion policy
  audit authority at national level, 88
  certification authority, 88
  COCOF (Coordination Committee of the Funds) notes, 79–80
  control process schematic, 87
  control system, 84, 86–90
  differences between 2007–2013 and 2014–2020, 84, 85
  examples in Europe, 95–7
  financial instruments in, 2014–2020, 80–4
  main amendments, 82–4
  managing authority, 86, 88
  microfinance programme through structural funds, 92–5
  monitoring process phases, 90
  regulatory framework in period 2000–2006, 75–6
  regulatory framework of period 2007–2013, 76–80
  structural funds and microfinance, 90–2
  use of EU funds, 89
competition
  EU domestic market, 11–12, 16, 98n12
  European SME system, 17
Competitiveness and Innovation Framework Programme, 43, 70n28, 70n36, 70n38, 71n43–4, 150
Consolidated Banking Act, 156, 252
COSME (Competitiveness of Enterprises and Small and Medium-Sized Enterprises), 40, 62–3, 105, 150
CPI (credit protection insurance policies), 157, 178
credit
  European Commission's view of access to, 39–40
  problem of access for microenterprises, 102–5
  supply in years of crisis, 26–38
credit card overdrafts, 29

credit line overdrafts, 29
credit rating
  economic self-sustainability, 60, 72n58
  MicroFinanza Rating (MFR), 60, 72n59
  Planet Rating, 60, 73n60
crisis years, supply of credit, 26–38

developing countries, microinsurance for, 167–9
DG Enterprise and Industry, 115, 144n20, 145n33
disability, 219, 225, 226
DMI (Deutsches Mikrofinanz Institut), credit access overview, 111, 112, 114

EAFRD (European Agricultural Fund for Rural Development), 150, 223, 250n7
EASI (programme for employment and social innovation), 125, 126, 145–6n41
ECB (European Central Bank), credit measures, 143n5
economic self-sustainability, 60, 72n58
Edquist, Charles, 217, 250n5
education, ESF (European Social Fund), 107
EFG (Equity Facility Growth), 63–4, 67
EIB (European Investment Bank)
  microfinance support, 149
  mission and operating methods, 40–1
  projects financed by, 42, 43
EIF (European Investment Fund), 41, 42, 44, 149
EMFF (European Maritime and Fisheries Fund), 223, 250n7
empowerment, non-financial service, 128
energy poverty, France, 197–8
England, microfinance programmes, 96, 97
enterprise life cycle, non-financial services in, 131

enterprises
  financing gap by firm size, 31
  financing sources by size, 29
  numbers from 2008–2012, 18–19, 20
entrepreneurial finance, 160
entrepreneurs
  role of, 15–16
  SMEs, 38–9
Entrepreneurship 2020 Action Plan, 119–20, 121, 123–6
  creation of business-friendly environment, 121–2
  education and training, 119–20
  promoting business culture change, 122, 123
  supporting elderly, 123, 124
  supporting immigrants, 123, 124
  supporting unemployed individuals, 125, 126
  unemployment and issues affecting youth, 123–5, 126
Entrepreneurship and Innovation Programme, 40, 49, 69n25, 70n37
environmental legislation, 219, 225, 226
EPPI (Evidence for Policy and Practice Information and Coordinating Centre), 162, 204n10–11
ERDF (European Regional Development Fund), 62, 99n18, 223
  cohesion policy, 74, 76–7, 94, 97
  contributions of, 72n49
  JEREMIE programme, 52, 53
  JESSICA programme, 56
ESF (European Social Fund), 91, 94, 97, 150, 223
  capacity of public authorities and stakeholders, 107
  case study from Germany, 110–15
  credit access of microenterprises, 105–10
  education and training, 107, 185
  Italy providing microcredit measures, 108–10
  objectives and investment priorities of, 106–7
  role of, 5–6
  social inclusion, 107

support for microcredit in Germany, 113–15
EUCoGC (European Code of Good Conduct of Microcredit Provision), 134, 147n64
EU (European Union)
  housing development policies, 183–6
  research methodology, 7–8
  small businesses and microenterprises in economy, 9–11
  see also cohesion policy
Eurom Consultancy, 135–8, 140, 147n63
Europe, microfinance programmes, 96–7
European Commission
  credit access, 39–40
  methodology, 3, 7
  new European plans, 118–26
  non-financial services, 117–18
European microfinance, microleasing, microinsurance and social housing, 154–6
European Microfinance Network (EMN), 90, 132, 136, 147n57, 227

factoring, 29
FEASR (European Agriculture Fund for Rural Development), 117, 121–3
Federcasa, 193, 208n42
financial engineering instruments
  data collected on, 61–2
  JASMINE, 40, 58–60
  JASPERS, 40, 56–8
  JEREMIE, 40, 51–3
  JESSICA, 40, 53–6
  number reported at end of 2011 and 2013, 61
financial growth cycle, theory, 22
financial hierarchy, 22
financial instruments
  CBS (Capacity Building Scheme), 45, 46, 49–51
  cohesion policy 2014–2020, 80–4
  communication, 99n17
  EFG (Equity Facility Growth), 63–4, 67

282 *Index*

financial instruments – *continued*
  EU from 2007–2013, 43–5, 46
  expansion of, 253
  GIF (Growth and Innovative Facility), 45, 46, 47–8, 66
  LGF (Loan Guarantee Facility), 64–5, 67
  Progress Microfinance, 91, 105, 134, 150
  SMEG (Small Medium Enterprise Guarantee Facility), 45, 46, 48–9, 50, 66
financial profiles, microenterprises, 20–6
Finland, microfinance programmes, 96, 97
France
  case for housing microcredit, 196–203
  energy poverty, 197–8
  microfinance programmes, 96, 97
  overview of personal microcredit in, 196–7

gazelle enterprises, 16, 102
gender equality, 219, 225, 226
Germany
  appraisal of ESF support for microcredit in, 113–15
  consolidation phase of initiatives, 111–12
  DMI (Deutsches Mikrofinanz Institute), 111, 112
  history of microfinance in, 110–15
  loan volumes, 114
  pilot phase of microcredit initiatives, 110–11
  roll-out of credit access, 113
GIF (Growth and Innovative Facility), 45, 46, 47–8, 66

hire purchase, 29
House Plan, 191, 208n39
housing microcredit
  contribution for stakeholders, 202
  credit assessment methodology, 199
  environmental impact, 200
  France, 196–203
  impact on beneficiaries, 200–201

  lessons learned, 201–3
  main characteristics of, 198–9
  obstacles, 202–3
  shared-value approach, 200–201
  sustainability, 201
housing microfinance
  Capacity Building project, 161
  definition, 206–7n33
  social housing and, 186–91
  see also social housing
housing policies
  demand for affordable housing, 188
  developments in European Union, 183–6
  social inclusion, 187–91
  social microcredit, 191–4

IAIS (International Association of Insurance Supervisors), 156, 171, 205n19
ICPs (Insurance Core Principles), 171
Italy
  ESF, providing microcredit, 108–10
  financing methods, 242
  microcredit/microfinance activity, 238, 239, 240
  microinsurance market, 259
  National Body for Microcredit, 165
  regulatory framework of microcredit/microfinance, 246
  reporting activity, 244
  social housing, 194–5, 207n37
  websites of microcredit programmes, 245

JASMINE (Joint Action to Support Microfinance Institutions), 40, 58–62
  budget, 59
  financial engineering instrument, 40, 58–60
  microfinance support, 149, 151
  summary of, 67
JASPERS (Joint Assistance to Support Projects in European Regions)
  financial engineering instrument, 40, 56–8
  performance, 58
  summary of, 67

Index 283

JEREMIE (Joint European Resources for Micro to Medium Enterprises), 40, 71n47, 77, 92
  advantages of, 53
  financial engineering instrument, 51–3
  Lombardy Regional Administration, 100n37
  microfinance support, 150, 151
  social inclusion, 190
  summary of, 66
JESSICA (Joint European Support for Sustainable Investment in City Areas), 72n50, 77
  financial engineering instrument, 40, 53–6
  summary of, 67

labour supply theory, 14–15
Latvia
  financing methods, 242
  microcredit/microfinance activity, 238, 239, 240
  regulatory framework of microcredit/microfinance, 247
  reporting activity, 244
  websites of microcredit programmes, 245
leasing, 29
Lega Cooperative Abitanti, 193, 208n42
LGF (Loan Guarantee Facility), 64–5, 67

managing authorities
  control process, 86, 87, 88
  financial management, 232, 234
  implementation, 229–31
  interest and needs in capacity building, 216–17
  management, 229, 231
  operational management, 232, 234
  programming, 227–9
MFIs (microfinance institutions), 59–60, 67, 73n60
microcredit, 4, 5
  definition, 249
  economic growth and employment, 149
  housing, in French case, 196–203
  new EU programmes, 148–50
  process for building model, 257–8
  scoring system for, 258–9
  social, supporting housing policies, 191–4
  target of programmes, 241
Microcredit and Employment Services project, 152
Microcredit Fund, Sardinia, 92–3
microenterprises
  definition, 204n16
  indebtedness levels of, 24–5
  EU economy, 9–11
  European Social Fund (ESF) and access to credit of, 105–10
  financial profiles, 20–6
  funding, 32
  numbers from 2008–2012, 19, 20
  problem of access to credit, 102–5
  weaknesses of, 16
microentrepreneurs, 10, 113, 157
  development and growth of economy, 175
  financing, 253, 258
  microfinance providers, 117, 140, 147n64
  microinsurance, 176–8, 180, 182
  microleasing, 159, 161, 164–5, 167
microentrepreneurship, 91, 152, 258
microfinance, 4–5
  cohesion policy, 90–2
  defining different models of, 146n50
  definition of, 4, 10, 203n2
  example programmes in Europe, 95–7
  history of, in Germany, 110–15
  non-financial services, 115–18
  strengthening culture, 258
  see also housing microfinance
MicroFinanza Rating (MFR), 60, 72n59
microinsurance, 154–6, 167–9, 182–3, 205n19
  Capacity Building project, 156–9
  vs. conventional insurance, 172
  definition, 169–70
  demand for, 173–6
  ICPs (Insurance Core Principles), 172
  legal status of providers, 174
  literature, 170–1
  market in Italy, 259

microinsurance – *continued*
  products and distribution channels, 176–9
  provision of, 173
  regulatory profiles, 171–3
  risks, 176–7
  strengths, 179–81
  weaknesses, 181–2
microleasing, 154–6
  advantages to small enterprises, 164
  Capacity Building project, 159–61, 161–7
  public administration, 165–6
  risk assessment, 166–7

N+2 rule calculation, 56, 72n52
NAPs (national action plans), 91, 99n32
National Agency for Microcredit (Italian)
  Capacity Building survey, 235–7, 255
  microfinance sector, 252
  role in Capacity Building project, 150–4, 155
National Body for Microcredit, Italy, 165
National Operational Programme Metropolitan Cities, 195
NBFI (non-bank financial institutions), 132, 134–6
networking, non-financial services in, 131, 132
non-financial services
  advantages and operational features, 126–32
  enterprise life cycle, 131
  funding by, 132, 133
  methods of provision, 133
  microfinance and, 115–18
  networking, 131, 132
  tutoring service, 129–30, 131, 132
  types of, 128–32
NRP (National Reform Programme), 92, 100n34

operational programme, structural funds, 60, 62, 71n46
output-demand theory, 15

partnership action, CBS (Capacity Building Scheme), 51
pecking order theory, 22
Planet Rating, 60, 73n60
Poland
  financing methods, 242
  microcredit/microfinance activity, 238, 239, 240
  regulatory framework of microcredit/microfinance, 246
  reporting activity, 244
  websites of microcredit programmes, 245
Portugal
  financing methods, 242
  microcredit/microfinance activity, 238, 239, 240
  microfinance programmes, 96–7
  reporting activity, 244
  websites of microcredit programmes, 245
private label, 12
product marketing, innovative projects, 68n10
programming
  managing authorities, 227–9
  microcredit/microfinance activity, 237–41
Progress Microfinance (Programme for Employment and Social Solidarity), 91, 105, 134, 150, 190
public procurement, 219, 225, 226

Region Abruzzo, 108
Region Apulia, 109
Region Basilicata, 109
Region Calabria, 109
Region Campania, 108–9
Region Sardinia, 110
regulation (EC) no. 448/2004, 75–6, 97n3
regulation (EC) no. 1083/2006, 51–2, 71n46, 76–9, 98n15, 98n8, 99n18
regulation (EC) no. 1260/1999, 71n46, 75, 97n4, 97n6, 98n7, 98n9
regulation (EC) no. 1303/2013, 81, 82–4, 106

regulation (EC) no. 1685/2000, 75, 97*n*6, 98*n*7
regulation (EC) no. 1828/2006, 52, 76, 78
regulation (EU) no. 1304/2013, 106–7, 143*n*10–13
regulatory framework, microcredit/microfinance sector, 243, 246–7
RoCredit, 135–40, 142
Romania
  case studies for financial and nonfinancial service delivery, 134–42
  FAER NBFI and FAER Foundation, 134–5
  RoCredit-NBFIF and Eurom Consultancy, 135–42

SAFE (Survey on access to finance of small and medium enterprises), 32, 34–5, 39
Sardinia, 92–3, 110
SBA (Small Business Act), 25
  objective, 117
  principles, 25, 68–9*n*12
Scotland, microfinance programmes, 96
seed capital action, CBS (Capacity Building Scheme), 50–1
Slovenia
  financing methods, 242
  microcredit/microfinance activity, 238, 239, 240
  regulatory framework of microcredit/microfinance, 246
  reporting activity, 244
  websites of microcredit programmes, 245
SMAF (SMEs' Access to Finance) Index, 27–8
small business, 13
small loans, 32
SMEG (Small Medium Enterprise Guarantee Facility), 45, 46, 48–9, 50, 66
SMEs (small and medium-sized enterprises)
  access to finance, 27–8
  bank borrowing, 23–4
  bank loans, 35, 36, 37
  credit supply in years of crisis, 26–38
  criticalities perceived by European SMEs, 104
  employment contributions, 17, 18
  EU economy, 9–11
  European economy, 11–19
  financial considerations, 38–9
  financial health of euro area, 30
  financial profiles, 21–3
  interest rates, 32, 33
  internal and external financing, 36, 37
  microfinance programmes, 25–6
  numbers from 2008–2012, 18–19, 20
  problem of access to credit for, 102–5
  socio-economic role of, 13–14
Social European Fund, 79, 106
social housing, 154–6
  common features, 186
  definitions, 187
  demand for affordable housing, 188
  developments in European Union, 183–6
  and housing microfinance, 186–91
  interventions, 194–5
  Italy, 207*n*37
  social inclusion, 187–91
  structural measures, 205*n*24
  sustainability, 205*n*23
social inclusion
  Capacity Building project, 191–4
  ESF (European Social Fund), 107
  housing policies, 187–91
social microcredit, 5, 191–4
social solidarity, 74, 91, 100*n*37, 145–6*n*41
state aid, 219, 225, 226
statistical system, 219, 225, 226
structural funds
  cohesion policy, 90–2
  evolution of EU, programming, 74–5
  implementing a microfinance programme, 92–5

286 *Index*

structural funds – *continued*
  operational programme, 60, 62, 71*n*46
  utilisation of, 255, 256
surveys
  access to financing, 103, 143*n*6
  see also Capacity Building surveys

topo, 16
trade credit, 29, 30
training
  ESF (European Social Fund), 107
  Non-financial services in, 130, 131

UDF (urban development funds), 54, 56, 67, 72*n*49

United Kingdom, microfinance programmes, 96, 97

Wales
  financing methods, 242
  microcredit/microfinance activity, 238, 239, 240
  regulatory framework of microcredit/microfinance, 243, 247
  reporting activity, 244
  websites of microcredit programmes, 245

youth entrepreneurship, 145*n*32, 145*n*39, 246
Youth Guarantee, 106, 120, 125, 126

 Except where otherwise noted, this work is licensed under a Creative Commons Attribution 3.0 Unported License. To view a copy of this license, visit http://creativecommons.org/licenses/by/3.0/

The manufacturer's authorised representative in the EU is Springer Nature Customer Service Centre GmbH, Europaplatz 3, 69115 Heidelberg, Germany. If you have any concerns regarding our products, please contact ProductSafety@springernature.com

Printed and bound by CPI Group (UK) Ltd, Croydon, CR0 4YY

23/03/2026

02076663-0019